the *Special Service*

WORSHIP
architect

the *Special Service* WORSHIP architect

Blueprints for Weddings, Funerals, Baptisms, Holy Communion, and Other Occasions

Constance M. Cherry

Baker Academic
a division of Baker Publishing Group
Grand Rapids, Michigan

© 2013 by Constance M. Cherry

Published by Baker Academic
a division of Baker Publishing Group
P.O. Box 6287, Grand Rapids, MI 49516-6287
www.bakeracademic.com

Printed in the United States of America

Library of Congress Cataloging-in-Publication Data is on file at the Library of Congress, Washington, DC.

ISBN 978-0-8010-4895-1 (pbk.)

13   14   15   16   17   18   19   7   6   5   4   3   2   1

This book is dedicated to
Richard Kevin Cherry,
brother, friend, and exemplary pastor

Contents

Acknowledgments   ix

Introduction   1

1. Foundations for Sacred Actions   11

2. The Christian Wedding   35

3. The Christian Funeral   61

4. Christian Baptism   95

5. The Table of the Lord   143

6. The Healing Service   191

7. The Foot Washing Service and the Love Feast   219

8. Child Dedication and Alternative Rites   243

9. Serving as a Rituals Architect: How to Create Meaningful Rituals for Corporate Worship   279

Appendix A: Prayer Forms   287

Appendix B: Orders of Services   291

Notes   299

Index   315

Acknowledgments

This book has been a labor of love for all of my students—past, present, and future—who are preparing for worship leadership in the local church. I often tell them, "I love you, but I love Christ's church more." By that I mean that I am passionate about the worship ministry of the local church. I therefore do not concentrate on what is popular or pragmatic, though these matters are not irrelevant, and we discuss them in class. Instead, I look beyond my students' faces into the faces of countless people worshiping in their future or current congregations who will benefit from a well-prepared worship leader. I am thankful for the hundreds of students with whom I am a co-learner, not only at Indiana Wesleyan University, but at other institutions in various parts of the world. They challenge me to become a better teacher and pastor. They stretch my thinking, deepen my reflection, and expand my prayer life. I am certain that I benefit more from my students than they do from me. For this I am grateful.

I am also thankful for the opportunity to teach at Indiana Wesleyan University and for the sabbatical that allowed me time for research related to this manuscript. In particular, my sisters and brothers in the School of Theology and Ministry provide frequent collegial encouragement in my endeavors; thank you.

I also recognize that my thinking is dramatically formed by real people in real congregations whom I have served beside over many years. It has been the *doing* of sacred actions of worship that has influenced me more than anything else, calling me to explore how God is at work in these significant moments of the worshiping community. Thank you for your patience as I learned to lead over the years, often by trial and error.

I am greatly indebted to the late Robert E. Webber, who shaped my thinking beyond measure in all matters related to worship. His influence upon my worship worldview is serving me well and continues to be a personal priceless treasure.

I had prayer partners—family and friends—who committed to pray for me over the eighteen months this book was being written. These special people have included my dad, a retired pastor and man of prayer, who has been faithful to daily lift up this endeavor. And I am certain that the prayers of my mother, now voiced in heaven on my behalf, have joined those prayers of all the saints who make petition around the altar of God. I have felt and deeply appreciated the prayers of each one, for there were many days when I felt inadequate for this task.

I wish to express sincere thanks to Bob Hosack and Baker Academic for believing in my ongoing work and affording me the opportunity for my teaching to reach beyond my own physical classrooms by the publication of this book.

Last, but not least, several people have played key support roles. Special thanks go to Kelly Bixler for assisting me with edits and formatting, to Chris Bounds and Lester Ruth for freely sharing their knowledge and insights with me when I felt the need to consult with theological and historical experts, and to Mary Brown and Joyce Thornton for serving as frequent morale boosters. To each of you I owe a debt of gratitude.

Introduction

The class demonstration was over, but no one moved or spoke. The room was completely quiet except for the sound of water running down over the massive stone wall of the baptismal pool. The sunlight of high noon shone brilliantly throughout the atrium of the church, where my upper-level ministry class, Church Rituals, had just participated in a practicum on believer's baptism by immersion led by a team of students in the class. At the end of the baptism, the leaders had eloquently incorporated a renewal of baptism service—a first-time experience for most of the students in the class. The last notes of the guitar-led singing had faded, and everyone had returned to their seats after having gathered near the water. Ordinarily we would begin to evaluate the service, but not this time—at least not now. There was a holy hush that had simply taken over in the church-turned-classroom.

Eventually Sarah broke the silence with one audible word: "Wow." Her exclamation called me back from worshiper to professor; I asked what she meant. "I have never felt like I truly worshiped in a class before. I thought this would just be a class exercise for a grade, but I am so moved by the Holy Spirit right now! I have just experienced the power of what baptism is all about." Several other students echoed the same sentiments. Somehow evaluation just didn't seem to fit at that moment. Instead, we spent some time in silence, then prayer, and quietly left the church—my students to go on to another class, and me to praise God that classes can be times of worship too.

Why a Book about Sacred Actions in Corporate Worship?

It is said that necessity is the mother of invention. This proverb was certainly true in the writing of this book. All corporate worship is significant, for each

1

time the people of God gather in a given locale, they experience the presence of the risen Christ. The weekly rhythm of Lord's Day worship is the foundation for the relationship between God and people. But within and in addition to Sunday worship, there are occasions that may not occur weekly but hold great potential for our experiencing God in exceptionally moving ways. On these occasions God is not more present to us, but we may be more present to God as certain events alert us to God's presence and power. This book is about these particular worship events in the life of Christian communities.

In my vocation as professor I prepare women and men for local church ministry. In this role, at both the seminary and undergraduate levels, I have regularly taught courses in "church rituals"—courses that prepare students for their first years of pastoral ministry by introducing them to particular services of worship that are related to special moments in the life of the Christian community, such as baptism, Holy Communion, weddings, funerals, healing services, foot washing, and more. These types of services involve sacred actions that are specific to experiencing and even validating the event. We explore how to plan for and preside at the "service within a service" that these occasions afford.

Throughout my years of teaching I have not found a source that covers all of these types of services thoroughly—one that not only explains *what* to do but also *why* we do what we do in order to lead these types of services effectively. I found some books that contained multiple service orders with information on how to lead the service but provided no substantial biblical, theological, or historical rationale for the actions (books such as minister's handbooks, denominational resource books, and collections of prayers and liturgies come to mind). I found other books with more historical and theological information, but they tended to provide less practical application and addressed only one or two of the services—perhaps a book on the sacraments or only one of the other types of services (funerals, weddings, healing, etc). Both of these types of resources are very helpful, but a pastor just entering the ministry would need to acquire a significant number of these books to have the basic resources at hand. In short, I wrote this book out of necessity. I needed a textbook that was broad enough to cover the basic services at which any pastor must be able to preside, and deep enough to give the student an introductory understanding of the biblical, theological, historical, and pastoral underpinnings for planning and leading each service.

The passion I have for the topics covered in this book comes not only from my teaching but from decades of local church ministry. I am a vocational minister as well as a teacher. Services of worship are not academic exercises; they form the dynamic dialogue of a relationship between God and people.

In the pages of this book you will find not only a theoretical "how to" but a passionate "why we must"; these two streams become inseparable in the life of the experienced minister. Theory and practice, reflection and action must always be joined for the mature Christian leader.

With these purposes in mind, this book is written for anyone involved in preparing and leading services related to the primary sacred actions of the church as expressed in the sacraments/ordinances, life passages, and various other occasional services. This book is useful for the student preparing for a vocational career in ministry or for those who have never had the benefit of formal training in these specialized areas. It is also beneficial for the seasoned minister who would profit from a refreshing review of the basics, with some new insights to ponder as well. *The Special Service Worship Architect* is not only for ordained ministers who are generally expected to preside at these types of services but also for other worship leaders who have responsibility for developing worship in the local community, including musicians, other artists, altar guild or worship committees, seasonal planners, and so on.

Life Passages, Sacraments (Ordinances), and Other Occasional Services

This book examines seven types of special services that fall into three broad categories: life passages (weddings and funerals), the sacraments/ordinances (baptism and Holy Communion), and other occasional services (healing service, foot washing with love feast, and child dedication). The focus is on rituals that (1) are widely practiced by many Protestants and (2) call for pastoral leadership. The categories I have chosen are somewhat generic in title in order to speak to a broad audience. Various terms used by others also hold merit. For example, the late James White refers to all of these particular services as types of sacraments (though he is not suggesting equal sacramental weight). Actions that are common to all humanity, such as marriage and caring for the dead, he designates as *natural sacraments*; those actions spoken of in the Acts of the Apostles and in various epistles, such as healing and penance, he labels as *apostolic sacraments*; and the primary sacraments of baptism and the Lord's Supper—those instituted by Jesus in the Gospels—he refers to as *gospel sacraments*.[1] Exactly how the categories are labeled is not critical; simply note that these categories represent a broad range of services. Precisely because these services do not constitute an exhaustive list of possibilities, the final chapter of this book demonstrates how the leader may go about designing *any type* of sacred ritual using particular and fitting sacred actions.

Sacred Actions in the Context of Corporate Worship

The sacred actions presented in this book are not viewed as independent or (worse yet) private services that address the individual needs of a few people. Rather, the sacred actions belonging to these various services are always rendered in the public worship of a local congregation. All of the services addressed in this volume are viewed and presented as occasions of worship in the truest sense. Each service—a wedding, a funeral, a baptism, a foot washing service, or any number of other possibilities—is cast as a gathering to which the community is called to focus on and glorify God in Christ Jesus. As such, the normative principles of worship apply. There will be special themes and considerations, but the services will nevertheless be consistent with the best Christian worship practices.

Because of this perspective, I conceived of this book as a sequel to my first book, *The Worship Architect: A Blueprint for Designing Culturally Relevant and Biblically Faithful Services* (Baker Academic, 2010). In *The Worship Architect* I explain how the weekly Lord's Day duties of the worship leader resemble the duties of an architect. Worship architects care for the general, weekly worship services of a Christian community. They function much like a building architect; however, a building architect designs a *building*, whereas a worship architect designs a *relational experience* between God and people. Yet I am struck with how the metaphor also sustains the idea of creating and leading *special* sacred rituals—those worship events that may not occur on a weekly basis. The term "rituals architect" is used in this book to refer to a worship architect working with specialized sacred actions pertaining to particular services of corporate worship. How is this metaphor developed?

First, a building architect begins with visiting the site. She or he does this to discover the parameters of the project—the exact boundaries as set by the local authorities as well as how the building will be situated on the property. The architect investigates such things as the soil content (with implications for the type of foundation the building will require); whether the terrain is hilly or level and the type of structural adaptations that may be imposed by the terrain on the building; and what surrounds the property, be it commercial buildings or housing developments, freeways, or woods.

Likewise, rituals architects must "visit the site" by noting the setting for each sacred ritual. They must consider the *whole* worship service, of which any significant ritual is only one part. Too often sacred rituals appear as a tag-on to a regular service. When this is the case, parts of the service don't appear to belong with the other parts. Perhaps it's time for Communion simply because it's on the church calendar; so Communion gets inserted into the service without thought as to how it is dynamically connected to the whole service. Baptism sometimes gets treated the same way. A rituals architect understands that, like a building, any primary ritual has surroundings to consider. What comes before and after the ritual? How does it lead from and to other worship acts? Also, as with a building site, foundations are to be considered. What are the foundational principles that undergird each ritual? What beliefs will give stability to those worship words and actions a leader invites worshipers to say and do? At the beginning of each chapter we will lay some biblical, theological, and historical foundations for each ritual. This cannot possibly be comprehensive (for this book has its own parameters!), but laying good foundations for any worship endeavor is imperative.

Setting the Cornerstone

Cornerstones no longer function architecturally as they did centuries ago. Today they are largely symbolic or cosmetic. Prior to the development of modern construction techniques, the cornerstone was critical to the structure of an edifice. In previous generations the cornerstone was laid on the foundation first. It was perfectly situated as a corner anchor; as such, it served as the reference point from which all other measurements were taken and all of the walls erected. If the cornerstone was true, the entire building would be stable, providing the occupants with security and peace. If the cornerstone was not well laid, the entire structure of the building was compromised.

Christian worship is *Christian* because of Christ. Therefore, the centerpiece of all sacred rituals is Jesus Christ. Throughout this book I will be careful to note how critical the role of Jesus Christ is in each ritual, thereby affirming the Christo-centric nature of the ritual. The glorification of Jesus Christ, enabled by the Holy Spirit, who reminds believers of the Son, is well pleasing to God. It is critical to lay the cornerstone for all sacred actions on the person and work of Christ. He is true; we therefore do well to build our worship rituals centered on him, for in him "the whole structure is joined together and grows into a holy temple in the Lord; in whom you also are built together spiritually into a dwelling-place for God" (Eph. 2:21–22).

I recently visited the magnificent, modern Coventry Cathedral in Coventry, England, rebuilt after the original cathedral was destroyed during World War II by incendiary bombs. There, strategically positioned as a cornerstone to catch every worshiper's eye, is a large masonry piece, perfectly set as part of the building. The cornerstone was laid to the glory of God by Queen Elizabeth the Second on March 23, 1956. It is inscribed with these words: "Other foundation can no man lay than that which is laid which is JESUS CHRIST." The cornerstone was not needed for structural reasons, but it certainly is valued for spiritual reasons. It reminds worshipers from all over the world that Christian worship is founded on the person and work of our Lord and Savior, Jesus Christ.

Building the Structure

When a building architect begins to erect walls on the foundation, he is really "ordering the building." He is deciding which room comes first and which rooms lead naturally to other rooms. With the establishment of doorways in the walls, a traffic flow pattern is made possible for the occupants. The order and flow of rooms is extremely important, for it will help or hinder the purposes of the building; those engaging in activities inside will feel either natural or awkward as they use the building. Probably all of us have gone through a house and wondered, "What was the architect thinking?" when we noticed that there was no apparent logical explanation for the arrangement of rooms. In the parsonage where I lived as a young child, there were two bedrooms upstairs connected by a single doorway. The only way to my bedroom was through my brothers' bedroom—much to their dismay. When I could, I made the grandest of entrances as I made my way through their territory into my own. They risked my walking in on them as they changed clothes; I risked getting shot at with rubber bands. We would have appreciated a more efficient traffic flow to our bedrooms. Good structure facilitates good flow.

Each significant sacred ritual will have a logical sequence to its elements. Rituals architects prayerfully think through what order of words and actions will best facilitate the purpose of the ritual (as opposed to interrupting it), all the while remembering the foundations on which the structure is built. Sometimes the order is not a matter of wrong or right, but simply a matter of good versus better. Just as we seek to place worship acts in a well-planned order for our weekly worship services, the flow of the elements needed for particular sacred actions also must be well thought through. The order isn't rigid; be flexible where possible. But let's resist the idea that *any* order works. I suppose that could be the case if our goal was efficiency. However, the primary sacred rituals of the church are not a matter of pragmatics but of profoundness—the opportunity to experience holy moments as God works through the Spirit in the community. The order of events will definitely play a role in achieving this or hindering it.

Installing Doors and Windows

After the structure is in place, the architect installs windows, which let in light, allowing occupants to see. Doors are also set in place to help people move through the facility, encountering others or performing their duties. Doors and windows facilitate vision and relationship.

The rituals architect is interested in discovering means by which worshipers can encounter God and one another through *experiencing* primary sacred actions. The architect considers which particular elements will shed light on the ritual and its meaning and which elements will help worshipers "see" God and experience his presence. We want to expand our vision of and relationship with God and others. For each of the rituals explored in this book, we examine various types of prayers and songs that will aid worshipers in encountering God as the service unfolds. We explore how various symbols and the Christian year can shed light on the ritual as well. These are thought of as doors and windows that help us encounter God in the ritual. They are means of spiritual illumination. This aspect of designing church rituals is a very important one, for you can have a solid order of service in mind, but without making use of appropriate and effective prayers, songs, symbols, and seasons, the encounter is limited; participants remain somewhat in the dark.

Serving as Hospitable Host

Last, an architect's job is not finished until the building serves its purpose. If you have ever been to the dedication of a new building, you might have seen the architect (as head of the project) participating as a vital part of the ceremony. An architect's work is not done until people inhabit the facility and are engaged in relationships appropriate to the purpose of the building.

A most crucial aspect of being a rituals architect is that of serving as host to the community as it enters into sacred actions. As one who presides, you will be the channel between God and people, helping to connect them to God and one another as they open themselves to profound mysteries that await them. A rituals architect's work is not done until she or he effectively serves the community as host for an event. Just as when you entertain guests in your home for dinner, your actions as host (your demeanor, gestures of hospitality, conversational words, and welcoming tone) are critical to enabling others to fully engage in the event. Likewise, this book will address the important role of one who presides over each of these sacred rituals. There are certain words, gestures, and demeanors that nuance each ritual, allowing leaders to function as especially gracious hosts. Frankly, there are effective and ineffective ways to lead each ritual. Implementing the suggestions for leading effectively will take practice, but in time hosts can become very comfortable in playing the role.

Using the architect metaphor, then, each chapter that addresses a specific ritual will include these sections: Laying the Foundations (biblical, historical, and theological considerations); Building the Structure (designing the order of service, with one or more sample services included); Installing Doors and Windows (employing songs, Scriptures, prayers, symbols, and the Christian year); Serving as Hospitable Host (the duties and attributes of the effective leader); Key Terms (important vocabulary specific to each ritual); and To Learn More (suggested readings for further study). (Chapters may include other sections as well.)

Also, in order to enable group study, each chapter begins with "Explore" (questions to initiate reflection before reading the chapter) and ends with "Engage" (practical suggestions for immediate application of the content).

What the Reader Can Expect

This book is a guide to effective leadership in the sacred actions of Christian worship. It will invite the reader to participate through reflection on and the performance of certain standard rituals that have developed over time and have found accepted practice in their general features while remaining adaptable to various denominational distinctives. I have intended to voice the content in broadly Protestant terms. While I write out of the greater Wesleyan tradition that I claim, I am sincere in my attempt to welcome and speak to other traditions within the body of Christ. I trust you will see that attempt reflected throughout the book. I am confident that each reader will be able to nuance the principles and practices suggested to suit his or her own denominational reference points. I make no attempt to be all things to all people. Still, there is much common ground to be enjoyed and celebrated.

Chapter 1 will introduce the reader to the vocabulary of sacred actions by defining some terms used throughout the book—terms such as "ritual," "rite," "liturgy," "rubric," "sacrament," and "ordinance." The reader will note that throughout the book I use the terms "sacred actions" and "rituals" interchangeably, a practice reminiscent of the influence of my mentor, the late Robert E. Webber. Chapter 1 will then set forth five foundational principles of all Christian sacred action (a nonexhaustive list). These fundamental aspects assert that sacred actions are corporate, formational, symbolic, Christo-centric, and outwardly focused in nature.

Chapters 2 and 3 present services related to life passages: the Christian wedding and the Christian funeral.

Chapters 4 and 5, the heart of the book, discuss services related to the sacraments/ordinances: baptism and the Lord's Table.

Chapters 6, 7, and 8 examine services related to other occasions: healing, foot washing with love feast, and child dedications. (Not only are child dedications, most common within the so-called Free Church tradition,[2] explained, but alternative approaches are also suggested, which may commend this ritual to wider consideration.)

Chapter 9 is a unique feature of the book. It answers the question, How does the leader go about designing other types of sacred actions? This chapter includes five dimensions of sacred ritual for corporate worship, additional considerations, the general order of sacred actions, particular features of dedications, and ten basic steps in designing sacred actions for corporate worship.

If this volume enriches your experience and understanding of the various sacred actions employed in your future or present congregation, my prayers will have been answered. May the Holy Spirit, poured out at Pentecost, empower every act of worship placed in service to the glory of God and for the sake of the world.

Constance M. Cherry
Pentecost Sunday, 2012

1

Foundations
for Sacred Actions

Ryan and Jason landed jobs in the same town after graduation. They knew each other in college but had never hung out in the same circle of friends. Once they realized that they were going to be living in the same town, and given the high cost of rent, they decided to become housemates in order to share expenses. They met at a local coffee shop one Friday night to talk over the details. After they discussed the housing arrangements, they turned to how things would work in the mornings; after all, they would leave for work around the same time. "I have my own routine in the morning," Ryan said. "When the alarm goes off and my feet hit the floor, I do the same things, the same way, in the same order every morning. It's efficient. I make some coffee, let the dog out, take a shower, sip my first cup of coffee, brush my teeth, shave (drink coffee), let the dog in, get dressed (drink more coffee), eat some cereal, fill my travel mug with the last of the coffee, and start the car."

"Do you ever vary the routine?" Jason asked.

"Rarely," Ryan replied. "There's no reason to change it, really; it gets me where I'm going just fine. Besides, I don't have to think about it; I just *do* it!" He paused. "So, how does your morning go?"

"Well, I hit the snooze bar, get up eventually, run to the shower, dress, and dash out the door. I grab breakfast at a drive-through."

Both agreed that they wouldn't be in each other's way and that things should work out just fine—as long as somebody let the dog out.

A regular morning routine is a kind of *ritual*. It consists of performing the necessary tasks in a certain sequence to prepare us for the day. We often maintain the same routine because it's just plain efficient. We probably all have our morning ritual. What's yours?

When we think about the sacred actions of Christian worship, we are thinking of sacred rituals performed in the context of the church; and while they are ordered actions, they are far from routine. The rituals of Christianity performed in public worship are much more than things we do without having to think about it. The sacred rituals of Christian worship are about relationship. They are about a chosen people on a journey with the triune God. The sacred actions that mark this journey *signify the type of relationship* we have with God and others; and they also *provide opportunities for ever-increasing depth in this holy relationship*. Rituals provide us the ways and means to express the relationship between God and God's people. Keep the following two features in mind as you proceed through this book:

- Rituals signify the believer's relationship with God.
- Rituals aid in deepening this relationship.

Every relationship transpires in stages; it's like a journey taking place over time. The primary sacred rituals of the Christian faith, that have been practiced by the church for millennia, provide markers for the stages of our journey with God. Some rituals have been practiced by believers since the time of Christ and are understood to "belong to the *esse* of the church"; that is, they are "essential practices . . . that constitute the church as church."[1] The proclamation of the Word and participation in the sacraments/ordinances are two examples of essential practices. Other rituals have been claimed by the church over time because, while they may not constitute the church in the same way, they are, nevertheless, to the great benefit of the church. These rituals are believed to be *bene esse*,[2] practices that are beneficial for the church. Many of the time-honored church rituals, such as services of healing, funerals, ordination, and weddings, may be considered in this category. So one way of thinking about the rituals of corporate Christian worship is to consider them as essential or highly beneficial. These ecclesial practices are related in that out of the church's commitment to Word and sacraments (both primary means for relationship with God) flows the context for the other more occasional practices.

The sacred actions that serve as markers on our journey with God can be categorized in other ways too. Some relate to common life passages, while others do not. For instance, weddings and funerals represent significant transitions from one way of life to another—a time when "life before" is very different than "life after." Some rituals relate to personal spiritual life passages, such as conversion, baptism, and confirmation. These occasions also represent lifestyles that are very different before and after, as individuals take on Christ and pursue life as citizens of the kingdom of God.[3] Some rituals are celebrated frequently, for instance the Table of the Lord; others are more occasional and need-specific, such as a healing rite. So while there are many types of rituals that Christians practice, each serves as a marker of some sort, as God's people progress on their faith journey, making pilgrimage in stages.

In this book we will explore several different types of sacred actions used in corporate worship settings. While they will vary in purpose and approach, you will discover how much they have in common. This chapter will examine some significant aspects all rituals share. These important commonalities form the biblical, theological, historical, cultural, pastoral, and missiological foundations for sacred ritual.

But first, every discipline has its own terminology, and ritual studies is no different. This chapter begins by explaining some basic and important terms so that as we learn about sacred actions central to Christian faith, we will have command of the vocabulary related to our craft as rituals architects. Many more vocabulary words that pertain to specific rituals are explained in succeeding chapters.

The Vocabulary of Sacred Ritual

As we get started, it is possible that you may not have heard of some of the words defined below; or if you have, perhaps you have held a very different opinion of their meaning. It's even possible that you have a negative bias about one or more of these words. If so, simply remember that we are venturing into vocabulary that has been accepted by church leaders throughout the centuries in many places and in many Christian traditions. If you are one who has had little or no acclimation to such terminology, simply try to take each meaning at face value. Many fine liturgical dictionaries and glossaries are available to offer helpful definitions as well; I encourage you to examine several of these sources to further round out your understanding of each concept. In doing so you will probably find that the words are nuanced a little differently depending upon the source. That's okay. It usually takes several good definitions to strike at the heart of the meaning of these words.

Here are a few key terms, then, that will be used repeatedly throughout the book as we become rituals architects. For each one, you will find a very simple definition; I have tried to keep them as succinct and as basic as possible. Each definition will be followed by some important things to note about the term.

Ritual

An authoritative *event*, sanctioned by the church, which uses formalized actions, words, gestures, and symbols that are repeated to enable some particular aspect of the corporate worship of God.[4]

Things to Note

ALL WORSHIPING COMMUNITIES EMPLOY RITUALS

Every worshiping community employs rituals to enable their worship, regardless of their history or tradition. Even those worshipers who are rooted in a very free and spontaneous tradition use actions, words, and gestures that are repeated in order to facilitate their experience of worship. Repeated actions, words, and gestures used by any community to enable some aspect of the worship of God are considered rituals. The question will not be *whether* we have or use rituals but the *degree to which* we reflect on and employ the rituals that we use in worship so that they glorify God and edify believers.

THEY'RE OLDER THAN YOU THINK

Worship rituals are not practices that originated over the past several hundred years of Western church history. Though every religion known to humankind employs ritual, our use of ritual is rooted in the Judeo-Christian practices we claim in the Old and New Testaments. Even a cursory reading of the Old Testament yields an astounding number of examples of worship rituals ordered by God to maintain the relationship between Israel and Yahweh. These include such things as circumcision, purification rites, entrance rites to the temple, sacrifices, offerings, and seasonal observances. Carefully constructed rituals, given by God, were the central features of Jewish worship. Many of these do not carry forward to the New Testament;[5] yet it is clear from the apostles' writings that while many rituals changed or were no longer needed, the early church nevertheless was not "rituals free." There too we find repeated actions and words that became necessary for Christian worship from God's point of view. This is seen, for instance, in the commands surrounding the Lord's Supper (1 Cor. 11:17–34),[6] the act of corporate prayer (see 1 Tim. 2:1–4), the giving of offerings for those in need (see 1 Cor. 16:1–4), and so on. The new community was expected to repeat these rituals to enable worship, though the manner varied from place to place. As various rituals developed and were formalized, certain features became normative and were passed on for widespread use.

Rituals Have Special Features

Rituals commonly share certain important features; I will highlight three. First, sacred rituals have significance—they are not "just actions and words." Worship rituals employ actions, words, gestures, and symbols in such a way that they express a deeper meaning than what is evident on the surface. Something profound is being experienced in these agents of communication, even if one holds a nonsacramental view of sacred actions. I was raised in a tradition that referred to baptism and the Lord's Supper as ordinances. ("Sacrament" and "ordinance" will be explained soon—hold on!) While we did not conceive of these actions as conveying any divine activity, even as a child I can remember experiencing a profound sense of the presence of Christ as I knelt at a Communion rail with other believers to receive bread and juice. For me those occasions were not void of God's activity in my young heart; they were extremely significant in advancing my spiritual journey. Regardless of your view of God's role in rituals practiced by the church, never make the mistake of underestimating the power of God-ordained rituals to communicate a spiritual truth and grace well beyond the words and actions themselves.

Second, rituals bear repetition—their actions, words, gestures, and symbols are repeated from time to time and place to place. That is one of the things that makes them rituals. If you've ever attended a Major League baseball game, perhaps you have noticed the sports rituals that surround the event—and have for well over a century. The same routine manifests itself from place to place: the players do warm-ups, the umpire yells "play ball," the organ background music pumps up the crowd, the announcer uses his familiar phrases, the seventh-inning stretch allows for the singing of "Take Me Out to the Ball Game," some hot dogs are eaten, and much more. These very actions and words together constitute what it means to *experience* baseball the good old American way. Baseball in America is not just a routine—it's an experience! It has its rituals, and they bear repeating; for each time people attend a game, they desire to engage in the same routine that helps them to participate in the event in all its fullness.

Actions, words, gestures, and symbols, when repeated over time in the context of Christian worship, likewise provide a means for participating in a holy event in all its fullness. The experience becomes recognizable through the very repetition of the rituals from time to time and place to place. It is in the repetition that the ritual becomes recognizable precisely as the event that it is, giving shape and character to the experience which, in turn, gives it its meaning.

A third feature of ritual is that it becomes formalized over time. Some folks have an aversion to the word "formalized." All that is meant here is that there has become a normative way of carrying out most sacred actions among Christians—for good reason. Certain ways of doing things have earned the church's seal of approval not because the rituals police are on patrol, but because there is typically a good and rich and full way of engaging in the actions that reflect biblical and theological soundness. In some cases, certain aspects of a ritual are formalized because of a direct command from Scripture. A good example of this is the use of particularly chosen words that Paul used at the Lord's Supper and, by implication, commends to the next generation of believers to use as well. These very words, Paul indicates, were passed on to him from the Lord: "The Lord Jesus on the night when he was betrayed took a loaf of bread, and when he had given thanks, he broke it and said, 'This is my body that is for you. Do this in remembrance of me'" (1 Cor. 11:23–24). These words of institution, used almost universally at the Lord's Table, are an instance of formalized liturgy. It's the same principle at work when we baptize using the Trinitarian formula of Father, Son, and Holy Spirit (Matt. 28:19). The singing of hymns during a foot washing service, the use of oil during healing services, the exchange of rings during a wedding ceremony, the eulogy during a funeral—all of these are instances of formalized liturgy. The exact actions, words, gestures, symbols, and orders of service have always varied according to context, of course. Yet there is amazingly widespread continuity in the general practice of sacred rituals because, over time, the church has viewed certain things as necessary or helpful to the ritual for effectiveness and for authenticity to scriptural expectations.

Rite

The particular combination of actions, words, gestures, and symbols that constitute the order and content for a designated ritual.[7]

Things to Note

The word "rite" is used in a variety of ways, which can get confusing. It can refer to the combination of actions, words, gestures, and symbols that relate to *a particular aspect of a worship service*. For instance, sometimes we refer to Gathering rites—those worship acts that are employed at the beginning of a service to help worshipers enter properly into God's presence as a community. (Remember, every church has Gathering rites, whether they call them that or not.) Other times the word "rite" refers to the combined worship elements of *a particular sacred ritual*. For instance, a baptismal rite consists of the actions, words, gestures, and symbols employed by a community to carry out Christ's command to baptize disciples of all nations.

Either way, rites are primarily the content choices and ordering of those words and actions considered to be important for experiencing the ritual event at hand. A rite creates a "rituals journey"; it forms a pathway for taking the community from point A to point B in a sensible way so that the relationship between God and people is deepened as they progress through the various worship acts related to the ritual. Rites can be contemporary or traditional in style (or any other type of stylistic expression); they may be formally or informally led. Simply think of rites as the plan you will follow to convey the ritual event.

Liturgy

The complete collection of actions, words, gestures, and symbols that facilitates the prayerful worship and full participation of all worshipers in the context of corporate worship.

Things to Note

The English word "liturgy" is from the Greek word *leitourgia*, translated as "the work of the people." In its broadest sense, "liturgy" refers to the sum total of worship acts that the people do in the course of any given worship service. In its original context in ancient Greece, *leitourgia* had to do with service in municipalities, the public works of civic employees as they served the community. Service is the key to understanding the word's original Greek use. In fact, it can be translated as "service" and is, of course, why we refer to a worship event as a "worship service." *Leitourgia* is a favored term in the New Testament, used numerous times to refer to the various worship acts rendered by persons as they serve God in public worship.

Liturgy is often identified with the content of worship. However, it is more than that. Liturgy is active—participatory. It refers to all that is entailed as the people offer themselves to God through sacred texts and actions. It includes not only what is verbalized but also what is unspoken—gestures, movements, signs, symbols, and more. Liturgy focuses on "participatory knowledge" rather than "propositional knowledge."[8] *Leitourgia* suggests that all worshipers should be highly invested in serving God through the corporate acts of the liturgy.

Like the word "rite," the word "liturgy" can refer to either a part of a service (for example, the Liturgy of the Word, the Liturgy of Baptism) or the entire worship service (the Divine Liturgy).[9] It is important to realize that the whole liturgy is, in itself, prayer. While there are prayers *in* worship, *all* of what we do in the holy occupation of corporate worship should be viewed as prayer—God communicating to worshipers, and worshipers communicating to God. Because sacred rituals are so intricately dependent on the use of the body, the early church father Tertullian emphasized that sacramental liturgy is inescapably a prayer of the body.[10] Worshipers engage their bodies through gestures and actions in order to "do" the ritual. The body both shows (portrays) and tells (announces) the central truths of the gospel represented in the ritual. Sometimes the most profoundly beautiful aspect of sacred ritual is the embodiment of the truth expressed in the ritual as prayer.

By now you may be thinking that there is overlap in the definitions of the three terms presented thus far: ritual, rite, and liturgy. You're right. It's sort of difficult to define one without resorting to the use of one of the other terms. In fact, you will notice this very problem when you study the words using authoritative sources. At times some of them are interchanged.[11] That's okay; the words do intersect. There is no reason to force differentiations between them that do not exist. Nevertheless, I would like to emphasize a central feature of each of these terms to help us as we make our way through the seven sacred actions explained in the following chapters.

Ritual is an *event*. We will think of rituals primarily as events in which we participate.

Example: Baptism is a ritual. (Baptism is an event.)

Rite is the intentional *content and order* of the event.

Example: A baptism ritual uses a particular set of worship elements in a sensible order that constitute a baptism (i.e., the baptismal rite).

Liturgy is the corporate words and actions that provide for the *prayerful participation* of worshipers.

Example: The baptismal liturgy contains all of the appropriate actions, words, gestures, and symbols for all worshipers to prayerfully participate in the baptismal service (the baptismal liturgy).

I hope to "lean into" these meanings of the terms as we proceed through the chapters of this book. There will always be some overlap of definitions, but this need not frustrate us. As rituals architects, we must understand how these words are used in certain contexts and also how they can shed light on our holy duties as we seek to lead God's people in most sacred moments.

Rubric

Instructions for leading and participating in a ritual.

Things to Note

Guidance for those leading sacred rituals is very important, for two reasons. First, there are sometimes very specific things to say and do that are considered necessary for the ritual to truly function as the ritual that is intended. For example, a rubric for a baptismal service will tell the minister how and when to use the symbol of water in the baptismal rite (appropriate to your tradition), as well as what words to say and when (for example, "in the name of the Father, and of the Son, and of the Holy Spirit"). The rituals instituted by Christ and his church are *sacred* rituals. As such, it is very important that the integrity of each ritual is maintained. This does not mean that all Christians will perform the rituals in exactly the same way. But rubrics make sure we are performing the ritual well, biblically, theologically, and pastorally.

Second, because Christian rituals hold the potential for a congregation to experience profound moments of deep spiritual meaning, the way leaders approach each ritual really matters. Rubrics provide helpful things to note to enrich the potential experience of the ritual event. Good leaders avail themselves of appropriate rubrics as a way of minimizing attention on themselves, drawing the attention instead to the God-moments of the ritual.

Rubrics, of course, are used in any number of events for good reason. Boy Scout leaders are provided rubrics for leading the Pledge of Allegiance. Written instructions advise the leader first to invite the audience to stand, then to turn and face the flag, place his right hand over his heart, begin with a strong voice, and lead at an appropriate pace. These are things expected of anyone leading the Pledge of Allegiance in order to fulfill the demands of the ritual.

Rubrics appear as written instructions found within denominational worship manuals or minister's handbooks.[12] Some rubrics are very detailed; others are less so. You will most often see rubrics appearing in red print. (The word "rubric" is derived from the Latin word *ruber*, for "red.") Some rubrics are indicated as *prescriptive* (required of leaders in order to fulfill the demands of the ritual from the church's point of view), while others are *descriptive* only (suggested for effective leadership). One can typically discern between prescriptive and descriptive by the use of the terms "shall" (prescriptive) or "may" (descriptive).

Rubrics should not be viewed as hard-and-fast rules to follow; often it's not a matter of right or wrong. Rather, rubrics are helpful guides that, if followed, coach the leader in performing the sacred action properly and pastorally from one's ecclesial point of view (in some cases authorized by one's denomination). Rubrics, then, are specific directions that help a leader preserve the integrity of the ritual and lead it effectively in the community.

Sacrament

A sacred ritual, instituted and commanded by Christ to be practiced by all believers of all times and places, which serves as a means of grace.

Things to Note

TWO SACRAMENTS/ORDINANCES

Protestants almost universally embrace two rituals that are called either "sacraments" or "ordinances."[13] These two are baptism and the Lord's Supper.[14] Some Christian groups have determined that other rituals also qualify as sacraments. Many Anabaptist traditions designate three ordinances by including feet washing. Roman Catholics designate seven sacraments: baptism, confirmation, Eucharist, penance, anointing of the sick, holy orders, and matrimony. Eastern Orthodox churches likewise embrace the same seven sacraments (though confirmation is referred to as "chrismation," due to the anointing with oil, "chrism," in the ritual).[15]

However, following the Reformation of the early sixteenth century, Protestant groups largely endorsed the two sacraments of baptism and the Lord's Supper. They were identified as such because both were (1) mandated by Christ for his followers, (2) to be practiced by all believers for all time, and (3) the only two actions that joined promise and visible sign; that is, both baptism and the Lord's Supper are based on a promise of God that cannot be separated from a visible sign that enacts the promise. As James White explains, "Sacraments are promises connected to visible signs, and those promises are contained in scripture."[16] Baptismal promises are contained in Scripture; for example, "The one who believes and is baptized will be saved" (Mark 16:16) and "This is my body . . . this is my blood of the covenant, which is poured out for many for the forgiveness of sins" (Matt. 26:26, 28). It is important to note that receiving the promise is not simply intellectual but includes "a deep sense of assurance that the sacrament actually conveys the promise that accompanies it."[17] This last dimension was most prominent in Martin Luther's theology; in fact, it was central to official Lutheran teaching.[18] John Calvin nuanced this same truth differently, choosing to view the sacraments as seals of God's promises.[19] For Calvin, the signs were extremely important, for they effected what they signified. The Church of England articulated its view in its Articles of Religion: "Sacraments ordained of Christ be not only badges or tokens of Christian men's profession, but rather they be certain sure witnesses, and effectual signs of grace, and God's good will toward us, by the which he doth work invisibly in us, and doth not only quicken, but also strengthen and confirm our Faith in him."[20] As you can see, most of the Reformers, in some measure, embraced the view that a sacrament is "an outward and visible sign of an inward and spiritual grace."[21]

For reasons addressed above, then, most Protestants have designated baptism and the Lord's Supper as the only true sacraments/ordinances to be practiced by the church. They are sometimes referred to as "dominical actions"—those actions ordered by Christ for his followers to practice. ("Ecclesial actions" refers to those sacred actions that are recommended and valued by virtue of common historical practice but are not explicitly commanded by Jesus.)

ROOTS OF THE WORD

Our English word "sacrament" comes from the Latin word *sacramentum*, which means "sacred pledge."[22] The term was used in ancient Rome to refer to a military oath of allegiance that a soldier took in pledge to his commanding officer—an oath not to desert his place of duty. The first part of the word comes from *sacer*, and refers to that which is sacred, set apart, consecrated, made holy in contradistinction to the profane or the secular. When we participate in the sacraments, we are engaged with sacred entities, tangible items (water, bread, wine) that have been set apart (consecrated) for holy use. By God's grace, what was common is now made uncommon to serve God's purposes. And all this is understood to be in the context of a sacred pledge—a covenant, if you will. In baptism we receive God's pledge of cleansing from sin and salvation; we pledge ourselves to repentance and to being faithful disciples of Jesus Christ, serving him as Lord. At the Table, Christ reminds us of his ongoing pledge to us of salvation from sin, of victory over evil, and his promise to return; we then renew our pledge to follow him as his true disciples and give ourselves anew in service to the kingdom of God. A mutual, sacred pledge transpires at the sacraments. Some traditions refer to the sacrament of the Lord's Supper as a mystery. This reference comes from the Greek word *mystērion*, a word Paul uses often in his New Testament letters. Indeed, how great a mystery God's love in Jesus Christ truly is, recalled in the sacraments of baptism and the Lord's Supper.

Yet when we use the word "sacrament," caution is in order. We must not be too quick to cast all traditions that use the word "sacrament" into the same pile. While many Protestants favor the term "sacrament" when referring to baptism and the Lord's Supper, a broad range of meanings is intended, depending on the official doctrinal perspective of one's denomination. The degree of supernatural significance that is understood to be at play varies widely. Some would take the "softer" sacramental view: "By faith we believe that God is somehow supernaturally at work in the event, though we may not know exactly how." Others would affirm a more assertive view: "We believe that God is supernaturally at work performing eternal salvation in and through the ritual." There are also a number of views that appear between these two extremes, much like a continuum.

As you can see, there's quite a variance of understanding among those who use the term "sacrament." They may agree on the term but disagree on the meaning of the actual ritual event. Those who use the term "sacrament" will agree, however, that divine activity is at work in and through baptism and the Lord's Supper, and that the Holy Spirit is expected to empower believers in their discipleship and spiritual formation (seen or unseen, recognized or not) when they sincerely participate in these events by faith. This position considers the sacraments to be "means of grace." They are a means, a way in which believers receive the gift of God's sustaining grace; they serve as a God-appointed avenue through which God meets us and changes us for God's glory.

Again, caution is in order. First, the phrase "means of grace" has a range of meanings, depending upon where you find yourself on this sacramental continuum. The majority of traditions that use the phrase are not referring to a means for eternal salvation apart from individual faith. Second, remember that grace is a multifaceted word, as there are several dimensions to grace. John Wesley noted four dimensions of grace: prevenient grace, justifying grace, sanctifying grace, and perfecting grace. Wesley said these episodes of grace were a way to explain the several movements of God's grace in our journey; in each of these movements God comes to us to impart that which we cannot provide for ourselves. We are not talking about more grace or less grace here; grace is grace. It's not about an amount of grace. Those who use the phrase "means of grace" are simply saying that the sacraments are God's venue for God to be at work calling us, saving us, sanctifying us, and perfecting us for God's glory and for the sake of God's kingdom.

In summary, the sacramental view of baptism and the Lord's Supper can be articulated this way: "When God speaks, God shows; and when God shows, God gives."[23]

Ordinance

A purely symbolic sacred ritual, instituted and commanded by Christ to be practiced by all believers of all times and places, which does not serve as a means of grace.

Things to Note

Christians who favor the term "ordinance" practice the same two rituals instituted by Jesus—baptism and the Lord's Supper—but they view the events very differently from Christians who hold a sacramental view. Ordinance folks take a highly symbolic view and believe that these events are *only* symbolic, that the events do not provide a means of grace,[24] while sacramental folks value the symbols related to the rituals of baptism and the Lord's Supper but understand the event to be more than symbolic. Ordinance folks perform the ordinances because they are ordained by God in Scripture through the commands of Jesus. Ordinance people say, "We baptize because Jesus said to; we take the Lord's Supper because Jesus said to. In so doing we use the symbols associated with the biblical accounts of these events, but we do not expect God to be at work supernaturally. We are simply obeying our Lord by doing what he told us to do concerning these two occasions."

At the risk of oversimplification, here is a very simple (nonexhaustive) comparison of the sacramental view and ordinance view as they pertain to baptism and the Lord's Supper.

Sacramental View	Ordinance View
Sacraments are a means of grace.	Ordinances are not a means of grace.
Sacraments are observed because Jesus told us to do so *and* we need God's ongoing and renewing grace.	Ordinances are observed because Jesus told us to do so.
The emphasis is on God's activity.	The emphasis is on the participant's activity.
The sacraments are more than symbolic.	The ordinances are purely symbolic in nature.
The Lord's Supper tends to be celebrated more frequently because it is a means of grace.	The Lord's Supper tends to be celebrated less frequently because it is not a means of grace.

Both positions are time-honored Christian views. This is one of those areas where we extend Christian charity, whether believers use the term "sacrament" or "ordinance." There are many things that divide us; this need not be one of them. Deeply spiritual people have used either of these two terms over the centuries, having simply arrived at a different viewpoint as a result of their interpretation of Scripture. In this book, especially as we get into the chapters on the Lord's Supper and baptism, I will approach the matter from the standpoint of sacrament, because that is the view I hold as a pastor and teacher and also because it is the position of my denomination and the institution in which I teach. Nevertheless, I honor my "ordinance" sisters and brothers and will continue to speak to their view also, as you will see.

Officiate

To perform a religious ceremony by virtue of office.

Things to Note

Most denominations have a stated position on exactly who may officiate at various church rituals. It may be the clergy, an elder, or a layperson, depending on the event and the denomination's polity. If someone officiates at a ritual, they do so by virtue of their ecclesial office. A pastor generally officiates at a wedding or a funeral and is most often required for baptism and the Lord's Supper. If you are a pastor-to-be, get comfortable with the funeral director's phone call with the invitation, "Will you officiate at your parishioner's funeral?"

Preside

To direct proceedings by virtue of exercising control over the event.

Things to Note

If you run into the word "president" in a rituals context, it is not referring to someone holding political or civic office; it simply means "the one who presides" at the ritual event. He or she is the one who controls what happens. There is no real difference between the meaning of the terms "preside" and "officiate"; both are used extensively in pastoral literature. For whatever reason, it is more common to find the word "officiate" in relation to leading weddings and funerals and "preside" when referring to the sacraments of the Lord's Supper and baptism.[25]

We have begun with exploring some basic terms that are important for the understanding of sacred rituals. It's important to learn these long-standing terms first, for they form the basic vocabulary of the rituals architect. Now let us turn to some foundational principles that will undergird our services of sacred actions.

The Corporate Nature of Sacred Rituals

Individualism has become a problem in modern Western worship. While it is true that God relates to individual persons and that the invitation to salvation and Christian discipleship is extended to individuals with the expectation of a personal response to the triune God, we are called to live out our faith in community. We are not isolated believers seeking to follow God on our own; rather, we are members of the body of Christ, operating within a fellowship of Christ-followers who are committed to living as residents of the kingdom of God.

All primary church rituals are to be offered within the context of corporate worship,[26] for it is in the communal worship setting where we experience the presence of the living Lord in a most unique way. In addition, we are on life's journey together; as a collective body we must gather ourselves, at God's invitation, to engage in the wondrous work of each sacred action. It is the body of Christ that must form the context for celebrating the significant occasions of spiritual pilgrimage and life passages.

Corporate worship is the primary avenue God uses to relate to any Christian community.[27] When faithful followers are gathered weekly for worship, they are holding a corporate conversation with God in Christ as empowered by the Holy Spirit. God is understood to be present, through Christ, among the believers who come together to hear from God and to offer themselves in love and service in response. Worshiping in community is a core value described in both the Old and New Testaments. In the Scriptures we read of dozens of occasions when God met with people of faith to receive their worship and to impart God's own self in return. The priority afforded in Scripture to weekly community gatherings of worship is unmistakable. It is through corporate worship that the God-human relationship is fostered and secured.

But there is more. Corporate worship is not only the scriptural means through which God and community relate; the meeting itself helps to form our corporate identity as the people of God. The truth is that we are shaped by our regular meeting with one another in God's presence. Like a biological family, we take on values, beliefs, language, and priorities simply by participation in the events of the family. Just when you think you are not your father or mother, you discover how very much like them you really are; we *are* our parents' children. Much of whom each of us has become has been *caught* rather than taught. Likewise, when we regularly place ourselves under the influence of the liturgy of our church, we will find ourselves becoming transformed by that which we hear, speak, think, taste, feel, and imagine. The ancient maxim *lex orandi, lex credendi* (as we pray, so we believe) is widely embraced to be true:[28] we pray (engage in the whole liturgy) only to find that we come to believe that which we are speaking and doing through worship. Certainly it is a two-way street; our theological understanding should influence the way we worship as well. In that sense, *lex orandi, lex credendi* is reciprocal. Nevertheless, this basic premise we find to be true: we worship in faith first, and then find ourselves shaped by that to which we have surrendered. That is why it is so very important to have young children participating regularly in the liturgy. In doing so we are discipling them in the faith; we are forming their

Christian worldview. Worship in community is, therefore, a profound arena for participating in the primary sacred rituals of the church, for in corporate worship we encounter the presence of the risen Lord and are positioning ourselves to be shaped by that very encounter.

It is imperative, then, that the liturgies for church rituals are communal in nature. Much care must be given to involve the worshiping community at every possible opportunity. It is not appropriate for the liturgy to take place between the pastor and one or two persons alone, with the congregation merely looking on. While we may be witnessing an individual person making a life passage (a funeral) or spiritual pilgrimage (a baptism), the person is understood to be undertaking this journey from, through, or into the community of faith. It is the unison voice of the community that must become the dominant voice of the ritual. Liturgical theologian Nathan Mitchell argues that "the gathered assembly is the primary *subject* (agent) of liturgical action and is not only the 'object' or passive recipient of ministry from the ordained."[29] Mitchell is not dismissing the agency of the Holy Spirit at work in liturgical action when he refers to the assembly as the primary subject; rather, he is simply emphasizing the critical role the community plays in corporate worship. The danger of individualism in worship is that the clergy and one or two "recipients" of liturgical action form a passive approach to church rituals, when instead it is the assembly *together*—the congregants, clergy, and particular participants in the ritual (a wedding couple, a youth to be baptized)—that is fully engaged throughout. That is why, for instance, *corporate* pledges are made in most rituals. When a congregation states their intent to pray for a newly baptized believer or pledge their support of the bride and groom, when it proclaims a creed of the church, or when worshipers sing a blessing, the ritual is centered in community. Remember that sacred rituals are about relationship—not just individual worshipers' relationships with God but also our relationship with one another before God. With the communal nature of sacred rituals in mind, we discover that rituals are both vertical *and* horizontal—they are directed to God and one another. Each of the primary sacred rituals of our Christian faith is intended to be celebrated publicly, with one's sisters and brothers of faith forming the arena for the ritual and serving as energetic participants throughout. There is little room for individual piety when it comes to the rituals of the church.

The Formational Nature of Sacred Rituals

We have just noted how sacred rituals shape us as we present ourselves to God in worship. And so, in a way, *lex orandi, lex credendi* happens somewhat informally.[30]

This formational aspect of the liturgy just "happens" over time as the sincere worshiper participates fully in communal worship. That true worship fosters faith through our full participation in the liturgy cannot be underestimated. At the same time, rituals offer us an opportunity for intentional spiritual formation.

The term "spiritual formation" is used in different ways today.[31] I am using the term to refer to our growth in Christlikeness, which comes when we intentionally cooperate with God for our transformation, especially through the ongoing use of the spiritual disciplines. M. Robert Mulholland offers a helpful definition: "Spiritual formation is the process of being conformed to the image of Christ for the sake of others."[32] The key words provide much insight. First, spiritual formation is always a *process*. There is no such thing as instantaneous spiritual formation. It happens over a long period of time—a lifetime, in fact. Second, spiritual formation is a process of *being conformed*. This suggests that surrender is involved. While our contemporary culture shouts, "*Be* yourself," God's Spirit is calling, "*Surrender* yourself." The point of spiritual formation is to become what God has in mind and to resist what we have in mind. Third, spiritual formation has only one goal: growth in Christlikeness. Spiritual formation is not about *knowing* more or *doing* more; it is about *being* more—more like Jesus. The fourth part of the definition is incredibly significant: our pursuit of Christlikeness is *for the sake of others*. We often have the mistaken idea that we are to become like Jesus so that we can be more spiritual people. Not really. Any progress in Christlikeness has a more important goal, that of benefiting others in their perception and experience of the triune God. The more we are like Christ, the greater the chances that others will comprehend who God is and experience aspects of his love.

This all raises the question, How does spiritual formation happen? One of the primary means through which we are formed is the practice of time-honored spiritual disciplines. Spiritual disciplines are those means that believers employ to place themselves before God in order for God to change them according to his will. They are intentional things we do (disciplines of engagement),[33] or cease to do (disciplines of abstinence),[34] in order to open ourselves to God for intervention—for allowing God's Spirit to transform our ungodly nature into God's holy nature. Spiritual disciplines are useful avenues that help facilitate the sanctification of the believer.[35] It is in and through the disciplines that we cooperate with God in our transformation. We have a part (offering ourselves to God by engaging with the disciplines), and God has a part (transforming us in the process). Simon Chan states it well:

> In other words, we do the work, and yet it is ultimately the work of grace, something freely given to us, something that we could only receive as a gift. . . .

We cannot predetermine the outcome of our practices no matter how correctly they are carried out. For ultimately it is grace that forms us and not practices per se, and yet it forms us not apart from practice.[36]

Worship is a spiritual discipline.[37] As we meet to offer worship to God regularly, sincerely, and intentionally, we create an opportunity for God to meet us and change us for his glory. Often the changes that take place in us as a result of true worship are unexpected, perhaps even unseen at first; but they are happening nevertheless. The fruit of spiritual disciplines is most often slow-growing. We must be patient as we look for ways in which God transforms us through corporate worship. When we view worship as a spiritual discipline that we undertake to honor God, when we commit ourselves to the work of worship, when we intentionally participate personally, and when we contribute to the worship experience of others, we are engaging in formal or intentional formation.

Now we come to sacred rituals in particular and their relationship to spiritual formation. Rituals function as corporate spiritual disciplines. As we engage in the sacraments and other rituals, we present ourselves to God, trusting that he will use these as transformational moments in the lives of individual believers and of the community. Intentional participation in many of the sacred rituals, when undertaken as a spiritual discipline, is an important means for individuals and communities to be transformed. For instance, in the ritual of foot washing, we engage in a process (washing feet) of being conformed (self-humbling) to the image of Christ (who not only modeled the ritual for us but commanded us to carry it on) for the sake of others (so that others receive the blessing of being served). The remarkable phenomenon is that in willfully participating in the spiritual discipline of the ritual of foot washing, we find ourselves changed for God's glory for the sake of others. *Sacred rituals provide a ways and means to be spiritually transformed.*

The Symbolic Nature of Sacred Rituals

Another thing that sacred rituals share in common is their prominent use of symbol and sign.[38] It doesn't take very long as a participant of worship to realize that rituals of the church speak about and portray some very profound truths of our faith. These realities of faith are not readily understood at first pass; indeed, perhaps none are ever fully comprehended. For instance, at one level we can understand what is *done* in the act of baptism (someone gets wet) and even what it *signifies* (identification with Jesus Christ in his dying and rising [Rom. 6:1–4]). But who of us can truly comprehend what this *means*—exactly how the

Holy Spirit is at work in baptism or what this sacrament implies in all its fullness? Symbols move us from the known to the unknown, from what is familiar to a truth yet unfamiliar. "That is what gives rituals and symbols their power to point to an inexhaustible 'surplus' of truth and reality that it is impossible for reason alone to discern. That is also why rituals and symbols invite *faith*."[39]

Believers in the West today have inherited the Enlightenment mind-set, which is still very much alive and well. One of the less fortunate results of the Enlightenment was the belief that almost anything could be understood given the proper information. The intellectual capabilities of the human mind were glorified; embracing mystery was devalued. Yet every religion

> is an immense symbol-system about the meaning of the past, value in the present, and imagination about the future. Religions propose to the community what ought to be considered ultimate and mysterious. . . . Since this system of the ultimate and mysterious is, by definition, beyond human knowledge, religion relies on symbols to radiate something of this ultimate mystery. . . . By the power of an especially effective symbol, the past is brought into the present, the commonplace is transformed by the exceptional, the individual is united with the community, and sorrow meets up with joy.[40]

So from the beginning of every religion, symbols have been used to communicate aspects of faith with which the human mind struggles to grasp. Verbal explanation only goes so far. The nonverbal language of symbols speaks of ritual's meaning at a deeper, more intuitive level than the purely rational. Symbols are useful because the sheer image itself speaks volumes. An obvious example of the unspoken power of image is one's national flag. Young children in schools in every developed country learn of their nation's history, its significant leaders, its political system, and so on. They are also instructed in the symbolic figures and colors of the flag. At first the young child simply learns to salute the flag and recite its pledge. Over time, the symbol grows in meaning until, when the flag is unfurled at a sports event or on a national holiday, the mere sight of the flag instantaneously represents far more to the youth or adult than the facts once learned about it; it calls up deep-seated feelings of patriotism, honor, and love of country.

Particular symbols are used for Christian rituals primarily because the event and the symbol are linked in Scripture. Water is the symbol for baptism, oil for healing, the rainbow for covenant, a towel and basin for feet washing, bread and wine for the Lord's Supper, and so forth. Worshipers have not been faced with the task of creating all symbols out of nothing; many are gifts to us, specified by God.

The whole idea of symbol is rooted in the doctrines of creation and incarnation. When God created the heavens and the earth, every aspect of creation was declared to be good; therefore, all things may be used for God's purposes. Jesus used tangible aspects of creation (salt, light, weather patterns, stones) as symbols of the truth he was teaching. Material items are not disqualified for spiritual purposes because of our fallen world. Jesus proved otherwise. Creation is still good. With the incarnation, God proved that what was beyond us (the physical presence of God) would come among us in human form (Jesus). Therefore the incarnation is God's ultimate symbol: the Word became flesh and dwelt among us.

The English word "symbol" is derived from the Greek noun *symbolon*, a token by which one infers something.[41] The verb form, *symballo*, means "to compare."[42] Essentially a symbol is an object or action that represents a meaning or truth greater than the symbol. That which is tangible represents that which is intangible. All symbols have external, internal, and spiritual qualities. The external quality is the physical property itself (water); the internal quality is the interpretation given to a symbol by the group employing it (the water is a symbol of washing/cleansing); the spiritual quality is the spiritual transformation that is received by faith so that the worshiper is transformed to the glory of God (by faith I am purified by the waters of baptism and seek to walk in my baptism daily as I am conformed to the image of Christ).

Here are a few important things to note about the use of symbols as you prepare to be a rituals architect. Symbols

- are bidirectional (God speaks to us through symbols, and we speak to God in response by using symbols);
- are not ends in themselves;
- come in many forms: an item (cross), a gesture (kneeling), a color (white), a time of the year (Pentecost), a word (Passover);
- both reveal and conceal (they reveal truth to the believer; they conceal truth to the unbeliever [1 Cor. 2:11–16; Mark 4:11–12]);
- are the point at which the finiteness of humanity meets the mystery of God;
- are grounded in material, tangible forms;
- are culturally understood (symbols can have variable meanings based on culture);
- are polyvalent (symbols can have more than one inference at once);
- are limited in scope (they can infer only to a certain extent);
- are used to glorify God and edify believers.[43]

A word of caution is in order regarding symbols. Symbols have assigned meanings. That is to say that the symbol refers to something because someone says it does. Jesus gave assigned meaning to bread and wine. He said that the bread is his body, the wine is his blood. We inherit our symbols; they are therefore precious and to be valued. That is not to say that it is wrong for us to infer appropriate meanings for other symbols. In a Good Friday service it may be helpful to use the symbol of a large nail to represent the suffering of Christ. That inference is not found in Scripture, but it can be useful. However, be careful to (1) preserve the meanings assigned in Scripture and by the church, and (2) take up the leader's responsibility to teach what symbols mean. We must not only describe the symbol but also prescribe its meaning. We have the theological task of training believers in the faith; it is a matter of discipleship to explain and claim the meaning of sacred symbol and sign. I fear that in recent decades the church has been less diligent in clearly prescribing the intent of symbols and signs. I urge rituals architects to assume their pastoral duties not only in creating and leading sacred rituals but also in communicating the intended meaning of the symbols implicit in them.

Two virtues are especially helpful to pursue as we contemplate the importance of symbols and signs. First is the virtue of humility. We don't call all the shots as to the meaning and role of symbols in worship. Remember that "in liturgy and sacrament the church does not 'invent' its own identity, but receives it from . . . God."[44] Humility is critical, for worshipers must seek to surrender their desire to make worship into their own form. It is imperative that the church serve *God* in worship "by performing a gesture which is not from itself, by saying words which are not its own, by receiving elements which it has not chosen."[45] The second helpful virtue is patience. Symbols grow in significance as we mature in faith. Because of this we must learn the discipline of contentment as we await the understanding that will come in time.

As you prepare and lead sacred rituals for your congregation, do not underestimate the power of symbol, especially when people influenced by postmodern culture are highly image-driven. Thoughtfully and prayerfully employ symbols as a means of experiencing that which cannot always be explained, for we will never exhaust the mystery of God.

The Christo-centric Nature of Sacred Rituals

In all of our discussion about symbols, the most important point is yet to be made: symbols must enable the centrality of Christ to be perceived in worship. Christian worship is *Christian* precisely because of the ongoing presence and ministry of the incarnate Son of God in the gathered community. Each and every symbol used in worship does not, of course, directly represent Christ. At the same time, all symbols must ultimately enable worship that properly glorifies God through the exaltation of Jesus Christ by the power of the Holy Spirit. Worship that glorifies God is worship that (1) magnifies God's Son (Phil. 2:9–11; Heb. 1:6; Rev. 5:12) and (2) is offered through the priestly ministry of God's Son (Heb. 2:10–13; 7:25; 8:1–2; 1 Tim. 2:5). While symbols are significant, even necessary, to Christian worship, they are not so because they are thought-provoking or because they offer a modality to satisfy certain types of learning styles of worshipers, helpful as these are. Symbols are of ultimate importance in worship to the degree that they enable worship that is truly *Christian*—worship understood to be properly centered in the person and work of Jesus Christ.

In focusing on Christ, symbols play an important role in remembrance. Christian worship is essentially a remembrance of who God is and what God has done. By remembering, believers recall, re-present, and anticipate the marvelous works of the triune God for the purpose of glorifying the One who has acted throughout human history.[46] Symbols greatly aid in our ability to recall ("remembering backward"), re-present ("remembering in the present"), and anticipate God's reign in the future ("remembering forward"). While the sweeping story of salvation history is vast, it culminates in the greatest of God's saving acts on behalf of humankind: the giving of Jesus, God's incarnate Son, for the redemption of all who will believe.

Nowhere are the symbols of remembrance more profoundly obvious than in the symbols related to the sacraments of baptism and the Lord's Table. The waters of baptism recall how God has saved people through water in the past (Noah and the great flood, Moses and the Red Sea); how God is saving people through the waters of baptism today (1 Pet. 3:21); and how those whose robes have been washed will have a special place near the river of the water of life in the heavenly kingdom (Rev. 22:1, 14). The bread and the wine of the Lord's Supper recall the Passover of God (Luke 22:15), provide an ongoing remembrance of Christ's body and blood until he returns (Luke 22:19–20), and anticipate the heavenly supper of the Lamb (Rev. 19:9). The symbols of remembrance attached to the sacraments are Christ symbols, for it is only in Christ that we are saved and baptized, and it is only in Christ that we feed on him by faith at his Table.

As you engage in leadership as a rituals architect, I urge you to consider how you will set Christ as the cornerstone of each and every ritual. Allow the person and work of Christ to be obvious in your actions, words, gestures, and symbols, for this is well pleasing to God.

Sacred Rituals for the Sake of the World

By now I trust the reader is more energized as to the purpose and value of sacred actions in corporate worship. But we must end this chapter where we began, by clearly stating that rituals are not valuable for their own sake. What's more, in many ways, neither are they valuable for the participants' sake exclusively. No, they have a much larger role to play. When the time-honored sacred rituals approved by the church of Jesus Christ are offered with devotion and sincerity, they are done so for the sake of the world. Church rituals have strong witnessing power—they present to the world a picture of the church in relationship with God through Jesus Christ. It is *that* final role that they must ultimately assume. Returning to Mulholland's definition, we recall that "spiritual formation is the process of being conformed to the image of Christ *for the sake of others*" (emphasis mine).[47] Whatever holy moment we experience is not for our own satisfaction but to glorify God in the face of a defiant world. Remember that rituals are primarily about relationship; they help us mirror the eternal relationship of the triune God. A beautiful relationship that is well demonstrated is prophetic in nature. Jesus prayed, "As you, Father, are in me and I am in you, may they also be in us, so that the world may believe that you have sent me" (John 17:21). Sacred rituals express the very relationship Jesus prayed for: an expression of oneness between God and God's people, and all for the greater purpose that the world may believe. This is the missiological piece to sacred rituals. In our faithful devotion to participating in those actions deemed necessary and beneficial by the church, we proclaim to the world the truth that the rituals portray. And we do so with Jesus's prayer on our lips that "the world may believe."

Conclusion

In this chapter I have attempted to lay some critical foundation pieces that will ground all of the sacred rituals practiced in the church. The next seven chapters will reflect these foundations as individual rituals are examined. Before you turn the page, however, remember the two propositions with which we started:

1. Rituals signify the believer's relationship with God. "Christian worship is not doctrine disguised in ritual shorthand but action that draws us into the dynamic, hospitable, yet perilous space of God's own life."[48] In short, "Liturgy's goal isn't meaning but *meeting*."[49]
2. Rituals aid in deepening this relationship. "Liturgies are, finally, about *connection*; about *being* connected and *making* connections—to God,

people, and planet; to space, time, culture, and history; to difference
and otherness; to memory and expectation."[50]

Key Terms

liturgy The complete collection of actions, words, gestures, and symbols that
facilitates the prayerful worship and full participation of all worshipers in
the context of corporate worship.

officiate To perform a religious ceremony by virtue of office.

ordinance A purely symbolic sacred ritual, instituted and commanded by
Christ to be practiced by all believers of all times and places, which does
not serve as a means of grace.

preside To direct proceedings by virtue of exercising control over the event.

rite The particular combination of actions, words, gestures, and symbols that
constitute the order and content for a designated ritual.

ritual An authoritative *event*, sanctioned by the church, which uses formalized actions, words, gestures, and symbols that are repeated to enable some
particular aspect of the corporate worship of God.

rubric Instructions for leading and participating in a ritual.

sacrament A sacred ritual, instituted and commanded by Christ to be practiced
by all believers of all times and places, which serves as a means of grace.

2

The Christian Wedding

Explore

Before reading chapter 2, reflect on your own experience of attending weddings.

- Describe in detail the first wedding you remember attending.
- What do you imagine would be the difference between a Christian wedding service in a church and a civil ceremony?
- In the weddings you have attended, what was the role of the wedding guests?
- Have you ever attended a wedding ceremony for unbelievers that was held in a church? Was it any different than for believers?

Now that you have begun to reflect on weddings, expand your thinking by reading chapter 2.

Expand

Pastor Andrew really cared for Zane and Hannah. He had watched Zane grow up in the church. Zane was an energetic kid who liked to follow Pastor Andrew around after services, helping to tidy the sanctuary after most of the people had gone. When Zane entered high school, he brought his friend Hannah to youth group. Their friendship took a romantic turn in college, and after graduation they became engaged. There was no other option, as far as they were concerned, than to be married in the church of their youth by Pastor Andrew.

Eventually, when the three of them met to discuss the wedding service, Zane and Hannah excitedly told their pastor about some of their ideas for the wedding. Pastor Andrew listened eagerly; he wisely considered their ideas while guiding them toward worshipful choices. For instance, together they agreed that the best man and maid of honor would each read Scripture during the wedding service. Later, they would each give a speech at the reception. Pastor Andrew enjoyed Zach and Hannah's youthful enthusiasm. He smiled to himself as they said their good-byes, realizing once again that planning wedding services with engaged couples proves to be a wonderful opportunity to help them see their wedding as an occasion for corporate worship—an event where God is truly at the center.

Wedding ceremonies in the local church have been commonplace for centuries, though it might surprise the reader to find that this has not always been the case. While the early church had things to say concerning marriage, weddings were largely viewed as civil events that the church merely recognized; in fact, "church participation was not required until the eleventh century."[1] Weddings performed by the church have had a bit of an erratic history, as they moved from early church ambivalence to full church endorsement when marriage became a sacrament in the early medieval period. A turn of events occurred again with the early Reformers' rejection of the sacramental view of marriage, resulting in less enthusiasm for church weddings once more. Today churches tend toward the high view of weddings as a spiritual occasion and sacred rite—one that lends itself to holding ceremonies in church sanctuaries, so much so that even couples with no religious background often seek out a church for their wedding. While the church has always considered *marriage* to be a holy estate instituted by God (which has spiritual ramifications addressed in Scripture), *weddings* were a different matter; the church and weddings have had a rocky relationship.

This chapter addresses marriage and wedding ceremonies for Christian believers. Later in this chapter I will touch on weddings for unbelievers.

Laying the Foundations

Christian Marriage Is Grounded in God's Gift of Creation

The crowning glory of God's magnificent creation was humans created in his image; "in the image of God he created them; male and female he created them" (Gen. 1:27). The man and woman God formed were created as equals, both heirs of the *imago dei* ("the image of God"). Paul echoes this affirmation when he teaches, "As many of you as were baptized into Christ have clothed yourselves with Christ. There is no longer Jew or Greek, there is no longer slave or free, there is no longer male and female; for all of you are one in Christ Jesus" (Gal. 3:27–28). The purposes God had in mind for marriage are clearly stated in the creation accounts. God gave the gift of man and woman to each other for companionship (Gen. 2:18), for co-regency over the earth (Gen. 1:26), and for procreation (Gen. 1:28). God's intention for Adam and Eve was physical and spiritual union. It was God's desire that they would be bone of the same bone, flesh of the same flesh (Gen. 2:23). This miraculous union was spoken of by Jesus when he cited the Genesis account in his teaching on divorce (Mark 10:6). The union is depicted as the two becoming one flesh: "So they are no longer two, but one flesh. Therefore what God has joined together, let no one separate" (Mark 10:8–9). Marriage is the relationship established by God for one man and one woman joined together to serve God's purposes.

At the end of God's season of creation, "God saw everything that he had made, and indeed, it was very good" (Gen. 1:31). God created the two sexes, and God created sexual intercourse as the natural means for pleasure and procreation, and it was all good. It didn't take long for things to go awry, for distrust and infidelity between couples to occur; nevertheless, the gift was perfect and pure from the beginning and remains God's arrangement to fulfill his purposes for all time. There is no other place to begin than with affirming that marriage was instituted by God from the beginning of time, and that it is good.

Christian Marriage Is Rooted in the Gift of Covenant

A man and a woman who share a deep love and who are convinced that God's will is for their permanent union elect to enter into the covenant of marriage. A covenant resembles a contract, but it is more. A contract specifies the legal role each party will play and includes the consequences for breaking the contract. Generally speaking, contracts enable each party to protect themselves. Contracts provide the legal language necessary to satisfy civil authorities. But a marriage covenant goes beyond the legal requirements of the law, though it does involve legal steps to validate the relationship in the eyes of society. A marriage covenant is more about pledging godly love to the partner in a way that protects the *other*, rather than oneself. The solemn covenant undertaken between two Christians involves each person giving of himself or herself to the other's benefit unreservedly. It is a costly giving, for one cannot predict the future, and there is no way to know what will be required of either party. Nevertheless, it is a covenantal relationship to which God calls the couple, expecting that the holy pledge taken between two humans includes the ongoing presence of the One who created them—the "threefold cord [which] is not quickly broken" (Eccles. 4:12).

Christian Marriage Is Centered in Jesus Christ

The New Testament has much to say about the role our Lord plays in the union of man and wife. Paul admonishes husbands and wives to be subject to each other out of reverence for Christ (Eph. 5:21–32). The husband's role in the relationship is compared to Christ's role as head of the church (Eph. 5:23); the subjection of the church to Christ is compared to wives being subject to their husbands (Eph. 5:24); the love expected from the husband to his wife is compared to the love Christ has for the church (Eph. 5:25); the nurture and tender care the husband is to offer his wife is compared to that same tender care that Christ provides to the church (Eph. 5:28–29). Paul admits that the oneness experienced by husband and wife is a great mystery comparable to the great mystery of Christ and the church (Eph. 5:32). The christological focus of the Christian marriage is unmistakable; it is the centerpiece of the relationship.

A Christian Marriage Forms a Community Reflective of the Kingdom of God

The real purpose of a family is *mission*—to live together in a way that inspires true citizenship in the sphere over which God reigns. Couples give birth to, or adopt, children whom they rear as citizens of this eternal kingdom. They teach them to love God and others, to serve God and others. A marriage constitutes the formation of a covenantal bond among related persons that, through their mutual demonstration of love, fidelity, and the honoring of one another, offers a picture to the world of what the kingdom of God is like—a domain where those who name Jesus as Lord extend selfless service and unconditional love to all in their circle of influence. Such a relationship begins with the husband and wife, whose "fidelity is the strongest indication we have that the Christian life is possible in our world."[2] The husband and wife, walking in their baptism, comprise a "little family within the household of God; a 'little church' in the body of Christ."[3] The Christian couple (family) is a local expression of the global reality of the kingdom of God. One worship resource book affirms,

> Therefore, the purpose of Christian marriage is not only to fulfill the needs of domestic intimacy, but also to enable the family to accept duties and responsibilities in the Christian community for society at large. The church witnesses to God's justice and love in both private and public life. Christian families are members of the church and citizens of the state.[4]

The church is blessed when couples grasp this expansive view of their purpose in being united in marriage.

Amid these several claims of what marriage *is*, there is a point to be made for what Christian marriage is *not*: for Protestants it is not considered a sacrament (or ordinance) of the church.[5] It is not a sacrament because it does not qualify as something instituted and commanded by Christ to be practiced by all believers of all times and places. Christ did not enter into marriage, and Paul encouraged singleness (1 Cor. 7:8). During the medieval period (due largely to scholastic theologians such as Albert the Great and Thomas Aquinas), marriage came to be viewed as one of the sacraments of the church. But the early Reformers did not see it that way and generally concurred that marriage was a civil institution to be governed by civil authority, not the church, harking back to the view of the earliest centuries of Christianity. Its sacramental status was stripped, and that remains the case for Protestants. But while it is not ranked as a sacrament, marriage certainly is a means of grace through which God forms the couple in the image of Jesus Christ. The joys and challenges of marriage are occasions for iron sharpening iron, with the result being individuals who are more reflective of their Lord. God fills couples with all spiritual graces and virtues needed to fulfill God's purposes in the family. Their holy union is a means to receive these benefits.

Implications/Considerations

In light of these foundations for Christian marriage, implications arise for the wedding service. There are things to consider in the biblical, theological, and historical practices of the church as they relate to weddings.

First, the Christian wedding is a worship service rather than a civil ceremony. Both are vehicles for accomplishing the legal union of a woman and a man, but the civil ceremony accomplishes *only* that, while the Christian wedding signifies much more. Like any worship service, several important features characterize the wedding service. Here is a partial list:

- The service is focused on God (not the bride, the groom, the wedding party, the attire, or the bride's mother!). God initiates worship and is the focal point.
- The ministry of the Word and the response to the Word form the dialogical nature of the service. Christian weddings must include the preached word (a brief homily). This is followed by the response to the Word, which consists of the marriage vows taken by the couple, along with other worship acts to help worshipers respond affirmatively to God's proclaimed Word.
- The service is Christo-centric. An awareness of Jesus Christ is fostered through prayers, music, spoken words, and possibly the Eucharist.[6]

- The Holy Spirit's power and presence is welcomed to seal the pledges made as a result of the Word. (The Trinitarian ethos is profoundly important.)
- The service is corporate in nature. The gathered community of believers is the normative context for worship. As such, they, along with the bride and groom, are the primary participants in offering praise and thanksgiving and petition to God for this marriage.
- Worship is centered on God's acts of love and salvation. In the Christian wedding, the couple testifies to God's love demonstrated in their union.

Presuming that a Christian wedding is a worship service—and it should be—one might want to reconsider some of the common wedding traditions that have their roots in age-old, pre-Christian practices. Many of these have made their way into the traditional wedding ceremony in the West, including such things as reciting the betrothal vow, giving away the woman in marriage, joining right hands, wearing a veil, throwing rice, and exchanging rings. Perhaps none of these are wrong per se, though some, like the giving away of the woman by her father, are questionable Christian practices. This gesture is an ancient practice that confirmed the young woman to be a piece of property, owned by her father, with the transfer of ownership occurring by the giving away of the bride. The giving of a woman's hand in marriage was the accepted gesture legalizing the groom's acceptance of his wife as property with accompanying dowry. It is helpful to sort through what are inappropriate pre-Christian practices (eliminating them from the wedding), innocent pre-Christian practices (allowing some if suitable), and truly *Christian* practices (giving priority to these).

A wedding that is viewed as a worship service will also lean toward a church sanctuary as the preferred location for the solemnization of vows. It is not wrong to hold the ceremony at other appropriate places (an outdoor park setting, a home, and so on), but the church offers a stronger context for the vows, for a church has (1) been dedicated as sacred space—a place given to God and blessed by God as a special meeting place for God and people—and (2) is the normative location for the gathered community to meet. Churches provide surroundings that naturally depict the Christian faith, complete with architecture, symbols, and furnishings that facilitate the actions of worship. Sacred space is not neutral space; it is the natural arena for church rituals, such as the wedding ceremony, to come alive when God meets a couple in community. Civil ceremonies, by contrast, may occur in any number of places, including the county courthouse. In this case the surroundings also suit the ceremony—a binding legal contract is entered into that satisfies the event as a marriage in the eyes of the state. Void of scriptural or religious language, the script for the civil ceremony consists of straightforward *contract* language, but little if any *covenant* language. There would be little point in providing a religious space for a secular ceremony. Again, a Christian couple may opt for the civil ceremony, but it is a missed opportunity, given the church's view of marriage as a holy union between man and wife with Christ at the center.

If the Christian wedding is a service of worship, partaking of Holy Communion is an option in the service. Like any worship service, the Word is preached, and when Communion is offered, it provides an opportunity for the community to respond to the Word of the Lord. If Communion is being discussed as a possibility for the wedding service, certain parameters should be clearly in place so as to maintain the appropriate approach to the Table of the Lord:

- Communion is not a private act between the bride and groom. Communion is a corporate act of the church—always. It is given to the church as a means of fellowship with God and with believers. Christ is the Host of the meal; he is the one who issues the invitation and invites *all* believers to the Table.
- If Communion is served to the congregation, it is best to serve it in the pews for logistical and pastoral reasons. First, it is far less interruptive than to have people come to the front to receive it, especially when the front of the church will have extra persons, equipment, and decorations. Second, passing the bread and cup in the pews allows nonbelievers to discreetly "pass" on participating, which is encouraged.
- Make sure the clergy indicates that this is a meal for those who profess Christ as Lord.
- Use an abbreviated Communion liturgy.

Many other worship elements are useful in establishing the wedding as a worship service. Weddings should include joyful congregational singing! They should also include various prayers, statements of faith, affirmations, Scripture readings, and more. Viewing the wedding as a worship service changes the whole perspective of the event. God is established as the audience of the day to whom all praises and petitions are directed. There is no better beginning to the Christian couple's journey than to understand their wedding ceremony to be a service of worship that truly honors God and involves all who attend.

Building the Structure

With these foundations and implications in mind, let's turn our attention to the structure for the Christian wedding ritual. Remember that the order of service, in its very sequence of worship acts, is a telling of the story of God (God seeks us, God speaks, we reply, God empowers for mission). In the case of the wedding, the story line centers on (1) God's love in calling the couple to holy union, (2) God's speaking promises of divine faithfulness, (3) the couple's reply to God's expression of love through the taking of vows, and then (4) the couple's being sent into the world to engage in ministries of love and justice for the sake of others. For these reasons, the order of the wedding worship service matters; it should follow this general fourfold purpose.

Certain components of worship remain fairly fixed (for instance, the taking of vows and the declaration of marriage). However, weddings are very personal occasions, and there is still lots of room for personalizing the liturgy while maintaining the God-focus. Especially in Western culture, couples spend a lot of time making it "their" wedding day. Songs, Scripture passages, types of prayers, various symbols—these and many other options afford the couple, in concert with the clergy, the opportunity to fashion a God-honoring, yet personally meaningful, service. The large-frame, fourfold order beautifully allows for worship acts such as those listed below. As you maintain the general fourfold order, remember that the sequence of worship acts *within* each movement is not fixed and allows for your creativity and needs.

The suggested order of service below is annotated, making it appear lengthier than it is. A basic outline without annotation is found in appendix B and provides a much clearer picture of exactly what is involved. The worship elements shown with titles on the left side of the page are considered necessary to the service; the elements shown with centered titles within brackets [ ] are considered optional.

The Order of the Christian Wedding

Gathering (God Calls Us to Worship)

Pre-service Music (Prelude)

Appropriate instrumental and/or vocal music prepares the congregation for worship.[7]

The Processional

The clergy and members of the wedding party enter the worship space.

Note: This can be accomplished through various means. The traditional entrance of the bride coming down the aisle beside her father is one option.[8] In this case she is typically preceded by attendants, the clergy having led the male attendants into the chancel area from the side, awaiting the arrival of the bride at the front. Occasionally the bride and groom enter together down the aisle.⁹ Sometimes the male attendants accompany the female attendants down the aisle. There are several possibilities. Think through which option makes sense in light of your circumstances and preferences.

Greeting

Greet the congregation warmly in the name of the Father, Son, and Holy Spirit, followed by a few words from Scripture. After this, feel free to offer a personal welcome.

SAMPLE OF SCRIPTURAL GREETINGS

- "Grace to you and peace from God our Father and the Lord Jesus Christ." (One of Paul's favorite greetings; see Rom. 1:7; 1 Cor. 1:3; 2 Cor. 1:2, and so on.)
- "This is the day that the LORD has made; let us rejoice and be glad in it" (Ps. 118:24). Welcome to this special day as we rejoice in the Lord and celebrate the union of [name] and [name]. Thank you for coming to participate in this holy occasion.

Note: Don't ad lib too much when it comes to the greeting. A nervous bride and groom will look to you for a steady and calm presence in the midst of an emotional event. Prepared words will lend a sense of reverence and calm and get the service off to a better start.

Call to Worship

Remind the congregation that we are gathered at God's invitation. Invite them to be full participants in the service.

SAMPLE CALL TO WORSHIP

Pastor: Make a joyful noise to the Lord, all the earth. Worship the Lord with gladness; come into his presence with singing.

People: Know that the Lord is God. It is he who made us, and we are his; we are his people, and the sheep of his pasture.

Pastor: "Enter his gates with thanksgiving, and his courts with praise. Give thanks to him, bless his name. For the LORD is good; his steadfast love endures forever, and his faithfulness to all generations" (Ps. 100:4–5).

Note: A call to worship may be read by the pastor or another worship leader, or spoken responsively by the congregation. (Words are printed in the order of service or projected.)

Invocation

Invite/welcome God's presence into the service of worship (see appendix A).

Statement of the Meaning of Marriage

Succinctly and formally state the meaning of marriage.

SAMPLE STATEMENTS OF THE MEANING OF MARRIAGE

1. "God gave us marriage as a holy mystery in which a man and a woman are joined together, and become one, just as Christ is one with the church. In marriage, husband and wife are called to a new way of life—created, ordered, and blessed by God. This way of life must not be entered into carelessly or from selfish motives but responsibly and prayerfully. We rejoice that marriage is given by God, blessed by our Lord Jesus Christ, and sustained by the Holy Spirit. Therefore, let marriage be held in honor by all."[10]

2. Dear Friends, we have come together in the presence of God to witness and affirm the joining together of this man and this woman in marriage. The bond of marriage was established by God at creation, and our Lord Jesus Christ himself adorned this manner of life by his presence and first miracle at a wedding in Cana of Galilee. This bond signifies to us the union between Christ and his church, and Holy Scripture commends it to be honored among all people. Marriage is intended by God for mutual joy; for the help and comfort given in prosperity and adversity; and, when it is God's will, for the procreation of children and their nurture in the knowledge and love of the Lord. Therefore, marriage is not to be entered into unadvisedly or lightly, but reverently, deliberately, and in accord with the purposes for which it was instituted by God.[11]

Declaration of Intent

This is a brief but important public affirmation by the couple that they are entering into the marriage covenant intentionally; they are declaring their desire to be joined in holy matrimony.[12]

SAMPLE DECLARATION OF INTENT

Pastor: [*Name*], understanding that God has created, ordered, and blessed the covenant of marriage, do you affirm your desire and intention to enter this covenant?[13]

Response: I do.

Note: The declaration of intent is asked of the groom and bride individually.

Affirmation of the Families

Family members of both bride and groom declare their affirmation that this union comes with their blessing.

Pastor: Who affirms and blesses the union of this man and woman?
Response (spoken by both sides at once): We believe God has brought [*name*] and [*name*] together for the purposes of holy union. We offer our love and support now and always.[14]

Note: For many years in Western practice, the father gave the bride away. When the pastor asked, "Who gives this woman . . . ?" her father replied, "I do." This harks back to the ancient patriarchal view that a father's daughter was property to be given to the husband. Today, some families have taken a step away from this by simply asking both sets of parents to answer, "We do." Yet this still presents the problem of the bride being given away. Many couples now shift the question from "Who gives this woman to be married to this man?" to "Who affirms and blesses the union of this man and woman?" Both sets of parents or whole family units from both sides, as decided on by the couple, offer an affirmation of this union. It is appropriate to have these family members stand for this brief exchange.

Affirmation of the Congregation

The congregation is asked to affirm their support of the union as well.

Pastor: Will all of you witnessing these vows do everything in your power to uphold [*name*] and [*name*] in their marriage?
Response: We will.[15]

[A Congregational Hymn or Song]

[A Corporate Prayer of Confession and Assurance of Pardon]

Word (God Speaks to Worshipers)

The Reading of Scripture

A Scripture passage is read that is the text for the homily.
Note: A well-prepared lay reader is one more way for the worship service to lend itself to participation of the congregation. Examples of Scripture passages suitable for the Christian wedding are given in the section below (see "Installing Doors and Windows").

The Homily

The minister offers a brief sermon related to Christian marriage. The homily:

- should not be lengthy; keep it succinct;
- should engage both the couple and the congregation;
- may include personal references related to the couple and humor where appropriate; however, remember that entertainment is not its focus.

Response to the Word (Worshipers Respond to God's Word)

The Exchange of Vows

The vows are the high point of the service in the sense that they are the very reason for which the community has gathered—to witness the legal and spiritual commitment made between husband and wife. The couple should face each other and hold hands when making these promises.

SAMPLES OF VOWS

1. (Traditional) "I, [*name*], take you, [*name*],[16] to be my wedded [*husband/ wife*], to have and to hold, from this day forward, for better, for worse, for richer, for poorer, in sickness and in health, to love and to cherish, till death do us part, according to God's holy law; and thereto I pledge you my faith."[17]
2. "I, [*name*], take you, [*name*] to be my [*wife/husband*]; and I promise, before God and these witnesses, to be your loving and faithful [*wife/ husband*]; in plenty and in want; in joy and in sorrow; in sickness and in health; as long as we both shall live."[18]

Note: While some couples wish to write their own vows, this can be a dangerous practice unless (1) it is done under the supervision of the officiating pastor, and (2) the content conforms to the type of wording that is necessary; in other words, *certain* vows must be spoken (for instance, faithfulness until death), not just the vows upon which a couple may singlehandedly agree. Couples should not be turned loose to write their vows. It could be an enlightening undertaking—a type of discipleship moment—when done with the proper guidance of the pastor.

[The Exchange of Rings or Tokens]

While many couples elect to exchange rings or other tokens of the vow, it is not necessary to the wedding ceremony.

SAMPLE WORDS FOR THE EXCHANGE OF RINGS

Pastor: What do you bring as a sign of your promise?
Response: Rings.

1. "These rings are the outward and visible sign of an inward and spiritual grace, signifying to all the uniting of [*name*] and [*name*] in holy marriage."[19]

2. The couple, in turn, speaks these words (repeated after the pastor):

   "This ring I give you, as a sign of our constant faith and abiding love, in the name of the Father, and of the Son, and of the Holy Spirit."[20]

3. [*Name*], I give you this ring as a sign of my vow, and with all that I am, and all that I have, I honor you; in the name of the Father, and of the Son, and of the Holy Spirit. Amen.[21]

Note: Following the exchange of rings, an optional prayer of blessing by the pastor for the giving of the rings is offered.[22] This may, if desired, be subsumed into the larger prayer of consecration for the couple that follows next.

[A Congregational Song or Vocal Solo]

[Holy Communion, when included, is offered here.][23]

Prayer of Consecration (Blessing of the Marriage)

The pastor offers a pastoral prayer on behalf of the couple, consisting of praise and petition. (The standard form for the pastoral prayer is found in appendix A.)

Note: The couple is encouraged to kneel, if possible, for this prayer. It may also include confession of sin if not offered as a separate prayer above.

Other examples of prayers of consecration are found below in "Installing Doors and Windows."

[The Lord's Prayer]

The Lord's Prayer may be prayed by the congregation in unison, sung by the congregation, or sung by a soloist.

The Sending (God Sends the Couple to Live to the Glory of God)

Charge to the Couple

The pastor addresses the couple with a final charge.

SAMPLE CHARGES TO THE COUPLE

1. "As God's own, clothe yourselves with compassion, kindness, and patience, forgiving each other as the Lord has forgiven you, and crown

all these things with love, which binds everything together in perfect harmony" (Col. 3:12–14, adapted).[24]

2. "Whatever you do, in word or deed, do everything in the name of the Lord Jesus, giving thanks to God the Father through him" (Col. 3:17).

Declaration of Marriage

The minister addresses the congregation and announces the couple to be officially joined in marriage. If the couple includes a public kiss, it appears here following the Declaration of Marriage.

SAMPLE DECLARATIONS OF MARRIAGE

1. "Before God and in the presence of this congregation, [*name*] and [*name*] have made their solemn vows to each other. They have confirmed their promises by the joining of hands (and by the giving and receiving of rings). Therefore, I proclaim that they are now husband and wife. Blessed be the Father and the Son and the Holy Spirit now and forever. Amen."[25]

2. "And now, by the powers vested in me by the church and by the State of [*name of state*], I present to you [*first and last names*] as officially married. What God has done let no one change."[26]

[Closing Congregational Hymn]

The Benediction

The minister offers a scriptural benediction.

SAMPLE BENEDICTIONS

1. "The LORD bless you and keep you; the LORD make his face to shine upon you, and be gracious to you; the LORD lift up his countenance upon you, and give you peace" (Num. 6:24–26).

2. "God the Father, God the Son, God the Holy Spirit, bless, preserve and keep you; the Lord mercifully with his favor look upon you, and so fill you with all spiritual benediction and grace, that you may so live together in this life, that in the world to come you may have life everlasting. Amen."[27]

The Recessional

All wedding participants leave the worship space.

Note: As with the processional, options for this abound. Most common is the wedding couple walking out together (wedding party following) and forming a reception line to greet guests. Some couples elect to stop at each row of seating to dismiss the people, thereby greeting those who attend. Music should be played as the congregation leaves the worship space.

Installing Doors and Windows

After the rituals architect has carefully arranged the service order for the Christian wedding, she or he begins to think about specific choices of songs, Scriptures, prayers, and symbols that will provide much of the dialogue between God and people. Your vision of the service is moving from the larger, more general vision (the order of the conversation) to the more particular part of the vision (choice of words and symbols that will actually carry the conversation).

Songs

Selecting music to be used in Christian weddings poses a very interesting challenge. Because the Christian wedding is a worship service, most of the same principles are in operation regarding the selection of worship elements as would be for a worship service in a local church. At the same time, a wedding is different in many ways from a typical worship service. The music selected for church weddings can be a contentious and controversial topic. The basic principle to be considered is this: wedding music must be God-honoring just as worship music must be God-honoring. The psalms, hymns, and spiritual songs suitable for the church are the corpus of song from which wedding music is drawn. Songs that do not contain explicit references to God and Christian truths are to be avoided, as are the instrumental versions of the same songs. Christian songs are best for Christian weddings because they allow the focus to remain on the triune God.

It is fairly common for couples to request favorite songs from popular culture to be used in the wedding ceremony—perhaps songs with sentimental value. But remember that the *human* perspective of love, cherished and legitimate as it is, is not the central theme for the Christian wedding; *God's* love is. Basically, the *text* of the song (how explicitly it refers to God and God's story) and the *standard use of the song* (the venue with which it is associated) will determine whether or not a song is suitable for the Christian wedding. Songs that do not enable worship may be appropriate for the reception or other wedding-related celebrations. As for instrumental music, much from the classical repertoire can add a great deal to the service. Much classical music was never associated with *any* text and would thereby be considered religiously "neutral," so classical music can be helpful in providing a worshipful tone for the service or for the accompaniment of the actions in the wedding ceremony, such as the procession.

In our music discussion thus far, we have not been discussing style but content. There is room in the wedding ceremony for any number of musical styles, as long as the text qualifies as helpful to the conversation with God. The stylistic song choices one makes will naturally be influenced by the bride's and groom's tastes, as well as by the style of worship common to the gathered worshiping community. Two rules of thumb are helpful in the whole process. First, churches should establish policies regarding the music to be used in weddings within their purview. This eliminates many potential problems. Such a policy is presented to the couple when they first speak to the pastor about the use of the church. A policy helps clarify everything from the start and helps to avoid confusion and miscommunication. Second, all musical selections should be done in consultation with the organist, music director, pastor, or other appointed representative from the church. This assures quality control.

To list possibilities for wedding instrumental music is beyond the scope of this chapter. Trained church musicians will be able to offer the couple many fine recommendations. However, here are a few suggestions for appropriate wedding hymns and songs in the Christian worship service. The author's name is included to help you in locating the song.[28]

Be Thou My Vision (ancient Irish text)
Christ, We Come with Joy and Gladness (Constance Cherry)
Come Down, O Love Divine (Bianco of Siena)
Come to a Wedding (Shirley Erena Murray)
Joyful, Joyful, We Adore Thee (Henry F. Van Dyke)
Love Divine, All Loves Excelling (Charles Wesley)
Now Thank We All Our God (Martin Rinkart)
O God, Our Help in Ages Past (Isaac Watts)
O Perfect Love (Dorothy F. Gurney)
Praise, My Soul, the King of Heaven (Henry F. Lyte)
Praise to the Lord, the Almighty (Joachim Neander)
The Gift of Love (Hal Hopson)
The Grace of Life Is Theirs (Fred Pratt Green)
The King of Love My Shepherd Is (Henry W. Baker)
The Servant Song (Richard Gillard)
When Love Is Found (Brian Wren)
Your Love, O God, Has Called Us (Russell Schultz-Widmar)

Scripture Passages

The pastor will select the primary Scripture passage as the text for his or her homily. Here are a few examples to help you start to form your own list of passages appropriate for the Christian wedding:

Genesis 1:26–28, 31a   Romans 12:1–2, 9–18

Psalm 67   1 Corinthians 13

Song of Solomon 2:10–14; 8:6–7   Ephesians 3:14–21

Matthew 5:1–10   Colossians 3:12–17

Matthew 22:35–40   1 John 3:18–24

Mark 10:42–45   1 John 4:7–16

Prayers

As is the case for every worship service, the use of various types of prayers assists us in voicing our part of the conversation with God. Prayers especially useful for the Christian wedding include the invocation, the confession of sin, the prayer of consecration, and the benediction. The components for formulating all of these prayers are found in appendix A. When following these forms, be sure to incorporate biblical allusion and scriptural phrases (even *praying* certain Scripture passages), relating them specifically to the wedding.

Sample Prayer of Consecration and Blessing

1. "(Let us pray.) Heavenly Father, we thank you for the lives of [*name*] and [*name*] and for the families that have nurtured them as they matured into adulthood. We thank you for the loving care that was given them and for bringing them to this place. Most of all, hear our prayers of gratitude for *your* steadfast love—the love of God that is at work in their lives today. For we are convinced that neither death, nor life, nor angels, nor rulers, nor things present, nor things to come, nor powers, nor height, nor depth, nor anything else in all creation, will be able to separate us from the love of God in Christ Jesus our Lord. For this we give you heartfelt thanks.

   "We come before you, God, asking that you will enable [*name*] and [*name*] to live within your will. Our world will confront them with many options. Give them discernment to be wise. Give them strength to follow your will and your ways even when others around them do not. Bless their marriage, protect them from harm, increase their love for you and for each other, and fill their home with peace and joy. Give them resolve to establish a Christian home, and cause their union to bring great blessing to many other people. These mercies we pray in the name of our Lord and Savior, Jesus Christ. Amen."[29]

2. "Most gracious God, we give you thanks for your tender love in making us a covenant people through our Savior Jesus Christ and for consecrating in his name the marriage covenant of [*name*] and [*name*]. Grant that their love for each other may reflect the love of Christ for us and

grow from strength to strength as they faithfully serve you in the world. Defend them from every enemy. Lead them into all peace. Let their love for each other be a seal upon their hearts, a mantle about their shoulders, and a crown upon their heads. Bless them in their work and in their companionship; in their sleeping and in their waking; in their joys and in their sorrows; in their lives and in their deaths. Finally by your grace, bring them and all of us to that table where your saints feast forever in your heavenly home; through Jesus Christ our Lord, who with you and the Holy Spirit lives and reigns, one God, for ever and ever. Amen."[30]

Symbols

Certain symbols are especially appropriate for the Christian wedding to help worshipers connect with God. Most of the symbols listed below arose through common popular practice (which doesn't necessarily discount a symbol). Symbols always have assigned meanings; some are established by God, many are established by the church, and others developed over time by local cultures. Some symbols helpful for the Christian wedding include

- Cross
- Banners
- Unity candle
- Other candles
- Wedding rings

- Trinitarian triangle
- Kneeling bench
- Bread and the cup of Eucharist
- The color white (purity)
- Liturgical dancers

The Christian Year

Christian weddings are appropriate anytime during the Christian year. Each wedding tells God's story in terms of human love, which is an expression of God's eternal love for all creation.

Serving as Hospitable Host

The pastor who officiates at a wedding plays a very important role. It is a privilege and a joy (and a *lot* of work!) to walk with a couple from the point of engagement through the wedding and into the first few months of marriage. The minister's shepherding and priestly roles once again come to the forefront as the couple, under the pastor's care, is tenderly guided down the path of becoming one flesh. Certain duties, attributes, and skills are needed to guide this journey successfully.

Duties

Certain primary duties will emerge for the pastor; these occur in several key stages. Performing a wedding ceremony is one thing; taking responsibility for the full range of duties required to establish a marriage on sound footing is quite another. The duties of the pastor fall into three broad categories: pre-wedding responsibilities, ceremonial responsibilities, and post-wedding responsibilities.

Pre-Wedding Responsibilities

Pre-wedding responsibilities primarily involve premarital counseling and the preparation of the wedding worship service. Premarital counseling is a must. Under normal circumstances, no pastor should consider performing a ceremony where he or she has not invested in multiple sessions of premarital counseling with the couple. Experience will guide you as to how many sessions you will need; more is better than fewer. There are many, many issues to be discussed so that there are fewer surprises and bumps in the road after the sounds of the wedding bells have faded. Premarital counseling sessions will address such things as the bride's and groom's families of origin, personality types, habits for spending money, sharing of home responsibilities, expectations for bearing children, religious faith issues, expectations related to intimacy, decision making, roles in the marriage, and more.[31] As these meetings unfold, you will find that you are developing a close relationship with the couple. This will benefit you when it comes time to perform the ceremony, for you will have established a solid relationship well before the "I dos" are spoken.

Beware of performing premarital counseling sessions for family members and close friends—in fact, don't do it. If you have been invited to perform a wedding for a child, sibling, or other close relative, you could agree to do the ceremony but arrange for another qualified pastor or counselor to handle the premarital counseling sessions. There is no way that the couple or you can remain objective while discussing sensitive matters. If you really care about the couple, you will step out of the role of premarital counselor.

A second pre-wedding duty for the pastor is preparing the wedding service in conjunction with the couple. Begin this process early—at least eight to ten weeks before the wedding date. Schedule face-to-face meetings with the bride and groom *together* to explain the nature of the service and what is typically included. It is wise to have a first draft on paper to which the couple can respond; it serves as a starting place. Explain any church and/or personal service policies in place related to the service. (Other policies related to the use of the building will have been agreed on much earlier.) The pastor must reinforce the spiritual nature of the ceremony, resist secular influences, and represent the standards of the church. The pastor is "the keeper of the gate" when it comes to weddings. He or she must be prepared to say no when necessary—something much easier to do if policies are in place. That way the pastor doesn't have to bear the whole weight of decision making. Instead, the pastor serves as the representative of the congregation.

Ceremonial Responsibilities

A number of duties are required of the one who officiates at the wedding ceremony, including those listed below.

- Provide a time line to the couple for when things need to occur (deposits, marriage license, preparation of printed order of service, when decorating the church may begin, and so on).
- Clearly establish the pastor's role in relation to the wedding planner's role. More and more couples enlist the help of an official wedding planner. The pastor must make clear that ultimately she or he is responsible for what is allowed or not allowed in the church wedding. The wedding reception is another matter; it is beyond the purview of the pastor unless it is held on church property. Working with wedding planners can be challenging, so make sure that the couple understands who is responsible for what and who has the ultimate authority in matters related to the church and the ceremony—the pastor.
- Serve as the contractor for services rendered by church personnel. Certain people will perform services for the wedding—custodian(s), organist, other church musicians, and so on. Arrange for the couple to give you the payment for these individuals on the day of the rehearsal. Dispense the checks promptly to these people following the wedding. It is not that rare for couples to fail to keep their commitment to these people, and it is awkward for the ones providing services to ask for the money due them. As pastor, it is much easier for you to make sure that it is all taken care of and that no one goes without.
- Prepare and lead the wedding rehearsal. This is a *very important responsibility*. Spend a significant amount of time preparing for the success of the rehearsal. Before the rehearsal, communicate to the couple how it will be handled. Show them the agenda for the rehearsal. Clarify as many details as possible with them in advance to reduce the number of times in the rehearsal that decisions will need to be made. When uncertainty occurs at the rehearsal (and it will), there are usually too many voices offering conflicting opinions, which adds great strain to the couple and the pastor. Much of this is alleviated with an agreed-upon rehearsal plan.

Here are a few suggestions for running a smooth rehearsal.

1. Inform the couple as to the length of the rehearsal, and set the start time well in advance of any rehearsal dinner or party plans. This will help you avoid running out of rehearsal time because of a reservation at a restaurant.
2. Establish the positioning of the bridal party, parents, and speakers with the couple *before* the rehearsal. Ask them to communicate the order of the attendants to the participants. This helps to avoid surprises and hurt feelings the day before the wedding.
3. Ask the groom to bring the marriage license to the rehearsal. It *must* be present the day of the wedding; having it at the rehearsal ensures it will be there.

A suggested order for the rehearsal follows.

- Welcome by the pastor
- Verbal explanation of the purpose and goals of the rehearsal
- Opening prayer
- Introduction of wedding party and family members (bride introduces her side; groom introduces his side)
- Assemble the wedding party in place at the front
- Go through the entire service once with instructions (explain who moves where when, and so on)
- Move to the back in reverse order (this rehearses the recessional)
- Practice the processional (participants are now in place to process)
- Go through the complete service a second time without commentary
- Clarify any remaining details
- Entertain questions
- Announce the required arrival time at the church for the wedding
- Close in prayer

4. Meet with the ushers directly after the rehearsal. Inform them of all duties and the timeline for the service.

Post-Wedding Responsibilities

It is the pastor's responsibility to return the marriage license to the county courthouse. This officially registers the marriage. Do so promptly, the very next business day.

Make personal contact with the couple approximately two weeks after the wedding to inquire as to how things are going. About three months after the wedding, make contact again and arrange for a home visit to encourage them and offer prayer. Determine if a pastoral counseling session is needed as they adjust to married life.

Attributes for Officiating

The pastor will pursue certain attributes that will assist her or him in becoming a very effective shepherd to a couple seeking to be married. Here are some suggestions for fostering personal and professional attributes.

- Cultivate a spirit of servanthood; view yourself as a shepherd. Accompanying a couple toward their wedding day is really a matter of pastoral care. It is an excellent opportunity to draw them closer to Christ. Conduct yourself in the most professional of ways.

- Dress professionally at premarital counseling sessions, the rehearsal, and all functions. You are making an impression on a variety of people; you will want to represent the couple, your profession, and your church well. Your best attire is necessary for the wedding service. If clergy robes are not worn, men should wear a plain dark suit with dress shirt and tie; women clergy should wear equally professional attire—a business suit (with skirt) or tailored dress.[32] Occasionally pastors will conclude that they should take their cues for dress from the family or the crowd or their own preference. Even if a family dresses casually, your presence is viewed differently, and you risk being perceived as disrespectful if you are dressed in anything other than professional attire.

- Exude the appropriate balance between reverence and joy. Maintain a reverent tone, yet express joyfulness—smile! Reverence and joy are not mutually exclusive. A certain degree of humor and lightheartedness is appropriate as you lead in the service, but let it happen naturally. Don't try to be funny, and don't steal the show. Remember, "little is much" when it comes to public humor in settings such as this. Just gently, naturally, and joyfully preside.

- Be prepared. Prepare a manuscript for leading the service; without it you could easily say something you regret. Most pastors use some sort of pastor's manual for the wedding service, which contains the official language for the prayers, vows, and so on. Prepare the entire script, complete with notes about what to do when, and you will feel much more secure in your leadership.

- Be flexible. Almost every wedding ceremony has some glitches. Stuff happens. If something unexpected occurs (the groom faints, the organ key sticks, the flower girl starts crying), just roll with it. Do your best to help and not panic. The truth is that it will all work out. Such things become stories we laugh about later.

Administration

There are administrative responsibilities related to any wedding. These become all the more important given the legal ramifications of a wedding. Here are a few suggestions for caring for the details.

- File the wedding license with the county courthouse immediately after the wedding.
- Make sure you have the legal paperwork in hand to perform a wedding. Keep it on file. In the United States, each state regulates the matters related to who may officiate. Ordination or a pastoral license or proof that you are a duly appointed pastor of a legitimate congregation, is required to legally perform a wedding. Judges are also legally permitted to perform weddings. Do not agree to perform a wedding in a state other than where you reside without investigating the legal criteria of that state. Allow plenty of time to receive out-of-state permission, as clerical timelines can be slow.
- While it is the responsibility of the couple to obtain a marriage license, it is helpful to know that the marriage license is always obtained in the *county where the wedding ceremony is to occur.*
- Keep a record of each wedding at which you officiate. Maintaining an accurate record of weddings you perform can come in handy, for families occasionally need documentation concerning wedding records.
- Create your own wedding performance policy as pastor. Revise it regularly; communicate it to church officials. This will include such things as your own purpose statement in performing weddings, any limitations for weddings you will not perform (for instance, whether or not you will marry divorced individuals, couples of mixed faith, and so on), whether or not you will accept an honorarium for performing the wedding, under what circumstances you will permit guest clergy to officiate in the wedding service with you, and so on.
- For tax purposes, keep a record of any wedding fees that you are paid.
- Provide the couple with a wedding certificate. *This is not the same as the marriage license.* A wedding certificate is a professionally produced document with the information concerning the wedding filled in: the date, names of couple, name(s) of clergy, place, and so on. It serves as a handy reference and memento of the event.
- Develop a church wedding policy. This provides a smoother path for clergy and church alike when the facility is requested for use. For example, is your church comfortable with an unknown clergyperson officiating at a wedding in your sanctuary? Will wedding receptions be held in your church? Is the throwing of rice allowed? Alcoholic beverages? What freedom will you allow the photographer/videographer?

- Guide your church in deciding whether or not a fee is required for the use of the church. Under what circumstances would there not be a fee?

Exceptionally Difficult Circumstances

There are various marriage scenarios that can be quite complicated and challenging. The number of ways in which a wedding can pose problems for the church, the clergy, and the couple is increasing. Pastors must be more prepared than ever to make their way through difficult situations. It is beyond the scope of this book to address in any detail these types of weddings. What can be said is that the alert and caring pastor will need to do much study, prayer, and soul-searching to resolve his or her own roles and responsibilities in relation to each circumstance. It will likely come down to a case-by-case basis, as there are no more "one size fits all" answers to these difficult types of questions. Consider a few representative dilemmas.

What is right regarding divorced individuals remarrying? The Protestant community is mixed on this issue. The New Testament speaks to divorce, yet honest, faithful, qualified pastors arrive at different conclusions after having studied the Scriptures. There is no question that the percentage of people divorcing and remarrying has increased dramatically over the years. Will you marry anyone who is divorced? Will it be conditional (for instance, when the former partner committed adultery)? Take your time to come to a conclusion that you feel is right in light of Scripture. Talk to pastors who hold various views. After arriving at the position you feel is right for you, hold your view loosely; it may be shaped differently in the future as you gain more insights into divorce and remarriage.

What should you do if family members are in conflict surrounding the marriage? For instance, should you marry a young couple whose parents do not support the marriage? This may suggest "cause for pause" as you sort out the reasons for the parental reservations. Couples not only marry their partner; they marry an extended family. It would be very helpful if the pastor could gain understanding as to the issues surrounding the lack of support. This is not to say that the couple absolutely should not be married, but much is to be gained by resolving any extended family conflicts prior to the wedding.

Would you marry a couple who is living together? Would you join a Christian with an unbeliever? Would you join a Christian with a person of another faith? Why or why not? Again, arrive at a decision; at the same time, allow yourself space to review your position as you continue to study and pray.

Ethical Considerations

Situations will arise occasionally that present an ethical dilemma to the pastor. He or she will have to work these out by seeking wise counsel. One unwritten code of conduct among clergy is that it is unethical to accept the invitation to marry a couple at a church other than your own without the knowledge and blessing of that pastor. Each pastor is responsible for every worship occasion in his or her church. Never proceed without inquiring directly with the appointed pastor. Often this matter is worked out by sharing duties. If so, remember that you are the guest in such a situation; you are there by invitation of the appointed clergy. Don't take over in someone else's setting.

Other Wedding-Related Services

Other occasions related to Christian marriage may call for a pastoral role. Examples of these include the blessing of a civil wedding and the renewing of wedding vows. The former is an affirmation/celebration of a wedding that was solemnized elsewhere; it is not a second wedding. The latter is an occasion, usually in recognition of a significant anniversary, whereby the couple wishes to publicly renew their vows for the purpose of reaffirming their love and covenantal commitment. Again, this is not a second wedding. Adapt the wedding service accordingly, or consult various minister's handbooks for assistance with these services.

Conclusion

Zane and Hannah's wedding day was exuberant—full of the type of joy and celebration indicative of a Christian wedding. At the reception, several people remarked that there was something special about that service; they couldn't quite put their finger on it, but it just felt different in a good way. Thanks to Pastor Andrew who guided them toward a God-focused service, those who gathered became worshipers, not just observers, and that made all the difference in the world.

Key Terms

bann The public posting or reading of an intended marriage in advance of the wedding.

crash The white strip of cloth/paper that covers the aisle before the bride enters.

homily From the Greek for "discourse." A brief sermon; devotional.

solemnization The legal act of joining two persons in marriage.

To Learn More

Langford, Andy. *Christian Weddings: Resources to Make Your Ceremony Unique.* 2nd ed. Nashville: Abingdon, 2008.

Engage

To get practical, here are a few more suggestions.

1. Write a personal mission statement for performing weddings.
2. Try your hand at writing a wedding policy in two parts: (1) a policy for the church; and (2) your personal/professional performance policy. Attempting this will quickly put you in touch with many of the critical issues you need to begin to resolve.
3. Suppose a couple has called you, the pastor of their church, asking that a friend of the family, also a pastor, officiate at their wedding to be held in your church. What process would you follow to handle this scenario?

3

The Christian Funeral

Before reading chapter 3, reflect on your own experience of attending funerals.

- Approximately how many funerals have you attended (that you did not officiate)?
- Were the services similarly designed and led? If not, how were they different?
- Which features of the various funerals have struck you as helpful? Which features have appeared inappropriate?
- Reflect on those funerals you have attended that have been for a Christian and those for a non-Christian. How have they differed?
- Do funeral services held in churches versus those held in funeral homes seem different to you? If so, in what ways?

Now that you have begun to reflect on funerals, expand your thinking by reading chapter 3.

Expand

The top of Amy's head was about the same height as the casket that rested in the curve of the parlor's bay window in the stately, southern home with the wraparound porch. The patterned, navy blue rug was surrounded by chairs for the mourners who had begun to arrive and were now filling the room. Baskets of flowers were placed here and there. Granddaddy had died. Amy hadn't seen him very many times; she was only seven years old, and her family lived many states away. They had made the trip in one very long day and were now staying with Grandma through the long weekend, which would culminate in the funeral at the country church. Amy had never seen a dead body in a house before. Where she lived, people who died were taken immediately to funeral homes, where they were kept until they were buried. This felt strange.

The strangers in the parlor spoke quietly. They told Grandma they were sorry for her loss and hugged her. People came and went all evening. Amy hung back, fearful of getting too close to the casket, but when Mama took Grandma's arm and walked her forward, Amy went with them. Both women, ordinarily strong, cried pretty hard. Grandma spoke to Granddaddy as if he were alive, wiping her eyes with a big white hankie with embroidered purple flowers. Amy didn't know what to do. She wondered why people were gathering in a house instead of a funeral home. Would Granddaddy stay there all night? What should she say to Grandma? Should she talk to Granddaddy too? If so, what would she say? Not certain what to do, Amy found an empty chair near the old upright piano and sat down to wait until she could figure things out. Before long, she fell asleep to the whispers of the crowd.

The practice of burying the dead ceremonially has existed from the earliest of times. Each culture and civilization has found its own way to handle the inevitable end to mortal life among its citizens. Interestingly, nowhere in Scripture is there any indication of how the early Christians performed burials, nor is there advice on how to do so. Nevertheless, Christians have connected death and burial with acts of worship from the beginning.[1] The funeral liturgy has become a profound moment for the church to recapitulate the truth concerning mortality and immortality.

In this chapter we will primarily discuss the funeral for a Christian. Adjustments for designing and leading a funeral for a nonbeliever as well as for officiating under special circumstances will be suggested later in this chapter.

Laying the Foundations

As we begin our discussion of funerals, the best place to start is to recognize that the movement from life to death to new life is the cosmic theme of the story of God as found in Scripture. It is seen in the fall, the flood, the Passover, the exodus, the exile, and more. Most of all, it is seen in the magnificent earthly journey of our Lord and Savior, Jesus Christ, through his incarnation, death, and resurrection. Whereas all humans experience death, not all experience resurrection to eternal life. This pattern of death and resurrection is recognized and celebrated in the Christian funeral. For believers, the funeral is an occasion, like no other, to confidently proclaim that those who die in the Lord will likewise rise with him (1 Cor. 15:20–22; 1 Thess. 4:16–17). "Fundamental to any Christian funeral service is the proclamation of Jesus Christ as Savior from death and sin and as Lord of Life. Here, as elsewhere in Christian worship, Christ holds the service. He is host; the worshipers are guests."[2] Christ is the cornerstone for all worship services, including the funeral.

The Purposes of the Christian Funeral

There are two primary purposes for the Christian funeral: worship and witness. In doing these well, another significant purpose is achieved, that of ministering to those who mourn. Notice that we did not begin with the purpose of the funeral being that of providing comfort to the bereaved, though it certainly should. Of course we are concerned with comforting those who mourn. But this comfort is provided through the greater ministries of worship and witness. Someone has said that as our funerals become more intentionally theological, they will become more pastorally helpful. The biblical and theological reference points found in both worship and witness serve the grieving individuals very well in time of need.

A Service of Worship

Perhaps the most important thing a rituals architect must grasp from the very beginning is that *a Christian funeral is a service of worship*. While it should seem obvious that a funeral for a believer must center on God and dynamically involve the community in worship, unfortunately funerals have succumbed (no pun intended) to many secular and popular practices that are so far removed from a service of worship that it is unrecognizable as such.[3] Thomas Long, a professor of preaching, bemoans the secularization of funerals, recognizing that "a general cultural and generational shift toward experimentation, customization, and personalization has impacted the social network of death customs and the Christian funeral along with it"[4] as demonstrated by "such features as open-mike speeches by friends and relatives, multimedia presentations of the life of the deceased, NASCAR logos on caskets, the deceased's favorite pop music played from CDs, [and] the release of butterflies." In Western culture today, Christian culture included, funerals are "about me." We must beware: "If Christian meanings are not kept sovereign the integrity of the service is lost."[5]

When we make the claim that a funeral is a service of worship, we shift the focus from self to God. In worship the focus is always on God. This actually becomes a source of comfort, for in looking to the One who created us and sustains us, we are looking to the One who will likewise re-create us to fit us for eternal life in God's kingdom. In worship we surround ourselves with elements of faith—songs, Holy Scripture, prayers, and symbols—that recall the universal truths concerning all who die in the Lord. In a funeral service the deceased is certainly not ignored (as you will soon see); however, for believers, we worship the risen Lord in the midst of death, for "[Christ] is the beginning, the firstborn from the dead, so that he might come to have first place in everything" (Col. 1:18). Funerals are occasions for worship where God in Christ is exalted, and as a result the Holy Spirit's comforting presence is experienced.

A Service of Witness

The Christian funeral is likewise a service of witness. There really is no more profound venue for testifying to our faith than a funeral. When life meets death, truth meets falsehood. During the funeral we will make direct and personal reference to our loved one who has died, but more importantly we will stake our claim on the truth of Scripture that Jesus has returned to the Father so as to prepare a place where our loved one and all believers will reside with him forever (John 14:1–3). Truth is the essence of our witness. During a funeral we rehearse reality—we restate what we know to be true by faith. All attendees, whether believers or not, must hear the clarion voice of Christians announcing the hope of eternity thanks to the goodness and mercy of God.

A Biblical View of Death

Christians in the last several centuries have been highly influenced by the Platonic view of dualism—"that human beings are essentially nonmaterial and immortal souls temporarily housed in disposable and somewhat loathsome bodies."[6] We have inherited a theology of disembodiment that considers the body to be merely a profane shell to house the soul, which is viewed as sacred. But the biblical story of creation lends itself much more to the affirmation of both body *and* soul and the interplay between the two. As Long reminds us,

> God creates the first human being, not by snatching some immortal soul out of the air, sticking it into a body and forcing it to work the garden. The picture is far more tender. God takes dust, ordinary dust from the ground, and breathes into the dust "the breath of life." Dust into which God has breathed life: that is what living human beings are in biblical understanding. Christians . . . do not believe that human beings are *only* bodies, nor do they believe that they are souls who, for the time being, *have* bodies; Christians affirm, rather, that human

beings are *embodied*. What others call "the soul" and "the body," Christians call the "breath of God" and dust; and when it comes to living human beings, they form an inseparable unity.[7]

But while the Christian view of embodiment is important to embrace, nevertheless a distinction is made between the essence of the body and the essence of the soul. All bodies eventually cease to exist and decompose; it's a biological fact. They return to the earth from which they came (Gen. 2:7). The Hebrew word for "man" is *adam*, which sounds like and may be related to the Hebrew word for "ground" or "earth"—*adamah*. So "Adam" literally means "earth man." Likewise, the English word "human" is likely derived from the Latin *humanus*, related to *homo* (man) and *humus* (earth). Humans, like all animals, are given physical bodies that decay and die. They have a beginning and an end; we are mortal in that sense. Humans, however, unlike animals, are given a soul, which has a beginning but does not have an end. The human soul is created for eternity and therefore lives on past the demise of the human body. The souls of those persons who are in Christ live eternally in the presence of the Lord; the souls of those who are not in Christ live eternally apart from the presence of the Lord. For the Christian, the earthly body, worn out, is replaced with a heavenly body—a glorified body—fit for the heavenly environment as a new dwelling for the soul. While the physical presence of the deceased will no longer be visible on earth, the funeral joyously acknowledges the believer as truly alive in the presence of God. One of the significant roles of the Christian funeral, then, is to mark the end of one's residence on earth as a mortal and to celebrate the transition from earth to heaven where residency in a new place is begun.

Unfortunately, there are many serious misunderstandings concerning God, death, and heaven that abound today, even in the church. The incredibly pagan or mythical ideas about death that persist communicate poor theology at best and heresy at worst. Much of our view of heaven is shaped by cultural myths perpetuated by popular culture, most especially the film and television industries. The number of afterlife theories posited today is growing exponentially. The death of a Christian is a prime opportunity to clearly communicate what the Bible teaches about life, death, and eternity. A Christian funeral is also a time to pause before the profound mystery of life and death and own it as just that: a holy mystery, beyond our complete understanding. At the Christian funeral we embrace the mystery and place our trust in God who understands all things; we express our faith in salvation, resurrection, and eternal life, giving God thanks for these gifts and celebrating their reality even in the midst of our remaining questions.

Implications/Considerations

When planning funerals, some choices need to be made. Our decisions should be grounded in God's truth concerning life, death, and eternity.

To Evangelize or Not to Evangelize?

When claiming that a funeral service bears witness to the gospel, a word of caution is in order: beware of turning it into an evangelistic enterprise. Some pastors are tempted to take advantage of a captive audience and seize the opportunity to make emotional appeals for conversion. There are at least two reasons to avoid this. First, the setting is emotionally charged to begin with; therefore, most attendees will not be able to think and act objectively in such a circumstance. Because the mourners' emotions are heightened from their loss, to turn the funeral into a stage for evangelistic purposes is to take advantage of the raw emotional state of the attendees. Invitations to follow Christ are best kept for occasions when nonbelievers are able to clearly consider what it means to commit to a life of true discipleship with its vast demands. Second, the leader risks being perceived as someone who is using the occasion for an ulterior motive; it will smack of manipulation. Let the funeral be the funeral. Altar calls at funerals are not appropriate.

Yet while preempting the funeral for conversions is not fitting, the proclamation of the gospel *is* most fitting—indeed a necessity. To say that a funeral should bear witness to the gospel is simply to suggest that believers should testify that they believe in the triune God and in all of the accompanying promises such trust in God includes. There is nothing more fitting than the community sharing its faith during the time of death. It will impact unbelievers or those who are weak in faith to draw closer to Christ. I know a seasoned pastor who does not support the public invitation for salvation at funerals but does make a general statement offering his availability to meet in the future with anyone who wishes to know more about the faith proclaimed in the funeral—the faith of the church as evidenced in the faith of the deceased. On more than one occasion, persons have contacted him weeks and even months later, desiring to learn more about becoming a disciple of Jesus Christ. When the tears had dried and the emotions were under control, they were able to contemplate matters of faith more deeply and respond to the Holy Spirit's persistence with greater clarity and commitment than in the convoluted mix of thoughts and emotions so prevalent the day of the funeral. The power of witness at a funeral cannot be overestimated; it will serve the purposes that God intends through the Spirit.

A Funeral Home or a Church?

An important consideration for any funeral is where it will be held. By far the most popular choice in current Western practice is a funeral home or a church.[8] The location for a funeral is typically not a matter of right and wrong, but of one's vision of the service. Many Christians arrange for their funeral to be held in a funeral home. Others insist that their funeral be held in their church. Whatever one's choice, the place is not neutral. Simply recognize that the environment itself communicates a message and that certain challenges are posed with either venue. It is very fitting for a Christian's funeral to take place in the church. The sacred space of a church sanctuary has been set apart for holy purposes. It offers a setting where the symbols of faith (Word, Table, baptismal pool, cross, flame, and so on) surround worshipers with reminders of God's presence throughout the journey from birth to death. Simply put, when the funeral is held in a church, it is easier to conceive of and lead a funeral service as a *worship* service (and the gathered mourners will more easily see themselves as a congregation assembled for worship). One consideration for holding a funeral in a church is the additional cost to the family for the transportation of the body and the setup of the casket and other items (charged by the funeral home). Most churches do not assess a fee for the use of their facility for funerals.

Leading a funeral in a funeral home poses a greater challenge to the rituals architect, because the service is less likely to be perceived as a worship service. The attendees will more naturally view themselves as passive observers rather than as worshipers. Leaders will need to be very intentional about shaping the service so as to maintain the God-focus and to involve the people congregationally. The obstacles may include such things as a lack of organ or piano (many funeral homes no longer provide a keyboardist or even have these instruments on site), no hymnals or Bibles readily available for use, no screens for projection of worship words for congregational use (you will need to print a detailed order of service), and no religious symbols.

Where a funeral is held may even hold implication for what the service is called. "A Service of Death and Resurrection" is an excellent title for the service held in a church (though it is also appropriate for a service held anywhere for a Christian). The word "funeral" is appropriate for the service in the funeral home. Regardless, I hope the reader can see that what you envision the service to be in its essence has implications for other related decisions.

In-Person or iPerson?

The technological advances of our day present some exciting possibilities as well as some hazards. Most folks by now have witnessed the use of technology at some point in the funeral industry. Website obituaries, complete with online condolences, have been common practice for years. Digital tributes consisting of photos accompanied by background music (representative of the dead person's musical tastes) are commonplace. These programs are typically running nonstop during hours of visitation and are often used in the service itself (when not viewed as a *worship* service!). An increasing number of funeral homes are taping funerals and then immediately launching them via the internet through streaming video on the funeral home website, a service to those who could not attend in person.

How should Christians view technologies as they relate to funerals? There are many ways that technology can positively influence our ministries to the grieving. There is no way to address all of the possibilities or to anticipate every technological scenario. But here is a rule of thumb for making wise pastoral decisions: let technology perform in the way it is best suited—for *delivery*, not for *content*. Let me explain. The unique benefit of modern-day communications technologies has largely to do with (1) ways to deliver information to others instantaneously and (2) highlighting the visual. Where you believe it is appropriate, use technology in these ways. But in experimenting with different delivery systems (such as multimedia slides, video streaming, websites, and social network sites), do not compromise the *content* of the visitation and funeral. *How* something is delivered must not make the decisions for *what* will be delivered. Sometimes we confuse the message with the medium. Technology must always serve the honorable purposes of the endeavor, not the other way around. Remember too that copyright issues must be considered when broadcasting via the internet. Make sure to obtain written permission from those legally authorized to give it before you use or broadcast any material.

Burial or Cremation?

Deciding between burial or cremation is a very relevant question today. The widely held view among Christians is that either one is a legitimate option. While there are no examples of cremation in Scripture, neither is there any prohibition against it. Because the human body, upon death, no longer houses the soul, it may be disposed of in more than one respectful way.

Cremations are dramatically on the rise for many reasons: lower cost, more ecologically sound, increased flexibility, and so on. The average cost of a basic funeral and burial (funeral director/funeral home fees, embalming, metal casket, and vault) in the United States at the time of this writing is $7,755.[9] The basic cost of cremation (cremation, funeral director fees, and cardboard/fiberboard container) is $2,070. Cremation is the process of committing the body to flames and then preserving the ashes. Approximately 97 percent of the body disappears in the form of vapors. The remaining 3 percent, in the form of gray ashes, is given to the survivors for safekeeping or for ceremonial distribution at a time and place to be determined. Containers for ashes (called urns) may be placed in a columbarium, a repository for urns. Columbaria exist in cemeteries as well as in a variety of other places. More and more churches are providing columbaria gardens on their grounds. A columbarium in a churchyard or in a designated room in the building is similar to a church providing a graveyard. Where better for the Christian's final resting place than in the church?

Close in process to cremation is incineration, a technique also used for the disposal of a body. While cremation exposes the body to flames, incineration exposes the body to intense heat. The result is effectively the same, in that the body is reduced to ashes. Typically found in larger towns and cities, cremato-ries are used for both cremation and incineration. Most local funeral directors do not have crematories on-site (though these are increasing, reflective of the growing interest in cremation); they therefore secure the services of a nearby crematory, handling all of the arrangements for the family.

Funeral or Memorial Service?

There is essentially only one distinction between a funeral and a memorial service: the presence or absence of the corpse. Typically, the word "funeral" is used when the corpse is present in the casket; the phrase "memorial service" is used when a service is held without the body present. So if cremation has oc-curred and there is a service of remembrance, it is called a memorial service even if the urn of ashes is present. Sometimes a funeral is held in one location with the body present, followed by a memorial service in another location, without the body, to accommodate a group of persons who could not attend the first service.

While memorial services are extremely common today, we should rethink the advisability of the absence of the body in a service of remembrance. This hearkens again to our Platonian view of the body. Long suggests, "If the 'real me' is a soul and not the body, then the presence of my body at a funeral is unnecessary . . . even a morbid and vulgar embarrassment to the more rarefied spirituality of the moment."[10] You might say it is a problem that the body is a problem. Long cites Mark Duffey, owner of a funeral concierge service, who remarks, "The body's a downer, especially for boomers. . . . If the body doesn't have to be there [at a memorial service] . . . it frees us up to do what we want. They may want to have it in a country club or a bar or their favorite restaurant. That's where consumers want to go."[11] Unfortunately, there is a growing view that the presence of the body somehow limits our self-expression, as if that is the central issue. To the contrary, there is something to be said for the presence

of the human body, given by our Creator at birth, at the service; the reality of
death is more vivid with the corpse present. If cremation is preferred, it can
take place following the funeral. Such a practice would, of course, defeat the
purpose of a less costly funeral but would allow the family to proceed with
cremation for reasons other than cost.

Open or Closed Casket?

One important decision to be made is that of the open or closed casket for the
service. It is a good and recommended practice to have the open casket during
public visitations when the family greets their loved ones. Sometimes the closed
casket at viewing is necessary, depending on the circumstances of death (for instance, if the body was greatly disfigured for one reason or another in the course
of dying). But when at all possible, have an open casket, because witnessing the
reality of their loved one now being dead will help the mourners in their grieving
process. This witness establishes the finality of the mourners' earthly relationship with the deceased. Young children, too, need to become acquainted with
the realities of life and death, thereby avoiding confusion and misunderstanding.

However, for the funeral service itself, the closed casket is highly recommended, because it greatly facilitates the shift in focus from the deceased to
God. As we have said, the funeral is a worship service that centers primarily
on God. That is difficult to accomplish with the congregants staring at their
loved one before them. A closed casket is also a great advantage in turning the
corner on the emotionalism inherent in any funeral by its very nature. The
closed casket will be front and center, but the eyes and ears of congregants
will be lifted to the words and actions of the funeral liturgy much more readily
than with an open casket. A closed casket redirects emotions away from the
body to the greater themes of God's love and mercy.

If a closed casket is elected, the family will still have their poignant final
moments. The best time for this is at the conclusion of the last visitation. For
instance, if there is a public viewing just prior to the service (especially possible
in a church where a large foyer or nearby room is available for the casket to
be placed prior to entering the sanctuary), the funeral directors will dismiss
the general public at the end of the stated time for visitation and offer a few
moments of private time wherein the family can view their loved one for the
last time and offer final sentiments before the funeral begins. The family is
then led from their private viewing into the sanctuary to take their seats or to
participate in the processional, the casket is closed, the clergy accompany the
casket in procession to the front of the sanctuary, and the service begins. If
the service is in a funeral home, it works best if the final family viewing takes

place well prior to the service, preferably the previous day as the last visitation concludes. This is advisable because the casket will likely already be placed in the spot for the service before the gathering crowd arrives, making it all but impossible for final family time to be private. Occasionally, the casket is closed for the service and reopened at the end of the service to facilitate final good-byes, but this (1) is practically challenging (the funeral directors have already lowered the body in the casket to accommodate the closing of the lid) and (2) only prolongs the inevitable. Let the service be the concluding memory.

While the closed casket for the funeral is recommended, it is not an issue upon which the pastor should insist. In many of these instances, it is not a matter of wrong or right but of good versus better. Often local practice will determine what is normative. If there is strong sentiment either way, let your best pastoral instincts guide you. Leaders can get in the way; this is not an occasion to alienate oneself from the family. It does seem that if the funeral is held in a church, the closed casket is most appropriate, because the intent of the worship service is to focus on God. However, if the funeral is held in a funeral home, where the challenge is always greater to pull off a true worship service, it could be argued more strongly to have an open casket.

Rites of Fraternal Order or Not?

If the deceased was a member of a fraternal order (e.g., Freemasonry, the Loyal Order of Moose, the Knights of Columbus), there is sometimes a special service related to that membership. If so, it must be held separately from the Christian funeral. They are not to be intermixed, for each service has different emphases. The organization will make its own arrangements in conjunction with the funeral director and must have concluded its proceedings prior to the Christian funeral and burial. Military rites for former members of the armed services tend to be simple traditional acts done at the cemetery (playing of taps, firing of guns, presentation of flag to the family, and so on) and do not compromise the committal when handled properly. If this is the case, plan to arrange for the best place to incorporate the rites into the committal. In all circumstances the final service and burial must be thoroughly Christian.

Holy Communion or Not?

It may surprise some readers to know that "the Eucharist was celebrated in connection with the Christian funeral at least as early as the third century."[12] It may have originated as a practice intended to counter or "Christianize" the Greek practice of placing a coin under the tongue of the deceased in order "to pay the fare of Charon, the ferryman of the dead, for passage to the next world."[13]

Christians adapted the corresponding custom of placing the food of the Lord's Supper under the tongue of the believer prior to death to provide nourishment for his or her journey to God.[14] Eventually, the practice changed to having the Christian community celebrate the eucharistic meal at the conclusion of the burial.

Today in the United States it is uncommon to include Holy Communion at a Protestant funeral.[15] A few denominations are reclaiming this aspect of the funeral worship service, as evidenced by their official worship books, which include eucharistic rites.[16] Including Communion at funeral services may be recognized as an appropriate liturgy, but it is rarely done. I remember an occasion when I experienced the Eucharist during a Service of Death and Resurrection that left a strong impression. Upon the death of Robert Webber, the Institute for Worship Studies community gathered for a memorial worship service. I cannot explain it, but for the very first time I became acutely aware of how thin the veil is between saints on earth and saints in heaven. I had been trained to view heaven as far away, but that was not my experience that evening. At the Table, our earthly praise was joined with the praise of the hosts of heaven into one mighty chorus. I found that the communion of saints is incredibly real at the Communion table during a Service of Death and Resurrection.

Including the Eucharist as a part of the funeral worship service is a wonderful option, even recommended, for the devout Christian, but it is not without its challenges. You can probably surmise that it works best, for symbolic and logistical reasons, when the service is held in a church. The symbols of faith are in place in the local church, and the facilities and personnel are equipped for handling the practical aspects of delivering the elements. Funeral directors would find it a logistical challenge to pull off Communion in the funeral home, though it could be done. Another issue to consider is the number of non-Christians who may be present at a funeral and what difficulties that may bring. Whether or not Communion is included will require pastoral guidance on your part. If it is not typically done in your setting, it will take some education and, most of all, doing it thoughtfully and appropriately when it is included.

Building the Structure

With these foundations in mind, it is time to consider the structure for the Christian funeral service. Remember that the order of service, in its very sequence of worship acts, is a telling of the story of God (God seeks us; God speaks; we reply; God empowers for mission). In the case of the funeral, the story line centers on God's love in life and in death. For these reasons, the order matters. Yet there is certainly flexibility in how we go about it as long as the story is told and the worship service is preserved as worship. The large-frame, fourfold order beautifully allows for worship acts such as those listed below. Maintain the general fourfold order, remembering that *the sequence of worship acts within each movement is not fixed and allows for your creativity and needs.* Also remember the corporate nature of the Christian funeral: "Every person is potentially both a mourner and a comforter of others, and all are to do the work of worship together."[17]

This service is developed as a Service of Death and Resurrection held in a local church. It is easily adapted for a funeral home setting with minimal adjustments.[18] While it may look lengthy on paper, this order of service can be accomplished in thirty minutes or sixty minutes, depending upon how developed you make it.

The Order of the Christian Funeral or Memorial Service

The basic outline alone appears in appendix B.

Gathering

Pre-service Music (Prelude)

Appropriate instrumental and/or vocal music prepares the congregation for worship.[19]

If the service is held at a funeral home, the clergy enters the room during the final selection of the pre-service music. If the service is held in a church, a processional occurs during the final selection of pre-service music or during the opening hymn. The pastor meets pall bearers and funeral director(s) at the rear of the church and then precedes the coffin down the center aisle to the designated place at the front of the sanctuary. The congregation will stand when the coffin is brought into the church as a sign of respect. Silence is also appropriate for the processional. Participants in the processional may be as many or as few as appropriate for the context. The following processional order is traditional (simply maintain the order while eliminating some features as needed):

- The light (an acolyte carrying the Paschal/Christ candle or other light)[20]
- The cross
- The officiant(s)
- The coffin (if an urn is used, the officiant may carry the urn)
- Members of the family

Greeting

Greet the congregation warmly.

SAMPLE GREETINGS (SCRIPTURE IS BEST)

- "Grace to you and peace from God our Father and the Lord Jesus Christ." (One of Paul's favorite greetings; see Rom. 1:7; 1 Cor. 1:3; 2 Cor. 1:2, and so on.)
- "In the name of the Father and of the Son and of the Holy Spirit." (A Trinitarian greeting establishes the funeral as a truly Christian event.)
- "The Lord be with you." The people respond, "And also with you."
- "Our help is in the name of the LORD, who made heaven and earth" (Ps. 124:8).
- "'Be still, and know that I am God! I am exalted among the nations, I am exalted in the earth.' The LORD of hosts is with us; the God of Jacob is our refuge" (Ps. 46:10–11).

Note: Don't ad lib when it comes to the greeting. People find immediate comfort in well-chosen words offered with assurance.

Opening Words from Scripture

Read a few verses of appropriate Scripture.

SAMPLE OPENING SCRIPTURE PASSAGES[21]

- Psalm 46:1–7
- Psalm 90:1–2
- Psalm 91:1–2

- John 14:1–3
- Romans 8:35–39
- 2 Corinthians 1:3–4

- Revelation 14:13
- Revelation 21:1–5

Note: Verses may be combined from more than one passage. Do not offer a lengthy introduction—simply read. The power of the scriptural words is profoundly felt in their stark simplicity. Because of its predictability, reserve Psalm 23 for later if requested.

Statement of Purpose

Make a simple statement as to why you have gathered.

SAMPLES

- "We are here today to worship God, to celebrate the good news of the resurrection, to offer thanks for [*name*], to recommit ourselves to God's purposes, and to be reminded of the promise of Scripture that 'neither death, nor life . . . will be able to separate us from the love of God in Christ Jesus our Lord' (Rom. 8:38–39). Let us pray."[22]

- "We are gathered in the name of our risen Lord to bring praise and thanks to God as we accompany [*name*] on [*her/his*] journey home to [*her/his*] heavenly Father. May God's Spirit abide with us as we seek to glorify God in this service. Let us pray."[23]

Invocation

Pray a prayer that acknowledges that we are in God's presence, and calls upon the Spirit's comfort and power to enable God-pleasing worship.

Note: This is not a long prayer petitioning for comfort, though comfort may certainly be mentioned. Later, intercessions are made for the family. The traditional parts to an invocation are found in appendix A.

Opening Hymn/Song

Sing the faith.

SAMPLES

See "Installing Doors and Windows" (below) for suggestions regarding song choices.

Note: Avoid highly sentimental, emotional songs for the opening of the service. Choose strong, faith-oriented, familiar texts. Though a vocal solo is appropriate to include in a funeral service, it is best not to replace the opening congregational song with a solo, because (1) we seek to establish the corporate nature of the event from the beginning, (2) the community can find great meaning in singing words of faith at this poignant moment, and (3) a solo can heighten emotionalism, depending on the choice.

Naming

Read a prepared summary of the deceased person's life.

Note: The official obituary, adapted, can serve quite well for this. This is best presented by the officiating clergy. This is not the eulogy (see below). This is not the time to share personal memories or entertaining stories; it is simply the time to objectively state the facts regarding the life and service of the deceased. Keep it somewhat formal.

Eulogy (optional)

If deemed important, previously designated individual(s) may share their memories or thoughts on the passing of their loved one.

Note: Make sure these are brief by suggesting a time limit to the speaker. (Offer the speaker less time than you really hope for, knowing that it typically goes longer rather than shorter.) Make sure the speaker is prepared. Ask him or her to prepare notes in advance. Limit the number of persons delivering eulogies. Do not allow for an "open microphone." This has the potential for a great number of problems, for there is no way to control what may be said. I have heard inappropriate statements made, confidences broken, speakers taking an exorbitant amount of time, and so on. In addition, emotional outbursts can occur that are all but impossible to handle. Not all things must be shared publicly. Remember, the focus of the worship service is on God.

Word

Scripture Lesson
Read the passage(s) that constitute the primary text(s) for the homily.

Prayer for Understanding
Pray that the Holy Spirit will impart understanding to the listeners.
Note: The traditional parts to the prayer for understanding (the Prayer for Illumination) are found in appendix A.

Homily
Deliver a brief sermon.
Note: Funeral sermons should be briefer in scope than the typical Sunday sermon preached in church. Given the nature of this service, ten to twelve minutes is plenty. Like any good sermon, it should be based on the text, providing scriptural interpretation that is inspirational for the mourners. The sermon is not about the life of the deceased but about the truth of the text. At the same time, *do* be careful to make direct reference to the deceased, connecting his or her life to that of the point(s) of your homily and/or the text.

Response (We Commit Ourselves to God's Purposes)

Prayer of Intercession
Offer a pastoral prayer that includes thanksgiving for the life, witness, and work of the deceased saint, petitions for those who mourn, and prayers of intercession for others and the world. Pray for comfort for those who mourn. Pray for peace in the days ahead. Pray for all those who mourn this day.
Note: It is best that these are prepared in advance so as to avoid fumbling around for words at such a grief-filled time.
Silence within the prayer may also be a fitting and moving dimension to the prayer of intercession. I recommend that the Lord's Prayer be prayed later, at the conclusion of the committal service, but if it is not going to be prayed there, it is a great idea to add it here as a conclusion to the prayer of intercession.

Other Response-Oriented Worship Acts
(as fitting given the homily)

The worship act(s) following the sermon provide appropriate opportunities for persons to consider how they can best love and serve God and others as a result of hearing the Word. It is a wonderful time for believers to recommit themselves to fulfilling God's purposes in this life.

SAMPLES

- Recite a creed (a most fitting corporate act in the face of death).
- Give an exhortation. (A designated and prepared individual of notable Christian maturity urges the congregation to live in a way that brings honor to Jesus Christ. An example of a scriptural exhortation is Romans 8:11–17.)
- Share Holy Communion (see above, "Holy Communion or Not?").
- Have an appropriate vocal solo.
- Have an appropriate reading.

Note: Do not overdevelop this part of the service, as significant as it is. Choose only one or two worship acts for the response (in addition to the prayer of intercession). Well-chosen, succinct worship acts bring the service to a fitting close. If a vocal solo or reading is offered, strive to select one that has a strong, objective text; avoid weak, sentimental texts and tunes.

Sending

Closing Hymn/Song

Sing about resurrection, hope, commitment to Christ, and so on.

SAMPLES

See "Installing Doors and Windows" (below) for suggestions regarding song choices.

Note: Seek a hymn or song that is uplifting in text and tone. Choose strong, faith-filled texts.

Closing Prayer

Conclude with a brief prayer that (1) offers thanks for God's divine assistance in the service and (2) invites continued presence as we journey to the cemetery (or other burial site if done that day).

Note: Save the benediction for the committal service. This will help worshipers to view the service and the committal as one extended and unified service. If there is no immediate service of committal, this prayer becomes a benediction. The traditional parts to the benediction are found in appendix A.

Transition to the Final Resting Place

Upon the conclusion of the funeral, it is most common to proceed to the cemetery.[24] It may be impossible to bury the body the same day in climates where winter is too cold to dig graves. If so, move from the funeral service directly into the liturgy for the committal. The body will be held and buried at a later date. A small, intimate graveside service may be desired at that time. Assuming that the attendees move to a place of burial or repose when the funeral concludes, it is important to view the funeral service and the committal service as one whole event divided into two parts. The journey to the final resting place is part of the service too. The events between the funeral and the committal will vary slightly due to local custom and the particular funeral director's practice; however, the following sequence is fairly common.

- The funeral directors dismiss the attendees while the immediate family remains seated. Often this includes a final pass by the casket if it is open.
- The family is dismissed last and either leaves (closed casket) or says their final good-byes at the casket prior to leaving (open casket).
- The presiding clergyperson remains in the room while the funeral directors secure the casket, readying it for the hearse.
- The officiating clergy moves to the head of the casket and leads the procession from the service room to the hearse, standing at the open rear door of the hearse until the casket is in and the door is closed.
- Upon arrival at the cemetery, the clergy stands at the door of the hearse again, leads the procession to the head of the grave, and remains there for the committal service.
- The funeral director indicates when to begin the service of committal.

The Service of Committal

The service of committal is led as a continuation of the funeral service. It has three basic features: the committal of the remains (the disposing of the physical body to the elements), the committal of the deceased to God (referred to as "commendation"), and the recommittal of the living to serve God's purposes (sometimes referred to as "offering").[25] Note the beautiful flow to these movements within the committal service: worshipers are confronted with the finality of death through the words that commit the bodily remains (committal), the loved one is entrusted to God and God's mercy (commendation), and those who remain are challenged to live faithfully, walking in their baptism, until they too are gathered to God (offering). The rhythm of the committal is the rhythm of life-death-life inherent in creation and in Jesus's own journey.

The Graveside Service

A graveside service is exactly what the term indicates: a service at the grave. It is different from the committal in that the funeral is not held just prior to the burial. Essentially, the funeral and committal are collapsed into one very brief service. Graveside services are often related to special circumstances surrounding death, such as a stillborn child or the death of an indigent person, or when the primary funeral/memorial service was held a great distance from the burial site at an earlier time. Sometimes graveside services are requested for other reasons, perhaps due to sheer efficiency or cost, or simply because the benefits of a public funeral are not valued by the family. Most graveside services tend to be private, without public attendance expected.

When planning a graveside service, expect that it will be brief, largely for practical reasons. To begin with, a graveside service is typically chosen over a funeral to avoid a full-fledged funeral or memorial service. If so, it is counterproductive to the family's wishes to provide a lengthy service at the grave. Second, it is held outside (unless at an indoor columbarium), and people will be standing. Think of the service as an embellished committal. You may wish to include, at most, some opening words from Scripture, the statement of purpose, an invocation, and brief words in memoriam, followed by the committal. A graveside service would not include a homily.

The Order of the Christian Committal Service

The basic outline alone appears in appendix B.

Scripture

Read brief verses of Scripture.[26]

Sample Passages

- Job 19:25–27
- Psalm 16:9, 11
- John 11:25
- John 12:23–26
- 1 Corinthians 15:39–44, 50–58
- 1 Peter 1:3–9

Note: Choose verses of hope, especially passages about the resurrection.

The Committal of Remains

Commit the remains to the earth (or final resting place).

Sample Words of Committal[27]

- "Into your hands, merciful God, we commend the soul of [*name*], as we commit (her/his) body to the ground, earth to earth, ashes to ashes, dust to dust, in sure and certain hope of life in the world to come; through our Lord Jesus Christ, who shall fashion anew our earthly body that it may be like unto his own glorious body, according to his might working whereby he is able to subdue all things unto himself."[28]

- "Unto you, almighty God, we commend the soul of [*name*], and to the elements we commit (her/his) body, in sure and steadfast faith that as (she/he) has borne the image of the earthly, so also (she/he) now bears the image of the heavenly."[29]

- "And now, we commit this body to its resting place; and we commit the spirit, O our Father, together with every sacred interest of our hearts, into Your keeping; praying that You will deal graciously and mercifully with each of us, until we too shall come to You in glory, through the riches of grace in Jesus our Lord."[30]

Note: Gestures can be helpful here. Options include placing your hand on the casket as you read/say the words of committal, or gently sprinkling a small handful of dirt upon the casket.

The Commendation

Commend the deceased into the hands of God.

Sample Words of Commendation

- "Depart, O Christian soul, out of this world;
  In the Name of God the Father Almighty who created you;
  In the Name of Jesus Christ who redeemed you;
  In the Name of the Holy Spirit who sanctifies you.
  May your rest be this day in peace,
  and your dwelling place in the Paradise of God."[31]

- "Into your hands, O merciful Savior, we commend your servant [*name*]. Acknowledge, we humbly beseech you, a sheep of your own fold, a lamb of your own flock, a sinner of your own redeeming. Receive [*her/him*] into the arms of your mercy, into the blessed rest of everlasting peace, and into the glorious company of the saints in light. Amen."[32]

The Prayer of Offering (Concluding Prayer)

Pray a *brief* prayer of thanks for receiving the deceased into God's heavenly kingdom, peace for those who remain separated from their loved one, and strength to live pure and purposeful lives until we too meet our Maker.

Samples

- "O God, King Eternal, whose light divides the day from the night and turns the shadow of death into the morning: Drive from us all wrong desires, bring our hearts to keep your law, and guide our feet into the way of peace; that, having done your will with cheerfulness during the day, we may, when night comes, rejoice to give you thanks; through Jesus Christ our Lord. Amen."[33]
- "O Lord, support us all the day long of this troubled life, until the shadows lengthen and the evening comes and the busy world is hushed, the fever of life is over, and our work is done. Then, in your mercy, grant us a safe lodging, and a holy rest, and peace at the last, through Jesus Christ our Lord. Amen."[34] (Especially appropriate for a mature/older adult.)

The Lord's Prayer

Praying the Lord's Prayer can be a powerful conclusion to the committal service.
Note: Even given the secular society today, there are typically enough people who know the prayer to carry it without printed text.

Hymn/Song (optional)

There is nothing quite so moving as a well-chosen congregational song sung a cappella at a graveside. If there is a good song leader available, able to pitch and carry the tune well, consider singing as the loved one is laid to rest.

Samples

See "Installing Doors and Windows" (below) for suggestions regarding song choices.

Benediction

Offer a true benediction with raised hand of blessing, looking at the recipients.

Samples of Benedictions for the Committal

- Numbers 6:24–26
- 2 Corinthians 4:6
- Philippians 4:7 or 4:6–7
- 2 Thessalonians 2:16
- Hebrews 13:20–21
- "Almighty God, Father, Son, and Holy Spirit, bless you now and forever. Amen."

Note: The traditional parts to the benediction are found in appendix A. A fitting conclusion to the benediction is also found in Luke 2:29–32 (adapt as appropriate).

Charge

Look directly into the faces of the congregation and offer simple words of challenge.

Sample of Dismissal

- "Fight the good fight of faith; take hold of the eternal life, to which you were called. . . . I charge you to keep the commandment without spot or blame until the manifestation of our Lord Jesus Christ, which he will bring about at the right time—he who is the blessed and only Sovereign, the King of kings and Lord of lords. It is he alone who has immortality and dwells in unapproachable light, whom no one has ever seen or can see; to him be honor and eternal dominion. Amen" (1 Tim. 6:12a, 13b–16).

The clergy or funeral director will indicate that the service is over. Sometimes announcements are given, such as an invitation to a fellowship meal at the church.

Greet the Family

The officiating clergy moves directly to the immediate family, seated closest to the casket, to offer them final condolences and words of hope as the crowd disperses.[35]

The entire committal service is very brief, perhaps as brief as five to ten minutes. There is no need to linger at the site, as it forms the conclusion to the primary part of the service held earlier. While committals tend to be brief, they are nevertheless important. Don't appear rushed; at the same time, don't lengthen the committal fearful that it seems too short.

We have been focusing on the spiritual and liturgical dimensions of the deceased person's final hours and the church's role in commemoration and burial, but it is also important to note several significant sociological and psychological benefits afforded by the funeral and committal. The service allows the community, sociologically speaking, to take up its responsibility to offer a respectful and dignified conclusion to the life of a valued member, honoring a life lived in community. In addition, the psychological benefits as a result of participating in the funeral and committal are enormous. The service provides a sense of closure and finality that greatly facilitates the grief process.

Installing Doors and Windows

After the rituals architect has provided order for the funeral service and committal, one must begin to make choices as to the songs, prayers, Scriptures, and other worship acts given to the community for them to carry out the service of worship, all the while conscious of appropriate symbols and the Christian year. These worship acts, like doors and windows, "let in light" and enable relationship, both with God (vertical) and others (horizontal). They help worshipers *experience* the ritual.

Suggested Songs

The song choices one makes will naturally be influenced by the style of worship common to the community in which the deceased worshiped. A few songs with appropriate texts for a Service of Death and Resurrection and/or Committal are listed below and represent several styles (classic hymns, gospel songs, modern worship music, and spirituals). There are many more hymns appropriate to a Christian funeral than there are other types of congregational song, hence, the preponderance of hymns listed below. These songs are merely suggestions; plan on compiling a comprehensive list, over time, appropriate to your context.

Abide with Me (Henry F. Lyte)
Amazing Grace (John Newton)
Be Still, My Soul (Katherina von Schlegel)
Borning Cry (John C. Ylvisaker)
By the Sea of Crystal (William Kuipers)

Children of the Heavenly Father (Carolina Sandell Berg)

Deep River (traditional spiritual)

For All the Saints (William W. How)

Give Me Jesus (traditional spiritual)

He Leadeth Me (Joseph H. Gilmore)

How Great Thou Art (Stuart K. Hine)

I Will Rise (Chris Tomlin)

I'll Fly Away (Albert E. Brumley)

I'll Praise My Maker While I've Breath (Isaac Watts)

In Christ Alone (Keith Getty and Stuart Townend)

In the Bulb There Is a Flower (Natalie Sleeth)

Lift High the Cross (George W. Kitchin)

My Faith Looks Up to Thee (Ray Palmer)

My Jesus, I Love Thee (William R. Featherstone)

Nearer My God to Thee (Sarah F. Adams)

O God, Our Help in Ages Past (Isaac Watts)

O Thou in Whose Presence (Joseph Swain)

On Eagle's Wings (Michael Joncas)

On Jordan's Stormy Banks I Stand (Samuel Stennett)

Precious Lord, Take My Hand (Thomas A. Dorsey)

Shall We Gather at the River (Robert Lowry)

Shepherd Me, O God (Marty Haugen)

Soon and Very Soon (André Crouch)

Stand by Me (Charles A. Tindley)

Steal Away to Jesus (traditional spiritual)

Swing Low, Sweet Chariot (traditional spiritual)

The Lord's My Shepherd (anonymous; *Scottish Psalter*)

There'll Be Joy in the Morning (Natalie Sleeth)

There's a Land That Is Fairer than Day (Sanford Fillmore Bennett)

We Shall Walk through the Valley in Peace (A. L. Hatter)

We're Marching to Zion (Isaac Watts)

When Peace like a River (Horatio G. Spafford)

When the Saints Go Marchin' In (traditional spiritual)

When We All Get to Heaven (Eliza E. Hewitt)

Scripture Passages

The possible Scripture passages appropriate for a Christian funeral are numerous. Here are a few to help you get started with building your own list.

Job 19:25–27a

Psalm 39:4–7

Psalm 46 (selected verses)

Psalm 90 (selected verses)

Psalm 118 (selected verses)

Psalm 121

Isaiah 35:6–9

Lamentations 3:22–26, 31–33

John 5:24–27

John 6:37–40

John 11:21–27

John 14:1–6

1 Corinthians 15:20–26, 51–52, 54–58

2 Corinthians 5:1–10

Philippians 3:7–21

1 Thessalonians 4:13–5:11

2 Timothy 4:6–8

Revelation 7:9–17

Revelation 21:1–7

Revelation 22:1–5

Prayers

Various types of prayers helpful to the funeral and committal are explained elsewhere (see "Building the Structure" above and appendix B). In addition to these, consider the Prayer of Confession as especially useful for the funeral. It can serve the congregants well in providing them a chance to confess the types of regrets, sins of omissions, or feelings of ill will which so often surface at the time of death. The Prayer of Confession and the Assurance of Pardon can play a liberating role for those who mourn. If used, a good place to add it to the order of service is after the opening hymn and before the naming.

Symbols

Certain symbols are especially appropriate for the funeral to help people connect with God and the great mysteries of our faith. These symbols will be more or less significant depending upon your liturgical tradition; however, consider these possibilities.

- Pall (white)
- Baptismal font
- Cross
- Crown
- Grains/stalks of wheat

The Christian Year

All Saints' Day (November 1) is the day on the Christian calendar designated to remember the saints victorious—those gone on to their reward. (It is
appropriate to celebrate All Saints' Day on the Sunday immediately following
November 1.) It is a great time to remember all those who have died in the
congregation during the year and to offer God thanks for the great cloud of
witnesses that surrounds us (Heb. 12:1). The service does not have to have a
somber tone; indeed, it can be festive as we focus on the resurrection! Holy
Communion observed on this day is especially ripe with possibilities for words
and images referring to the Communion of saints.

Serving as Hospitable Host

The role of the pastor at the time of death is that of hospitable host who
accompanies the loved ones of the deceased through a series of events in a
way that helps them feel welcomed and that their needs are provided for. The
minister shepherds the body from preparation to committal and walks with
the family through this journey. The hospitable host extends spiritual care,
direction, and support. Of special importance is pastoral care to the children.
Young children and youth have a lot of confusion and sorrow when someone
close to them dies. Their theology of death and the afterlife is underdeveloped.
Include them; speak to them; hug them. Let them know that their feelings
matter. Pay attention to their body language. Invite them to participate as
they are able in the viewing and funeral. Answer their questions honestly and
directly with age-appropriate information. Don't shy away from using the
words "died" or "dead." If we revert exclusively to vague terminology, such
as "passed on" or "lost my loved one," in order to soften the blow, we risk
confusion. The occasion of death is a priceless opportunity to instruct young
people in the Christian view of death. Don't miss it.

So far, most of our discussion has surrounded *creating* the funeral service
for a Christian. But a funeral is not designed to be admired on paper; it is
designed to be experienced. *Leading* a funeral service is a most critical piece
of the successful funeral. The officiating clergy must (1) provide a pastoral
approach throughout the entire journey through death (from notification to
postfuneral care) and (2) preside with confidence and skill during the funeral
and committal. Certain duties and attributes are necessary to serve as a hospitable host at a funeral. As you provide pastoral care to a family, remember
that you are representing not only yourself but your own local congregation
and, to some extent, even the church at large, for those who are uninitiated

to the church will form views and opinions of God and the church as a result of encountering your leadership.

Duties

A certain logical sequence of duties will naturally unfold. A sample time-line is given below. The pastor should carefully balance being available when needed yet not hovering. People need their space as well as your attention. Experience will help you find the right balance. It is unusual for a family to let you know directly what they need; frankly, they are expecting you to know what to do and when to do it. It is necessary for you to be present at certain points and optional at others. For example, occasionally a family will desire that the pastor be present when working through the arrangements with the funeral director(s). They may want some experienced guidance in picking out a casket, how much to spend on various items, and so on. But this invitation should come from the family, not from the pastor inserting herself or him-self into the consultation. Recently I learned of a pastor who announced to the family that he would be present to make arrangements with them at the funeral home, though they had not asked for his assistance. Because he was much loved by the family, they did not resist. However, they were very uncom-fortable that he became privy to their financial situation, that he overheard sensitive discussions, and that he was present when the amount to be given to the clergy was discussed. When in doubt concerning which events to attend, a rule of thumb to follow is to offer to be available and let the family decide whether your presence is needed.

A Common Timeline

- Clergyperson is notified of death (or imminent death).
- Make plans to be present with the immediate survivor(s) as soon as pos-sible. Extend comfort and offer prayer.
- At this initial meeting, be fully present to the family for the sole purpose of pastoral care. Never worry about what you will say. Your presence and a brief prayer communicate the most. Do not assume you will be asked to officiate at the funeral, and do not begin to make funeral plans at this time. If they extend the invitation for you to officiate, feel free to respond regarding your availability and interest, but let them know you will make a subsequent appointment for the purpose of planning the service.
- Set the time for a special meeting to receive input regarding the service.
- Meet with the family to receive input for the service. Invite their stories; take time to listen; take notes; ask about favorite songs, Scripture passages,

poems, treasured items, memories, hobbies, and so on. Welcome input and suggestions, but weigh all of these in light of best worship and funeral practices. Remember, *the pastor is ultimately responsible for the integrity of the service.*

- Design the service and prepare the homily.

- Arrange to meet the family just before the first viewing to pray with them as a group prior to seeing the body; then follow them into the room. It is an emotional moment as they see their loved one in the casket for the first time. Let them move to the casket first. Hold back but be available.

- Remain with the family for the beginning of the public viewing, which typically follows. You do not need to remain for the entire time, but stay long enough to see it off to a solid start.

- Arrive at the funeral home well in advance of the funeral. Do not make the funeral director or family become anxious because you are cutting it close. Ask the funeral director for final cues as to the setup, sound system, and so on.

- Officiate at the funeral and committal.

- Attend any dinner or gathering immediately following the committal, if invited. Use this time to build relationships with the extended family.

- Make follow-up calls to check on family members. A phone call a day or two after the funeral is a good idea. An in-home visit is recommended one to two weeks after the funeral.

- Make periodic phone calls for the first six months.[36]

- Send a note on the first anniversary of the death, letting the family know that they are in your thoughts and prayers.

Attributes for Presiding

An appropriate demeanor is needed for presiding at a funeral. Your effectiveness will come as much from your way of leading as from the content of the service. Here are some tips for approaching the funeral.

- Dress professionally. At each private and public gathering—from meeting with the family to the funeral to the postfuneral house calls—remember that appearance matters. Your best attire is necessary for the funeral service. If clergy robes are not worn, men should wear a plain, dark suit with dress shirt and tie; women clergy should wear equally professional attire—a business suit (with skirt) or tailored dress.[37] Even if a family dresses casually, your presence is viewed differently, and you will be perceived as disrespectful if dressed in anything other than professional attire. At the very least, you do not want to dress less professionally than the funeral director(s).

- Be authentic. Your relationship with the deceased will naturally be reflected as the service unfolds, but avoid dwelling on your own personal stories of her or him. It's not about you. Sometimes you will be called on to officiate at a funeral for someone you did not know well or even at all. Again, be authentic. I remember officiating at the service of someone who was born and raised in the community but had lived in a different state all of her adult life. However, she had chosen to have her funeral and burial in her hometown. I began the homily this way: "I never personally met Helen. But I felt as if I knew her from what I learned about her life from family and friends." Afterward the local funeral director expressed appreciation for my honesty. He remarked that too many pastors pretend a relationship that wasn't there. He appreciated authenticity.

- Be your natural self; avoid using an overly somber voice or demeanor. Maintain a reverent but hopeful tone. Smiles and an inviting countenance are a welcome gift during a time of sorrow.

- Prepare a manuscript for leading the service; without it you will find yourself at risk of saying something you might regret. Extemporaneous comments tend to come off poorly in this more serious setting. The family will appreciate a pastor who cares enough to fully prepare for their loved one's funeral.

- Be personal; mention the deceased's name; refer to family members (spouse and children) by name. Look directly at them at intended points so as to personalize the message.

Administration

The job isn't done until administrative duties have been handled. Here are a few representative suggestions:

- Keep a record of each funeral at which you officiate.
- Know your local funeral directors. Build trust with them. If they do not take initiative to welcome you to the community, seek them out to introduce yourself. Become acquainted before you are called on to work together, and you will have a head start when the first funeral occurs.
- Research funeral costs in your area. Every funeral home has a price list. Keeping current on costs can provide you with knowledge as you help others through the maze of decisions ahead.
- Develop a church funeral policy. This provides a smoother path for clergy and church when the facility is requested for use. For example, is your

church comfortable with an unknown clergyperson leading a funeral in your sanctuary? Will funeral dinners be held in your church? Is it okay for unknown musicians to perform? Would they be paid? Think of these things in advance—when no funeral is pending and emotions are not running high.

Exceptionally Difficult Circumstances

It is beyond the scope of this book to address in detail exactly how to officiate at funerals for those who have suffered extreme circumstances, such as tragic deaths, suicide, the death of children and youth, stillborn babies, SIDS deaths, murder, those declared missing, and so on. There are many minister's handbooks available to consult that alert pastors to special considerations and wordings in order to help them through these situations. I strongly suggest that you seek out several sample services as a guide for whatever type of death you are facing. In many of these circumstances, you may experience self-imposed pressure to have answers or to say just the right thing. The truth is, no one has all of the answers, and sometimes nothing can be said. Here is where your pastoral presence becomes the most important thing. It is perfectly appropriate to say, "I don't understand this, but God is holding us in the palm of his hand." While promises concerning the destiny of the deceased may not be possible or appropriate, the promise of God's presence *is* possible. God is with us. That is what we know for sure. Admitting the unknown is a very wise posture in the face of unexplainable deaths.

The funeral for a non-Christian will need to be adjusted in content and approach in order to faithfully serve the deceased and his or her family. Interestingly, very often Christian ministers are still called on to officiate at services for non-Christians. Here are a few adjustments that may need to be made; experience will likely suggest others.

- Develop the service as a reflective and even inspirational time, rather than a formal worship service per se. In light of this, you will call it a funeral rather than a Service of Death and Resurrection. Certainly, many of the features of a worship service will be useful, without forming the event as a worship service. Use Scripture passages, prayers, and a modified homily; but choose Scriptures that speak of who God is and of divine love for all humankind rather than passages that describe the blessedness of a saint who dies in the Lord. Songs are less likely to be used under these circumstances.
- Assume the attendees are more of an audience than a congregation. This is not to say that there are no Christians attending the service. It is simply that the approach to the funeral service has shifted somewhat. Therefore, call for less active participation in acts of worship by those who attend.

- Keep the focus on God. Instead of emphasizing the deceased's relationship with God, emphasize the character of God. God's goodness and faithfulness and love must still be proclaimed; it will simply not be able to be demonstrated through the personal witness of the one who has died. For example, you can offer a prayer thanking God for creating Thomas without mentioning Thomas's lack of response to God. By doing so, you have emphasized God's character (as Creator) without making false connections between God and Thomas's faith (or lack thereof).

- Maintain your spiritual presence. Do not compromise your role as a minister of the gospel while officiating at the funeral of a nonbeliever. While you will make adjustments in your choices, do not lay aside the beliefs, symbols, and vocabulary of faith simply because of a non-Christian audience. Your calling is not well served if you create a totally secular service in order for the liturgy to sit well with nonbelievers. Be sensitive that you proceed in ways that are meaningful in this context without stripping the service of God's story—yes, even in the life of one who never owned that story.

- Avoid bold statements concerning the nonbeliever's eternal state. While it is appropriate—indeed a wonderful thing—to speak with assurance about the deceased *Christian* being present with the Lord, don't make promises that do not apply to the *unbeliever*. Of course, we are not the judge of anyone's eternal destiny. Still, we have no cause for doubting that upon death a Christian is with Christ, and we should rejoice in affirming that truth with all boldness at a Christian funeral. But if the deceased has provided no obvious evidence of devotion to Jesus Christ, it is not appropriate to make false promises. Announce God's love and grace, without playing judge in this case.

- The committal will include the committal of remains and the commendation, but may or may not include the prayer of offering, depending on the circumstances. All human flesh returns to the earth (committal of remains), and all souls (both the believer and nonbeliever) should be commended to God's care . If those gathered are primarily Christians, it is not inappropriate to include the prayer of offering. If it appears to be primarily a secular crowd, it may be excluded. Appropriate Scripture, a prayer for comfort and peace, and a benediction are very fitting for the committal of anyone, believer or otherwise.

Ethical Considerations

The hospitable host must make several ethical or thoughtful considerations. First, there is a widely held ethical principle that any clergyperson should *not* officiate at the funeral of a former parishioner. Some denominations go so far as to put this principle in writing, so that all parties are clear: pastors are not to cross over church lines in order to serve persons not currently appointed to their care. The relationship between pastor and parishioner is a sacred trust. Bluntly stated, it is a violation of professional ethics to officiate at a funeral when the deceased person's own pastor is available. It is through moments of critical pastoral care that the deepest bonds of relationship are forged between pastor and parishioner. If the shepherd of the flock is denied the opportunity to care for her or his sheep, by virtue of the intrusion of another pastor, a great deal of potential bonding is lost. Two factors may moderate this firm position. First, if the pastor of the deceased issues an invitation to an outside clergyperson to conduct the funeral, it may be considered. Second, co-officiating is an option, with the understanding that the home pastor is the lead pastor and the visiting pastor assists.

Another circumstance to consider as you formulate your professional positions regarding funerals is more of a personal matter. Will you officiate at the funeral of a family member? While many pastors enjoy the honor of being asked to conduct the funeral of a loved one, consider drawing the line on this unless the relative is more distant in family lineage. There is something to be said for simply playing your role as a family member like everyone else rather than finding your identity so strongly tied to your function as pastor. Again, let the family member's pastor have the privilege of shepherding your loved one. What's more, you may have more emotional trouble performing the funeral than you anticipate.

Also, consider the issue of excessive floral displays sent in honor of the deceased. It may be advisable to encourage people to express sympathy in more permanent ways that benefit others in an ongoing manner, such as donating money to noteworthy humanitarian, not-for-profit organizations or to a memorial fund at the church. This is an excellent way of honoring the dead with life-giving results. It is also a way of offering Christian sensitivity to those family members and friends who do not have the financial means to purchase a large floral spray. They are able to give to a mission-oriented organization in any amount and not feel embarrassed.

Last is the matter of the funeral fee. Decide whether or not you will accept money for officiating at a funeral. Some pastors believe they should not receive any honorarium for performing services that fall under expected pastoral duties. Others believe it is appropriate to receive a token amount, given the extraordinary number of hours spent in the process of ministering to a family at the time of death. A case can be built for either view. Simply think this through prayerfully, and arrive at a decision that is comfortable for you.

Conclusion

To summarize what we have said, Thomas Long offers us exceptional insight in stating eight purposes of a good funeral.[38] I summarize them here. Good funerals are

1. kergymatic—they announce the gospel story;
2. oblational—they are an occasion to offer the deceased and the living to God;
3. ecclesial—they are the work of the whole church at worship;
4. therapeutic—they provide comfort;
5. eucharistic—they are an expression of thanksgiving, with or without the Lord's Supper;
6. commemorative—they help mourners remember attributes of the deceased;
7. missional—they reorient survivors for serving God and others in the world;
8. educational—they provide an opportunity to learn about the biblical view of life and death.

Amy awoke in one of Grandma's big poster beds upstairs. She guessed that Dad had carried her upstairs and tucked her in after she had fallen asleep at the wake. As she descended the stately staircase, she wondered if Granddaddy was still in the house. She discovered that no one was in the parlor, and her family was quietly getting dressed for the funeral. As they drove to the country church, she remembered her many questions. When she arrived, the pastor who led the funeral called her by name and smiled at her. When he prayed and spoke during the service, she somehow felt that things were all right and that even if all of her questions were not answered, many of them would be someday.

Key Terms

columbarium A designated place where the urns of ashes repose following cremation.

committal service Following the funeral, a brief, final committal of the body and soul to God.

cremation Committing the body to flames and then preserving the ashes.

crematory A facility that performs cremation and incineration.

embalming The process of preserving the corpse (delaying decay) by way of draining natural fluids from the body and replacing them with preservative fluids.

eulogy Spoken words honoring the deceased during the funeral or memorial service.

graveside service A brief combination of the funeral and committal held only at the burial site.

incineration The body is exposed to intense heat, but not directly to the flames, resulting in ashes.

interment The ritual placing of the corpse in the grave.

memorial service A full service of remembrance when the body is not present; often held at a time more removed from the death than is the case with a funeral.

pall From the Latin word *pallium* (meaning a cover); a cloth covering for a casket, usually white to represent Christian baptism; it is often embroidered with symbols of faith.[39]

pall bearers Persons who help carry the casket to and from the hearse.

wake With the corpse present, a gathering of mourners who wait with the family to grieve and comfort one another as a community.[40]

To Learn More

Long, Thomas G. *Accompany Them with Singing: The Christian Funeral*. Louisville: Westminster John Knox, 2009.

Sheppy, Paul. *In Sure and Certain Hope: Liturgies, Prayers, and Readings for Funerals and Memorials*. Nashville: Abingdon, 2003.

Engage

After expanding your understanding of officiating at a funeral, you are ready to try your hand at two very important statements that can offer you guidance now and in the future.

1. First, try writing your own mission statement for a Christian funeral in one sentence.
2. Second, try writing a funeral policy for a local church.

4

Christian Baptism

Explore

Before reading chapter 4, reflect on your own experience of baptism.

- Have you been baptized? If so, at what stage in your spiritual journey?
- How much preparation did you receive prior to baptism? Did anyone intentionally disciple you immediately following baptism?
- Have you ever participated in a "renewal of baptism" service? If so, describe it.
- Reflect on baptismal services you have attended. What features seemed to be the most important?
- To what degree have the baptismal services you have witnessed been corporate in nature? Describe what specifically made them corporate.

Now that you have begun to reflect on baptismal services, expand your thinking by reading chapter 4.

Expand

The white cotton robe hung loosely over Megan's shirt and shorts underneath, coming to rest on the top of her toes. Megan's mother had dressed her in clothing that could get wet and not be ruined. She knew whatever her eight-year-old daughter wore into the baptismal pool would be covered up anyway, since every person to be baptized that Sunday evening—young and old, male and female—would be wearing a covering of white. After her baptism Megan could put on the Sunday school dress from this morning, which was hanging in a room behind the chancel—a place where all of the women change into dry clothing. The boys had their room on the other side.

It was a special afternoon for Megan, as her two brothers would be baptized also. Earlier, the pastor had explained the meaning of baptism to everyone. The whole thing didn't seem too strange to Megan, for she had always heard about it and had even attended some baptismal services. Baptism was what Christians did to please God and to witness that they believed in Jesus. Megan remembered asking Jesus to forgive her sins last year during a prayer time at Vacation Bible School. This seemed to be the next step, as the pastor explained it. Though she was eager to be baptized, when it came down to it, Megan was glad that her brothers would be baptized too. Somehow the concerns she had about swallowing water or slipping in the pool were alleviated knowing she was not alone.

It was over before she knew it. She walked into the pool, felt the strong arm of the pastor across her back, saw his smile, closed her eyes, and the next thing she knew a kind lady with a towel was helping her up the steps out of the water. Megan wondered how she would feel when it was over. While she really didn't feel any surge of excitement, she did remember feeling at peace, even as an eight-year-old.

If you have been in the church for any length of time, you have no doubt observed that the approach to Christian rituals varies widely. This is understandable, given our various historical and theological heritages. This reality is particularly true of the sacraments (or ordinances):[1] baptism and the Lord's Supper. As you can imagine, to address these subjects among a diverse group of believers is challenging, for likely these rituals, more than others, pose greater obstacles for agreement as to meaning and practice. In this chapter I will attempt to simply lay out the "what, why, who, when, where, how" of baptism. Within these headings I hope to explain a range of thought and practice among Protestants, believing that you will be able to find your place among your sisters and brothers who are, like you, devoted disciples of our Lord Jesus Christ. As you read this chapter, try not to focus on the differences; instead, look for that which all Christians share in common, for indeed there is much that unites us. As for those areas of difference, I appeal to wise words: "In essentials, unity; in nonessentials, liberty; in all things, charity."[2] Better still, the Scriptures remind us that there is "one Lord, one faith, one baptism, one God and Father of all, who is above all and through all and in all" (Eph. 4:5–6).

When we come to the "who" section of this chapter, I will separate two approaches to the service of baptism—one for infant baptism and one for believer's baptism.

Laying the Foundations

What Is Baptism?

The ritual of Christian baptism has been practiced from the inception of the church. Indeed, the story of the first instance of *Christian* baptism is recounted as early as the day of Pentecost, the occasion the church was birthed (see Acts 2). It was only a few weeks earlier that Peter had heard his Master command his disciples to baptize believers of all nations. No doubt Jesus's words were still ringing in Peter's ears when, after delivering a blazing sermon to the international crowd gathered in Jerusalem to keep the Jewish festival of Pentecost, he issued the invitation: "Repent, and be baptized every one of you in the name of Jesus Christ so that your sins may be forgiven; and you will receive the gift of the Holy Spirit" (Acts 2:38). With Peter's words, Jesus's message was fulfilled: disciples from many nations were baptized on that day.

The occasion of Acts 2 is not the first incidence of baptism reported in the New Testament, however. All four Gospels tell of the ministry of John the Baptist and of Jesus's own baptism by John.[3] John's baptismal message was straightforward: "Repent, for the kingdom of heaven has come near" (Matt. 3:2). John preached the necessity for the Jews to turn from their ungodly ways and "bear fruit worthy of repentance" (Matt. 3:8). But he viewed his ministry as distinctly different from the baptism that would soon come, the baptism to be brought by way of Jesus Christ, for, John said, "He will baptize you with the Holy Spirit and fire" (Matt. 3:11).

The roots of New Testament baptisms can be traced to even more ancient practices—those of the purification rites of the Mosaic law. Various ceremonial washings were required of the priests and the Levites in order to fulfill their liturgical responsibilities. The Levites were sprinkled with water during their ordination ceremony (Num. 8:6–13), the priests washed their hands and feet before performing the sacrifices (Exod. 30:17–21), and the high priest bathed himself in preparation for the day of Atonement (Lev. 16:4, 23–24). Common citizens were required to wash themselves in pure water after having come in contact with a defiled article or person (Lev. 16:24–40). Washing was required after intercourse, menstruation, or giving birth, as well as for rituals associated with leprosy (see Lev. 12–15).[4] Any Gentile wishing to convert to Judaism was required to take a ritual bath (a type of baptism) to wash away the impurities associated with their pagan background.[5] Biblical scholar Grant R. Osborne notes, "The parallels between this and the Christian practice are easily observable: the act as an initiation rite, similar terminology, similar theology (the person was reborn)."[6] These and other uses of water for ritual cleansing in the Old Testament provide a notable foreshadowing of water baptism as practiced by the New Testament church.

The English word "baptism" is from the Greek word *baptizō*, which is translated "to dip, immerse, wash, plunge, sink, drench, overwhelm."[7] The very definition of the word is understood by some Christian groups to be a mandate for the exclusive practice of immersion when baptizing. Other groups do not consider the definition to be a command for practicing a particular method for water baptism. For instance, the same Greek word, *baptizō*, is used when referring to the washing of the Pharisees (Mark 7:4) and to the lack of washing by Jesus before coming to the table for a meal (Luke 11:38), instances when a full bath would certainly not have been the case. The point is that there are plenty of times when the word *baptizō* is used that do not refer to complete immersion. "To dip" can refer either to dipping something into a liquid or pouring the liquid on something. This is an issue for various Christian traditions to settle for themselves. Nevertheless, baptism is understood to be a sign-act involving getting believers wet with water.

The New Testament speaks of baptism using a number of significant themes and metaphors. I will identify four of these as important building blocks for laying a solid foundation for the practice of Christian baptism.[8] First, baptism provides the occasion for *union with Christ* by participating in his suffering, death, and resurrection (Rom. 6:3; Col. 2:12). Baptism not only *represents* the symbolic dying and rising with Christ; it signifies the *actual* dying and rising with Christ. In other words, through baptism we are made to participate in Christ's death and resurrection. Paul instructs that "when you were buried with him in baptism, you were also raised with him through faith in the power of God, who raised him from the dead" (Col. 2:12). Paul also writes, "Therefore we have been buried with him by baptism into death, so that, just as Christ was raised from the dead by the glory of the Father, so we too might walk in newness of life" (Rom. 6:4). The early church picked up this metaphor of dying and rising with Christ, which has proven to be a strong and consistent depiction of baptism throughout the centuries. Liturgical historian James White notes that some early baptisteries facilitated immersion while also replicating the form of a mausoleum.[9]

Second, baptism is an *act of initiation* into Christ's holy church—the family of God (1 Cor. 12:13). Even as baptism is the occasion for union with Christ, it is also the occasion for union with all other Christians who follow Jesus with full devotion. In our baptism we are incorporated into the body of Christ—past, present, and future. Our baptismal unity is expressed as one holy, catholic, apostolic church to which we belong as representatives of the kingdom of God on earth. It is through our baptism that we are made one in

Christ Jesus; therefore, "There is no longer Jew or Greek, there is no longer slave or free, there is no longer male and female" (Gal. 3:28).

The development of the catechumenate over the first few centuries of the early church provides an impressive and detailed account of the relationship between baptism and becoming a member of Christ's holy church. The catechumenate is a lengthy and involved process of inquiry and spiritual formation, and it provided an intense preparation for baptism. This process could take up to three years. The catechumens (persons engaged in the process) progressed through seven stages of instruction and ceremonies as they moved toward baptism. The rite of baptism, occurring very early on Easter morning, did not just represent the culmination of the catechetical process; more important, it signified the initiation into the community of Christians as full members of the body of Christ. With baptism came all of the privileges, responsibilities, and joys of previously baptized Christians, including receiving the Lord's Supper, which had been denied the catechumens prior to baptism. So tied was baptism to initiation into the community that the catechumens were allowed to call themselves "Christian" only after their baptism. There is a very long history—indeed, from the New Testament to today—of baptism signifying membership in the community of faith.

Third, baptism is the *recognition of new birth* (Mark 16:16; John 3:5; Acts 2:38; 22:16; Titus 3:5; 1 Pet. 3:21). Jesus said that "no one can enter the kingdom of God without being born of water and Spirit" (John 3:5). Paul's words to Titus affirm that "he saved us . . . according to his mercy, through the water of rebirth and renewal by the Holy Spirit" (Titus 3:5). These sentiments became dogma in the words of the Nicene Creed: "we acknowledge one baptism for the remission of sins." It is critical to boldly state that faith on the part of the baptized is a necessity for baptism. While it is true that faith in Jesus Christ (not the act of baptism in and of itself) saves us, faith is appropriated or embodied in the act of baptism as a sign and seal of God's promise of salvation. Regardless of one's particular theology of baptism, one thing is all but universally embraced within Protestantism: faith in Christ, resulting in confession of sin, repentance, and the commitment to live as a devoted disciple of our one Lord, is required for salvation.[10] This faith is sealed in baptism.

Fourth, baptism is the occasion for *receiving the Holy Spirit* (Matt. 3:11, 16; Mark 1:8; John 1:33; Acts 2:38). At baptism, God gives the gift of the Holy Spirit, both as realized indwelling now and also as a promise of the inheritance yet to be received—a guarantee of the future eternal kingdom still to come (2 Cor. 1:21–22; Eph. 1:13). Jesus's own baptism is the harbinger of our own: the Holy Spirit descended upon him at his baptism (Matt. 3:16; Mark 1:10; Luke 3:22; John 1:32). Protestants have understood the ways and means of the gift of the Holy Spirit at baptism differently, but virtually all have embraced the connection between Spirit and baptism in some measure.

There are other subthemes for baptism that can be mentioned; however, these four themes just described form the major biblical foundations for Christian baptism and will serve us very well historically, theologically, and biblically. Some Christian communities hold the more sacramental view of baptism, believing it to be both symbolic and instrumental, while others acknowledge the same metaphors but view them as purely representative in nature (baptism is symbolic rather than instrumental). Readers are urged to look for what Christians share in common (the biblical themes/metaphors) and then let the theological perspective(s) of their liturgical tradition direct their teaching and practice. Remember also that sometimes it is not "either/or." There is an innate tension within most theological positions. For example, while John Wesley affirmed the Articles of Religion of the Anglican Church (a communion he served as priest until his death), which indicated that baptism administered to infants is a sign of regeneration, he nevertheless also envisioned regeneration to be the result of "a conscious conversion experience."[11]

In discussing the sacraments,[12] we are quickly faced with the question of God's role in the event. Chapter 1 included a detailed explanation of the two predominant views of baptism and the Lord's Table (the sacramental view and the ordinance view). I don't repeat that entire discussion here, though I touch on it briefly; rather, later in this chapter I indicate how each view impacts the *practice* of baptism, for the theological position one takes has implications for the services one develops and leads.

The sacramental view of baptism considers God to have the primary role in the event. That is to say that God is both calling *and* bestowing; the sacrament is both symbolic *and* instrumental. Both the calling of the disciple, which leads to baptism, and what is imparted at baptism are understood to be actions of God's grace. God has called an individual to become a disciple of Jesus Christ, either by virtue of his or her birth into a Christian family (a family of the covenant) or as a result of his or her own personal conversion upon hearing the good news and personal repentance. In either case, God offers prevenient grace—grace that is operative before the recipient is even aware that God's Holy Spirit is drawing him or her to faith in Christ. In fact, that's what "prevenient" means: to go before, to precede.[13] "Prevenient," when referring to grace, is the antecedent to human action.[14] Therefore, before I can *see* God at work, God is at work! This is grace in action out of God's sheer love for humans—persons created in God's image whom God wishes to reconcile to himself.

The ordinance view of baptism considers the believer to have the primary role in the event. Baptism is understood to rest primarily on what a person decides to do as a way of demonstrating his or her willingness to follow Christ. Like those who hold the sacramental view, they share the claim that God calls people to faith through the convicting agency of the Holy Spirit. However, those who hold the ordinance view would not typically label the conviction stage as grace per se. Ordinance folks would claim that God's action is at work in salvation, yes, but is limited to the event of salvation, not baptism. Human action is the impetus for entering into the baptismal waters; the event is initiated and undertaken by the believer.

The point of departure between the two views comes most clearly in that those who hold the ordinance view believe that the ritual of water baptism is a purely symbolic act—a sign-act that only *represents* one's dying and rising with Christ. They would not assert that any gracious action is bestowed by God in the baptismal event, only that baptism is something advisable to do, given Christ's command to baptize disciples. The sacramental view, by contrast, asserts that in the act of baptism God is also bestowing a measure of grace, especially in the form of cleansing from sin and giving the gift of the Holy Spirit (Acts 2:38). In all of the ways the Scriptures speak of baptism—union with Christ in his death and resurrection, initiation into the community of faith, signification of new birth, receiving the deposit of the Holy Spirit—*God* is really the one performing the action: unifying, initiating, bestowing the Spirit, and providing new birth. So for those holding the sacramental view, baptism is not only *advisable* by virtue of obeying Christ's command but is also *beneficial*, given that the baptized one receives the miraculous benefits of God's action. In this sense, then, baptism is truly a means of grace. It is a means through which God in Christ administers grace through the power of the Holy Spirit—grace to hear God's call to discipleship, grace to die to self, and grace for Holy Spirit empowerment to live the life of a true disciple.

If a sacrament is a pledge (see chapter 1), who pledges to whom? Does God pledge himself to the believer, or does the believer pledge herself to God? I submit that the answer is "yes." As in a marriage ceremony, two parties engage in a mutual promise. Like Luther, we can affirm that "through my baptism God, who cannot lie, has bound himself in a covenant with me."[15] At the same time, we, like the early catechumens, pledge undying faithfulness to God in Christ, empowered by the Holy Spirit. Robert Webber describes this very event in the ancient baptismal rite:

> [The candidate pledged his or her] allegiance to the triune God in the words of the ancient creed, the forerunner of the Apostles' Creed, known as the interrogatory

creed. It asks for allegiance to the faith of the church, citing what the candidate believes about the Father, the Son, and the Holy Spirit. Faith is seen not merely as truth passed down from apostolic times but as a pact with Christ that replaces the pact with the devil.[16]

One more thing to mention here is that Christian baptism as a sacrament is understood to be both sign and seal. (The same is true for the Lord's Supper.) It is a sign in that it provides a visible depiction of an invisible reality; what is unseen is seen by virtue of the sign. Baptism is also a seal in that it confirms the reality of the event; it authenticates the promise of grace found in the baptismal act. Although we have neatly described them as two separate entities, sign and seal are not mutually exclusive. Indeed, as a sacrament, the sign itself comes to mean the event. The sign of water baptism (the visible depicting the invisible) seals the event as the spiritual occasion that it is.

Why Do We Baptize?

For more than two thousand years Christians have participated in water baptism for three primary reasons: Jesus was baptized, Jesus commanded the ritual of baptism, and the New Testament provides both stories of and teaching on the importance of baptism.

First, Jesus's own baptism is the foundation on which the church bases its practice of ongoing baptism. We enter the waters of baptism first of all because our Lord showed us the way. It is mystifying why Jesus was baptized, for John preached a baptism of repentance, and certainly Jesus—as the sinless One—had no need of repentance. But Jesus did participate in water baptism and for at least three grand purposes. First, it was an act of obedience to the Father. John recognized the absurdity, from a human point of view, of Jesus submitting himself to John for baptism—a baptism of repentance—and so John protested. But Jesus clarified that it was necessary "to fulfill all righteousness" (Matt. 3:15). In his obedience to the Father, Jesus demonstrated full solidarity with humanity; the very persons who *did* stand in need of repentance witnessed the Messiah identifying with them in their spiritual need. In this way, Jesus's baptism is seen as one occasion in a long line of self-abasements, from his incarnation to his cross. Second, at his baptism, Jesus's identity as the Son of God was unequivocally established. God the Father made a clear and audible statement, leaving no doubt as to the identity of Jesus as well as God's relationship with him. Jesus was the Son of God whom the Father loved (Mark 1:11). At the occasion of Jesus's baptism, God the Father graciously affirmed his relationship for the sake of his Son, securing Jesus's identity before others. Third, Jesus's baptism was the occasion for the filling of the Holy Spirit. The Holy Spirit descended on Jesus as he rose from the water and would be the central force that would guide, direct, and sustain him through to the completion of his mission (Luke 4:18–19). The purposes accomplished in Jesus's baptism are not unlike those accomplished in our baptism: we surrender to baptism as an act of obedience, we are identified as God's child, and we receive the gift of the Holy Spirit. The foundations for Christian baptism are first laid in Jesus's baptism.

Another reason we baptize is that Jesus gave a direct command for his disciples to do so until the end of the age. After his resurrection and immediately prior to returning to the Father, Jesus gave the eleven disciples the mission they were to carry out. This mission included baptizing disciples of all nations in the name of the Father and of the Son and of the Holy Spirit (Matt. 28:19). This very clear and direct command has been taken seriously in every age.

Third, the many occasions of water baptism cited in the New Testament, beginning in the book of Acts, suggest that it was a very important priority of the early church. The first incident of baptism began with the three thousand who were baptized on the day of Pentecost (Acts 2:41). The stories continue with the accounts of the baptism of Saul, the Ethiopian eunuch, the crowd baptized by Philip in Samaria, Cornelius's household, Lydia's household, the Philippian jailer's household, Crispus's household, and more. Today, when we baptize we stand in a long, uninterrupted line of Christians, beginning with Jesus, who obeyed Christ's command.

Who Is Baptized?

Who is baptized? At one level it is an easy answer: disciples of Jesus Christ. Jesus said, "Go therefore and make disciples . . . baptizing them" (Matt: 28:19). Yet it is precisely here that the waters get a little muddy (pun intended). The question is raised: Who are disciples? This question has been answered in different ways over the centuries and consequently has resulted in various approaches to Christian baptism. We will focus on the two primary Protestant practices since the time of the Reformation: infant baptism and believer's baptism.

Infant Baptism

Many Protestant denominations practice infant baptism (pedobaptism). The historical precedent for baptizing infants is deep and wide. Infant baptism, though not mentioned explicitly in the New Testament, was consistently practiced relatively soon after the New Testament period. As church historian James White asserts,

Beyond any doubt . . . by the third century, children are being baptized. . . . *The Apostolic Tradition* also gives unmistakable evidence that children are being baptized, many of them still too young to "speak for themselves." From this point on, there is no doubt about the baptism of infants. Theological developments in the fourth century were to make it the normal practice everywhere for well over a millennium.[17]

Most of the Reformers (Menno Simons and other Anabaptist leaders being notable exceptions) maintained the practice of infant baptism. Even Ulrich Zwingli compared it to the covenant between God and Israel, with circumcision providing a clear parallel to baptism.[18]

Those who dispute the practice of infant baptism claim that there is no reference to such a ritual in the New Testament. It is true that the baptism of infants is not explicitly mentioned in the Scriptures. Those who baptize infants counter that it is more than likely that the several "household baptisms" reported in the book of Acts would have included very young children. This argument is helpful, but at best it relies solely on what is *implied*, not what is stated explicitly. However, those who baptize infants are not without additional biblical and theological support. Two such considerations are baptism as covenant and Jesus's acceptance of children.

Baptism as Covenant

Infant baptism is grounded in God's covenant with his people—the covenant established with Abram and which remains in place today for all believers who are considered to be heirs of the covenant. *God* initiated the covenant with the patriarch, whereby God promised to bless him and his offspring so that all of the families of the earth would be blessed (Gen. 12:3). The covenant included protection, prosperity, and real estate (Gen. 13:14–17; 17:1–8), but in the end it was all about relationship. In fact, the covenant is summed up as a holy relationship between God and God's people—all of the descendants of Abraham, Isaac, and Jacob—past, present, and future. The relationship was unique among all of the peoples of the earth. God pledged himself exclusively to Abraham and his descendants and asked complete fidelity in return (Gen. 17:9). The one true God became the God of Israel exclusively.

The sign of the covenant was circumcision (Gen. 17:10–14), which was performed in a special ritual and served as a perpetual reminder of the relationship between God and his people. The first generation of the covenant, consisting of adult male descendants ages thirteen and older (Gen. 17:23–27) *and their households* (including foreigners and slaves), was circumcised so as to bear the sign of the covenant. Abraham was circumcised as an adult expressing faith, yet God told him to circumcise his children before they had faith. Beginning with the second generation of the covenant (since by this point in time the adults had all been circumcised), infants were circumcised on the eighth day after birth (Gen. 17:12; Lev. 12:1–3). The rite of circumcision was the rite of initiation into the covenant. Circumcision was the sign of the promise; it was "an expression of faith that God's promises would be realized" in the future.[19] The sign-act of circumcision served as both a sign of the covenant and a seal of the covenant.

Covenant and circumcision in the Old Testament is connected to baptism and spiritual circumcision in the New Testament. The apostle Paul argues, "In him [Christ] also you were circumcised with a spiritual circumcision, by putting off the body of the flesh in the circumcision of Christ; when you were buried with him in baptism, you were also raised with him through faith in the power of God, who raised him from the dead" (Col. 2:11–12). In the case of infants, like circumcision, baptism became a sign of the promise—an expression of faith that God's promises for salvation and the gift of the Spirit will be fully realized in time. Note that the sign of the promise is for entire households. Therefore, one primary rationale for infant baptism is that children are born into families who are communities of the covenant. As such, they are baptized as a promise that, given necessary and intentional spiritual nurture, faith is all but assured in the newborns when they are able to claim that faith as their own in the future. The faith expressed at infant baptism is that of the parents and the church on behalf of the child. That is not to say that the child is saved on the basis of others' faith; it is to say that others' faith provides the foundation on which the child's own faith will eventually come to fruition. At baptism the child is afforded the seal of the Holy Spirit—the deposit of things yet to come. Even as circumcision was a rite of initiation into the old covenantal community, baptism is the rite of initiation into the new covenantal community, the church universal.

Infant baptism is therefore a ritual whereby adult covenantal members of the body of Christ (parents and church) affirm their faith and pledge their devoted attention to the Christian education and love of the baptized infant so as to qualify themselves, by God's grace, to bring their child to a place where he or she claims Jesus Christ as Savior and Lord. Because the parents of the infant are speaking on behalf of the child, it is necessary that at least one of the parents is a committed Christian who is able to provide the consistent spiritual nurture necessary for the child to come to saving faith in time.[20] If you think infant baptism sounds remarkably like a "child dedication" practiced by many Free Church traditions today, you are right, except for a few very noteworthy differences. These differences are not many, but they are significant. The differences between infant baptism and child dedication will be explained in chapter 8.

JESUS'S ACCEPTANCE OF CHILDREN

In the Gospels, Jesus is clear: children are a part of God's kingdom. While it is true that there is no recorded instance of Jesus supporting the baptism of children, nevertheless his view of children in the kingdom of God is important to those who practice infant baptism. When Jesus's disciples attempted to prevent children from spending time with him, his response was insistent: "Let the little children come to me, and do not stop them; for it is to such as these that the kingdom of heaven belongs" (Matt. 19:14; see also Mark 10:14 and Luke 18:16). Such sentiment is in keeping with bringing young children to the waters of baptism for the purpose of relationship with Jesus. It is interesting that both those who advocate for baptism and those who advocate for child dedication appeal to this same story for rationale to support their position. Of course, neither baptism nor child dedication is directly addressed in the incident, but it does demonstrate Jesus's love for children.

On these grounds, especially that of covenant, infant baptism has been practiced by all or some branch of Christendom since at least the third century AD. It does not (according to the majority Protestant view) provide regeneration,[21] remove the curse of original sin, or indicate the parents' dedication of the child to God. Rather, infant baptism is essentially understood to be

- a means of grace whereby God is believed to be providentially at work in the life of the child;
- focused on what God has already done in providing salvation through the death and resurrection of Christ and placing the young child into a family and community of faith who are able to immerse the child in the story of God, thereby helping the child to find his or her place in that story;
- the pledge *of God* to claim and keep this child as a citizen of the kingdom of God, and a pledge taken by both *the church and parents* to provide the nurture, love, and spiritual formation needed for the child to come to personal faith in Jesus Christ;
- a sign of God's work of salvation under way (to be owned when the child is of age and intent).

With the baptism of infants, the trajectory of the child is emphasized over the specific one-point-in-time occasion of salvation: "The direction is indicated rather than the arrival."[22] Hence the *promises* found in infant baptism are key.

The practice of confirmation was a natural development as infant baptisms became the norm. Originally confirmation referred to the anointing of oil by the bishop immediately after baptism as a sign of sealing the baptism. At first, baptism was one singular event that included several rites, such as baptism, anointing with oil (chrismation), and participating in Eucharist for the first time. Eventually, the act of chrismation became known as confirmation—the confirming of the presence of the Holy Spirit in the baptized person—and was separated from the act of water baptism. Once separated, confirmation was delayed and became an occasion for the taking of postbaptismal vows once the child had reached the age of reason (typically seven years or older).[23] Confirmation, practiced by many denominations today, refers to a point in time when a baptized youth publicly states his or her intention to follow Christ (confirming the faith that was claimed in his or her baptism) as a result of receiving comprehensive education in the faith; likewise, the church confirms the work of the Holy Spirit evidenced in the baptized youth, which is signified by anointing her or him with oil.

Believer's Baptism

Believer's baptism refers to the baptism of those persons who have reached the "age of accountability"—an inexact age whereby one is developmentally old enough and intellectually able to hear, understand, and respond to the good news. Typically, those thus able to respond would be an older child, youth, or adult. Practically speaking, all groups that baptize infants also practice believer's baptism, since in every era there are unbaptized people who first come to hear the good news and respond in faith well after their infancy. However, generally those who baptize *only* believers do not baptize infants.

Examples of believer's baptism are obvious on many occasions in the New Testament, especially in the book of Acts, including three thousand converts on the day of Pentecost, the Ethiopian eunuch, Simon the magician, Saul, and many others. Jesus was also baptized as an adult. Those who baptize only believers point to the several verses in the New Testament, primarily in Acts, that mention repentance followed by baptism as opposed to the reverse. (In addition to Matthew 28:19, see Acts 2:38, 41; 8:13; 18:8.) Certainly the baptism practiced by John, a pre-Christian model for baptism, assumes repentance followed by water baptism. There is much to commend believer's baptism as an appropriate rite.

The practice of adult baptisms continued into the first several centuries, which saw an extensive process for spiritual formation culminating in baptism. Given the severe persecution of the church by the Emperor Diocletian in the late third to early fourth centuries, the commitment undertaken in baptism was of utmost consequence, for the pledge one made in baptism was a pledge of fidelity to Christ and the Christian community at the possible cost of martyrdom. One can see how only adults were capable of undertaking the up-to-three-year regimen of education and making such a dramatic decision regarding their discipleship. It was later in the fourth century, a time when the Roman Empire was influenced by its emperor's conversion to Christianity, that the age for a believer to be baptized grew younger.

Believer's baptism presumes repentance and faith on the part of the disciple prior to baptism. The individual must hear the gospel explained and experience the Holy Spirit convincing her or him of the need for reconciliation with God through Jesus Christ. This, in turn, must lead to repentance, a turning from one way of life to another. All of this happens through the gift of faith, given to the believer so that he or she may trust in God's promises made good on the cross of Christ. Believers are baptized after hearing the gospel, understanding the truth, and responding to God's invitation made clear through the Holy Spirit.

Believer's baptism is more common among groups that refer to baptism as an ordinance rather than a sacrament.[24] (And infant baptism is more common among groups that take a sacramental view.) Believer's baptism therefore enjoys a wider practice among those groups that see it as subsequent to saving faith, as a testimony of salvation, and as a symbolic event only. Most Baptist denominations, Christian Churches/Churches of Christ, and other Free Church traditions hold that through baptism, salvation is "not initiated, augmented, or completed."[25] Traditions representing the more sacramental view, however, view adult baptism as grace bestowed and not purely symbolic.

Essentially believer's baptism is understood to be

- a public testimony of one's intention to be a true disciple of Jesus Christ;
- a sign of repentance and faith in Christ alone for salvation;
- a spiritual cleansing;
- a symbol of dying and rising with Christ;
- initiation into the body of Christ.

I have endeavored to explain some of the differences between the baptism of infants and the baptism of believers, but there are more ways in which they are alike than ways in which they differ. Consider these aspects that all baptisms share.

- They take place within the Christian community.
- They require confession of faith.[26]
- There is an expectation of growth in understanding and discipleship following the baptism.
- They are Christ-centered.

- The baptized person has or is experiencing God's prevenient grace.
- The whole gathered community proclaims their corporate faith.[27]

To summarize, the four building blocks of baptism (identified earlier in this chapter) serve both infant and believer's baptism. In either circumstance, baptism is understood to be union with Christ, initiation into the body of Christ, new birth, and the receiving of the Holy Spirit.

When Is Baptism Administered?

It should come as no surprise that there are differing views as to when baptism should be administered. In both infant baptism and believer's baptism, the questions arise as to timing: how long after birth, how long after conversion? If a church supports infant baptism, the sacrament can occur relatively soon after the baby's birth. For those Protestants who hold the view that baptism is regeneration (a minority view), baptisms tend to occur sooner rather than later. For those who subscribe to infant baptism but view it as a rite of initiation into the covenant community without regenerative powers, urgency is less of an issue. In either case infant baptism should occur only after due preparation of the parents (or others who speak on the child's behalf). As a minimum this should include a meeting with the pastor to counsel the parents as to the meaning of baptism and their important role both in the ritual and in the years to come. Periodic classes in the meaning of baptism are highly advisable not only for those anticipating infant baptism but for the whole church. The more members of the community who grasp the meaning of baptism, the better, especially since baptism is not altogether an individual matter.

All groups that hold to believer's baptism (remember, every Christian denomination that practices infant baptism also practices believer's baptism) agree that baptism should follow personal conversion. The question then becomes, How long after conversion? Some groups, such as the Christian Churches/Churches of Christ and certain Baptist groups, are committed to immediate baptism upon confession of sin and commitment to following Christ. In these instances it is not uncommon for the new convert, upon surrendering his or her life to Christ, to be led to the baptismal pool in the chancel area of the church and immersed within the hour. This practice is reminiscent of the conversion of the Ethiopian eunuch who, after hearing the good news of Jesus, exclaimed to Philip, "Look, here is water! What is to prevent me from being baptized?" (Acts 8:36). Those who practice immediate baptism tend to have a higher view of the need for baptism; some go so far as to say that "confession of sin + baptism = salvation." In other words, baptism is absolutely required to be truly saved. It seems ironic that certain groups that hold that baptism is only a symbol are the very ones that require it immediately upon conversion. In this case it seems to assume the urgency of a sacrament, yet is referred to as an ordinance.

Others who practice believer's baptism do not require baptism immediately following conversion. Instead, they believe that there is merit in a concentrated time of spiritual education, as the new disciple comes to understand the cost of discipleship. Spiritual instruction is required so that the believer is strengthened to enter into the baptismal waters with greater understanding of and commitment to Christ and his church. In this case, not only a testimony of faith is required for baptism but also the completion of some discipleship training and/or mentoring by mature Christian leaders. This paradigm for baptism resembles the catechumenate of the second through fourth centuries, though our modern version is not typically as demanding as was the case for our ancient sisters and brothers. Remember that the faith of early Christians had to undergo testing by church leaders to make sure that the pledge of baptism was taken with the greatest of resolve; the safety of the whole church was at risk should a traitor be in the camp.

The latter paradigm is the model in operation in the Methodist Church of Cuba. I taught for a number of years at the Methodist Pastoral Training School in Havana. While there I saw a tile baptismal pool, deep enough for adult immersion, recently built at a large Methodist church. The church's pastor, Pastor Ricardo, who was also a senior leader among other Methodist pastors, told me of the importance of prebaptismal training for the Cubans. He reported that at the time of the Revolution (1959), church membership classes consisted of two weeks of training before reception into membership (conversion, of course, was a prerequisite to the membership classes). But when Fidel Castro forbade church attendance and forced missionaries out of the country, there were many deserters of the faith; church attendance plummeted, and a few faithful believers were left to carry on the mission of Jesus Christ on their own. Three teenage Cuban leaders, one of whom was Ricardo, held the remnant of Methodist believers together over many years. While they did so, they determined that church membership would no longer be so easy to achieve. They saw a direct relationship between the easy requirements of preparation for church membership and the ease with which church members forsook the active practice of their faith. Today the governmental religious restrictions have been alleviated somewhat, and church attendance is permitted in most cases. Churches are burgeoning but not because of a quick and easy process for church membership. Instead, Pastor Ricardo and others created a fifty-two-week preparation class for baptism and church membership. These weekly meetings go for hours and cover many important topics, including Bible study, theology, Methodism, the importance of the church, marriage education, evangelism, and the role of suffering for one's faith. Interestingly, the number of baptisms soared in spite of costlier discipleship.

Each church will need to prayerfully and thoughtfully discern the appropriate time to baptize people. Most denominations hold a particular viewpoint on this; as a member of your denomination, your integrity calls for you to honor that position. Those groups that view baptism as a means of grace could make an argument that a lengthy trial period (either for parents taking vows for children or for adult candidates) should not be needed. After all, why delay the means of grace? Nevertheless, the merits for preparation for baptism have been noted. There may not be one and only one answer to the question, even within one community; nevertheless, it is important and wise to take a position on when to baptize. This should serve you well on most occasions. Because our present, post-Christian culture is not unlike the pre-Christian culture of the early church, I favor a significant period of training and spiritual formation in preparation for believer's baptism. The greater the training, the greater the possibility for vital and faithful participation in the mission of the church. Jesus said, "From everyone to whom much has been given, much will be required; and from the one to whom much has been entrusted, even more will be demanded" (Luke 12:48).

Where Is Baptism Administered?

Like the "who" question addressed above, the "where" question has a simple answer as well. Where should baptism be administered? (Get ready for the obvious.) Where there is water! Given the many possibilities for water supply in the Western world, many options are within reach. Many churches have their own baptismal pools constructed in the sanctuary. Other facilities, built in year-round warm climates, have baptismal pools outside on the grounds of the church. Some congregations baptize in nearby rivers or lakes; others go to a home with a swimming pool. Many churches do not have baptismal pools designed for immersion but do have baptismal fonts (a pedestal with a bowl for water), which facilitate sprinkling or pouring rather than immersion. Some congregations that practice immersion but do not have a baptismal pool on the premises of their church are extended the privilege of holding their baptismal services at a church nearby. It's a wonderful, neighborly thing to do—not to mention a statement of the unity of the church.

The early church held an opinion regarding where baptism should be administered. In one of the earliest extant documents concerning early church practices, the *Didache*, we are told that a place with running water was preferable (as a symbol of living water), and cold water was preferable to warm. "If you do not have running water, baptize in other water. If you are not able to use cold water, use warm. And if you have neither, pour water on the head three times, in the name of the Father, the Son, and the Holy Spirit."[28]

But the question of "where" not only refers to the location of the water; it also refers to the location of the community. Where should baptism occur? The answer: wherever the community is gathered for worship. Both infant and believer's baptisms are covenantal in nature. Therefore, it is imperative that baptisms are administered as the people of the covenant are gathered for worship. Baptism is always a communal act. In fact, private baptisms were one of the abuses of the church addressed by the Reformers. It is a great privilege and joy and, yes, even a mandate for the members of the household of God to be present to (1) glorify God and (2) make their own pledge before God to enter into covenant with the newly baptized. The earliest editions of *The Book of Common Prayer* indicate that baptisms should be administered only on Sundays and other holy days so that the greatest number of people could be present to testify of the reception of the baptized into Christ's church and to remember their own baptism.[29] John Wesley eliminated the rite of private baptism in his development of worship practices for America.[30]

Because baptism is always a corporate event, it is not appropriate to hold a private service for an intimate gathering of family members or to accommodate someone who does not want to be seen with their hair all wet![31] Baptism is a public event. In fact, it is the public nature of the event that is the point. A gathered community of worshipers (preferably one's local church) is necessary for baptism for two reasons: to fulfill the declarative nature of baptism and to fulfill the communal nature of baptism. First, baptism is declarative in nature. The event of baptism is the premier opportunity to announce one's faith and stake one's claim to the truth of Jesus Christ *before others*. Jesus said, "Everyone therefore who acknowledges me before others, I also will acknowledge before my Father in heaven; but whoever denies me before others, I also will deny before my Father in heaven" (Matt. 10:32–33). Not only does the church have a vested interest in hearing new converts or parents of infants attest to the Christian faith; it's a great occasion for unbelievers who are present to witness the bold proclamation of faith given by believers. Candidates for baptism should be encouraged to invite non-Christian acquaintances to the service. Observing this ritual can powerfully stimulate one to consider Jesus Christ as Lord.

Baptism is also communal in nature; that is, the community, as well as the pastor and the candidate, has a role to play in the event. It is the local church community that rejoices, encourages, remembers their own baptisms, affirms the apostolic faith, and receives the newly baptized into the fellowship of the saints. The ritual of baptism is enriched by the energetic participation of the church, and each member adds to the sanctity of the moment. Baptism is always done in the context of a developed worship service, which includes the proclamation of the Word. Baptism is not thrown in first to "get it out of the way,"""; nor is it tagged on at the end as an addendum. It should not be rushed. Baptism should be a well-developed "service within a service" that forms the primary response to the preached word. It takes a community to perform the service to the glory of God.

The *best* community to gather for worship at a baptismal service consists of the members of the local church to which the candidate belongs. Sometimes people desire other venues for their baptism—during church camp, for instance. While this may not be wrong per se, it should be highly discouraged. Baptism is a sacrament of the church; and while, technically, believers from anywhere are members of the church universal, and while believers are baptized into the church universal, it is the local congregation that is the representative of the church universal. The congretation comprises the particular people with whom the candidate is in dynamic fellowship; these people should therefore constitute the crowd witnessing baptisms. They are the ones with whom the candidate is in mission; they are the ones who can best hold her or him accountable for living the life of true discipleship. Baptism was properly to be received only "in the midst of the *ecclesia*, because only in and through the church does a christian [sic] receive either incorporation into Christ or the gift of His Spirit."[32] Yes, baptism is a communal event. As for the group best able to serve as coparticipants in the ritual of baptism, the popular adage is most appropriate: Think globally, act locally.

How Is Baptism Administered?

To answer the question of how baptism is administered, I will address several general issues here; in a later section, "Serving as Hospitable Host," I will speak to the more particular issues related to clergy presiding at baptismal services.

The Mode

Three modes for water baptism have been practiced widely throughout the centuries of Christianity. The three traditional modes for baptism are

- immersion (the entire body is submerged into a body of water);
- pouring (a substantial amount of water is poured on the head);
- sprinkling (a relatively small amount of water is sprinkled on the head).

All three represent long-standing historical practices. Both immersion and pouring seem to have been commonly practiced in the first several centuries of the church. Liturgical historian James White comments on archaeological findings: "The earliest surviving baptismal pools . . . indicate that the adult candidate stood in water a couple of feet deep while it was poured over his or her head."[33] Some groups feel strongly about one particular mode as preferable—even necessary—in order for baptism to be properly administered. For instance, Anabaptists, Baptists, members of Churches of Christ/Christian Churches, and others (especially from the Free Church tradition) *require* immersion.[34] They ground their mandate on several things, including (1) the translation of the Greek word for "baptize" (one translation of which is "immerse"), and (2) their interpretation of Jesus's example in the Jordan, assuming that when Jesus came "up out of the water," this indicated a full immersion had taken place (though he could have been waist-high and still come "up out of the water"). However, those groups that practice sprinkling or pouring also immerse. In other words, baptismal modes seem to fall into two categories: those who only immerse, and those who are permitted to use any of the three modes in order to baptize. Most Lutheran, Reformed, and Wesleyan traditions fall into this latter category.

The Quantity of Water

Believe it or not, the amount of water to be used in baptism has been a topic of debate, sometimes contentious, over the years. Obviously, those who immerse would support the presence of a great amount of water—enough to cover the body. The mode of pouring, especially in the earlier centuries, emphasized getting the candidate drenched. Though the person is not technically dipped in this case, he or she is nevertheless thoroughly water-soaked, often by kneeling in a shallow pool. Less water was used for sprinkling, and in some cases the amount was downright stingy. Recent worship renewal movements of the twentieth century have advocated for the liberal use of water in whatever mode is used, so as to maximize the effect of the symbol. Much water is needed to take full advantage of the inherent symbolism, especially the metaphors of cleansing and dying/rising with Christ. Regardless of the mode of baptism, we should not shy away from getting the candidate wet! The more water used, the better. The words of Professor Arlo Duba, as cited by James White, say it all: "How much water is necessary for baptism? . . . Enough to die in."[35]

Trinitarian Formula

Baptisms must be performed in the name of all persons of the Godhead: Father, Son, and Holy Spirit. The most obvious reason for the use of the Trinitarian formula at baptism is simple: Jesus commanded it. After his resurrection and before his ascension, Jesus instructed his followers to make disciples, "baptizing them in the name of the Father and of the Son and of the Holy Spirit" (Matt. 28:19). In addition, Jesus's own baptism in the Jordan expressed the full participation of all three persons: the Father spoke words of approval ("This is my beloved Son"), the Spirit descended as a dove, and Jesus submitted himself to baptism.

Perhaps we can back up a step and speculate as to why the Trinitarian formula is a necessity for baptism. Before asking questions about modes of baptism, the most important question one can ask is, "*Who* is God?" God is triune. When baptism is performed in the name of the Father, Son, and Holy Spirit, the sacramental act is centered in the very identity of God. Our identity, through baptism, is immersed in the identity of the Holy One. Some pastors have gravitated to the phrase "Creator, Redeemer, Sustainer" when performing baptisms. However, consider that these terms refer to the *roles* of God, not the innate *identity* of God. We are baptized into the triune God; we are not baptized into the *functions* of the triune God. A secondary, albeit very important reason to baptize in the name of the Father, Son, and Holy Spirit is to preserve the unity of the church universal. Because the Trinitarian formula is universally accepted, to substitute other terminology at baptism could put ecumenical relations at risk. Some branches of Christendom—Roman Catholics and Orthodox Christians, to name two—would call into question baptisms using any other terminology. The Trinitarian formula prescribed for Christian baptism is a very tangible bond of unity that should not be jeopardized.

In the Context of Worship

Baptism is always to be administered in the context of a worship service that includes the preaching of the Word. Baptism is not a stand-alone ritual; it is a vital part of a well-developed worship service. As such, it is best understood as a response to the Word. Preaching must occur in the service of baptism; this is an established practice of long standing. All of the major Reformers emphasized the connection between preaching and the sacraments. Luther and Calvin were both adamant concerning the necessity of the preached word at baptism. They viewed baptism as complementary to the sermon. The sermon is the word spoken; baptism is the word made visible. The symbolic gestures of baptism portray the gospel in and of themselves. (The same is also true of the Lord's Supper.)

The Candidate's Name

When baptizing, it is common practice to use the first and middle names of the candidate but not to use the surname. There is symbolic reasoning for this practice, which also has a long history. When we are baptized, we are baptized into the church—the global family of God past, present, and future. We are not baptized into a nuclear family unit. By omitting the candidate's last name, we are indicating that the baptized person is now a member of Christ's holy church. Her or his identity is found in the community of all baptized believers who constitute the church of Jesus Christ. The community constitutes the baptized person's primary family.

Once Is Enough

The sacrament of baptism is done once for each individual and must never be repeated. First, we have no record in Scripture for rebaptism being recommended. Whereas the New Testament advises us to make the sacrament of the Eucharist an ongoing and repeated event (1 Cor. 11:26), no such command was given in relation to baptism. Perhaps more important, if God's grace is at work in baptism, this can never be improved on later. In other words, we can appear to discredit the efficacious nature of our first baptism if later we take matters into our own hands to be baptized again. The truth is, everyone I know who has been rebaptized (if there really is such a thing) has done so for one of two reasons: (1) they have been told that their first baptism was not legitimate ("the candidate wasn't old enough to understand," or denominational one-upmanship is at play—a later group does not respect or honor the group who first administered baptism); or (2) the individual wants to experience a feeling or have the memory of her or his moment of baptism. In this latter situation, someone has told the individual how important it is to be aware of the baptism while it is happening in order to remember it vividly and recall the warm feeling surrounding the event. Please notice, however, that denominational wrangling over whose baptism trumps another does not serve the scriptural goal of "one Lord, one faith, one baptism"; and vividly recalling the experience of baptism is a self-centered purpose rather than a God-centered purpose. I know a number of people who have taken trips to Israel and were offered the chance to be rebaptized in the Jordan River by a clergyperson on the tour. It was of little concern to the clergyperson making the offer or to the believer whether they had already been baptized. The emphasis was on what the person would feel *now*. They were promised new meaning if their baptism took place in the Jordan. Yet the meaning of baptism doesn't revolve around the fleeting rush a person might feel in the moment. The meaning of baptism revolves around God's several actions of grace, from giving the gift of the Spirit to engrafting the believer into the church. Baptism is largely an objective experience, not a subjective experience (although emotion is often involved as a result and is even valued). One's baptism is a state of being—a position we hold in Christ—not a warm, fuzzy feeling to be pursued.

In recent decades the number of services for "Remembering Your Baptism" has increased in many places.[36] These services help believers recall their baptism—not so they can *feel* it all over again, but so that they will *own* their baptism by reviewing its meaning. In these services, baptismal images, Scripture readings, songs, the presence of water, and testimonies remind us that as a result of our baptism we should daily "walk in newness of life" (Rom. 6:4). When we are urged to "remember our baptism," remembering does not mean calling up a specific memory of a particular event; rather, it means to remember in the *anamnesis* way[37]—remembering past, present, and future all at once as a cosmic reality. The Western mind-set thinks of "remembering" as recalling an event that is fully concluded. But "to remember, in the biblical sense, is when the present and the past come together; it is to claim that what God did in the past to benefit humankind is equally active and efficacious in this present moment."[38] To remember your baptism, then, is to let the objective truth of your past personal baptismal event carry forward in such a way that you realize your union with Christ, the Holy Spirit's power, your membership in the body of Christ *now*.

The idea of the renewal of one's baptismal vows can be compared to the renewal of marriage vows. Sometimes couples will decide to renew their marriage vows, perhaps in celebration of a wedding anniversary milestone. The couple was married once and only once. When the renewal of vows occurs, the couple is not remarried. They are simply recalling the benefits of that one past event in such a way that it positively affects their present life together and encourages them for the future. Marriage is a one-time occurrence; remembering the significance of the event takes place over a lifetime. So it is with Christian baptism.

Building the Structure

Two separate services are described below. The first is appropriate for infant baptism; the second, for believer's baptism.

The Order of Christian Baptism of an Infant

The basic outline alone appears in appendix B.

Those denominations that practice infant baptism usually provide an order of baptism in denominational resources, such as its approved book of worship.

I urge leaders to follow the orders of service authorized by their own denomination with care, for they consist of content that is in keeping with the historical, theological, and biblical reference points of the denomination. A generic order of baptism for an infant is suggested below.

The reader should assume that a worship service is under way, consisting of the Gathering and the Word (now completed), leading to the baptismal rite, which is viewed as the Response to the Word; this is then followed by the Sending. The order here is fairly flexible. The leader should feel free to adjust the sequence of elements to suit the service. The worship elements shown with titles on the left side of the page are considered essential to the service; the elements shown with centered titles within brackets [ ] are considered optional.

[Song transitioning from the Word]

Opening Words from Scripture

Read a few verses of appropriate Scripture.

Sample Opening Scripture Passages[39]

- Matthew 28:18–20   • Mark 10:13–16   • Romans 6:3–4

Note: Verses may be combined from more than one passage. Do not offer a lengthy introduction—simply read. The power of the words is profoundly felt in their stark simplicity.

Statement of Purpose

Make a simple statement as to the special nature of this part of the service.

Samples

- "Family of God, this is a day of great joy and celebration, because these precious young lives are presented to God and the church for holy baptism. By God's grace [*names*] were born to parents of faith who will raise them to love Jesus. Also by God's grace, they are surrounded by you, members of a spiritual family, who will see to their spiritual development and care so that in time each of them will confess their own need of a Savior and express personal faith in Jesus Christ."[40]

- "Members of the household of faith, we are gathered in God's presence to follow our Lord's command to baptize disciples in the Christian faith. 'Baptism is a means of grace through which God acts to seal the promises of the gospel.'[41] Through the rite of baptism, this child will receive the promise offered to all little ones who are presented by godly parents [*or other approved adult(s)*] committed to the virtues of the kingdom of God. This is a most joyous occasion as we celebrate this moment together."[42]

Presentation of Candidate(s)

Announce the name(s) of the child(ren) to be baptized.

Note: It is appropriate to have an official assistant (a lay leader, elder, or other leader) name the children (and the parents) as a way of presenting them publicly as approved for baptism.

Invocation

Acknowledge God's presence in this most important act. (For an outline of the invocation, see appendix A.)

Sample

"God of Abraham and Sarah, Joseph and Mary, and of our Lord Jesus Christ: Your faithfulness through all generations is evident in Scripture and the church. We joyously welcome your presence made known in the gathered community as we likewise welcome this child whom you have created to live for the praise of your glory. May your Spirit make us aware of your presence and your power as together we publicly claim this little one for Christ and his kingdom; to the glory of God the Father and in the name of the Son who saves [*her/him*]. Amen."[43]

The Pledges of the Parents[44]

Introduction

"Dear friends, you have brought these children whom God has given you to be baptized, thereby testifying to your own commitment of faith in Christ and the assurance you hold that the grace of God is even now at work in their lives. For as much as these children are now presented by you, it will be your duty as parents to teach them as soon as they are able to learn, the nature and meaning of this sacrament. In order to testify to your faith and to your desire to nurture your children within this faith, please respond to these questions."[45]

Renunciation of Evil

Questions are asked of and responses given by the parents (or other adults approved by the church) related to the rejection of Satan and all evil.[46]

SAMPLE

Pastor: On behalf of the whole church, I ask you: Do you renounce the spiritual forces of wickedness, reject the evil powers of this world, and repent of your sin?

Response: I do.

Pastor: Do you accept the freedom and power God gives you to resist evil, injustice, and oppression in whatever forms they present themselves?[47]

Response: I do.

Affirmation of Faith

Parents or other approved adults affirm their Christian faith.

SAMPLE 1

Pastor: Do you confess Jesus Christ as your Savior, put your whole trust in his grace, and promise to serve him as your Lord, in union with the church, which Christ has opened to people of all ages, nations, and races?

Response: I do.

Pastor: Do you believe in the triune God: Father, Son, and Holy Spirit? That Jesus Christ suffered, died, and was resurrected to reconcile you and all believers to God?

Response: I do.

Pastor: Do you believe the Holy Scriptures, both Old and New Testaments, to be the inspired Word of God?

Response: I do.

Pastor: Do you believe that the church universal, as expressed in the local assembly of believers, is God's agency for kingdom living, mission, and justice in this world now?

Response: I do.[48]

Pastor: Will you nurture these children in Christ's holy church, that by your teaching and example they may be guided to accept God's grace for themselves, to profess their faith openly, and to lead a Christian life?

Response: I will.[49]

SAMPLE 2

Pastor: Do you present your *children* for baptism as a sign of the grace of God which is extended even now to your *children* through the atoning work of Christ and declare *them* to be a part of the family of God?

Response: We do.

Pastor: Do you promise with the help of God to bring your *children* up in the instruction and discipline of the Lord, to pray with *them* and for *them* and to make every effort to so order your own life that you will not cause *these little ones* to stumble?

Response: We do.
Pastor: Do you intend to encourage your *children* as soon as *they* are able to comprehend its significance to acknowledge personally *their* own faith in the Lord Jesus Christ, and to serve God faithfully in the fellowship of his church?[50]
Response: With God's help, we will.

The Pledge of the Community

The gathered members of the local church pledge their allegiance to Christ and to the nurture of those being baptized.
Note: It is advised that the congregation stand for their pledge and remain standing through the corporate affirmation of faith.

Sample

Pastor: Do you, as Christ's body, the church, reaffirm both your rejection of sin and your commitment to Christ?
Response: We do.
Pastor: Will you nurture one another in the Christian faith and life and include these persons now before you in your care?
Response: With God's help we will proclaim the good news and live according to the example of Christ. We will surround these persons with a community of love and forgiveness, that they may grow in their trust of God, and be found faithful in their service to others. We will pray for them, that they may be true disciples who walk in the way that leads to life.[51]

A Corporate Affirmation of Faith

The congregation will affirm their faith together by stating a creed in unison. Alternative affirmations of faith or reading creedal-type Scripture passages in unison are options for those groups that do not ordinarily use creeds.

The Prayer for the Candidate(s)

A brief prayer of intercession may be prayed for the candidate(s), asking God to empower them to follow Jesus as Lord and to be filled with the Holy Spirit.

The Baptism

Note: The water is prepared in a way appropriate to the mode being used (for instance, water from a pitcher may be poured into the font). Let there be silence except for the sound of the water as it is transferred from pitcher to font.

The Prayer of Thanksgiving for the Water

Offer a prayer that gives God thanks for the gift of water and sets the water apart for holy use. (For samples, see "Installing Doors and Windows," below.)

The Water and the Words

SPRINKLING

The pastor, holding the child in his or her left arm, scoops an abundance of water with his or her right hand from the bowl and then places the hand on the head of the infant. Looking into the face of the child, the pastor says, "[*First and middle names*], I baptize you in the name of the Father, and of the Son, and of the Holy Spirit. Amen."

POURING

The procedure is identical, except instead of scooping water by hand from a bowl, the pastor lifts a small pitcher and gently pours water over the head of the infant. The same words are used.

IMMERSION

The procedure is identical except instead of pouring, the pastor immerses the infant into a large font or small pool. The infant is lifted high when coming out of the water. The same words are used.

Note: A few years ago I discovered an ancient text that is a beautiful lead-in to the Trinitarian baptismal words for infants:

> For you, baby Maria, God made the world out of nothing.
> For you, baby Maria, God called Israel out of Egypt.
> For you, baby Maria, God brought Israel back from Exile.
> For you, baby Maria, Christ came into the world to teach the children.
> For you, baby Maria, Christ died on the cross and rose again.
> For you, baby Maria, God sent his Holy Spirit to give you strength to
>   live as you ought.
> For you, baby Maria, Christ will come again and take us to God.
> Baby Maria, you know nothing of this.
> But we promise to tell you the story until you make it your own.
> And so I baptize you in the name of the Father, the Son, and the Holy
>   Spirit. Amen.[52]

[The Anointing with Oil]

From very early times, the bishop anointed the newly baptized with oil (chrismation) in an act that confirmed the presence of the Holy Spirit. In fact, a large amount of oil was poured on the heads of the baptized immediately following water baptism. This practice has been maintained in many places, though the exact manner has varied.

Note: The pastor may use a small amount of olive oil to anoint the forehead of the baptized infant with the sign of the cross and invoke the presence and work of the Holy Spirit upon the child. A larger amount of oil may be used if desired.

SAMPLE WORDS TO BE SPOKEN

"The Holy Spirit work with you, that being born through water and the Spirit, you may be a faithful disciple of Jesus Christ. Amen."[53]

The Blessing of the Candidate(s)

A prayer of blessing (benediction) is prayed over the newly baptized.

Note: There is nothing better than a scriptural benediction. (For samples, see "Installing Doors and Windows," below.)

[Presentation of Token]

Some churches like to give a small token or gift, such as a rose or a small, white New Testament. Giving the parents a baptismal certificate is a nice gesture as well as an official record of the baptism.

Introduction to the Community

While continuing to hold the child, the pastor moves closer to the congregation (and may even choose to stroll down the center aisle), introducing the child to the people. This is an informal moment with spontaneous words of introduction. The purpose in this gesture is to remind the congregation that this child is in relationship not only with the biological family but with the local family of God as well.

A Song of Faith

Invite the congregation to sing a joyous song of celebration or a thoughtful song of blessing.

The worship service resumes with the Sending.

The Order of Christian Baptism of Believers

The basic outline alone appears in appendix B.

A generic order of a baptism of a believer—someone who is old enough and is willing and able to repent of their sin and follow Christ as Savior and Lord—is suggested below. Remember that a baptismal service is a "service within a service"; it is most fitting as a Response to the Word. The order of service listed here presumes that a worship service is under way, consisting of the Gathering and the Word (now completed). The baptismal rite comes next; this is then followed by the Sending. The sequence of elements within the baptismal rite is fairly flexible. The necessary components are shown with titles on the left side of the page. Those elements shown with centered titles within brackets [ ] are ones that are optional but recommended. The leader should feel free to adjust the sequence of elements as suits the service. Additional samples of prayers, Scripture readings, and so on may be found in "Installing Doors and Windows," below. This service begins with an optional congregational song, which serves as a bridge from the Service of the Word to the Service of Baptism.

[Song transitioning from the Word]

Opening Words from Scripture

Read a few verses of appropriate Scripture.

Sample Opening Scripture Passages
• Matthew 28:18–20   • Romans 6:3–4   • Colossians 2:8–15

Statement of Purpose

Make a simple statement as to the special purpose of this part of the service.

Samples
• "Sisters and brothers, we are gathered in God's presence to follow our Lord's command to baptize disciples in the Christian faith. These persons standing before you have responded to the good news, have repented of their sin, and have claimed Jesus Christ as personal Savior and Lord. In obedience to Christ's call on their lives, they desire the sacrament of holy baptism. The church has examined them and found them sincere in faith and intent. This is a joyous occasion as we celebrate this momentous event in their spiritual journey."[54]
• "Family of God, this is a day of great joy and celebration because these new sisters and brothers in the faith are presented to God and the church for holy baptism. By God's grace they have been saved. In response to Christ's command, they desire to be baptized as a testimony to the saving

faith they have personally experienced. May we enthusiastically join together in acts of worship as we affirm this step in their spiritual journeys."

Presentation of Candidate(s)

Announce the name(s) of the candidates to be baptized.

Note: It is appropriate to have an official assistant (a lay leader, elder, or
other appropriate leader) name each candidate as a way of presenting them
publicly as approved for baptism.

Invocation

Acknowledge God's presence in this most important act. (For an outline
of the invocation, see appendix A.)

Sample

"God our Father, you called your Son to be baptized by John in the Jordan.
Your Son also charged his followers to preach the gospel and baptize believers
in the triune name of God. We thank you that the gospel has been proclaimed
to those presenting themselves for baptism and that the Holy Spirit has given
them the gift of faith and the will to obey. We joyously welcome your presence
made known in the gathered community as we celebrate your faithfulness in
the lives of those about to enter the waters of baptism. May your Spirit make
us aware of your presence and your power, as together we proclaim that Jesus
is Lord to the glory of God the Father. Amen."

The Testimony of the Candidate(s)

A brief time is given to each candidate so that they may verbally testify
that they have repented of their sin, accepted the salvation Christ offers, and
intend to follow him in true discipleship all of their earthly life.

Note: The verbal testimony is an important component in the baptismal
service. It gives the candidates the opportunity to speak of their faith to others; it also gives the community assurance of the Holy Spirit's work in the
lives of the candidates. This can be a very special part of the baptismal rite.

An alternative to the personal testimony is to ask examination questions.
These tend toward a more catechetical style of exchange, that of question
and answer concerning basic statements of Christian doctrine. Normally, I
recommend this taking place at an earlier time rather than in the baptismal
service itself.

There are many ways to approach the testimonials of the candidates. Sensitive consideration must be given to the following issues.

- *Time*. Specify brief time limits on those who give an extemporaneous testimony. Testimonies should not be lengthy.
  - *Shyness*. Some may feel too timid to speak in front of a group. Two options will ease this difficulty. First, consider the interview approach. The pastor will ask specific questions to which the candidate will offer simple answers. (Rehearsal/preparation is important; candidates should not be taken off guard. Instead, they should be given the advantage of thinking through their answers in advance.) A second option is to do brief video clips in advance that are played for the congregation just prior to an individual's baptism.
  - *Preparation*. Guide the candidates as to what should be included in their testimony, and then ask them to write it down. They can treat it as a letter to the community if they wish. The pastor should read such a letter in advance. This will serve as a great personal discussion starter between the pastor and candidate as they take the final steps of preparation for baptism, and it will also prevent any potentially embarrassing or inaccurate statements from being made at the baptism.

The Pledge of the Candidate(s)

Introduction

"Dear friends, you stand before your sisters and brothers of like faith to testify to the saving grace of God in your lives. You have heard the good news and chosen to surrender your lives to Jesus Christ. In preparation for baptism, you are invited to publicly proclaim your intention to follow him as Savior and Lord."

Renunciation of Evil

Questions are asked and responses given related to the rejection of Satan and all evil.[55]

SAMPLE

Pastor: On behalf of the whole church, I ask you: Do you renounce the spiritual forces of wickedness, reject the evil powers of this world, and repent of your sin?
Response: I do.
Pastor: Do you accept the freedom and power God gives you to resist evil, injustice, and oppression in whatever forms they present themselves?[56]
Response: I do.

Affirmation of Faith

SAMPLE

Pastor: Do you confess Jesus Christ as your Savior, put your whole trust in his grace, and promise to serve him as your Lord, in union with the church, which Christ has opened to people of all ages, nations, and races?

Response: I do.[57]

Pastor: Do you believe in the triune God: Father, Son, and Holy Spirit? That Jesus Christ suffered, died, and was resurrected to reconcile you and all believers to God?

Response: I do.

Pastor: Do you believe the Holy Scriptures, both Old and New Testaments, to be the inspired Word of God?

Response: I do.

Pastor: Do you believe that the church universal, as expressed in the local assembly of believers, is God's agency for kingdom living, mission, and justice in this world now?

Response: I do.

The Pledge of the Community

The gathered members of the local church pledge their allegiance to Christ and to the newly baptized as co-laborers in the kingdom of God.

Note: It is advised that the congregation stand for their pledge and remain standing through the corporate affirmation of faith.

Sample

Pastor: Do you, as Christ's body, the church, reaffirm both your rejection of sin and your commitment to Christ?

Response: We do.

Pastor: Will you support, exhort, and encourage these newly baptized sisters and brothers in the Christian faith so as to increase their resolve to pursue Christlikeness?

Response: With God's help we will live so as to encourage them in every good work, that God may be glorified and the kingdom of God is known on earth as it is in heaven. We will surround these persons with a community of love and forgiveness, that they may grow in their trust of God and be found faithful in their service to others. We will pray for them, that they may be true disciples who walk in the way that leads to life.[58]

A Corporate Affirmation of Faith

The congregation will affirm their faith together by stating a creed in unison. Alternative affirmations of faith or reading creedal-type Scripture passages in unison are options for those groups that do not ordinarily use creeds.

The Prayer for the Candidate(s)

A brief prayer of intercession may be prayed for the candidate(s), asking God to empower them to follow Jesus as Lord and to be filled with the Holy Spirit.

The Baptism

Note: The water is prepared in a way appropriate to the mode being used (for instance, water from a pitcher may be poured into the font). Let there be silence except for the sound of the water as it is transferred from pitcher to font.

The Prayer of Thanksgiving for the Water

Offer a prayer that gives God thanks for the gift of water and sets the water apart for holy use. (For samples, see "Installing Doors and Windows," below.)

The Water and the Words

IMMERSION

The pastor and assistant lead the candidate into a large body of water.[59] These words are spoken to the candidate: "[*First and middle names*], I baptize you in the name of the Father, and of the Son, and of the Holy Spirit. Amen."

The pastor immerses the candidate in a large body of water.

(Alternate words): "[*First and middle names*], in affirmation of the Holy Spirit's working in your life and upon your confession of Jesus Christ as Lord, I baptize you in the name of the Father, and of the Son, and of the Holy Spirit. Amen."

POURING

The pastor lifts a medium-sized glass pitcher and gently pours water over the head of the candidate. The same words are used.

SPRINKLING

The pastor scoops an abundance of water with his or her right hand from the font or bowl, places his or her hand on the head of the candidate, and looks directly into the face of the candidate as the words of baptism are pronounced.

[The Anointing with Oil]

From very early times, the bishop anointed the newly baptized with oil (chrismation) in an act that confirmed the presence of the Holy Spirit. In fact, a large amount of oil was poured on the heads of the baptized immediately following water baptism. This practice has been maintained in many places, though the exact manner has varied.

Note: The pastor may use a small amount of olive oil to anoint the forehead of the baptized person with the sign of the cross and invoke the presence and work of the Holy Spirit upon him or her. A larger amount of oil may be used if desired.

SAMPLE WORDS TO BE SPOKEN

"The Holy Spirit work with you, that being born through water and the Spirit, you may be a faithful disciple of Jesus Christ. Amen."[60]

The Blessing of the Baptized

A prayer of blessing (benediction) is prayed over the newly baptized.

Note: There is nothing better than a scriptural benediction. (For samples, see "Installing Doors and Windows," below.)

[Presentation of Token]

Some churches like to give a small token or gift, such as a Bible or small cross. Giving individuals a baptismal certificate (available at most Christian bookstores or found online) is a nice gesture as well as an official record of the baptism.

The Welcoming to the Community

The pastor invites the congregation to welcome them as baptized members of the community. Applause is appropriate here.

A Song of Faith

Invite the congregation to sing a joyous song of celebration or a thoughtful song of blessing.

The worship service resumes with the Sending.

A service of Holy Communion may follow the service of baptism. The connection between baptism and participating at the Table developed very early in the life of the church and became the normative pattern during the early centuries. The bread and the cup were withheld from the unbaptized; the tradition was that the catechumens were dismissed from worship following the sermon while the baptized believers continued worship with Communion. Initiation into the body of Christ (baptism) has been a prerequisite for Communion for the majority of traditions throughout the centuries. More recently, many evangelical and Pentecostal churches do not consider baptism a necessity for coming to the Table. Instead, personal repentance/conversion, but not necessarily baptism, is required for participating at the Table. Whether or not your tradition links baptism with first Eucharist, it is a fitting and marvelous thing to join baptism with the communal celebration of the Table of the Lord.

Installing Doors and Windows

After the rituals architect has arranged the general order for the service of baptism, more detailed choices need to be made for appropriate songs, prayers, Scriptures, and other worship acts, to enable participation in the service. In addition, thought should be given to relevant symbols related to baptism and the Christian year. All of these aspects, like doors and windows, "let in light" and enable relationship with both God and others. They help all worshipers truly *experience* the ritual of baptism.

Suggested Songs

Here is a starting list for appropriate baptismal hymns/songs. They represent a variety of styles of congregational song. Be sure to pay attention to each stanza; some may be better suited than others for a baptismal service. To help you locate these songs, the author's name is listed with the title.

A Charge to Keep I Have (Charles Wesley)
Almighty Father, Covenant God (Marie J. Post)
Baptized in Water (Michael Saward)
Child of Blessing, Child of Promise (Ronald S. Cole-Turner)
Children of the Heavenly Father (Carolina Sandell Berg)
Come, Be Baptized (Gary Alan Smith)
Come, Holy Spirit, Dove Divine (Adoniram Judson)
Come to the Water (John Foley)
Gather Us In (Marty Haugen)
Go, Make of All Disciples (Leon M. Adkins)
Go, My Children, with My Blessing (Jaroslav J. Vajda)
Go to the World! (Sylvia G. Dunstan)
Here I Am, Lord (Daniel L. Schutte)
Lift High the Cross (George W. Kitchin)
Loving Spirit (Shirley Erena Murray)
Now Thank We All Our God (Martin Rinkart)
O Happy Day (Philip Doddridge)

O Jesus, I Have Promised (John E. Bode)

On Eagle's Wings (Michael Joncas)

Take Me to the Water (African American spiritual)

The Church's One Foundation (Samuel J. Stone)

This Is the Day of New Beginnings (Brian Wren)

This Is the Spirit's Entry Now (Thomas E. Herbranson)

Wade in the Water (African American spiritual)

Wash, O God, Our Sons and Daughters (Ruth Duck)

We Are the Church (Richard K. Avery)

When Jesus Came to Jordan (Fred Pratt Green)

With Water Freely Flowing (Larry E. Schultz)

Scripture Passages

Start collecting Scripture passages that pertain to baptism. Here are a few to begin.

Genesis 17:1–14	Acts 2:37–42
Isaiah 43:1–2	Acts 8:26–39
Jeremiah 31:31–34	Romans 6:3–11
Ezekiel 36:25–28	Romans 8:14–17
Matthew 3:13–17	Galatians 3:27–28
Matthew 28:18–20	Ephesians 4:4–6
Mark 1:9–11	Colossians 2:11–12
Luke 3:21–22	Titus 3:4–8
John 1:29–34	1 Peter 2:9–10

Prayers

Some particular prayers are very helpful for conducting baptismal services. A few of these prayers are listed below with explanations.

Invocation

Acknowledging the need for God's presence in the sacrament/ordinance.[61]

Thanksgiving for the Water

It has been a common practice for many centuries to offer God thanks for the water of baptism. Throughout the Scriptures common entities are set apart to be used for God's purposes or given special meaning (bread, wine, water, oil, and so on). In this sense, certain items become holy instruments through which God achieves God's holy purposes. We do not believe that the properties of the water are altered when we bless it; offering this prayer is simply a means through which we receive with gratitude the gift of water to wash us in baptism and to pray that God will set it apart for its special use.

SAMPLE PRAYER

"We give you thanks, O God, for in the beginning your Spirit moved over the waters, and by your Word you created the world, calling forth life in which you took delight. Through the waters of the flood you delivered Noah and his family, and through the sea you led your people Israel from slavery into freedom. At the river your Son was baptized by John and anointed with the Holy Spirit. By the baptism of Jesus's death and resurrection you set us free from the power of sin and death and raise us up to live in you.

"Pour out your Holy Spirit, the power of your living Word, that those who are washed in the waters of baptism may be given new life. To you be given honor and praise through Jesus Christ our Lord, in the unity of the Holy Spirit, now and forever. Amen."[62]

Note: This prayer resembles the invocation of the Holy Spirit in the Great Thanksgiving—the prayer of thanks prayed at the Table (see chapter 5). The rituals for the two sacraments resemble each other in several significant ways.[63]

The Prayer for the Candidate(s)

A brief prayer of intercession may be prayed for the candidate(s), asking that God will empower them to follow Jesus as Lord and to be filled with the Holy Spirit.

SAMPLE

"Gracious God and heavenly Father, we thank you that you make us new persons in Jesus Christ through grace alone. We pray for [name(s)]. Bless and strengthen [them] daily with the gift of your Holy Spirit. Unfold to [them] the riches of your love. Deepen [their] faith. Keep [them] from the power of evil. Enable [them] to live a holy and blameless life until your kingdom comes."[64]

Benediction

Benedictions are blessings pronounced upon people. They are not prayers, for in the benediction we are directing our words to others, not to God. Appendix

A provides an outline for the traditional parts of a benediction. Scriptural benedictions are always favorable, especially at baptism. Here are a few to consider. Some may be used verbatim; others will require slight adaptation.

SCRIPTURAL PASSAGES FOR A BAPTISMAL BENEDICTION

- Romans 15:13
- Philippians 4:4–7, 8–9
- 1 Thessalonians 5:23–24
- Jude 24–25

Symbols

Obviously the primary symbol used at baptism is water. The presence of water should be prominent in the worship space. This can be aided by

- using clear glass pitchers and bowls so that water can be *seen*;
- pouring the water from container to container (that is, from pitcher to font) in complete silence—no background music for this—so that the water can be *heard*;
- finding ways for all worshipers to get a little wet (!) so that the water can be *felt*; this is best linked to moments of remembering one's baptism (see chapter 8);
- placing the baptismal font in the center of the worship space as a visual focal point, signifying the centrality of the act and the community gathered around the water;
- using a small fountain with running water, thereby strengthening the metaphor not only by engaging more than one sense—sight and sound—but also by portraying the idea of living water.

Secondary symbols are rich with meaning for Christian baptism as well. They assist the worshiper in perceiving the invisible actions of God through the visible means of common items or signs such as the following:

- Dove (symbolic of the Holy Spirit)
- Rainbow (symbolic of the covenant with Noah)
- Cross (symbolic of dying with Christ)
- Baptismal font/pitcher/pool (symbolic of the water)
- Shell (an instrument used by the early church to pour water during baptism)[65]
- The color white (symbolic of cleansing, purity, and holiness)
- Entering the baptismal waters in one direction, and exiting in the opposite direction (symbolic of beginning a new journey—not returning the same way from which one came)

The Christian Year

Certain days and seasons of the Christian year have served as meaning-ful occasions to remember God's story as it relates to baptism. Early Easter morning is one of those special days. The catechumens who had success-fully completed years of preparation and were deemed ready were chosen for baptism. The final three days of Lent (Maundy Thursday, Good Friday, and Holy Saturday) were given to fasting, intense personal examination, and daily exorcisms.[66] The candidates' expression of solemn willingness to die to self and live for God's purposes mirrored Jesus's own testing in his final hours as he wrestled with God over the cup of suffering that lay before him. Finally, now mirroring the victory of the resurrection, at the earliest dawn of Easter morning, the approved candidates entered the baptismal waters surrounded with much symbolic pageantry and jubilation from the community. This early ritual was rich in words and gestures, including renouncing Satan, anointing with oil, baptizing candidates naked, descending into the water, proclaiming creedal statements, re-dressing candidates in white robes, laying on hands by the bishop, invoking God's grace, pouring more oil on the heads of candidates, praying, kissing as a sign of peace, receiving the Eucharist, and receiving a cup of water and a cup of milk and honey.[67] For centuries (and even today in some traditions), Easter morning was seen as the perfect time to baptize, in light of its symbolic picture of dying and rising with Christ. Pentecost was another favored time for baptism in the early church, given its association with the coming of the Holy Spirit.[68] It was the day of Pentecost when Peter and the disciples baptized three thousand new believers. A fine rationale exists for performing baptisms when the church celebrates Pentecost.

As you, the rituals architect, prepare for baptisms in the local church, con-sider what exceptionally meaningful days or seasons would, by their very nature, represent the sacrament. It is not wrong to baptize on other days (though the Lord's Day is highly urged, given its own rich connection to the resurrection and the coming of the Holy Spirit). But the ritual can certainly be illuminated when it is positioned in relation to Jesus's own life, death, and resurrection. This is one more way for the disciple to identify with the Master.

Serving as Hospitable Host

Officiating at a baptism is a joyous privilege. It is also a great opportunity to serve as host for a big family event—the family of God celebrating the initiation of new members into the body of Christ. We have discussed the *content* for bap-tismal services, for both infants and for believers, but it takes a host to bring the service to life and to lead it with passion, sensitivity, and decorum. As is the case for each of the sacred rituals discussed, the worship architect needs to perform certain duties and possess certain attributes in order to be a hospitable host.

Credentials

Most denominations require that a person be ordained in order to perform baptisms.[69] This is because the pastor is understood to be a representative of God for both preaching and conducting the sacraments/ordinances. Formal pastoral training in the administration of the sacraments will have prepared the leader for this most holy event. What's more, a clergyperson not only acts as a representative of the local congregation (the context for the baptism) but also represents the universal church, since baptism ushers the believer into Christ's universal church. For these and other reasons, ordination is required. In addition, some denominations hold a very high view of apostolic succession; therefore, only those persons set apart by the church (pastor/priest or bishop) may preside at baptisms. Make sure you know your church's position on exactly who may administer baptism in your tradition.

Duties

As you have noticed from reading this chapter, the pastor has a number of responsibilities related to baptizing. It's not just designing a service and figuring out the details. *People* are the real responsibility. Baptismal responsibilities fall into three phases, all a matter of caring for people: providing instruction prior to baptism, preparing participants for the service, and providing consistent follow-up. These are all critical for the successful baptism event. Here are some guidelines for serving as host in these three phases of nurture and care.

Prior to Baptism

- Identify candidates who are ready for baptism.
- Meet with the candidates (or their parents/sponsors) to discuss the meaning of baptism and to inquire of their interest.
- For believer's baptism, hold a series of instructional classes to teach the basic tenets of the Christian faith. The length and number of these classes will vary from place to place.
- Link the baptismal candidates with congregational members who can serve as sponsors or prayer partners during the preparation process. It's great to involve more people so that a sense of community is developed and the congregation begins to understand its role as partner in the candidate's spiritual journey. Baptism really is a family celebration!

- Plan to have a final one-on-one interview with the baptismal candidate. Encourage the candidate, cover any remaining questions, and pray for him or her.
- Review the actual vows that will be taken at the baptismal service. On no occasion should a candidate for baptism be surprised by any questions asked of him or her in public. Make sure anyone taking baptismal vows—their own or on behalf of an infant—has had full disclosure and understanding of what is being asked of them.

Preparation for the Service

- Plan the baptismal service carefully and prepare the homily.
- Rehearse the ritual. Arrange to meet all of the participants at a separate time to walk through the service. In the case of infant baptisms, the rehearsal may be done early before the service; just be sure to allow plenty of time, so folks are not rushed. In the case of a believer's baptism, I recommend holding this walk-through a day or two before the service. This will allow everyone time to become familiar with the order of service, know where to stand and when to participate, view the setting for the pool or font, and so on. Have prayer at this rehearsal. Do not use the water in the rehearsal; save that for the actual event.
- Advise the participants in a believer's baptism on what to wear.
  - Two options are possible for baptismal attire. (If you want to keep your church job, I recommend not reclaiming the early church practice of baptizing candidates in the nude!) Some churches purchase or borrow white baptismal robes. These have a significant advantage in that (1) everyone is dressed alike, (2) they provide a modest extra layer of covering so that water-soaked clothing clinging to the body is less noticeable, and (3) the white robe is symbolic of purity/cleansing and of the white-robed martyrs mentioned in Revelation (Rev. 6:11). Baptismal robes have weights in the hems to prevent the fabric from rising when one enters the water.
  - If robes are not worn, I recommend that both women and men wear dark slacks and dark shirts. Skirts should not be worn, for they will rise in the water. Thinner material should not be used, because it will accentuate body parts when wet. All clothing should be plain—without writing or design. This helps keep everyone uniform and avoids distracting words or emblems.

Follow-up

- After the baptismal service, it's vital that you follow up with the baptized.
- Make a follow-up house call with the family of the infant who was baptized. Encourage the parents and pray with them. The visit doesn't have

to be long, but it will communicate your ongoing interest in the spiritual formation of the child and family.

- Plan to meet individually with believers who were baptized within the first month after baptism. Meet for an informal cup of coffee or make a house call. Ask how they are doing in their private devotions, prayer life, worship experience, and so on. Give them a short inspirational book. Remind them of ongoing spiritual formation classes available for their growth. Encourage them and pray with them.

Attributes for Presiding

The most important attribute for presiding at a baptism is your own pastoral preparation. Spend plenty of time not only designing the service but also rehearsing the wording, gestures, and movements you will use within the worship space. The better prepared the leader is, the more comfortable all participants will feel during the baptism. Preparation involves many aspects of one's leadership. Listed below are some attributes that you should nurture and develop as a leader.

- Have a natural, pastoral demeanor. As is the case for all rituals, the host's demeanor speaks volumes. Because baptism is a holy sacrament of the church, you should approach the service with a degree of seriousness. Jokes and an "entertainment" agenda have no place in a service of baptism. But don't confuse seriousness with sternness. Avoid a harsh approach, by all means. Simply maintain a natural, pleasant, pastoral demeanor throughout the service. Put people at ease by your own ease. Maintain a slow pace as you move from event to event within the service. Smile. Be personable.

- Dress professionally. For a baptism, present yourself as a professional clergyperson. You may not be convinced, but parishioners want their pastor to appear professional. What you wear will depend a great deal on the context. Some churches will expect their pastor to wear a robe, both during the baptismal service and even in the baptismal pool, if immersion is the mode used. Other churches will expect a male pastor to wear a suit with shirt and tie and a female pastor to wear a professional dress or suit (though the pastor will change clothes prior to entering the water). Others will have more casual expectations. Know your context. When in doubt, dress more formally than less formally; you will be glad you did.
    - If you are presiding during immersion, I recommend (1) a robe if the candidates are robed or (2) dark clothing similar to what the candidates wear. Some pastors actually use waders (waist-high, rubber fishing boots/pants). The main thing is not to stick out—wear clothing that

resembles the attire of those in the baptismal service. Also, remember that while you will not be immersed, your body will become fully wet in the process, so wear clothing that will reveal the least while clinging to wet skin.

- Keep the focus on God. The focus should be on God first, the baptismal candidates second, the other congregants third, and yourself as leader last. I've actually witnessed pastors who turn baptism into a show about themselves. A good leader will lead so effectively that he or she recedes into the background, and the really important aspects are what are remembered.

Administration

Remember to take care of the details.

- Keep a record of each baptism you perform. Not only will you need to report this in your clerical reports, but there are often occasions when a baptismal record is needed for civil or family reasons, church membership changes, or other occasions.
- Develop a baptismal brochure. Having a document available that explains your church's views on baptism can come in handy. This should be brief, simple, and attractive.

Unusual Circumstances

I met Shelly at the first church I served as pastor. She was about fourteen years old at the time we met. Shelly was physically and mentally challenged and was confined to a wheelchair. As I was organizing the youth for some activities, I spoke with her parents about her participation. In the course of that discussion, I learned that Shelly had not been baptized when some of her peers had been; a former pastor had assumed she should not be baptized or join the church because she could not understand its meaning. On hearing this, I asked if I could hold one-on-one discipleship classes with Shelly. I met with her over a series of weeks, using a confirmation curriculum for children with developmental difficulties. We regularly prayed together. Later it was my great joy to baptize Shelly and receive her into membership. As Jesus said, "Let the little children come to me."

Circumstances will occur in your ministry that will give you pause. Should mentally handicapped individuals be baptized? Should you force immersion upon someone who is physically impaired? What about people who have a real fear of water? Any number of situations can present themselves for which you will need to find a pastoral response. God will lead you. Remember, if baptism is *God's* work, then we are the channel between God and the work God wants to do in someone's life. That perspective will help supply you with wisdom.

Logistical Details

There are a number of items to which the pastor must attend. Some of these are a matter of life and death (protecting people near the water), and some are practical tips. Consider the following.

- Make sure there is absolutely no electrical current anywhere near the water! Deaths have occurred as a result of handheld microphones or other items near or in the water.
- Make sure all baptismal pools are emptied or securely covered and locked when not in use. Toddlers have drowned by innocently wandering into a body of water at the church.
- Allow plenty of time to heat the baptismal pool. It can take twenty-four hours or more, depending on your system.
- Train an assistant to be in the water with you for immersing very large people.
- When immersing,
  - keep your knees bent;
  - place your left arm across the back of the candidate;
  - ask the candidate to cross their arms over their chest in an "X";
  - cover the candidate's mouth and nose with a white handkerchief or cloth;
  - speak the actual Trinitarian formula ("I baptize you in the name of the Father, and of the Son, and of the Holy Spirit");
  - fully immerse the candidate and return up out of the water in one down/up motion;
  - let the individual get their footing and orientation;
  - lead them to an assistant who will help them out of the pool.
- Train assistants to help lead people into the pool and out of the pool.
- Have large towels ready immediately on their leaving the pool; have white hand towels handy for baptisms at fonts.
- Have a dressing room very close to the pool where the baptized may change clothing.
- Be attentive to privacy needs. Young women may be less comfortable with immersion at certain times of the month.

Conclusion

After baptism, Megan reentered the sanctuary from the front, along with everyone else who was baptized that evening. She enjoyed hearing the singing of the crowd as the door to the sanctuary opened and they made their way to sit together in the first pew. She also noticed how good it felt to be surrounded by people that loved God and loved her. This was a special service, and she was glad that she was included.

Key Terms

affusion The mode of pouring.

asperges The mode of sprinkling.

baptistery A pool of water built for immersing.

catechism Prebaptismal instruction in doctrine related to Christianity.

catechumen A new convert to Christianity in process toward baptism; a learner who is being instructed in the Christian faith; from the Greek meaning "to echo" (the catechumenate process involved question/answer learning).

charge The challenge given to someone making a pledge.

chrism The oil used at baptism.

chrismation The anointing of oil at baptism (historically administered by the bishop).

confirmation The rite of confirming one's baptism if baptized as an infant; an adult declaration of faith affirming the baptismal vows taken on one's behalf as a child; leads to full membership in the church.

font A receptacle to hold water for the administration of baptism; derived from the Latin *fons*, meaning "a spring of water."

godparents Adults who agree to (1) hold the parents accountable to spiritually nurture the child and (2) guide the spiritual growth of the baptized child in the event that parents are incapacitated. Not a legal responsibility.

initiation Baptism (initiation into Christ's holy church).

pedobaptists Those who baptize children.

To Learn More

Armstrong, John H., ed., and Paul E. Engle, series ed. *Understanding Four Views on Baptism*. Grand Rapids: Zondervan, 2007.

Baptism, Eucharist and Ministry. Geneva: World Council of Churches, 1982.

Webber, Robert E. *Journey to Jesus: The Worship, Evangelism, and Nurture Mission of the Church*. Nashville: Abingdon, 2001.

White, James F. *The Sacraments in Protestant Practice and Faith*. Nashville: Abingdon, 1999.

Engage

After expanding your understanding of the meaning of Christian baptism, begin to sharpen your skills as a rituals architect by doing two exercises.

1. Write a brief position statement on baptism consistent with your church's theology of baptism.
2. Create a simple printed guide for introducing your church's view on baptism to your youth group.

5

The Table of the Lord

Before reading chapter 5, reflect on your own experience of the Lord's Table.

- Do you remember the first time you took the Lord's Supper? How old were you? Where were you? Who was with you? Did it make any lasting impression? If so, in what way? Describe your experience to an acquaintance in your church or classroom, or describe it to a family member.
- Can you think of a Lord's Supper experience that really stood out to you as being noteworthy (for whatever reason)? If so, share this experience with someone as well.
- Did anyone ever explain to you personally the meaning of the Lord's Supper (other than in a formal Christian education setting)? If so, who was that?
- Recalling the churches in which you have received the Lord's Supper, what has been the predominant theme or tone of the service?

Now that you have begun to reflect on the Table of the Lord, expand your thinking by reading chapter 5.

Expand

Matthew knew that this Sunday dinner would be special, because by Saturday evening the dining room table was set beautifully. There was no time for

Matthew's mom to do anything extra in the morning while getting three young children ready for church. The tablecloth was pressed and draped perfectly across each corner of the table. The china was out of the cabinet, and real cloth napkins lay under the forks. Wooden candlesticks were perfectly placed at the center of the table. When the last rays of the evening sun caught the edge of the glassware, creating a brilliant sparkle, Matthew was pulled into the room. He stepped through the doorway into the dimming daylight, imagining the joy and delight tomorrow would bring and basking in silent anticipation of the meal. It would not be an average meal; it would be Mom's best, the most delicious she could afford. Matthew's older brother was returning home in the wee hours of the morning from military duty. He had been away a long time. "*This* meal will be special," he thought, "for there will be a lot of love around the table, we will share memories, and we will offer thanks." A faint smile crossed Matthew's face; he was thinking how the fellowship his family shared when gathered in the dining room was different from what he experienced anywhere else.

Food and drink are necessities for human existence. God created us with the need for daily nourishment and refreshment. If our bodies are denied such nourishment for very long, we begin to die. We eat because we must. At the same time, God not only has created us to be biologically dependent on food but has also mysteriously wired us to value the meal itself. Meals are social events. Some people eat meals alone out of necessity, while others prefer to eat alone; but most folks enjoy the company of friends or family as they share a meal together. That very common phrase, "share a meal," says a great deal. Meals are times of communal fellowship in which we not only share the food in the dishes on the table but also share our lives—our thoughts, our ideas, our concerns, our joys, our everyday experiences. Eating together is a sociological phenomenon of great importance in every culture.

In the Bible, meals hold not only sociological significance but liturgical significance as well. There are many stories of meals with eucharistic overtones: the meal of bread and wine shared between Abram and King Melchizedek of Salem (Gen. 14:17–24); the meal Abraham served the three visitors (Gen. 18:1–15); the Passover meal (Exod. 12:1–28); the feeding of the multitudes (Matt. 14:13–21); the breaking of bread with the Emmaus disciples (Luke 24:28–35); the fish fry with Jesus on the beach (John 21:9–14); the marriage supper of the Lamb (Rev. 19:9).

The meal of all meals is the one that Jesus Christ himself instituted for all of his followers to partake in often (1 Cor. 11:25) and always (Matt. 26:29). This meal is special, unlike all others. It is a simple table setting consisting only of a plate of bread and a cup of wine—food and drink that nourishes the body *and* the soul. This holy meal is a gift of God to the body of Christ, handed down from generation to generation (1 Cor. 11:23a). As such, we receive it with gratitude and wonder. The meal is known by many names, some of which have their source in Scripture, while others have emerged over time in the life of the church. I will use the phrases "the Table," "the Lord's Table," or "the Table of the Lord" as overarching references for any and all of the particular words used to refer to this sacred event. Several of these key terms are explained below.

In this chapter I will follow the same outline as I did for the sacrament of baptism (see chapter 4). I will endeavor to explain the "what, why, who, when, where, how" of the Lord's Table. Once again, it will be necessary to cover a range of thought and practices among Protestants in a very cursory manner. Nevertheless, I hope not only that you will find your spot somewhere in the theological spectrum that will serve as a reference point for your ministry; I also hope that as you encounter the differing viewpoints of the Table held by your sisters and brothers in Christ, you will remember that they, like you, passionately love the Lord Jesus Christ though they encounter him differently at the holy feast. I invite you into the dining room now, where you will see a table set for guests to partake in the oldest of all Christian rituals—a meal given to us by our Lord himself.

Laying the Foundations

What Is the Lord's Table?

Similar to our discussion surrounding baptism, there are many things to consider when answering the question, What is the Lord's Table? In this rather lengthy section I will try to address the Table much like gazing upon a prism: we will turn it slowly and see it from different angles so that we can begin to capture what God had in mind in giving us this wonderful gift. In the end, however, we must admit that many of its aspects we will never grasp in this life—it is a mystery.

The Lord's Table Is a Sacrament/Ordinance

The Lord's Table is given the special standing of sacrament or ordinance in the church. As such, it is a vitally important practice of the church and central to Christian worship. With very few exceptions, all Christians worship at the Table of the Lord.[1] Certain groups approach it very differently from others; yet *that* most Christian groups include the Table in worship is a sign of its importance to our faith. Remember from earlier discussions (see chapters 1 and

4) that Protestants generally approach the Table from one of two directions: as a sacrament or as an ordinance. Here we will apply these two views to the Lord's Table. In many respects the explanation that follows is oversimplified. If you wish to discover more, a few helpful resources for places to begin are listed at the end of this chapter (see "To Learn More").

THE TABLE AS SACRAMENT

To begin with, one basic question can be asked about the Table: From whom is the primary action arising? Is it God-initiated or human-initiated? Is God the primary agent of the action, or are individuals? A wide range of Protestant denominations refer to the Table of the Lord as a sacrament of the church. They may be quite far apart on how they interpret the meaning of sacrament, yet they share this view in common: at the Table, *God* is the primary force at work, making the meal what it is. People are important participants but are largely *recipients* of God's divine action rather than being *responsible* for God's divine action (as if that were possible). It's all about who is the agent of action at the Table.

As mentioned when discussing baptism, for those who view the Table as a sacrament, the event is both advisable *and* causative. That is, we come to the Table because we should; we are commanded to do so by our Lord, and we wish to obey our Master (therefore the Table is advisable). But we also come to the Table to receive the benefits of the meal that is blessed by God's Spirit. There is spiritual nourishment to be had in the bread and the cup; we are fortified for living as good citizens in the kingdom of God, a kingdom already here, in part. When the Holy Spirit's presence is invited to the feast, mere earthly elements of bread and wine take on new meaning and function, filling us and nourishing us for vibrant Christian living. In this way the Lord's Table is said to be a means of grace, like baptism. The Table is a means, a channel through which God's grace flows to us as eager recipients. Because of this, the Table is causative: divine action takes place.

Here we run into a dilemma similar to that of baptism: What kind of grace does the Table involve? A few Protestant groups make the claim that sincere participation in the Lord's Table offers pardoning grace—it is salvific in that sense. But remember that it is possible to make the claim that the Table is a sacrament and not claim that it is a primary means of salvation. Protestants would not claim that the bread and the cup alone provide our salvation. Faith, repentance, and true conversion (and in many cases baptism) are a prerequisite for coming to the Table. While there is a range of understanding regarding what happens at the Table, no one would encourage the unrepentant sinner to come to the Table; faith and repentance are necessary to partake in the meal.

John and Charles Wesley referred to the Lord's Table as a "converting ordinance." Here they seem to mean two things: (1) it is able to help those whose faith is weak, and (2) it could serve as the convicting call of the Holy Spirit to salvation. This latter sense is represented in Charles's hymn "Come, Sinners, to the Gospel Feast":

> Come, sinners, to the gospel feast,
> let every soul be Jesus' guest.
> Ye need not one be left behind,
> for God hath bid all humankind.
>
> Do not begin to make excuse;
> ah! do not you his grace refuse;
> your worldly cares and pleasures leave,
> and take what Jesus hath to give.
>
> Ye who believe his record true
> shall sup with him and he with you;
> come to the feast, be saved from sin,
> for Jesus waits to take you in.[2]

The Wesleys' view of grace at the Table went even further; they believed that God imparted to the one who came in faith whatever grace was needed: justifying, sanctifying, or perfecting grace. For them, the holy meal truly satisfied the spiritual hunger of the recipient at any and all levels.

The Table as Ordinance

Those who refer to the Table of the Lord as an ordinance partake of the elements because Jesus commanded his followers to do so. They observe the event primarily out of obedience to Christ's command. (The word "ordinance" is related to "ordained"; that is, Jesus ordained this holy meal.) Those who hold the sacramental view, as seen above, also come to the Table in reverence to Christ's command, but ordinance folks claim this as their primary, even singular, reason for doing so. Consequently, ordinance people lean toward a view that God is less active at the Table, resulting in an experience that is largely about individuals approaching the Table properly and remembering Christ's death sincerely so as to please God. In this sense *people* are given much of the responsibility for the effectiveness of the Table, whatever that is thought to be. Those who view the Table as an ordinance see it primarily as symbolic of a spiritual truth: that Christ suffered, died, and was buried for the forgiveness of our sins. Most within the ordinance camp would go so far as to declare that the bread and the cup are *only* symbols, nothing more, and that we come to the Table exclusively to remember and give thanks for the work God rendered in the past. For these brothers and sisters, the bread and the cup represent an event that was completed, one which we, as worshipers, recall in the past tense. This is sometimes referred to as the Memorialist view of Communion (emphasis on remembrance in the past tense) and is attributed largely to Ulrich Zwingli, one of the early Reformers of the sixteenth century.

The type of view held (either as sacrament or as ordinance) will greatly affect the spirit of the service and also the frequency with which the Table is offered. Those worshipers viewing the Table as an ordinance tend to favor a Memorialist view, which lends itself to a somber tone, for the death of Christ is emphasized, as well as the participants' unworthiness. Those worshipers viewing the Table as a sacrament, in which spiritual nourishment is given, are more likely to capture a spirit of celebration and may emphasize the resurrection.[3] As to frequency of observance, if the event is "symbolic only," the partaking of the bread and cup may not have the same sense of urgency as it would for a group who views it as manna from heaven to feed the hungry soul. It makes sense that those who view the Table as a sacrament would come to the Table more frequently to receive the grace God offers there. These contrasts are much too stark as I have laid them out, for there is definitely overlap in these matters. Nevertheless, for the sake of fostering a basic understanding, we can allow for these generalizations.

What sets the sacrament/ordinance apart as significant? Two actions distinguish it from other, more common aspects of worship. First, the use of the words of institution qualifies the event for what it is—words spoken by our Lord at his last Passover meal, then repeated by Paul, and consequently given to every generation since to practice continuously.

> The Lord Jesus on the night when he was betrayed took a loaf of bread, and when he had given thanks, he broke it and said, "This is my body that is for you. Do this in remembrance of me." In the same way he took the cup also, after supper, saying, "This cup is the new covenant in my blood. Do this, as often as you drink it, in remembrance of me." (1 Cor. 11:23–25)

Second, the invocation of the Holy Spirit upon the elements sets the meal apart as a gift of God to the people of God. This prayer is the prayer of consecration, a prayer that enables common items to serve uncommon purposes. Disputes concerning exactly what happens as a result of the prayer of consecration have been the source of much division throughout Christendom for centuries. It is precisely at this point that arguments arise. It is simply not possible (or needful) in this book to cover how these various opinions developed or to explain in detail what various theories are presently held. Again, at the risk of oversimplification, some traditions believe that the presence of the Spirit invoked on the elements directly causes material change in the bread and wine, turning them into the actual substance of Jesus's own body and blood (transubstantiation).[4] Others believe that the bread and the cup are truly the body and blood of Christ without material change.[5] Christians in yet other traditions believe in the spiritual presence of Christ in the elements. Christ's presence is real but in a nonobjective way.[6] Most churches in the Free Church traditions make no claim that any hint of the presence of Christ resides at the Table. Therefore, they do not pray an actual prayer of consecration. They may offer an extemporaneous prayer for forgiveness, or a prayer of thanks for Christ and his work, or a prayer for the people to increase in devotion, but would not consider invoking the Holy Spirit upon the elements.

The Lord's Table Is Part of the Dialogical Nature of Worship

Christian worship is a dialogue between the community and God. When the worshiping community gathers, it enters into a holy conversation with God. The various acts of worship facilitate this most important weekly conversation. Many elements of worship—songs, prayers, Scripture, offering, and so on—give us the words for our conversation. But the overall order of service gives us a framework for the conversation. In chapter 1, I explained the importance of the fourfold order (Gathering, Word, Table, Sending). Within this fourfold order is the twofold centerpiece of the conversation: Word and Table. In the Word, God speaks; at the Table, we return our sentiments in the form of praise, petitions, and offering ourselves in service to God and others.[7] Word and Table comprise revelation and response. These two movements of worship in particular form the core of the Christian worship service.

The Table, then, is best understood as one of several normative and significant movements of the service. Specifically, *it functions as the response to the Word*. In worship, the Word of God is preached, to which the people respond at the Table. For fifteen hundred years in the life of the church, this was the normative pattern. The pattern was altered after the Reformation, though at the dismay of most of the Reformers, who argued for the ongoing joining of Word and Table. It is very important to stress that preaching and Eucharist belong together. In much of Protestantism there has been a widespread separation of preaching and Eucharist in many traditions on many Sundays. The result has been that on those rare occasions when the Table *is* included in the worship service, it is then viewed as distinctly different, unique, or special. Such a treatment of the Lord's Supper is a grave departure from its original practice and intention. Frankly, some churches intentionally schedule it rarely, so that when it does occur, there will be goose bumps. Have you ever heard someone remark, "We wouldn't want to observe the Table too often; it might lose its meaning"? This sentiment demonstrates that leaders are after an effect. But the service of the Table should not be scheduled so rarely that when it does occur, people receive the impression that something very different from "normal" is happening.

The Lord's Table Signifies Several Motifs Simultaneously

Jesus's call to celebrate his Table is grounded in several key motifs or themes found in Scripture and which are central to our Christian faith. The Lord's Table is so vast, so multidimensional that it represents several truths all at once. Keep the idea of the prism in mind as you read this section. Slowly turn the prism so as to see the Table as an expression of these various motifs. Also remember that when we say that something *signifies* something or someone, we are simply saying that the sign points to a reality beyond itself—to something greater. The sign provides a visible depiction of an invisible reality. What is unseen is seen by virtue of the sign. In this sense the meal that believers share points to more than one meaning. Depending on your tradition, these motifs will vary in number and terminology. I will briefly identify six key themes on which there is much consensus in the broader Christian community.

AT THE MEAL WE REMEMBER

The Lord's Table is an occasion to remember the goodness of God for the many ways that God has provided salvation to his people throughout human history. God is a saving God. Our Bible includes a long and trustworthy record of God's perfect creation going awry at the hands of wicked mortals. But humanity is not left in its corrupt state. Time and again God's long arm of salvation reaches into the lives of God's people and delivers them. The story of God is marked by deliverance. Therefore at the Table we remember how, beginning with the first Adam, God restores broken relationships. The greatest act of salvation provided by God is the deliverance available in the second Adam, God's Son, Jesus Christ. It is very important to remember that God is to be praised for *all* of the times this cycle of creation–sin–re-creation has demonstrated God's faithfulness, both to our spiritual forebears and to us today. So at the Table we remember what God has done for his covenant people then and now, and most especially what God has done in giving us the gift of his Son. In this meal we remember the incarnation, earthly ministry, passion, death, resurrection, ascension, and anticipated return of Jesus the Christ. This is summed up in Jesus's own words, "Do this in remembrance of me" (Luke 22:19; 1 Cor. 11:24).

Remembrance at the Table occurs in a very special way. Our Western view of remembering predominantly focuses on recalling the past: an event has taken place, it is over and done with, and we remember it by reflecting back on it. However, the Greek word used often in the New Testament for remembering is *anamnesis*. The Greeks remembered in an active sense by bringing the past, present, and future together. In other words, the memory of an event relates dynamically to the experience of today and also anticipates what will be. This idea of remembering can be illustrated by way of celebrating a wedding anniversary. When a married couple wants to celebrate their anniversary, they remember their wedding day by reminding one another of the details of the event—where it was held, who officiated, the family and friends who attended, what was worn, the unexpected episodes of the day, and so on. But in doing so the couple not only delights in the events of their wedding day but also rejoices in the reality of their marriage today—where it stands as a result of the past—and also what it will be in the future. The past, present, and future converge for real celebration. It is the same at the Table. We rehearse the many ways in which God has saved us, most especially in the events we recall concerning Christ's life, death, and resurrection; however, we remember in a way that celebrates the meal as yet another moment of God's redemptive history—a continuous, unbroken line of God's mercy.

At the Meal We Give Thanks

Thanksgiving is the heart and soul of the Table. In fact, one of the Greek terms Paul uses for the Table is *eucharistesas*, translated as "thanksgiving." We offer thanks to God for the plan of salvation expressed in the gift of the Son. The primary prayer offered at the Table is referred to as the "Great Thanksgiving" or the "Great Prayer of Thanksgiving" precisely because giving thanks is at the core of the event. It is interesting that the early Christian prayers around the Table were modeled after the *berakhah*—an ancient Jewish prayer form that blesses God and expresses thanks for the care and provision of God's people. *Berakhah* is translated in the New Testament as *eucharistia* (thanksgiving) or *eulogia* (blessing). It has been and remains the principal prayer form in Jewish liturgy and spirituality. The *berakhah* fosters the disposition of wonder coupled with praise. In time the prayer form became standardized into three essential movements: praise, recitation of God's saving acts, and petition. There are numerous examples of this prayer form in the New Testament, including some of the prayers of blessing that Jesus prayed.[8] So, at the Table of the Lord we bless God, praise God for his mighty saving acts, and offer petitions according to our needs and the needs of the world. We revel in thanksgiving.

AT THE MEAL WE COMMUNE

The table, like any meal, affords us the opportunity to enjoy sweet fellowship with God and with one another. "Commune" is rich in meaning; it shares the same etymological roots with other significant words related to the Table, like "community," "unity," and "oneness." Fellowship happens at the Table in two directions at once—vertically and horizontally. We experience fellowship between us and God; we also experience fellowship person to person within the body of Christ. Persons gathered around the Table of the Lord portray a magnificent symbol of the unity for which Christ petitioned the Father (John 17:20–22). It is a physical demonstration of what it means to be the body of Christ. The gathered body doesn't only *represent* fellowship; the gathered body *is* fellowship. Fellowship happens as a result of eating the sacred meal through the power of the Holy Spirit. It's a reality! "Community" is not a noun; it's a verb. The act of eating consecrated bread and drinking consecrated wine together unifies us as we partake. It is a miraculous blessing that the Holy Spirit unites us with God and with one another to be the people we are called to be.

AT THE MEAL WE ANTICIPATE THE COMING KINGDOM OF GOD

God's kingdom is both "here" and "not yet"; it was inaugurated with Christ's first coming to earth (Mark 1:15) but will not come in its fullness until Christ's second coming. Eating at the heavenly banquet table plays a prominent role in the kingdom. The Lord's Table, therefore, has a highly eschatological dimension to it, as the sacred meal we share now is a foretaste of what is yet to come. When Jesus inaugurated the Lord's Supper, he gave hints that this was a meal that would make its way into eternity: "I tell you, I will never again drink of this fruit of the vine until that day when I drink it new with you in my Father's kingdom" (Matt. 26:29; see also Mark 14:25 and Luke 22:16). Christ promised his devoted disciples that one of the blessings they would share with him in the future kingdom is "that [they] may eat and drink at my table in my kingdom" (Luke 22:30). This is to be the joyful feast that all believers will attend, for in speaking of the end of time, Jesus said that "people will come from east and west, from north and south, and will eat in the kingdom of God" (Luke 13:29). Jesus makes the very strong connection between the bread and the cup that he instituted as the ongoing meal for his followers and the meal they would share again later when the kingdom had finally come. The bread and the cup we enjoy now anticipate the future reign of God.

AT THE MEAL WE RENEW OUR COVENANT WITH GOD

Both sacraments (baptism and the Lord's Table) are signs of the covenant God makes with his people. Long ago, God established covenantal worship with Moses and the Israelites at the foot of Mount Sinai. Upon receiving "all the words of the LORD and all the ordinances" (Exod. 24:3), the people pledged themselves to God in full obedience (Exod. 24:3, 7) and God pledged himself to the people (Exod. 34:6–7, 10). Symbolic gestures sealed the pledge, as was the ancient Near East custom. Moses took half of the blood of the sacrifices offered and dashed it against the altar and on the people as a seal of the covenant. As noted in chapter 1, the word "sacrament" comes from the Latin word *sacramentum*, meaning "sacred pledge."[9] Rooted in military parlance, it was used to confirm the allegiance of a soldier to his commanding officer. When worshipers receive the bread and the cup, it is a perfect occasion for renewing our pledge to Christ to be faithful in our discipleship and to offer ourselves anew in service to the kingdom of God. Like the ancient Israelites, we must say to God, "All that the LORD has spoken we will do, and we will be obedient" (Exod. 24:7). We have a Lord to whom we have pledged our allegiance. Maintaining our pledge is an important part of what happens at the Table. Also at the Table we receive again Christ's ongoing pledge to us of salvation from sin, victory over evil, and his promise to return. Similar to Old Testament practice, symbolic gestures ratify the pledge, in this case eating bread and drinking wine. In this way the two-party covenant is reestablished each time we gather at the Table. The renewal of the covenant is a way for us to once again offer ourselves to God in Christ through the Spirit, in response to God's first offering Christ to us through the Spirit.

At the Meal We Celebrate Christus Victor

This holy meal instituted by our Lord represents many things to Jesus's followers, but perhaps no theme sums it all up more comprehensively or powerfully than that of *Christus Victor*. This Latin term, appearing early in the writings of the church fathers, proclaims Christ as Victor! The meaning behind this glorious title could take volumes to unwrap. But the essence of it is this: when Christ was crucified, raised, and ascended, he accomplished *so much more* than providing personal salvation for lost individuals. These crowning events of Christ's incarnation not only provide forgiveness for the sins of those who believe in him (John 3:16) but completely and triumphantly severed once and for all Satan's ultimate power (Rev. 20:10).[10] The bondage with which the enemy of God held all creation—evil, sin, and death—was broken through the Christ Event; the chains of evil, seemingly so strong, fell limply to the ground like the ropes on Samson's arms that could not bind him, falling "off his arms like a thread" (Judg. 16:12). The magnificent truth is that Christ is shown as Victor in terms of the *whole cosmos*! *Christus Victor* presents Jesus Christ not only as the Savior of sinners but also as the One who created our world with God the Father (John 1:1–3) and would therefore re-create the entire created order when the kingdom is finally established (Rev. 21:1–2). The victory wrought through the resurrection effectively and practically triumphed over Satan so that believers are not only *saved* from sin but *delivered* from slavery to sin now; it no longer need reign in us. For a time we still suffer the results of evil in our world; as Paul notes, "The creation waits with eager longing" for the time when "the creation itself will be set free from its bondage to decay and will obtain the freedom of the glory of the children of God" (Rom. 8:19, 21). But when the Father signals the moment, ultimate triumph will belong to *Christus Victor*. Satan and his demons will be placed in eternal bondage, sentenced to their own pit of torment, never to rise again; they are rendered powerless forever (Rev. 20:1–3a, 10)! On that day no knee will bend to the evil one; that is a genuflection reserved only for the King of kings and Lord of lords (Phil. 2:10)!

Allow me to quote Robert Webber, historical theologian, at length:

> In the Incarnation the Creator *became* the creation and took upon himself the distortion of sin that extended not only into people but also into every corner of nature and every institution of society. By his death he, the Creator, destroyed the power of death and sin. And by his resurrection, he, the Creator, demonstrated the power to re-create.
>
> Consequently, by virtue of the incarnation, death, and resurrection, Christ has triumphed over the power of sin in his creation. And at his second coming he will completely destroy the power of sin over his creation, releasing it from the "bondage of decay" it is now under.
>
> In this view the Fathers taught that Christ not only died to satisfy the requirements of justice but also taught that he gained a victory over the power of evil that raged in his world. His work on the cross, which extends to all of life, is the downfall of the powers of evil. The havoc they have wrought in the entire created order cannot and will not prevail, for his victory over them is the promise of the ultimate restoration of his creation.[11]

When we come to the Table of the Lord, we are engaged in proclaiming so much more than our own forgiveness through the blood of the cross. We are engaged in a cosmic proclamation: Jesus Christ has triumphed over Satan; he repels the power of sin and death; and he will one day redeem all creation—the earth, the created order, his holy ones—and return it to the perfect, sparkling spectacle it was when it was first fashioned by his hands. Yes, we will thank God for saving us personally but only in light of the fact that God is making *all* things new (Rev. 21:5) through Christ who is *Christus Victor*! The next time you celebrate the Lord's Table, place your own personal appreciation for salvation in the context of the larger scope of Christ's cosmic triumph over all things. If you do, you may very well experience a fresh new wonder at the greatness of God.

The Lord's Table Invites Several Approaches

By now you have deduced that there are several terms universally used to refer to one event—the event we have been calling "the Table." We have bumped into some of them already. Consider these biblical terms: Eucharist, the Lord's Supper, Communion, breaking of bread. Other terms developed over time, and therefore have historical precedence for some churches. These include "the Divine Liturgy" (the Orthodox Church) and "the Mass" (the Roman Catholic Church). Each one of these terms refers to the same event—the Table of the Lord.[12] I will briefly explain the four primary terms used in the Scriptures for the sacred meal.[13] Again, much more could be said, and I urge you to further explore the rich meanings for each of them. As you reflect on the many sides to the Table, keep turning that prism slowly, and you will see the Table in greater fullness as you gaze from several angles.

EUCHARIST

The English word "Eucharist" is from the Greek *eucharistos*, meaning "thanksgiving." Both Mark (Mark 14:22–23) and the apostle Paul (1 Cor. 11:24) use the term, suggesting that there is reason to celebrate when we take the bread and cup! Indeed, there *is* much to celebrate. The emphasis of Eucharist is on the resurrection—rejoicing that the cross led to the empty grave. At the Table we not only remember the death of our Savior but celebrate the power of God that raised Christ from the dead. We rejoice in *Christus Victor*—the Lord who has triumphed over Satan and all evil powers of darkness. We are glad in the power the Spirit gives to every believer to live the holy and victorious life as we too triumph over the evil one.

Historians confirm that for the earliest believers, celebrating the Eucharist was a joyful time. Why not? For the resurrection was fresh in their minds; they had personally interacted with the risen Lord. The bread and the cup reminded them that Jesus was truly alive and with them through his Spirit. One biblical and historical approach to the Table, then, is "Eucharist"—joyful thanksgiving, celebration, and praise.

THE LORD'S SUPPER

"The Lord's Supper" is perhaps the most common term used among Protestants. It has direct connection to the Last Supper, which Jesus shared with his disciples the night before he was killed. The story of Jesus celebrating the Passover meal with his disciples is told in all four of the Gospels. During dinner, Jesus instituted the meal as a new covenant and commanded his followers to eat the bread (his body) and drink the wine (his blood) in remembrance of him. It was years later that Paul, in recalling the meal Jesus instituted, referred to the event as the Lord's Supper (*kuriakos deipnon*, 1 Cor. 11:20). The focus of the Lord's Supper is on recalling the suffering and death of Jesus. It is remembering Jesus in memoriam (hence the Memorialist view).

It is very common for the Lord's Supper to have a rather solemn atmosphere, reminiscent of the crucifixion. Emphasis is on the unworthiness of the participant, and therefore confession plays a prominent role in the service. The rituals architect will create a more somber format for approaching the bread and the cup if the Lord's Supper is the predominant means for coming to the Table.

COMMUNION

The English word "communion" is derived from the Greek *koinonia*, which is translated as "participation," "sharing," or "fellowship." In using this word, both Paul and Luke emphasize the communal nature of the meal. Luke uses *koinonia* in reference to the breaking of bread (Acts 2:42). Paul uses the same word in addressing the Corinthians regarding the importance of participation *together* in the bread and cup (1 Cor. 10:16–17). The real focus of the word "communion" is the unity of the body, the uncommon fellowship believers share through Christ. This sense of oneness transcends the local fellowship that physically gathers around the Table. Though we can see only the members of our church who are present, we remember that God's Spirit makes us one with the church universal—believers of every tribe and nation, past, present, and future, who name Jesus Christ as Lord. Unity is a gift from God that is recognized and welcomed at the Table.

So this approach to Holy Communion is with a spirit of love and appreciation for our sisters and brothers who gather locally and those who worship with us globally, even eternally. The approach will be warm, inviting, relational, thoughtful—all representative of the blessing of oneness, which is a gift from above. It is a sweet communion, a holy fellowship.

BREAKING OF BREAD

The earliest Christian community devoted itself to the breaking of bread (Acts 2:42). Part of their devotion to this practice was that they shared the meal often, presumably daily, for we are told that "day by day, as they spent much time together in the temple, they broke bread at home and ate their food with glad and generous hearts, praising God and having the goodwill of all the people" (Acts 2:46–47). Historians believe the breaking of bread referred to a regular daily meal at which the bread and the cup were celebrated. The two aspects of the Table were joined together: "We may reasonably deduce that a meal in Christian fellowship and the celebration of the Lord's Supper often took place together."[14] The love feast referred to in Jude 12 was perhaps reference to such a meal.[15] Many Anabaptists, Moravians, and Methodists historically observed the breaking of bread in the form of a love feast—a simple meal that included the bread and the cup. (See chapter 7 for the ritual of a love feast.)

A service of the Table could take place as a common meal shared by the members of a local church which also includes the bread and the cup, typically served at the conclusion of the meal, though it could be served any time during it. Such a service would be orchestrated around the theme of fellowship (similar to Communion) but with a more relaxed, somewhat spontaneous approach to the Table of the Lord.

As you can see, there is a vast richness in the ways to follow our Lord's command to "do this." All of these terms show preference for coming to the Table in a variety of ways. Sometimes we come rejoicing; sometimes we come with a solemnity befitting the sorrow Christ experienced; sometimes our hearts are warmed at the recognition that we are in community with other believers; and sometimes we sense an atmosphere similar to a family gathering for a common meal. Let the primary preaching text of the day as well as the time in the Christian year (more on this below) direct the approach you choose for any given observance of the Table. Just be sure to capture the various approaches over time in your local church so as to benefit from a fully orbed experience of the Table and to honor the many ways Christ comes to us in the bread and the cup. From this point forward in the book, I will more freely use these biblical terms interchangeably for "the Table," as appropriate. Keep turning that prism!

The Lord's Table Is Relational in Essence

The Lord's Table is essentially about relationship—relationship with God in Christ first, and also relationship with fellow believers. The basis for the relational nature of the Table is found in the eternal Trinitarian relationship of God the Father, God the Son, and God the Holy Spirit. This interrelationship of mutual love and self-giving is described by the church fathers as a *perichoresis*—derived from a combination of Greek words that means "to dance around in a chorus."[16] As William Dyrness affirms, "This image represents the most fundamental assertion one can make about the character of the Christian God: the nature of God is a dynamic movement of love and beauty."[17] And this eternal, mutual, and loving fellowship of the persons of the Godhead—the very fellowship that the Godhead enjoys—forms the ultimate fellowship into which all believers are invited. The fellowship that is the reality of the one God in three persons is the real basis for the oneness that is also our reality at the Table: we are one with Christ and one in fellowship with all true disciples of Jesus Christ.

Communion, therefore, is a profoundly *corporate* act. It is meant to be shared by the entire community of believers who are gathered in one place. There may be three who are present (such as when the two on the road to Emmaus met Jesus and shared Communion; see Luke 24:30) or a great multitude (such as the banquet of the Lamb; see Rev. 19:6–9), but one thing is for sure: Communion is designed for all of the people of God to partake of *together* and must never be received by particular individuals who insist on the privilege of receiving it under special circumstances. In the medieval period this was one of the grievances addressed by the Reformers: worshipers came to church and watched the priests receive the elements, while they were denied. Though this has been corrected today in every branch of Christendom, it does emerge in other ways, such as a bride and groom alone receiving Holy Communion during their wedding service while other believers merely observe (a practice to be discouraged; see chapter 2 for elaboration).

In examining the themes and motifs of the Table of the Lord, it is obvious that the focus is on what this meal represents: remembrance, thanksgiving, communion, anticipation, covenant, and victory. In coming to the Table, we are asserting certain affirmations of faith, and we are making these assertions in community. In emphasizing these motifs and the communal nature of the meal, we are not suggesting that the personal faith of the believer should be slighted or overlooked. We do not wish to understate in any way the personal dimension of taking the bread and the cup, for in the end the community gathered around the Table is composed of redeemed individuals who have personally accepted the claims of the gospel, who have received the gift of salvation through faith, and who name Jesus Christ as Lord.

Why Do We Celebrate the Feast?

We celebrate the Table of the Lord for a simple reason: because Jesus commanded us to do so. This meal of bread and wine shared first by the Rabbi and his disciples is accompanied by a directive from our Lord: "Do this in remembrance of me" (Luke 22:19). The earliest followers took their Master seriously and remembered him in this manner weekly, or even daily in some cases. Though Christ's command serves as the foundational rationale for our ongoing participation in the meal, we also have good reason for maintaining the practice, given that the apostolic tradition endorses the ongoing observance of the Table. Paul had much to say to the Corinthians about the necessity of being faithful to the meal. He completely embraced it, using Jesus's own words as those handed down *directly to him* for the purpose of handing on to others (1 Cor. 11:23–25). When we gather at the Table, we do so (1) in obedience to Christ's specific command and (2) as participants in a long line of faithful witnesses who have kept the practice alive and uninterrupted for more than two millennia.

There's one more aspect to consider when asking, "Why Communion?" When we accept Christ's invitation to the feast, we do so not only for ourselves but also for the sake of the world. We have said that the Table is a place of spiritual refreshing for the believer, but it is not only that. Much of what we gain at the Table is not for our own sakes but for the sake of others. This means that whatever strength we gain, whatever power we receive is not meant for our own gratification; it is not so that we can feel more "spiritual." Rather, it is meant to empower us to be agents of God's love and reconciliation to those in need of God's grace. Why do we celebrate the feast? To be fed so that we can feed others. The oneness we have as our reality, the oneness for which Christ prayed, the oneness truly demonstrated at the Table is "so that the world may know that you [the Father] have sent me [Jesus] and have loved them even as you have loved me" (John 17:23). The goal of Christian oneness, so profoundly expressed at the Table, is for the sake of the world. This is the clear picture of life in the earliest Christian community. The daily breaking of bread was in the context of sacrificial living on behalf of others, and this kind of living brought much favor among all the people (Acts 2:43–47).

Who May Eat?

The meal that Jesus established for remembering his life, death, and resurrection until his return is not to be offered to just anyone who is interested in bread and wine; it was instituted for a specific group of people. In chapter 4 we answered the question "Who is baptized?" with the simple response: disciples of Jesus Christ. When we consider who may come to the Table, the answer is the same. Both these sacraments/ordinances of the church are gifts from God for a well-defined group of people; they are open to persons who have committed themselves to the lordship of Jesus Christ. The Scriptures very clearly specify that the breaking of bread is a meal for those who are already citizens of the kingdom of God. Recall that the meal has its roots in the Passover feast of ancient Judaism. God's covenantal relationship with the descendants of Abraham was central to the Passover meal; only children of the covenant could celebrate the meal.[18] On the night in which Jesus celebrated his last Passover meal with his disciples, he established the new covenant of his body and blood. In this action he also established people of the new covenant. It was his disciples whom Jesus invited as guests at the inaugural meal and to whom he entrusted it as an ongoing practice. He gave it to his followers and all succeeding followers who would become people of the new covenant. The apostle Peter is referring to these people when he writes, "But you are a chosen race, a royal priesthood, a holy nation, God's own people. . . . Once you were not a people, but now you are God's people; once you had not received mercy, but now you have received mercy" (1 Pet. 2:9–10). From its inception, the meal was established for those who are in covenantal relationship with God through Jesus Christ.

The apostle Paul likewise assumes that the meal is for believers when he addresses the Corinthians concerning their approach to the Table. He forthrightly states that he is speaking to the church (1 Cor. 11:18)—the group of believers at Corinth—when he admonishes them concerning the Lord's Supper. The problems Paul was addressing were due to irregularities in practice among Christ-followers. Paul was not addressing nonbelievers. Finally, as we have seen, the breaking of bread is a foreshadowing of the heavenly banquet, a table set in the eternal kingdom for all who name Christ as Lord. For all of these reasons it is evident that the Table is a special meal to be offered only to those who trust in Christ for salvation and intend to follow him in true discipleship. This has been the stance of the Christian church since its inception.

Throughout history, the church has been very careful to protect the integrity of the Table. Exactly who may be admitted to the meal has been taken very seriously. Protecting the Table has come in many forms throughout church history. Some traditions established the practice of "fencing the table"—a phrase referring to denying Communion to those who were not in right standing in their relationship with God and others and were therefore deemed unqualified to partake. At first, "fencing" involved a round of face-to-face visits of elders in the homes of parishioners prior to each Communion so as to examine their readiness. John Calvin supported such rotations so that sins could be confessed and absolved, right relationships among members of the community were validated to be in good order, and fasting and prayer were encouraged. During some periods of church history, tokens or tickets were distributed to those approved for the Lord's Supper; such people were required to produce the token prior to receiving the elements. Of course, the idea of fencing the table was not original to the Reformers. It had already taken an unfortunate and heretical form during the height of the medieval period when fencing involved actual wood structures (called rood screens) that were installed in front of the altar table. These effectively established physical barriers between those who were worthy (priests) and those who were not (people) as the Mass was performed.

Much of the concern regarding spiritual readiness stems from Paul's warning that no one should eat the bread or drink the cup of the Lord in an unworthy manner (1 Cor. 11:27). The penalty for doing so is severe: it brings judgment in the form of illness or even death (1 Cor. 11:29–30). Unfortunately this admonition from the respected apostle has been misinterpreted. Many people mistakenly view this passage to mean that one may not receive the bread and cup if they are personally unworthy. They may be able to point to a recent offense against God or just simply feel guilty and thereby deem themselves unworthy. I was recently told by a local pastor that some people stay home from church on Communion Sunday (in churches where it is not offered weekly) because they don't feel good enough to take Communion and they don't want to be noticed for not receiving it. But these concerns are by no means what Paul is addressing in the passage. When Paul speaks of eating the Lord's Supper unworthily, he is addressing selfishness and inconsideration among the body of Christ as they come to partake of the meal. As Ben Worthington states, "With 'unworthy' Paul refers to those who are partaking in an unworthy manner, not to persons who are themselves unworthy. The examination called for in v. 28 is to be one's consideration of how properly to partake of the Supper, not an introspective assessment of one's worthiness to partake."[19] One pastoral favor you could provide to your people is to make sure that they are able to discern between personal feelings of unworthiness (which we all share) and willfully disrespecting the event or those with whom we commune.

Congregations today establish their own boundaries for who may or may not partake of the Table of the Lord in their church. Some practice what is known as "closed communion"—the Table is only open to those who are baptized members in good standing of a particular denomination. Many congregations practice "open communion"—all baptized believers (or in some cases even unbaptized believers) are welcome at the Table regardless of denominational affiliation. Confession of Christ as Savior and Lord is the prerequisite. A few groups observe "limited intercommunion"—fellowship at the Table under certain approved conditions.

So if the Lord's Table is a meal for disciples of Jesus, we're back to the same question asked at one's baptism: Who qualifies as a disciple? As you can imagine, there is an array of answers. Many churches in the Free Church tradition consider anyone who has intentionally and sincerely trusted Christ for salvation and follows him in true devotion as eligible to take the bread and cup. One's personal conversion is the qualifying marker. Typically in these churches children are discouraged from or even forbidden at the Table until they have made their own profession of faith. Other churches specify that baptism is the threshold for Communion. This practice hearkens back to the practices of the catechumenate of the early church. The catechumens were dismissed from worship after the service of the Word while only the baptized received Eucharist. Upon their baptism on Easter morning, the catechumens were immediately invited to participate in receiving the Eucharist with all baptized believers. As the church moved toward the baptism of infants, young children became eligible for Communion by virtue of their baptism. Today many denominations indicate that all baptized persons, including baptized children, may receive the bread and the cup. Still other churches designate confirmation as the point of first Communion. It is highly advisable that each Christian leader follow the pattern of their denomination. If no pattern is mandated, think and pray about your church's answer to this question. Whatever the case, Christ must be honored at the Table by those who name his name and call him Lord.

When Should the Table Be Offered?

It is fitting to offer the Lord's Table any time the church is gathered for worship and the Word is preached. Most often this is on the Lord's Day, a most appropriate occasion for receiving the Table, since Sunday is itself a symbol of the resurrection. It was the normal practice of the first Christians to partake of Eucharist each and every Lord's Day. As such, it set the course for the church's practice for more than fifteen hundred years. The weekly receiving of the Lord's Table was interrupted around the time of the Reformation. There were several reasons for this,[20] but initially it seemed largely due to the pressure which lay people applied to the clergy for infrequent Communion. Having witnessed grave abuses prior to the Reformation and having been effectively eliminated from the Table for years, lay people were not eager to make it a weekly observance. Most of the Reformers (Zwingli being a notable exception) pled for weekly Lord's Day Eucharist to no avail. Today our best understanding of worship practices suggests that a service of Word and Table is the normative pattern, scripturally and historically speaking. I highly recommended it for theological reasons as well: it maintains the dialogical nature of worship in revelation/response. Again, the leader's decision as to how frequently to offer Communion depends in large part on one's tradition and historical roots, while entertaining the possibility of influencing an increased number of occasions for it.

Regardless of how often a church celebrates the Table, it is very important to note that it should be served within the primary service of worship in the local church. That is not to say that additional opportunities for the Table will not be appropriate on other occasions; it *is* to say that to relegate Communion to any time other than when the whole church is gathered is to diminish the role of the Table. Some congregations schedule Communion for the Sunday evening service to avoid the funeral-like tone of the Table at the primary morning service, when things must appear energized; or they don't want to take the time during the Sunday morning service. I am aware of several churches that set the Table as an alternative experience for those who feel led to avail themselves of it in a service while others do not. One church simply has the elements set up in front, and during the extended time of singing in the Gathering, anyone is free to come and partake on their own if they wish. No words of institution, confession, or prayers are offered related to the Table; it's just there for the taking. Another church has Communion stations in the side aisles of the church, and after the service people can go there to take the bread and the cup if they so desire. Perhaps by now you can see how problematic some of these practices are. Communion is either to be taken by *all* believers gathered as an act of sweet fellowship in the Lord, or it should not be offered. It is fundamentally a communal act.

The pastoral leadership of the church must be diligent in teaching their people the meanings and practices of Holy Communion. The congregants' view of the significance of the meal will depend largely on when, where, and how it is celebrated. If it is placed to the side, or presented as an afterthought or as one of several options for the day, it is not able to function in the life of the people as intended. Pastors must provide regular teaching concerning the purpose of Communion and what is meant by receiving Communion in an unworthy manner. Sound teaching can correct much misunderstanding when it comes to the Table.

Where Is the Table Set?

The Table can be set in many different settings: retreats, meetings, classrooms, camps, ecumenical services, hospital rooms, prisons, and so on. But the primary time and place for celebrating the Table of the Lord is the Lord's Day worship service of the local church (with an approved officiant presiding). The regular services of the church are the first priority; the other settings, meaningful as they may be, are secondary. It's important to note that ordinarily the Lord's Supper is not to be observed privately.

How Are the Bread and the Cup Taken?

To answer the question of how the bread and the cup are taken, I will first address the general issues here; in a later section, "Serving as Hospitable Host," I will speak to the more particular issues related to clergy presiding at the Table of the Lord.

The Mode

There are a number of modes appropriate for serving the elements. While not an exhaustive list, here are a few common ways to distribute the bread and the wine:

- *In the pews.* People remain seated in the pews while ushers/deacons serve trays of bread (cubed) and wine/juice (in small cups).

- *Intinction*. People come forward and dip a piece of bread into the cup of wine/juice.
- *Common cup*. People come forward, eat a piece of bread, and drink from a common cup of wine/juice.
- *Seated at a table*. A table is set for an intimate meal. Worshipers come forward a few at a time to fill the places around the table. The elements are passed around the table much like at a meal. When finished, they leave and others come.
- *Standing around a table*. A good number of worshipers come forward to stand comfortably around the table. Each person serves the person next to him or her as the elements make their way around the circle.
- *Kneeling*. Another way to receive the elements is to kneel at kneeling benches in the front. It is a humbling position. Servers provide the bread and the cup either as individual pieces and small cups, as intinction, or as common cup.

Each of these modes (and others too) are fitting and meaningful ways to receive the elements of bread and wine/juice. You can imagine how each one carries its own symbolic meaning. Taking Communion while in the pews has a sort of community feel—all people receive at the same time while served by members of the community. Receiving by intinction emphasizes the Eucharist, for the early worshipers prayed standing up during the time surrounding Easter—a sign of joyfulness rather than somberness. Gathering around a table set for participants depicts the Lord's Supper. Kneeling suggests a more penitential approach. As you plan for services that include the Table, (1) vary how you come to the Table, and (2) be intentional about your choices—know why you are choosing one mode on any given day.

Building the Structure

A group of believers has gathered to worship God; they have celebrated God's presence in Jesus Christ and have offered their praise and thanksgiving. The Scriptures have been read, and the word has been proclaimed. Now it is time to set the Table and to invite believers to the feast where God nourishes us and strengthens us to live as true disciples of his Son. Holy Communion is the third movement of the fourfold order of worship. It is an opportunity for the community of believers to respond to the revelation of God as heard through the read and proclaimed Word.

The suggested order of Communion given below begins following the sermon. It is then succeeded by the fourth movement of the service, the Sending.

If your denomination provides authorized services of Holy Communion, consult them and follow them. (Some denominations require the use of approved Communion liturgies.) In most cases you do not need to follow the same order rigidly, but neither should you ignore the incredible assimilation of worship elements provided by your denomination that have stood the test of time historically and theologically and which contain the theological perspective of your liturgical tradition. The order of this "service within a service" is not as flexible as that of baptism, in that more of a sequential drama is portrayed as the liturgical narrative unfolds. Still, there is room for some freedom and creativity. Just remember to keep the main thing the main thing; make sure the *primary* parts are the focal point. Never draw attention away from the most significant words and actions at the Table.

The Order of the Table of the Lord

The basic outline without commentary appears in appendix B.

At the risk of oversimplification, there are two broad approaches to the liturgy of the Table among Protestants.[21] One approach, most common to those who view the Table as an ordinance, might be called "the warrant form" and focuses on the words of institution as spoken by Jesus in the Gospel accounts of the Lord's Supper (or by Paul in 1 Cor. 11:23–27). The action is rooted (warranted) in the command of Christ to "do this." Typically, the liturgy is short, consisting of an opportunity for confession and the words of institution (which form the heart of the brief liturgy), followed by a spontaneous prayer, which may vary in purpose. A second approach is a "narrative form." It is more elaborate and sequential in nature as it recalls a fairly comprehensive story line of God's actions in history. (This narrative approach, which I recommend, is explained below in greater detail as the "Great Thanksgiving.")

The service outlined here is a sort of hybrid of these two approaches. Communion services will differ in length according to what is included on various occasions for various reasons. Two questions will guide you as you prepare for the Table. First, what elements are critical for the story line of God's redemption in Jesus Christ to be clear? Second, what order of events will help believers best offer their response to God? Here, then, is one possible order of service, beginning with the option of a congregational song that serves as a bridge from the Service of the Word to the Service of the Table.

Note: Various portions of Isaiah 55 are used as samples for this model service. The worship elements shown with titles on the left side of the page are considered necessary to the service; the elements shown with centered titles within brackets [ ] are optional but would add much to the service if included.

[A creed/affirmation of faith is appropriate
immediately following the sermon to conclude the Service of the Word.]

[Song transitioning from the Word]

Invitation to the Table

Invite the congregation to the Table.

Note: The invitation can be extended in any number of ways, such as a Scripture reading, a song, a litany, well-prepared spoken words, and so on.

Sample Scriptural Invitation to the Table[22]

- "Ho, everyone who thirsts, come to the waters; and you that have no money, come, buy and eat! Come, buy wine and milk without money and without price. Why do you spend your money for that which is not bread, and your labor for that which does not satisfy? Listen carefully to me, and eat what is good, and delight yourselves in rich food. Incline your ear, and come to me; listen, so that you may live." (Isa. 55:1–3a)

Confession of Sin

Invite the congregation to confession of sin. (For an outline of the prayer of confession, see appendix A.)

Sample Scriptural Invitation to Confession

- "Seek the LORD while he may be found, call upon him while he is near; let the wicked forsake their way, and the unrighteous their thoughts." (Isa. 55:6–7a)

Note: The prayer of confession may come through spoken prayer, unison prayer, silent prayer, a song, Scripture—in short, a variety of ways.

Assurance of Pardon (refer to appendix A)

Sample Assurance of Pardon

- Hear the good news: "[We have returned] to the LORD, that he may have mercy on [us], and to our God, for he will abundantly pardon." (Isa. 55:7b; adapted)

[The Passing of the Peace]

Note: This element of worship is a very long-standing tradition dating back to the ancient church. It consists of an exchange of words (and often gestures such as an embrace, a holy kiss, or a handshake) that signify reconciliation and Christian love. It is grounded in Jesus's admonition concerning relationships in the community: "So when you are offering your gift at the altar, if you remember that your brother or sister has something against you, leave your gift there before the altar and go; first be reconciled to your brother or sister, and then come and offer your gift" (Matt. 5:23–24). Right relationships with others are a prerequisite for true worship.

Sample wording:

Pastor: The peace of Christ be with you all.
People: And also with you.
Pastor: As we have been reconciled to God through Jesus Christ, let us also be at peace with one another.

[Offering]

The presenting of tithes and offerings is fitting here. As these are brought forward for dedication, so also bread and cup may be brought forward by laity and presented at the table along with monetary gifts. Songs may be sung during the presentation of all of these offerings to God.

The Prayer of Thanksgiving[23]

Give God thanks for the many acts of love and deliverance God has rendered throughout salvation history, most especially his greatest act of love in giving his only Son, Jesus Christ, as Savior for lost humanity.

Note: This prayer, so central to the eucharistic liturgy, is discussed in greater detail below. (See "Installing Doors and Windows.")

The Words of Institution

Note: These words from Scripture form a very critical part of the service, for they authoritatively establish the event.

Recite this text from the writings of the apostle Paul (1 Cor. 11:23–25), who, in turn, is quoting Jesus at the Last Supper:

"The Lord Jesus on the night when he was betrayed took a loaf of bread, and when he had given thanks, he broke it and said, 'This is my body that is for you. Do this in remembrance of me.' In the same way he took the cup also, after supper, saying, 'This cup is the new covenant in my blood. Do this, as often as you drink it, in remembrance of me.'"

Consecration of the Elements

Offer a prayer of blessing on the elements.

Note: In many denominations this prayer is an invocation of the Holy Spirit to be present in the bread and wine/juice.

Sample Prayers of Consecration

1. "God of all power, send your Holy Spirit upon us, that in sharing the bread we may share in the body of Christ, that in sharing the cup we may share in his blood. Grant that, being joined together in Christ Jesus, we may become united in faith and in all things become mature in the one who is our head."[24]

2. "Pour out your Holy Spirit on us gathered here and on these gifts of bread and wine. Make them be for us the body and blood of Christ that we may be for the world the body of Christ redeemed by his blood. Make us one with Christ, one with each other, and one in ministry to all the world until Christ comes in final victory and we feast at his heavenly banquet."[25]

[The Lord's Prayer]

[The Breaking of the Bread]

Note: Earlier, in the fourfold action of take, bless, break, and give, the common loaf was torn in two. If the celebrant wishes to simply observe a separate breaking of bread (a large wafer or common loaf), it is advised that he or she does not break the bread earlier but reserves the action for here.

The Distribution and Partaking

Distribute the elements according to the mode determined for the day.

Note: Words of distribution are recommended prior to or during the receiving of the elements.

Sample Words of Distribution

1. (Suggested when elements are received all at once.) "The body of our Lord Jesus Christ, which was given for you, preserve your soul and body

unto everlasting life. Take and eat this remembering that Christ died for you, and feed on Him in your heart, by faith, with thanksgiving.

"The blood of our Lord Jesus Christ, which was shed for you, preserve your soul and body unto everlasting life. Drink this remembering that Christ's blood was shed for you, and be thankful."[26]

2. (Suggested when elements are received individually, such as with intinction.) "The body of Christ given for you. The blood of Christ shed for you."

Concluding Prayer

After all have received and the Table is returned to order, offer a brief concluding prayer of thanks and rededication of ourselves to God's purposes.

OR

Benediction

A blessing is offered.

Sample

• "The grace of the Lord Jesus Christ, and the love of God, and the communion of the Holy Spirit be with you all. Amen."

[A Song of Praise]

Invite the congregation to sing a joyous song of celebration for the gifts received at the Table.

The worship service now resumes with the Sending. In keeping with the use of Isaiah 55 throughout this service, consider concluding with Isaiah 55:12–13: "For you shall go out in joy, and be led back in peace; the mountains and the hills before you shall burst into song, and all the trees of the field shall clap their hands. Instead of the thorn shall come up the cypress; instead of the brier shall come up the myrtle; and it shall be to the LORD for a memorial, for an everlasting sign that shall not be cut off."

Do you see how the order of service provides the story line? Look back over the order of the Table, and you will note how the service moves from invitation to the meal, preparation to receive the meal, thanksgiving, instructions concerning the importance of the meal, sanctification of the meal, eating of the meal, and a concluding prayer that dedicates us to God's service as a result of being strengthened by the meal. The sequence of events portrays the good

news: we are called by God, are made right with God, celebrate God's acts
of salvation, receive instruction, are set apart for service, are nourished for
service, and offer ourselves anew to God's purposes. The Table of the Lord
depicts the story of God through word, action, and symbol!

Installing Doors and Windows

After the rituals architect has arranged the order for the Lord's Table, more
detailed choices can be made for appropriate songs, prayers, Scripture readings, and other worship acts, so that the community can engage as full participants in this movement of the worship service. Thought must also be given
to relevant symbols related to the Table and also to the Christian year. These
worship acts function like doors and windows; they "let in light" and encourage relationship with God and others. The rituals architect is interested in
discovering means by which worshipers can encounter God and one another
through *experiencing* the ritual.

Suggested Songs

The church has inherited many songs that communicate and facilitate the
Lord's Supper, and more are being written all the time. The ones suggested
below represent a variety of styles of congregational song. To help you locate
these songs, the author's name is included.

An Upper Room Did Our Lord Prepare (Fred Pratt Green)
As We Gather at Your Table (Carl P. Daw)
Bread of the World (Reginald Heber)
Come, Share the Feast (Bryan Jeffery Leech)
Come, Sinners, to the Gospel Feast (Charles Wesley)
Eat This Bread (from the Community of Taize and Robert Batastini)
For the Bread Which You Have Broken (Louis F. Benson)
Gather Us In (Marty Haugen)
Here, O My Lord, I See You Face to Face (Horatius Bonar)
I Come with Joy (Brian Wren)
In Remembrance of Me (Ragan Courtney)
Let All Mortal Flesh Keep Silence (Liturgy of St. James; ancient Latin hymn)
Let Us Break Bread Together (African American spiritual)
Now Let Us from This Table Rise (Fred Kaan)
One Bread, One Body (John B. Foley)

Table of Plenty (Daniel L. Schutte)
This Is the Threefold Truth (Fred Pratt Green)
We Remember You (Walt Harrah)
You Satisfy the Hungry Heart (Omer Westendorf)

Scripture Passages

Start collecting Scripture passages that pertain to the Table. Here are a few with which to begin your list.

Exodus 12:1–20	Luke 22:14–20	John 6:30–58
Psalm 103:1–12	Luke 24:28–35	1 Corinthians 11:23–26
Matthew 11:28–29	John 3:16–17	Revelation 5:11–14

Prayers

The service of Holy Communion uses various standard prayer types in order to facilitate the people-to-God conversation at the Table. The sample service above employed a prayer of confession, a prayer of thanksgiving, a prayer of consecration, and so on. Rather than exploring each of these individual prayer forms, some of which are addressed elsewhere in this book, let's devote our attention instead to a brief overview of a prayer that holds great significance for the church—the prayer known as the "Great Thanksgiving."[27]

The Great Thanksgiving is a eucharistic prayer with ancient roots that has developed over centuries and is still used widely today. It is called the Great Thanksgiving because the giving of thanks is the theme of the prayer throughout. It is truly a prayer of praise to God for all of God's activity in the world: creation, faithfulness after the fall, the gift of the covenant, deliverance from Egypt, the establishment of the Law, the sending of the prophets, and so on. It culminates in praise for the cosmic work of Jesus Christ—his life, death, resurrection, ascension, and coming again. Thanks are also given for the gift of the Holy Spirit and the establishment of the church. As you can see, the prayer is all-encompassing in scope and deeply rich in theological underpinnings. It is also highly biblical in content, for it traces God's story from creation to re-creation, using the biblical narrative to do so. The main thing to note is that when one prays the Great Thanksgiving, the entire service of Eucharist becomes one big prayer.

To our knowledge, the earliest worshiping communities who used this eucharistic prayer are Rome, Alexandria, and Antioch.[28] It is remarkable to consider that the earliest extant version of the Great Thanksgiving dates from

c. AD 215.[29] This eucharistic prayer is attributed to Hippolytus (AD 170–235), presbyter of the church at Rome, in his early liturgical treatise *Apostolic Tradition*. Even more remarkable are the comparisons between this prayer and liturgical material found in the writings of Justin Martyr as early as c. AD 155,[30] suggesting that the shape and content of the Great Thanksgiving are rooted in the earliest of apostolic times. In fact, the structure of the Great Thanksgiving "appears in documents written before the canon of New Testament Scriptures was finally determined and is at least as old as any creed."[31]

Historically the general outline of the prayer has remained relatively stable, yet "its text was subject to constant development and revision, so that it varied considerably from church to church and from period to period, and even . . . from celebrant to celebrant."[32] There is no such thing as *the* Great Thanksgiving if by that one means a sample prayer handed down in universal form from generation to generation. The prayer was never considered to be a rigid formula to be followed in the same way throughout Christendom; rather, the church allowed for flexibility and cultural expression. Over the centuries, numerous versions of the eucharistic prayer have appeared. The work of liturgical historians in the twentieth century has done much to acquaint modern Protestant worshipers with the richness of this prayer. Today many denominations have their own authorized version of it for use within their churches. At the same time, as has always been the case, the greater point is not that the "right" prayer is used but that the Eucharist is an occasion for giving thanks to God for *all* God has done throughout salvation history, especially in the person and work of Jesus Christ. Following the outline of this prayer simply assures us that we are comprehensive and true in our thanksgiving.

With the many eucharistic prayers in use today, it is not possible (nor desirable) to come to uniform practice. Nevertheless, a strong consensus of form is noteworthy.[33]

Opening Dialogue: An exchange between prayer participants (pastor and people)

Here the corporate and dialogical nature of the prayer is established. One common exchange between the "partners in prayer" is:

Pastor: The Lord be with you.
People: And also with you.
Pastor: Lift up your hearts.
People: We lift them up to the Lord.[34]
Pastor: Let us give thanks to the Lord our God.
People: It is right to give him thanks and praise!

Preface: Thanks and praise to God encompassing
a general narration of salvation history or a specific work
of God in Christ related to a particular season or occasion

The theme of the prayer is expressed beautifully in Ephesians 1:3: "Blessed
be the God and Father of our Lord Jesus Christ, who has blessed us in Christ
with every spiritual blessing in the heavenly places." [35]

Congregational Acclamation of Praise: A response of praise
for what God has done in Christ is offered by the people

The congregation recites together (or sings) these lines (from Isa. 6:3 and
Ps. 118:26):

Holy, holy, holy Lord, God of power and might,[36]
Heaven and earth are full of your glory.
Hosanna in the highest.
Blessed is he who comes in the name of the Lord.
Hosanna in the highest.

Words of Institution: A recitation of the authoritative words
used by Jesus to institute the Lord's Supper

The pastor states, "While they were eating, Jesus took a loaf of bread, and
after blessing it he broke it, gave it to the disciples, and said, 'Take, eat; this
is my body.' Then he took a cup, and after giving thanks he gave it to them,
saying, 'Drink from it, all of you; for this is my blood of the covenant, which
is poured out for many for the forgiveness of sins'" (Matt. 26:26–28).

Congregational Affirmation of Faith: A brief creedal statement
is affirmed

All state together, "Christ has died, Christ is risen, Christ will come
again."[37]

Remembering the Work of Jesus Christ: In praying this prayer
we remember all that Christ has done and offer ourselves anew
to God's service

"We remember the life, death, resurrection, ascension, and coming again
of Jesus Christ—his work past, present, and future."[38]

Invocation of the Holy Spirit:[39] God is asked to send
the Holy Spirit upon the gifts and the assembled congregation[40]

The Holy Spirit's presence causes us to benefit from Communion.

"Lord, our God, send your Holy Spirit so that this bread and cup may be for us the body and blood of our Lord Jesus Christ. May we and all your saints be united with Christ and remain faithful in hope and love. Gather your whole church, O Lord, into the glory of your kingdom."[41]

Trinitarian Doxology and Amen: Words (song) of praise for the triune God

The prayer concludes with a Trinitarian statement of praise.

SAMPLE

"Through him, with him, in him, in the unity of the Holy Spirit, all honor and glory are yours, Almighty Father, now and forever. Amen."[42]

(Often the Lord's Prayer follows as an additional corporate conclusion.)

Note four important aspects of the Great Thanksgiving: (1) it is Trinitarian in form (it begins by thanking God the Father, centers on the salvific work of Christ, and invokes the Holy Spirit); (2) it is a biblical narrative; (3) it is a corporate prayer—highly participatory in structure; and (4) it is creedal in nature.

Symbols

The primary symbols representing the Christ Event at the Table are the loaf of bread (symbolizing the body of Christ) and the cup of wine (symbolizing the blood of Christ). These are the primary symbols because they were assigned significance by Jesus while keeping the Passover feast with his disciples on the evening before his death (Mark 14:22–24). The loaf of bread and the chalice of wine are universally recognized symbols among Christians for the body and blood of our Lord—symbols of the new covenant instituted by Jesus for his followers.

Other symbols, such as the cross, may be useful as the meaning of Holy Communion unfolds, but the loaf and chalice are most representative of the meal.

The Christian Year

The Christian year is a celebration of the intersection of time: God's time with our time. When *kairos* (a Greek word for "time" suggesting God's momentous time of action) meets *chronos* (a Greek word for "time" suggesting the societal way we mark time chronologically), we experience the God who exists *outside* of time, meeting us *inside* our time for the purpose of relationship. When we celebrate the events of the Christian year, we are simply marking our calendar time (*chronos*) by noting how God has entered human time to perform mighty deeds of salvation throughout history (*kairos*).

Sunday to Sunday—Lord's Day to Lord's Day—is the fundamental cycle of time within the Christian year. For the earliest Christians, time was no longer marked by the recurring Sabbath but by the recurring Lord's Day. Because Jesus was raised to life on the first day of the week—Sunday—the earliest disciples celebrated the resurrection weekly as they gathered to worship. The weekly celebration of Eucharist became a central feature of Lord's Day worship. Every Sunday is Easter Sunday; therefore, every Sunday is appropriate for gathering around the Table of the Lord. That God raised Christ from the dead was a *kairos* moment; that we celebrate the greatest of all saving events on Sunday is a *chronos* moment. The weekly celebration of Eucharist is the most basic celebration of the Christian year in that it is the central piece to God's story. In short, it's always time for Eucharist!

While the celebration of Eucharist is fitting every time the church gathers for Lord's Day worship, other days and seasons of the Christian year are particularly fitting for Eucharist too. Many churches that do not celebrate weekly Eucharist plan for monthly or quarterly dates to ensure that it is received regularly. Approaching it that way may "get it taken care of," but that is hardly the point. Why not consider the many striking possibilities for partaking of the bread and the cup that are related to the Christian year? Here are a few suggestions for especially relevant times for celebrating the Table.

- The first Sunday of Advent (anticipating the Lord's return)
- Christmas Sunday (in celebration of the incarnation)
- Epiphany (Christ is manifested to the Gentiles)
- Ash Wednesday (the call to solemn reflection)
- Throughout the Lenten season (in recognition of Christ's passion)
- Maundy Thursday (recalling the Lord's institution of the meal)
- Good Friday (remembering Christ's death)
- Easter Sunday (remembering the resurrection)
- Ascension Day (foreshadowing the heavenly banquet to come)
- Pentecost Sunday (recalling how, as a result of Pentecost, the new community gathered often, perhaps daily, to break bread)

- World Communion Sunday (in celebration of the unity of the worldwide communion of Christians)[43]
- Christ the King Sunday (in celebration of the exaltation of Jesus Christ)

It is exciting to think about the many days and seasons of the Christian year that hold real meaning for experiencing the Lord's Table. Begin to connect the many dimensions of the bread and the cup with the story of God, and it will no longer be a matter of "scheduling Communion"; instead, you will experience your place in God's story through your place at the Table.

Serving as Hospitable Host

Presiding at the Eucharist is an incredible privilege and joy. It is also a wonderful opportunity to serve the community gathered before God. The Lord Jesus Christ is the real host at the Table, yet God uses people to serve as Christ's hands and voice as the community breaks bread. The physical and emotional presence of the presider is extremely important; gestures and words offered at the Table should contribute to rather than detract from the sacred action. Certain skills must be developed in order to lead well. An effective officiant will communicate the story of the Table through his or her dramatic presence and well-rehearsed actions. As you gain experience and skill in presiding at the Table of the Lord, keep your primary role in mind: *you are a host at a meal on behalf of Christ.*

Credentials

As was the case for baptism, most denominations require that a person be ordained in order to preside at the Table of the Lord.[44] The ordained clergyperson is understood to be fulfilling a priestly role in administration of the sacraments/ordinances. Make sure you know your church's view on exactly who may preside at the Table, and respect that position. The words and gestures used in Communion carry significance. Theological preparation, pastoral guidance, and skill in implementing and leading the service are critical, whether the leader is ordained or not, so that the sacrament can fulfill God's expectations for the event.

Duties

As you prepare for presiding at the Table, you will find there are several important duties that, when fulfilled well, will provide the service with integrity and instill greater confidence in the leader.

Pre-Communion Duties: The Preparation of Setting and Elements

- Center the Table in the chancel area (platform). Make sure that there is enough space to stand behind the table, facing the people, as you preside. Also leave room to walk all around the table in case you need to move back and forth to assist servers.

- Cover the table with a white cloth or other color appropriate to the liturgical season. Remove all other items from the table except those directly related to Communion. (Two candles may remain if so desired.)

- Arrange for a plate (paten) with a whole loaf of bread to be on the table. This visual image of one loaf provides a symbol of unity among God's people. Don't cover up the loaf; you don't want to hide the symbol.

- Plan for a large goblet (chalice) to sit beside the paten. If desired, include a pitcher (flagon) with grape juice/wine for pouring into the chalice. If the pitcher is present, it will sit behind the plate and chalice.

- The traditional placement of the vessels is (from the view of the congregant facing the table) paten on the left and chalice on the right.

- Do not cover the trays, plates, or cup with white cloths. This practice developed many years ago to prevent insects from having their own feast prior to the congregation partaking. Covering the elements bears no theological or liturgical purpose. Besides, it reduces the powerful symbolic communication available when the bread and the cup are *seen*.

- Prepare the elements according to the mode you have decided on for receiving Communion.

  NOTES

- Even if individual pieces of bread and cups are used, have the loaf and chalice on the table as symbols of the unity of the body.

- If servers will hold loaves of bread, wrap the bread in a white cloth or paper napkin. The server will break off a piece of bread and hand it to the communicant to alleviate sanitary concerns (as opposed to many people picking at the bread). It also assures an appropriate-sized piece is available for intinction.

- The use of leavened or unleavened bread is a decision for you to make. Either one is fine.

- Some communities accommodate those who have health issues related to the elements. You may wish to consider providing gluten-free bread.

- Most Protestants use grape juice instead of wine, but if wine is served, offer the option of alcohol-free wine for those who prefer or need it.

These considerations are issues of hospitality at the Table.

Communicating with Servers

I highly recommended that pastors train all persons who serve Communion on a regular basis. Educating parishioners in the background and importance of the Table is part of providing good discipleship. They will not only learn how to assist in Communion; the Table will take on a whole new meaning for them. Be careful to choose participants that represent diverse ages, races, and genders. Don't forget about inviting older children and youth to serve the elements, provided they are able to receive Communion in your community.

Communicate these things with servers:

1. when to come forward;
2. where to stand;
3. what to wear;
4. what to say ("The body of Christ," "The blood of Christ");
5. to look into the eyes of each communicant;
6. to smile;
7. what to do if they are finished before other servers;
8. when to serve each other;
9. how to serve musicians who are involved during Communion;
10. how to serve young children;
11. what to do with leftover elements.

Post-Communion Duties: Your Hospitality Is Extended

- If any bread or juice/wine remains after all have been served, it is first of all returned to the Table until the conclusion of the service. At that point, two options exist for disposing of the unused elements; either one is appropriate. Option 1: The elements are ingested immediately, typically by the officiant. Option 2: They are returned to the earth (placed/poured on the ground for nature to take its course). They are not to be casually discarded in the trash or sink. The elements have been consecrated. No matter what your view regarding the form of the elements after consecration, they have been set aside for a holy purpose and should therefore be handled in ways appropriate for sanctified items.[45]

- Plan to take Communion to church members who are physically unable to come to church, such as homebound people, those in nursing homes, those in prisons, and so on. It is the duty of the church to see to it that those who are physically prevented from attending are not without the sacrament. When bringing Communion to these church members, make every effort to take at least a few church members with you, so that the sense of community can be strengthened. Communion in these contexts differs in two ways. First, given that the Table was duly instituted and the elements have already been blessed in the worship service, it is not necessary to repeat these parts of the liturgy. Do read Scripture, pray, sing, pray the Lord's Prayer, and remind these parishioners of God's love and forgiveness through Jesus Christ. Second, most denominations do not require that ordained clergy preside on these occasions if the elements have been duly instituted, though it is appreciated by the recipients, and it affords one more occasion for personal contact and pastoral care. At the same time, it is appropriate, even special, for deacons, elders, or other appointed members to carry out this vital mission.

Attributes for Presiding

Any effective host will learn the art of excellent hospitality. Some pastors will not feel adequate or comfortable with this role at first. That's okay; it can be learned over time. Some leaders come by it naturally, but even so, there is always room for improvement. Here are a few relevant attributes that you should foster over time for presiding at the Table.

Demeanor

Seek to portray a welcoming demeanor at the Table by considering these aspects.

- Your facial expression should exude joy. Even if you emphasize the Memorialist view, the cross is *good* news!
- Appear relaxed without being nonchalant.
- Do not appear stern or harsh. You are inviting folks to a *meal*; be pleasant.
- Be *authentically* passionate and compelling as you lead. Do not appear unemotional or disengaged. Enter into the event in its fullness. This will convince others that it is important.
- Be personable. When you serve individuals, communicate personally, look directly into their eyes, and use their names.

Attire

What you wear at the Table matters. Some pastors wear robes. This has its benefits, for it removes the possibility for distractions stemming from one's clothes. It also helps to place the event in a liturgical context. If robes are not worn, male clergy should wear dress slacks and shirt, tie, and sports jacket or suit; women clergy should wear a professional-looking suit or dress. Each local congregation has different expectations. Nevertheless, presiders should dress respectfully and professionally, even in the most casual of churches.

Focus

As much as is possible, keep your focus on Jesus Christ as you preside. The best way to do this is to fully engage with whatever liturgy you are using. Enter into the prayers, the songs, the words, the gestures. Let the liturgy be *your* prayer on behalf of the people. This will help you to concentrate on what really matters in the event.

Administration

It's always a good idea to keep track of the facts related to taking Communion. Record the date each time you serve the Lord's Table at your church (which is easy to do if you serve it weekly!). Note the mode you used, who helped you serve, what Scriptures were read, and so on. Keeping this type of record will make sure that you are offering Communion often enough and that you are providing a variety of approaches, as suggested by the various words for the Table used in Scripture.

Skill

Presiding at Eucharist as an effective host requires some very particular skills. Words and gestures merge to become one dramatic moment of encounter with God. It will take time to hone these skills. Be patient. And try to think of them less as skills than as *prayer*. When you lead at the Table, you are *really* leading your people in prayer. If you can think of improving your leadership in *prayer* as opposed to improving a *skill set*, you will much more capture the spirit of these duties.

Some skills in leading at the Table have to do with leading the scriptural fourfold action, speaking the words, memorizing, and praying the liturgy.

The scriptural fourfold action involves gestures at the Table. Four incredibly important sequential actions are fundamental to presiding at the Table: take, bless, break, give. These actions were modeled for us when Jesus instituted the Lord's Supper the night before he died. The actions are very clearly stated in the Synoptic Gospel accounts: "Then he [Jesus] *took* a loaf of bread, and when he had *given thanks*, he *broke* it and *gave* it to them" (Luke 22:19, emphasis added; see also Matt. 26:26 and Mark 14:22).

First, Jesus *took*. He placed his hands on particular items (bread and wine) as a means of selecting them for his purposes. Second, he offered a prayer of *blessing* upon the items.[46] He gave thanks. Third, he *broke* the bread so that it could be shared. Fourth, he *gave* it to those who had gathered so they could be filled.

It is not insignificant that this same fourfold action is used at other meals over which Jesus presided prior to his ascension. The various accounts of

Jesus feeding the crowd of five thousand people indicate these identical actions: "taking the five loaves and the two fish, he looked up to heaven, and
blessed and broke the loaves, and gave them to the disciples, and the disciples
gave them to the crowds" (Matt. 14:19; see also Mark 6:41 and Luke 9:16).
Remarkably, the very same gestures are found when Jesus presided as host
for two of his disciples in Emmaus on the evening of his resurrection (Luke
24:30). Clearly, this fourfold action, by virtue of its chronic repetition in
Scripture, is a pattern for us to follow as we preside. It forms the core of our
words and gestures at the Table as we serve as host at the church's holy meals
just as Jesus did.

Make the most of these important gestures. Let them be four distinct,
dramatic movements in the liturgy. While speaking the words of institution,
physically demonstrate each one as you face the people while standing behind
the table: "On the night in which Jesus gave himself up for us[47]

- he took bread [pick up the loaf and lift it shoulder-high],
- gave thanks [raise the bread high before the people and glance heavenward],
- broke the bread [lower the loaf back to shoulder height and tear the loaf
  apart],
- gave it to his disciples [spread your arms apart at a natural elevation as
  in a gesture of giving; moving from the waist, gently and slowly sweep
  the congregation from left to right as you symbolically give to one and
  all, while scanning the crowd with your eyes and continuing the words of
  institution], and said, 'Take, eat; this is my body given for you. Do this
  in remembrance of me.' [Return the loaf to the plate.]

"When the supper was over

- he took the cup [pick up the chalice with both hands and lift it shoulder-
  high],
- gave thanks to you [raise the cup high, glancing heavenward],
- gave it to his disciples [lower the cup to shoulder height and, moving from
  the waist, gently and slowly sweep the congregation from left to right as
  you symbolically offer the cup to one and all, scanning the crowd with
  your eyes and continuing the words of institution], and said, 'Drink from
  this, all of you; this is my blood of the new covenant, poured out for you
  and for many for the forgiveness of sins. Do this, as often as you drink it
  in remembrance of me.'" [Return the cup to the table.]

Helpful tips for leading this aspect of Communion:

1. Take your time. Move slowly. Pause between each gesture. Draw out this meaningful action.
2. Score the bread. Ask those preparing the elements to partially slice the loaf of bread so that it will tear much more easily for you. It can help avoid an obvious tug-of-war between loaf and pastor!
3. Don't bounce. One of the most common mistakes that beginners make is that while holding the bread, the hands move up and down in rhythm to what is being spoken. Keep your hands still while you are speaking.

I have explained the scriptural fourfold actions at the Table in some detail because of their significance. In addition to their long-standing use historically, the four physical actions contain a more profound meaning; they are the symbolic portrayal of Jesus's passion. These actions are not only about food and drink; they reflect the grand, sweeping movements of the gospel itself, for in the fourfold action resides the good news: Jesus was taken by God the Father to be sent into the world (John 17:3, 8), Jesus was blessed by his Father at his baptism (Matt. 3:17), Jesus was broken by his Father as a sacrifice (Isa. 53:10), and Jesus was given to the world as Savior (John 3:16). When leaders employ the fourfold action of take, bless, break, and give, they not only emulate Jesus's own actions at the meals he served but announce the more significant work of God in Jesus Christ. This fourfold action both tells and portrays the good news!

The Words Spoken at the Table

A hospitable host at any event will recognize and use just the right words that will enable those present to be full participants in the action. If you recall someone who has the gift of hospitality, you will immediately be able to identify some of the things they normally say to make the gathering the meaningful occasion that it is. When you arrive at their house for a dinner party, for instance, you will be greeted warmly, invited in, introduced to others, be told how the meal will be served, where you will sit, and so on. Exactly *what* words are used and *how* they are spoken are very important to the success of the dinner.

An effective leader at the Table will carefully prepare the words she or he will speak and also how they will be spoken, so that others are fully able to enter into the meal in a manner that is honoring to Christ, the true Host of the dinner. In many churches within the Free Church tradition, these words are often performed ad lib, with the possible exception of the words of institution. Likewise, the prayers are offered extemporaneously. If you serve the Lord's Supper in this type of context, I urge you to begin to think carefully about what you will say at the service of the Table and start to place in order particular words you will use—words both to the community (horizontal direction) and to God (vertical direction). Preparation is highly advisable in any tradition. It will ensure that the meal is more in keeping with scriptural and historical expectations and will improve the sense of hope and joy your congregants will experience at the Table. If you serve within a tradition that has created resources for words to be used as you preside, take full advantage of these texts. They will bring richness and depth to worship and provide greater assurance that what you are doing as leader is in keeping with scriptural and historical norms.

Memorize your words! This is very important, for you want to be free to move and gesture throughout the Communion liturgy. However simple or involved, memorize the words you will speak, whatever they are. Be patient with yourself—remember that memorization takes time. Ease into it slowly by speaking only a small portion from memory if need be. Start with memorizing the words of institution, and then go from there. The key to memorization is repetition. I make it a habit to pray the Great Thanksgiving while on my daily walk or in daily devotions. This helps me to remember to review it and also enriches my time with God. The people you love who are gathered around the Table will greatly appreciate the intentionality and care with which you choose and use words in the service, for you will be able to better focus on them as guests on behalf of Christ.

Remember that your leadership is prayer. One of the skills you will need to nurture as leader is to remember that *all* of the words and gestures you offer at the Table constitute prayer. This one feature can transform your leadership as you preside at the Table. Begin to see yourself as one who is praying on behalf of those gathered, rather than someone who is simply trying to facilitate a portion of a worship service. The more that *you really pray the liturgy*, the more the participants will understand what is going on. The Communion liturgy, of course, will use corporate pronouns so that worshipers will understand that while it is your voice that is speaking, it's really the prayer of the community offered to God. I also encourage you to bring any of the prayers you lead in worship into your own prayer life (not vice versa). For instance, pray the invocation you will use for Sunday's worship during your own daily prayer times. It will transform your leadership to the glory of God and the benefit of others.

Other Considerations

Don't substitute the elements. Sometimes, in the interest of being clever or creative, leaders will suggest that elements other than bread and wine/juice are substituted for Communion. This is strongly discouraged.[48] In fact, some leaders believe that to serve anything other than bread and the fruit of the vine "is an act of disobedience,"[49] given Jesus's clear instructions concerning the symbols. He was very direct in saying that the bread specifically "is my body" and the wine "is my blood." In referring to substituting other elements, David P. Scaer writes, "Such a ritual can be sacramental . . . but it is not a sacrament instituted by Christ."[50] *Christ* established the relationship between the food and drink ingested at Communion and the truth each represents. "The external elements of the sacraments as signs correspond to what the sacraments are and do. Like water in baptism, bread and wine are not arbitrarily chosen, but their external forms convey and correspond to the heavenly things they contain. . . . Fittingly, Jesus describes himself as 'bread' (John 6:33, 35, 48, 51) and the 'vine' (John 15:1), which is the source of wine."[51] Be careful to be faithful to the symbols established by our Lord in instituting the Lord's Supper.

Anointing with Oil

There is no particularly strong historical connection between Communion and anointing with oil. The closest precedence we have for their combination in worship is the service of baptism in the early church, an occasion when anointing with oil (chrismation) and celebrating the Eucharist followed water baptism. Beyond this, little is available for suggesting their coexistence in worship. However, with the development of the charismatic renewal movement of the mid-twentieth century, offering the anointing with oil with prayers for healing and wholeness became a fairly common feature at Communion services in charismatic churches. This practice has spread and is now used in various denominations with great appreciation. Just because there are not substantial biblical or historical reasons for combining Eucharist and anointing with oil does not preclude the practice. It can be a very meaningful time to experience God. Some groups refer to the anointing with oil following Communion as "ministry time." Typically, it is handled in this way:

- After individual persons have taken the bread and cup, they are free, if they so desire, to approach a prayer station where one or two leaders are ready to anoint with oil and pray for each person as the Communion service proceeds. (Depending on the size of the crowd, more than one station may be helpful at different spots surrounding the seating.)
- The leaders at these stations should be persons of known integrity and prayer.
- The leaders should be prepared in advance by the clergy.
- The leaders ask the persons who approach in what way they desire prayer.
- Using olive oil (purchased in a small vial at Christian supply houses), put a small amount on your thumb and make the sign of the cross on the

forehead of the one requesting prayer. Slowly speak this blessing, "May God the Father, God the Son, and God the Holy Spirit bring peace to you—body, mind, soul, and spirit. Amen."

• Offer an extemporaneous prayer of intercession for the individual.

Anointing with oil following Communion serves as an extension of the Communion service and offers people yet another highly symbolic and sensory occasion to experience the holy touch of God. Remember that this part of the service is voluntary. The pastor should not pressure people to participate. Simply offer it as an option for those who desire it. Congregational singing during Communion and anointing with oil are especially powerful additions to the service.

Challenging Circumstances

Sometimes matters related to the Table pose awkward or challenging situations. Be prepared.

Children

There is a difference of opinion within Protestantism concerning the age that is considered appropriate for young children to fully participate in Holy Communion. Be sure to become acquainted with your church's position concerning children and Holy Communion. In many traditions baptism is the threshold for receiving Communion. If infants are baptized, then very young children may participate in the meal. Other traditions designate personal conversion as the criterion for baptism. In this case the age of the child will vary. Still others designate confirmation as the appropriate time for youth to receive their first Communion. Educate your congregation (especially parents of young children) concerning your church's view of children and Communion. If young children are not served Communion due to your church's particular theological position, I strongly advise that the children are nevertheless invited to come forward to receive a blessing. This will enable the children to feel welcomed and included in the experience. In this case the pastor should bend to look into the face of the young child, place a hand on the child's head, and speak a blessing upon him or her, reminding the child of God's love. These can be very special moments in the life of the child and, indeed, the whole community.

Not for the Wedding Couple Alone

The case has been made for the Lord's Supper as a corporate act of ecclesial communities. It is simply unbiblical to offer the bread and cup to some members of a community and not others. It has become popular in some circles for the wedding couple to desire private Holy Communion as a part of the ceremony. This practice is directly opposed to any New Testament or historical understanding of the nature of the Table. It should not be permitted. However, given that a Christian wedding is a service of worship, Communion could be offered to all Christians present. This would maintain the corporate nature of the Table while offering the bride and groom a meaningful experience (though having a meaningful experience isn't the goal of the Lord's Supper).

If the couple elects to have Holy Communion served to the gathered body, some obstacles and logistical considerations would need to be overcome. How would it be served? How would unbelievers be advised against the taking of the elements? How would the Communion and wedding liturgies merge? And so on. Resolutions to these questions can be achieved, but will take thought and preparation.

Ethical Considerations

Sometimes ethical considerations related to Communion come into play.

Refusing a Communicant

Are there occasions when someone desiring Communion should be denied? Now we're back to the discussion surrounding the fencing of the table. When confession was made in advance of Communion, as was John Calvin's practice in the sixteenth century, folks had the opportunity to become right with God and others prior to partaking of the elements. The refusing of communicants happened significantly *prior* to coming to the Table. Today in many churches, prayers of confession (if made at all) come at the same time the elements are offered, creating a situation whereby it is all but impossible for a pastor to know what is in the heart of those coming forward to receive the elements. I do not recommend that anyone be denied the bread and the cup on the spot, except under the most extreme circumstances.[52] If the pastor has very serious doubts as to a person's spiritual readiness for Communion based on hard evidence of faithless living, I advise that he or she initiate a conversation with the individual before Communion is served the next time, in order to discuss with them their spiritual state in relation to receiving the bread and cup. Such a conversation holds the potential for being a wonderfully redemptive opportunity. Generally, people appreciate accountability. Don't approach them with an accusatory or condemning spirit, but invite them to share where they presently are in their life of faith. Use the conversation as an open door to promote spiritual formation in the lives of others.

Wine or Juice

Deciding on serving real wine or grape juice doesn't have to be a big deal. Very likely your own denomination will specify which of these may be used. Be sure to know its position. However, if wine is served, I do recommend a nonalcoholic wine be available for those who must drink only nonalcoholic beverages.

Conclusion

Matthew was right. The family dinner was very special on Sunday—not because of the beautiful table or delicious food, but because the love that was shared that day warmed everyone's heart. It was good to be together as family, with everyone at the table once again. He would remember this event for a long time to come.

Key Terms

anaphora Another term for the Great Thanksgiving/eucharistic prayer.

canon Another term for the Great Thanksgiving/eucharistic prayer.

celebrant The individual who leads ("celebrates") Communion.

chalice The goblet containing the juice/wine.

closed Communion Communion that is available only to church members of a particular denomination.

common cup Communicants drink from one chalice.

Communion Partaking of the bread and the cup in a manner that emphasizes the fellowship of believers.

elements The bread, wine, and water used in the sacraments.

elevation The raising (elevating) of the bread and the cup.

epiclesis Calling upon the Holy Spirit to be present in the elements.

Eucharist "Thanksgiving"; suggests a joyful celebration at the Table.

eucharistic prayer Another name for the Great Thanksgiving.

fraction The physical breaking of the bread/wafer.

Great Thanksgiving The primary prayer at the Table, which (1) praises God, (2) rehearses God's saving acts, and (3) asks for a blessing on the elements and on us.

host From the Latin *hostia* (meaning "victim"); the large unleavened wafer used at Communion, signifying the body of Christ.

Institution The recitation of Jesus's words at the table in the upper room authorizing the new covenant.

intinction Dipping the bread/wafer into the chalice of juice/wine; from the Latin *intingo*, meaning "I dip in."

Memorialist view Perceiving Communion as a remembrance of a past event, the death of Christ; associated with the term "Lord's Supper"; often associated with Zwingli's nonsacramental view of the Table.

open Communion Communion that is available to anyone who is a disciple of Jesus Christ.

paten The plate containing the bread/wafers.

pedocommunion Serving Communion to young children.

sanctus Latin for "holy"; the response sung during Communion, "Holy, holy, holy Lord, God of power and might."

transubstantiation The belief that the material elements of bread and wine are miraculously transformed into the real body and blood of Jesus Christ.

To Learn More

Armstrong, John H., ed., and Paul E. Engle, series ed. *Understanding Four Views on the Lord's Supper*. Grand Rapids: Zondervan, 2007.

Baptism, Eucharist and Ministry. Geneva: World Council of Churches, 1982.

Galbreath, Paul. *Leading from the Table*. Herndon, VA: Alban Institute, 2008.

Watkins, Keith. *The Great Thanksgiving*. St. Louis: Chalice, 1995.

White, James F. *The Sacraments in Protestant Practice and Faith*. Nashville: Abingdon, 1999.

Wright, Tom. *The Meal Jesus Gave Us: Understanding Holy Communion*. Louisville: Westminster John Knox, 1999.

Engage

After expanding your understanding of the meaning of the Table of the Lord, individually or with others, evaluate your current practice of the Table. Here are a few approaches you may take:

1. Review the order of service for the last six times your church has served Communion. Take a look at the songs that surround Communion. What tone does the music establish for your service?

2. Review the prayers and other parts of the liturgy. If you had to describe the current focus of your Communion service in one word, what would it be?

3. Which of the four biblical terms for the Table most often represents your church's approach to the Table (Eucharist, Communion, Lord's Supper, breaking of bread)? If you wanted to move toward a different approach, which one would you choose? Why?

4. Write out an invitation to the Table that is well suited to your congregation.

6

The Healing Service

Explore

Before reading chapter 6, reflect on your own experience of prayers for healing.

- What is your favorite story of Jesus healing someone? Why?
- Have you ever attended a service that was advertised as a healing service? Describe the event as if you were a reporter. What occurred? Separately, describe your own impressions or thoughts concerning the event in journal form.
- Have you ever watched a television episode of a faith healer? What questions, if any, did it raise in your mind?
- Read Mark 5:25–34. Note five observations you make concerning this miracle.

Now that you have begun to reflect on the healing service, expand your thinking by reading chapter 6.

Expand

Laura's father, Ron, had been ill for a couple of months. He caught a very bad cold in October, but he thought he was getting over it. Things took a turn for the worse in November, when his congestion developed into pneumonia. His brief hospital stay relieved the fluid in his lungs, but his breathing had not yet returned to normal. He went back to work, though his chest still ached and he was exhausted. Now it was December, and Ron really needed a little more time off; but feeling lousy or not, he couldn't afford to miss any more work. His supervisor at the construction site was already unhappy about the week he had taken off while hospitalized. Now Ron was faced with a tough decision: return to work on Monday or lose his job.

Laura was worried about her dad. Her friend Allison suggested that Ron attend a Sunday evening healing service at her church. Laura had never heard of such a thing. Allison explained that her pastor held these services two Sunday evenings a month in the small chapel of her church. She said the services did not look at all like the healing services in big arenas the two girls had seen on TV one night during a sleepover. Allison had even attended once or twice with her mom. She explained that a few dozen folks from her church joined Pastor Harris for a brief worship service that included some soft singing and quiet prayers. He prayed for anyone who was hurting, for whatever reason, and he anointed them with oil. Laura wasn't too sure about this. She asked Allison whether everyone was healed. Allison replied, "I'm not sure, but I do know that people seem peaceful when they leave." Laura thought the whole thing sounded a little crazy. But she was very worried about her dad. What could it hurt? She would mention it to him that night and see what he thought. She wanted God to restore her dad to health; she wanted him to keep his job. Maybe it wasn't such a bad idea after all.

Prayers for healing have been a part of Judeo-Christian practice for millennia. Both Old and New Testaments provide numerous accounts of infirm individuals requesting the miraculous touch of God. Sometimes the individual directly prayed for divine intervention, as was the case with Hezekiah (2 Kings 20:1–6); other times the one who was ill sought out an agent of healing to offer prayer on his or her behalf, as Naaman did (2 Kings 5:1–5). Prayers for healing are nothing new to Christianity. What *is* a more recent phenomenon, relatively speaking, is the development of actual services for healing—corporate worship experiences with the central focus being prayers offered for those who are ill in body, mind, or spirit. The current practice of gathering to pray for the sick finds its roots in James 5:13–16 (which is discussed at length below). Whereas in the Old Testament prayers for healing seemed largely to have been individual persons appealing to God or to a holy person endowed with the power to heal, the passage in James seems to place healing squarely in the context of the Christian community, especially with its leadership—the elders. Since then its history has been spotty in practice. However, worship renewal efforts of the past half century among mainline denominations have sought to establish the healing service as normative in the life of local congregations, hence the many examples of healing services that have appeared in recent editions of approved worship manuals.[1]

It is significant to note that healing, when used in the context of healing services today, is used in a broad sense to encompass all manner of illnesses—any aspect of life that is deficient so as to rob one of wholeness. Prayer is offered for those who suffer from anxiety, are troubled of mind, are anguished from bad memories, experience ongoing fears, struggle with bitterness, and suffer broken relationships—as well as those with physical illnesses. A cursory reading of the Gospels should convince the reader that Jesus's healing ministry was very broad in scope; the healing service, likewise, exists to pray for wholeness of body, mind, soul, and spirit.

In this chapter we will discuss the content, order, and leading of healing services held in either a church, a hospital, a home, or another appropriate venue. We will focus on services designated exclusively for the purpose of praying for healing on behalf of people. The purpose of a service of healing is to provide believers the occasion to make intercession for those who are struggling, so that one's sister or brother in Christ may experience wholeness. This, in turn, renews and strengthens believers in their love of and service to Jesus Christ.

Laying the Foundations

Biblical Foundations

Many scriptural stories of healing serve as precedents for praying for the sick. Yet the number of biblical passages that provide an explicit appeal for the church to engage in prayers for healing is few. The most direct admonition for gathering the church together for this very purpose is found in James 5:13–16 and therefore serves as the primary rationale for services of healing today.

> Are any among you suffering? They should pray. Are any cheerful? They should sing songs of praise. Are any among you sick? They should call for the elders of the church and have them pray over them, anointing them with oil in the name of the Lord. The prayer of faith will save the sick, and the Lord will raise them up; and anyone who has committed sins will be forgiven. Therefore confess your sins to one another, and pray for one another, so that you may be healed. The prayer of the righteous is powerful and effective.

Note some key aspects of the above scenario.

- There is a simple connection between suffering/sickness and prayer. Do you suffer? You should pray. Are you sick? You should call for prayer.

- The prayers for healing are initiated by the one who is sick, not by a well-intentioned third party.
- Those called to this prayer ministry are the leaders of the church.
- The agency of oil is used in a sacramental way—a material entity becomes a means through which God's power is enacted.
- Faith is central to healing.
- Confession and forgiveness open the door to healing.

Let's examine each of these six principles briefly. First, illness invites intercession. To whom do we turn when faced with impairment? We look to the One who created us and can therefore as easily re-create us, making us new. When King Hezekiah became sick to the point of death, he prayed for healing while he wept bitterly. The Lord responded, "I have heard your prayer, I have seen your tears; I will add fifteen years to your life" (Isa. 38:5). Numerous persons in need of Jesus's healing touch cried out in prayer, begging to be healed. Bartimaeus pleaded, "Jesus, Son of David, have mercy on me!" (Mark 10:47). His request was simple: "Let me see again" (Mark 10:51). Jesus responded, "Go; your faith has made you well" (Mark 10:52). The psalmist captures the natural inclination to appeal to God when faced with physical and spiritual despair: "Have mercy on me, LORD, for I am faint; heal me, LORD, for my bones are in agony. My soul is in deep anguish. How long, LORD, how long?" (Ps. 6:2–3 NIV). Prayer is the instinctive reflex when illness comes. Just witness the number of nonreligious people who suddenly believe in prayer when illness strikes close to home!

Second, prayers for healing are requested by the one who desires healing. The individual seeking the healing touch of God is the most vital human part of the equation. This passage in James emphasizes the full participation of the one who is ill. Other individuals, no matter how sincere their intentions, cannot force the engagement of someone who is unwilling, unbelieving, or unrepentant. Jesus often asked sick people if they wanted to be made well prior to his divine intervention. Their active role in the event was a necessity; in the Gospels, Jesus always healed in response to the willing—indeed eager—request of the one in need.[2] The weight of responsibility falls upon the recipient of the prayers to fully participate in faith and sincerity.

Third, the leaders of the church are called to this prayer ministry. Notice that James is identifying office holders in the early church—elders (*presbyters*). As local church pastors, presumably these would be people of greater spiritual maturity and experience. Also note that they are not identified on the basis of some personal spiritual gift of healing; rather, they are identified by virtue of office. While healing is mentioned by the apostle Paul as a spiritual gift (1 Cor. 12:9), that does not seem to be a requirement for those called to pray for the sick. All leaders in the faith, not only those with the spiritual gift of healing, should consider themselves called and qualified to offer prayers for the sick. This prayer ministry is an urgent one, for "it is not a sin to be sick or to die. It is, however, a sin for sickness and death to go unchallenged because there is no one to pray."[3]

Fourth, oil is designated as an aid to healing. Both the Old and New Testaments make reference to the healing agency of oil in general. While God certainly heals without the anointing with oil, it is an ancient and commonly accepted practice to use oil to communicate the healing balm of God's renewing touch. There is no biblical reference to Jesus using oil in his healing ministry, though he did sometimes make use of various material compounds in the healing process (for example, mud and spittle). There *is* evidence, however, that Jesus's disciples anointed the sick with oil as they undertook their own missionary journeys of teaching and healing (Mark 6:13).

Fifth, faith is a key element for healing. How much faith is not specified—perhaps as little as a mustard seed (Luke 17:6). Jesus often connected faith and healing. He noted faith as a commendable virtue for healing when a Roman centurion requested healing for his personal servant by suggesting that Jesus need not appear in person but only speak the word from a distance and healing would come. To this Jesus remarked in amazement, "Truly I tell you, in no one in Israel have I found such faith" (Matt. 8:10). Paul healed a man who had never walked after "looking at him intently and seeing that he had faith to be healed" (Acts 14:9). Much theological confusion has led to erroneous conclusions about the role of faith in prayers for healing (more on this later). But thorny theological issues aside, this much can be said: faith and prayer are connected for the healing of the sick. James is explicit: "The prayer of faith will save the sick" (James 5:15).

Last, confession of sin (and forgiveness) is also related to healing. Here again, unfortunate interpretations of this verse (James 5:16) have led to false conclusions—that someone is *not* healed because of sin in his or her life. First, notice that the verse does not indicate that sin is the *only* cause for unsuccessful prayers for healing. Second, we are likely not talking about common, everyday-variety infractions; rather, the sins James has in mind here are mortal sins—those of a very grave nature.[4]

In a few short verses, this letter written by an apostle (James) provides insightful principles for services of healing. Fortunately, we do not have to lean entirely on this passage for our rationale for healing ministries. Jesus's expectation that his followers would continue his ministry of healing is clear.

The disciples' ministry of healing was rooted, of course, in Jesus's own healing ministry. His emphasis on healing is prominent throughout the Gospels: "Jesus went throughout Galilee . . . curing every disease and every sickness among the people . . . and they brought to him all the sick, those who were afflicted with various diseases and pains, demoniacs, epileptics, and paralytics, and he cured them" (Matt. 4:23–24). It wasn't long before "Jesus summoned his twelve disciples and gave them authority over unclean spirits, to cast them out, and to cure every disease and every sickness" (Matt. 10:1). Jesus prepared his followers to carry on and even expand (John 14:12) his ministry of announcing the kingdom of God through ministries of teaching and healing. Jesus commissioned others who would go out "as agents bearing the full authority of their sender."[5] The Acts of the Apostles provides a fantastic account of the disciples indeed carrying on this very ministry for which Jesus trained them. The tongues of fire had barely disappeared on the day of Pentecost when Peter and John were found healing a lame man lying at the temple gate. The healing miracles persist throughout the book of Acts.

The New Testament provides ample foundations for believers to engage in prayers for the sick. But how was this done? We turn now to a brief look at some of the historical practices surrounding the prayers for healing.

Historical Foundations

The historical evidence of early church practice seems to indicate that "ordinary Christians were anointing themselves and others with consecrated oil in the case of sickness."[6] Evidence from the first several centuries does not, however, indicate formal services of healing in the context of a gathered, worshiping community; this developed much later. Anglican scholar John Halliburton says, "Theologians like Origen (and after him John Chrysostom) use [James] 5 to illustrate their theology of the forgiveness of sins and not as a warrant for the practice of anointing the sick."[7] People brought their anointing oil to be blessed by the bishop and then took it with them for private use. "This taking home of oil for private consumption or application seems to have been wide-spread," Halliburton concludes.[8] He notes the "curious reluctance" during the first several centuries of the life of the church to associate James 5 directly to any rite of healing: "what to us seems obvious as a clear scriptural warrant is not the peg the Fathers use to hang their theology of anointing and healing."[9] Indeed, "to the end of the patristic period there is no actual rite or form known to us which gathers the presbyters round the bed of the sick and provides a text for their use."[10] While Christians did gather to pray for the sick, the practice does not seem to be formalized or conceived of as an official service; it "cannot be traced in the ante-Nicene Church."[11]

While there is little to glean from the early church in terms of the rites, rubrics, or liturgical structure for praying for the sick, there is significant information related to the oil used for anointing the sick. Frequently mentioned in Scripture, anointing with oil is one of the oldest of human rituals. The ancient practices reflected in the Old Testament depict the use of olive oil in several ways. First, oil served medicinal purposes. As such, it is viewed as an agent of healing (Isa. 1:6). Second, oil served consecration purposes. Kings, prophets, and priests were consecrated with oil for their sacred tasks (Lev. 8:30; 1 Sam. 10:1; 2 Sam. 2:4). Leaders are referred to as "the anointed of the Lord" (1 Sam. 12:3; 24:6). Third, oil served cosmetic purposes for both men and women (Ruth 3:3; 2 Sam. 12:20). In the New Testament the use of oil becomes more consistently associated with physical healing. The Samaritan poured wine and oil on the wounds of the man who was robbed, beaten, and left for dead on the road (Luke 10:34); Jesus's disciples anointed with oil to heal the sick (Mark 6:13); and as we have seen, James advised church leaders to pray for the sick and anoint them with oil (James 5:14).

The New Testament uses two different Greek verbs to designate two types of anointing. One, *aleiphō*, refers to the act of washing or pouring oil. It is the verb used in the Gospels in reference to the anointing of Jesus's body for burial; it is also the word used in reference to the anointing of the sick in James 5:14. The other, *chriō* (and its related verb forms), refers to the anointing upon the person and work of Christ, whose very title is to be interpreted "the Anointed One," the "Messiah." This verb also refers to the pouring out of the Holy Spirit at baptism (from which we get the English word "chrismation").[12] The former use of anointing is relevant for our discussion in this chapter. The long and distinguished practice of chrismation is discussed in the chapter on baptism (see chap. 4). The two terms are very much related, however. Very early in the life of the church, the anointing with oil at baptism came to symbolize the indwelling Holy Spirit. The members of James's church would have made the connection between the oil of baptism and the oil for anointing the sick.[13] Thomas Long makes this remarkable point: "To be anointed with oil at the time of sickness is to remember one's baptism and to remember that one ultimately belongs to God."[14] Some also hypothesize that this is why Jesus's disciples used oil when praying for the sick—a sign that they had been sent with a power not their own.[15]

The practice of blessing the oil, of setting it apart for holy use, developed quite early: "The provision of oil, duly blessed, for the healing of the sick seems to be more or less universal from the third century onwards."[16]

Authoritative figures, primarily the bishop, were qualified to bless the oil, though possibly a presbyter or occasionally a desert father was permitted to do so.[17] Cyril of Jerusalem believed that the invocation of the Holy Spirit on the oil changed it from mere ointment to "the gracious gift of Christ and the Holy Spirit, producing the advent of his deity."[18] A prayer of blessing from *Apostolic Constitutions* (fourth century) is noteworthy: "Do thou now sanctify this water and this oil through Christ in the name of him that offered or of her that offered, and give to these things a power of producing health and driving away diseases, of putting to flight demons and of dispersing every snare through Christ our hope."[19] Hippolytus, in *The Apostolic Tradition* (third century), instructs, "If anyone offers oil, let the bishop give thanks over it in the same way that he gives thanks for the offering of bread and wine."[20] With the blessing of the oil, the rite began to be viewed in a sacramental way.

In the twelfth century, anointing and prayer for the sick "was renamed 'extreme unction' and became a final preparation for dying through a final purgation of one's sins."[21] Eventually extreme unction made its way into the list of official sacraments of the Roman Church. However, today, while extreme unction remains a sacrament, the term is not used extensively among Catholics and refers not only to anointing those who are dying but also to those who are gravely ill. The anointing with oil for healing is not a sacrament or ordinance among Protestants.

Theological Foundations

Observing how anointing and healing was practiced from antiquity to the present is one thing; arriving at definitive theological positions on healing is quite another. Church leaders differ dramatically as to what can be claimed when it comes to illness and healing. Some Christians dismiss healing miracles as a thing of the past belonging to an era when God permitted healings for a special purpose during a special time (a kind of dispensational of view). Other Christians believe that God still heals today and that we should boldly approach the throne of grace to appeal to God's mercy to grant wholeness in the lives of others. Still others go so far as to claim that God *will always* heal if our faith is strong enough. A full theological discussion of healing is beyond the bounds of this chapter. Nevertheless, I invite you to consider establishing sound theological principles on which you will base your understanding and practice of the ministry of healing in your local church. I favor "the middle way," believing that God still heals today and we should ask for God's healing. I will offer some principles below that I hope will help those who believe that we are called today to anoint the sick and pray in faith for the well-being of our sisters and brothers.

God Welcomes Our Prayers for Healing and Wholeness

As elaborated above, there is scriptural evidence for healing prayers in James 5. Beyond this passage, others abound that show God as a loving God who invites us to bring our concerns to him in prayer. Consider just a few examples:

- "Cast your burden on the LORD, and he will sustain you; he will never permit the righteous to be moved" (Ps. 55:22).
- "Come to me, all you that are weary and are carrying heavy burdens, and I will give you rest" (Matt. 11:28).
- "Cast all your anxiety on him, because he cares for you" (1 Pet. 5:7).

God issues an open invitation for us to "come" and to "cast our cares" upon the One who will sustain us, heal us, and carry our burdens with us.

God Ultimately Heals

The God who created all things perfectly, declaring each aspect of creation "good," continues to do all things for our good (Rom. 8:28). The evil one comes to kill and to destroy, but God brings life and shalom. While we believe that God always has our well-being in mind, many times our prayers for healing do not yield the result we had hoped, and the recipients of our prayers do not experience improvement in body, mind, or spirit. Sometimes they decline in their condition or even die before their time, from our point of view. While there are many instances of healings throughout the Bible, the Scriptures do not promise that every prayer for healing that we offer will yield the results we anticipate. The bigger picture is that God *ultimately* heals. It may or may not occur in our desired time frame. Someone has wisely said that there are three possibilities for answered prayer: yes, no, or wait. We must recognize that all three are answers to prayer. The word translated "to be sick" (*astheneō*) in James 5:14 is neutral in tone. It is used in the New Testament either to refer to the general sense of being ill or in reference to mortal sickness (as was the case for Lazarus). The word translated as "raise up" (*egeirō*) in verse 15 is also ambivalent. It could simply mean to raise up from the sickbed (immediate healing), but it also is used regularly in the New Testament for resurrection from the dead (ultimate healing). Jeffrey John notes, "It could mean, as most naturally fits the context, 'The prayer of faith will *heal* the *sick* man and the Lord will *cure* him.' But it *could* also mean, 'The prayer of faith will *save* the *mortally ill/dead* man and the Lord will *resurrect* him.'"[22] John goes on to say that the first meaning is likely intended. Still, the "vocabulary is so strikingly and systematically ambiguous that one is forced to wonder whether the author himself made it deliberately so."[23] The apostle Paul taught the Philippians that Christ is exalted through life *or* death when he writes, "Christ will be exalted now as always in my body, whether by life or by death. For to me, living is Christ and dying is gain" (Phil. 1:20–21). The point is simply this: in the appropriate fashion from God's point of view, God will heal, not destroy. As Job so eloquently puts it, "After my skin has been thus destroyed, then in my flesh I shall see God" (Job 19:26). For the Christian, healing happens in God's way and in God's time.

God Is Sovereign

To believe that God is sovereign is to believe that God is in control—that God has ultimate knowledge, power, and authority over all people and things. The human body is positioned under the sovereignty of God. Simply put, God is in control of our debilitating circumstances. When we acknowledge that Jesus is Lord (our Sovereign), we view ourselves as citizens of a kingdom in which we are subject to the will of the Sovereign. God has purposes in mind for each of us; our days are numbered before we were born. When we offer prayers of faith for healing, we do so boldly, yes, but with this larger truth in mind: God is in control of the situation. We must ask according to God's will and willingly submit to it. Our peace in the midst of our circumstances comes in our recognition of the sovereignty of God. Some people discourage the practice of including the words "if it be your will" (referring to God) when offering prayers for healing; including these words is viewed as expressing a lack of faith or as an escape clause in case healing doesn't happen. These words must be embraced, however, by everyone who believes that God is sovereign. Though they may or may not be spoken aloud, they are an undergirding assumption, for God's will is our singular desire. Jesus included these very words when pleading with the Father to be delivered from death (Luke 22:42). When praying for healing, there is always a tension between praying with boldness and authority and submitting to God's will in every circumstance. These two approaches are not in conflict; they are in dialogue. We pray with boldness and faith while ultimately surrendering to God's sovereign purposes at the same time. Often it is necessary to live in the tension of two things at once: we pray the prayer of faith (Mark 11:24) and also submit to the Father's great purposes that are beyond our control (2 Cor. 12:9–10). It may not be "either/or"; we may find it to be "both/and."

Suffering Serves a Purpose

A sound theology of healing is directly related to a sound theology of suffering. Suffering is used by God to accomplish good things in our lives, including those benefits described in the Scripture passages below.

- Suffering allows us to console others in their suffering (2 Cor. 1:3–7).
- Suffering results in genuine faith, which, in turn, will bring praise and glory and honor to Jesus Christ (1 Pet. 1:6–7).
- Suffering identifies us with Christ's suffering (1 Pet. 2:20–21).
- Suffering is an opportunity to glorify God (1 Pet. 4:16).
- Suffering is the pathway to eternal life (Rev. 2:10).

While we may long for healing and pray for it, do not overlook the purposes God often accomplishes through prolonged suffering. Paul testified to this reality when he experienced ongoing suffering in his body—a deficiency from which he pled with the Lord for deliverance. But God chose to use this suffering as a means for growth in character. Paul became content in his weakness so that the power of Christ would be evident as a result (2 Cor. 12:7–10). Peter offers us sound advice: "Therefore, let those suffering in accordance with God's will entrust themselves to a faithful Creator, while continuing to do good" (1 Pet. 4:19).

Depend on the Holy Spirit for Wisdom and Discernment

There has been much false teaching surrounding the issue of healing. One erroneous teaching states that seemingly unanswered prayers are due to a lack of faith. While faith is a vital part of the equation for healing, the Bible does not claim that healing depends on a certain amount of faith. When healing fails to occur, sometimes leaders place the blame on the individual, associating their lack of healing with their lack of faith. But the truth is that there may be any number of reasons why healing does not occur. It is best not to pile guilt on the individual who is already in need, especially when there are multiple reasons why healing may not occur.

Another questionable explanation for the lack of healing is sometimes referred to as "sin in the camp"—a reference harking back to occasions in the Old Testament when God penalized the whole Israelite community for the sin of some members of the community (see 2 Sam. 24). While it is true that the blessing of God may be marginalized in a community when its members live in outright, ongoing disobedience to God's will, still God does not withhold the healing touch from a sincere member in the community because others around him or her may be living sinful lives.

A further prominent false teaching is that one need simply declare his or her intent to be healed; this is sometimes referred to as "name it and claim it." This view is a poor interpretation of Mark 11:24: "[Jesus answered them], 'So I tell you, whatever you ask for in prayer, believe that you have received it, and it will be yours.'" Prominent faith healers have misled others by teaching that if you proclaim your desire in prayer, it will be done. Actually, the context of this verse lies in the greater story of Jesus heading to Jerusalem to suffer and die. The backdrop is Monday of Holy Week and the cleansing of the temple; Jesus does not speak these words in the context of healing miracles. Healing does not take place by some magical incantation of naming and claiming. We do not manipulate words or demand to be made well. Healing, when it occurs, is a gift that serves the Father's purposes, rather than a response to the willful demand of someone who has physical relief as a goal.

Last, beware of self-serving faith healers. It is easy to be enamored with the charismatic presence of a true faith healer and the miracles that result. But even Jesus did not seek to be noticed as the healer. There are many occasions in the Gospels when Christ admonished other people to refrain from advertising who had healed them. Those who draw attention to themselves probably have their reward in full. The attention must go to Christ, for "He himself bore our sins in his body on the cross, so that, free from sins, we might live for righteousness; by his wounds you have been healed" (1 Pet. 2:24).

We must admit there are many unknowns when it comes to praying for the sick. Yet of these things we can be sure: God welcomes our prayers for healing, God ultimately heals, God is sovereign, suffering serves a purpose, and the Holy Spirit is our source for wisdom and discernment in these matters.

Building the Structure

The healing service can be thought of in one of two ways: it can be a stand-alone service with its singular purpose being prayers for healing, or it can be a "service within a service"—a response to the Word in a normally scheduled, primary worship service of the church. Some churches have established regular healing services, perhaps monthly or quarterly, on a Sunday evening. Others have intentionally planned for it in the primary service as appropriate. The suggested structure outlined below may be used in either scenario; it is developed enough to serve as a short, independent service of healing, yet brief enough to serve as a substantial response to the Word within the fourfold order of worship.

The structure for a service of healing is quite simple, consisting of three primary parts: the confession of sin, the anointing with oil, and the prayer of faith (as per James 5). These basic parts are surrounded with a few other relatively optional elements of worship that do, however, serve to embellish the service if desired. The order of service for healing offered below may be viewed in this way: worship elements shown with titles on the left side of the page are considered essential parts of the healing service and are included as a response to the Word (within a regularly held worship service); additional elements shown with centered titles within brackets [] are to be used in a stand-alone healing service. In the case of the first, a transitional congregational song and/or words spoken by the leader will form a bridge from the Service of the Word to the Response to the Word (the healing service). The basic elements listed on the left may be additionally streamlined at the leader's discretion to be suitable for hospital, home, or other nonchurch settings.

The Order of the Healing Service

The basic outline alone appears in appendix B.

[Pre-service Music]
(instrumental, vocal, or congregational singing)

OR

[Enter in Silence]
(Complete silence can be a most effective setting to begin a healing service.)

[Greeting/Welcome]
(This should be scriptural in content and pastoral in tone.)

Scripture Reading/Call to Worship

Read a few Bible verses that are invitational in nature and establish the context for the service. These do not have to be overtly about healing but should at least portray God as a caring God who welcomes our concerns and intercessions.

Sample Scripture Reading/Call to Worship[24]

- "Bless the LORD, O my soul, and all that is within me, bless his holy name. Bless the LORD, O my soul, and do not forget all his benefits—who forgives all your iniquity, who heals all your diseases, who redeems your life from the Pit, who crowns you with steadfast love and mercy, who satisfies you with good as long as you live so that your youth is renewed like the eagle's" (Ps. 103:1–5). This passage is particularly appropriate, for it makes reference to forgiveness *and* healing; it also describes healing in a very comprehensive manner.

Invocation

Pray a brief prayer that welcomes God's triune presence as we offer prayers for others.

Note: This is not a long prayer, nor is it yet the prayer for healing. It is particularly fitting to call upon the Holy Spirit to bring assurance, comfort, and power during this service. Remember, the traditional parts to standard prayers for worship are found in appendix A.

[Congregational Song]
(Select a song fitting for gathering the community into God's presence.)

Confession of Sin[25]

Invite the congregation to confession of sin. Pray the prayer of confession.

Note: This may incorporate both corporate and personal components. The personal time of confession is especially needed in this service for those who are asking for prayers for healing (see James 5:16).

Assurance of Pardon (refer to appendix A)

[The Passing of the Peace]
(This is especially fitting given the importance of reconciliation in healing and the strong sense of fellowship and intimacy inherent in this service.)

[Reading of a Biblical Account of Healing]
(Selecting a narrative depicting an actual healing is very helpful.)

[Homily]
(A brief reflection/meditation on the passage is best here.
The homily also covers the "Brief Scriptural Basis for Healing and Instructions" below; therefore, if a homily is given,
proceed directly to the instructions in item 2 below.)

Brief Scriptural Basis for Healing and Instructions

Offer a *very brief* rationale for this service, followed by simple instructions as to what will happen. Note:

1. This should not be an extensive teaching on the biblical view of healing. First, I highly advise pastors to provide teaching on healing in other congregational venues, such as a sermon series, Sunday school classes, small group meetings, and so on. Second, it is far more powerful to *experience* the service than to *learn about* the service. This is a moment to simply assert that the Scriptures emphasize healing and that the Christian church has always embraced it on that basis.

2. It is important to *clearly* and *briefly* state how the service will unfold logistically. This gives people greater comfort in participating by removing some of their potential uncertainties.

Thanksgiving for the Oil

Offer a brief prayer of thanksgiving and petition concerning the use of the oil. Note: This is a short and simple prayer that has two purposes: (1) to give God thanks for the gift of oil, which is used as a symbol of healing and wholeness, and (2) to set apart the oil (sanctify it) for God's holy use in healing.

[Congregational Song]
(Select a song that explicitly affirms God as divine healer
or invites persons to present themselves for prayer.)

Call for the Elders (Pastors or Other Leaders)

Invite those to come forward who will be anointing with oil and joining in prayer for the sick. Just a few (two or three) people should be called for this ministry at this point in the service. Note:

1. The scriptural term "elders" would normally have referred to pastors of local churches. However, there is no reason to believe that those who pray for the sick must be ordained. After all, Jesus sent his disciples out on healing expeditions. It is fitting for pastors to lead this service; it is likewise permissible for other mature leaders to be trained for this ministry as well.

2. More people may be invited to come forward shortly to join these leaders in prayer.

3. The leaders who will anoint with oil and lay hands on the sick must be discipled well in this ministry previous to participation.

Invitation to Receive Prayer for Healing

Invite any who wish to receive prayer for any type of healing (body, mind, soul, spirit, relationships, and so on) to come forward. Note:

1. Inviting them to kneel is greatly advantageous. If someone is unable to physically kneel, invite him or her to stand or sit. Depending on the size of the crowd, people may kneel or stand across the front of the church or form lines waiting for "prayer stations" to open up, similar to taking Communion by intinction. Another option is inviting those coming forward to sit in the front pew(s) as they await prayer.
2. After they have come forward, it is appropriate to invite other congregants to come forward also to surround them in prayer.

Anointing with Oil

The pastor or other designated laypersons will anoint with oil using their thumb to make the sign of the cross on the forehead, saying, "[Name], I anoint you in the name of the Father, and of the Son, and of the Holy Spirit. Amen." Note:

1. The oil itself is not the key factor; as a symbol it points beyond itself and beyond those who are anointing to the active presence of the triune God: the Father as the source of all healing, Christ who is the agent of healing, and the outpouring of the Holy Spirit bringing peace and shalom.
2. Olive oil is traditionally used, but other appropriate oils may likewise be used. Place the oil in a small bowl, flask, or bottle.[26]

Prayer for Healing

The pastor or other designated laypersons will (1) quietly ask the individual to state aloud his or her need for prayer and then, (2) placing their hands on the head of the person desiring prayer, pray an extemporaneous prayer for healing.[27]

Sample
Consider this model prayer for healing.

"As you are outwardly anointed with this holy oil, so may our heavenly Father grant you the inward anointing of the Holy Spirit. Of his great mercy, may he forgive you your sins, release you from suffering, and restore you to wholeness and strength. May he deliver you from all evil, preserve you in all goodness, and bring you to everlasting life; through Jesus Christ our Lord. Amen."[28]

Note: The congregation should be invited to join in silent prayer and/or meditate on an announced scriptural text during the prayer service. It is also appropriate to have soft instrumental music, vocal solos, or gentle congregational singing during this time. However, care must be taken that the music will not overpower or overshadow the primary event—prayers for healing.

Prayer of Thanksgiving

The pastor or designated layperson may offer a general prayer thanking God for hearing our prayers and emphasizing the goodness, mercy, and love of God in Jesus Christ.

Note: This prayer may take the form of a blessing, as in the following example.

"The Almighty Lord, who is a strong tower to all who put their trust in him, to whom all things in heaven, on earth, and under the earth bow and obey; Be now and evermore your defense, and make you know and feel that the only Name under heaven given for health and salvation is the Name of our Lord Jesus Christ." Amen.[29]

[Testimonies/Informal Sharing]
(Those having received prayers are welcome to testify of God's goodness, witnessing to what they experienced in the service. Others may also share here as appropriate.)

Song of Hope

The congregation is invited to affirm the Spirit's work by singing a song of hope, healing, forgiveness, victory, and so on.

Benediction

A scriptural benediction is especially meaningful following a service of healing, for it assures people of God's peace and shalom as they depart.

It is common (and appropriate) to conduct a service of healing in conjunction with the Eucharist; indeed, there is much precedence for doing so. Often the same liturgical spaces needed for Communion suit the service of healing very well; using Communion rails both for receiving the elements and for kneeling or standing to receive prayers for healing is one example.[30] Some traditions recommend that services of healing take place immediately preceding the distribution of the bread and cup,[31] while others suggest Communion followed by prayers for healing.[32] Arrange the order as is best suited to your service.

Installing Doors and Windows

A number of songs, Scriptures, prayers, and symbols are suitable for services of healing. While many songs are appropriate in the general sense, relatively few Christian hymns/songs explicitly address the topic of healing. Perhaps this is due to the sporadic history of services of healing throughout the centuries. Remember that songs, prayers, and symbols, among other things, help worshipers interact with God as we move through the order of service; they facilitate the dialogue by giving us a means to express ourselves to God and one another and, likewise, to receive from God and one another. They encourage the corporate nature of the healing service by providing a means of full participation.

Songs

A few relevant hymns/songs for the healing service are listed below.[33] While most are generally appropriate, a few are explicitly about healing.

And Jesus Said (Shirley Erena Murray)
Be Still, for the Spirit of the Lord (David Evans)
Be Still, My Soul (Katherina von Schlegel)
Bless the Lord, My Soul (the Community of Taizé)
Come to the Water (John Foley)
Create in Me a Clean Heart (anonymous)
For Freedom Christ Has Set Us Free! (Sylvia G. Dunstan)
Give Thanks with a Grateful Heart (Henry Smith)
Go, My Children, with My Blessing (Jaroslav J. Vajda)
God Will Take Care of You (Civilla D. Martin)
Have Thine Own Way, Lord (Adelaide A. Pollard)
He Is Able (Rory Noland and Greg Ferguson)
Heal Me, Hands of Jesus (Michael Perry)
Healer of My Soul (John Michael Talbot)
Healer of Our Every Ill (Marty Haugen)
His Strength Is Perfect (Steven Curtis Chapman and Jerry Salley)
I Lift My Eyes Up (Brian Doerkson)
If You and I Believe in Christ (Zimbabwe chorus)
If You Will Trust in God to Guide You (Georg Neumark)
Jesus Heard with Deep Compassion (Joy F. Patterson)

Jesus, Lover of My Soul (Charles Wesley)

Jesus, Your Name (Claire Cloninger)

Jesus's Hands Were Kind Hands (Margaret Cropper)

Just as I Am without One Plea (Charlotte Elliott)

My Faith Looks up to Thee (Ray Palmer)

My Soul in Stillness Waits (Marty Haugen)

Nothing Can Trouble (the Community of Taizé)

O Christ, the Healer, We Have Come (Fred Pratt Green)

O Lord, Hear My Prayer (the Community of Taizé)

On Eagle's Wings (Michael Joncas)

Spirit of the Living God (Daniel Iverson)

Spirit Song (John Wimber)

There Is a Balm in Gilead (traditional spiritual)

Through It All (André Crouch)

Wait for the Lord (the Community of Taizé)

We Cannot Measure How You Heal (John Bell)

We Shall Overcome (traditional spiritual)

What a Friend We Have in Jesus (Joseph M. Scriven)

When Jesus the Healer Passed through Galilee (Peter D. Smith)

When Peace like a River (Horatio G. Spafford)

When the Storms of Life Are Raging (Charles A. Tindley)

You Are My Hiding Place (Michael Ledner)

Scripture Passages

Relevant Scripture passages abound that affirm God's interest in healing his children. Here are a few examples to explore; however, begin now to form your own list of passages appropriate for a service of healing.

Job 7:11–21	Psalm 103:1–5	Matthew 5:1–12
Ecclesiastes 3:1–15	Psalm 146:5–9	Matthew 10:1–8
Psalm 23	Isaiah 35:1–10	Matthew 11:28–30
Psalm 30	Isaiah 38	Mark 6:7–13
Psalm 41	Isaiah 40:1–11	Acts 5:12–16
Psalm 46:1–7	Isaiah 40:28–31	Romans 8:15–27
Psalm 91	Isaiah 53	Romans 8:28–39

2 Corinthians 1:3–11	Hebrews 2:14–18	Revelation 21:1–4
Philippians 4:6–9	Hebrews 5:7–10	
Colossians 1:8–14	James 5:13–16	

Prayers

A few types of prayers are especially fitting for the healing service: the invocation, the prayer of confession, the thanksgiving/petition for the oil, and the prayer for healing.[34] Denominational worship books/service books are a gold mine of such prayers, which you may pray verbatim, adapt, or use as a model for forming your own. Many of these resources offer very specific prayers for healing, including prayers for a sick child, emotional or mental distress, anxiety, AIDS patients, Alzheimer's sufferers, and so on. The invocation and prayer of confession have been discussed previously; their forms are found in appendix A. Below are a few examples of the two prayers unique to this service: the thanksgiving/petition for the oil and the intercessory prayers for the sick. Examining these sample prayers will give you a sense of the nature of each one.

Prayer of Thanksgiving/Petition for the Oil

"O Lord, holy Father, giver of health and salvation: Send your Holy Spirit to sanctify this oil; that, as your holy apostles anointed many that were sick and healed them, so may those who in faith and repentance receive this holy unction be made whole; through Jesus Christ our Lord, who lives and reigns with you and the Holy Spirit, one God, for ever and ever. Amen."[35]

"O God, the giver of health and salvation, we give thanks to you for the gift of oil. As your holy apostles anointed many who were sick and healed them, so pour out your Holy Spirit on us and on this gift, that those who in faith and repentance receive this anointing may be made whole; through Jesus Christ our Lord. Amen."[36]

Prayer for Healing

"Merciful God: you bear the hurt of the world. Look with compassion on those who are sick (especially on [*name*]); cheer them by your word, and bring health as a sign that, in your promised kingdom, there will be no more pain or crying; through Jesus Christ our Lord. Amen."[37]

"May the power of God's indwelling presence heal you of all illnesses—of body, mind, spirit, and relationships—that you may serve God with a loving heart. Amen."[38]

Symbols

A few symbols come to mind that will help people connect with our healing God.

- Vial of oil
- Kneeling bench
- Sign of the cross (imposed on the forehead)
- Various Trinitarian symbols

The Christian Year

Services for healing are appropriate during any time of the Christian year, since they are best done when the need arises. After all, illness is no respecter of the liturgical calendar. Nevertheless, two seasons seem particularly appropriate in which to offer healing services. Epiphany celebrates Christ's manifestation as Son of God and recognizes his earthly ministry. As healing was such a vital aspect of his ministry, it is very fitting to offer special services of healing during this time. Another especially appropriate occasion is the season after Pentecost—a period of time in which we celebrate the expansion of the church. Christ commissioned his disciples to follow in his footsteps with regard to healing the sick; as we pursue the spreading of the gospel in light of Pentecost, we engage in the same ministries of teaching, preaching, and healing that Jesus did.

Serving as Hospitable Host

Presiding at a service of healing is a very special responsibility of the pastor and other church leaders. These occasions may very well yield awesome moments when an awareness of the presence of the Holy Spirit seems more evident. Healing services are great avenues for pastoral care; they should not be overlooked and get lost in the busy schedules of local church programming or be dismissed as unimportant. Pastors should be as trained in ministries of healing as they are for other pastoral care responsibilities. As is the case for all church rituals, certain duties, attributes, and skills are needed to escort those in the leader's care through a meaningful service of healing.

Duties

There are several general duties for which pastors/leaders are responsible. First, it is the duty of all pastors to educate their people concerning what the

Bible teaches about healing. Too much misinformation exists related to healing and miracles, even among well-educated, long-term believers. Before you
offer your first healing service, spend some time instructing those in your care
by providing them with a solid, biblical perspective on healing. A second duty
is simply to offer *regular* opportunities for prayers for healing. Some churches
offer this type of service quarterly or monthly. Regardless of how often you offer
concentrated prayers of intercession for healing, try to be consistent. Decide on
how often and when you will make these services available, place them on the
church calendar, and commit to them. Third, it is imperative to disciple some
key leaders in the ministry of healing prayer. Prayerfully discern who may serve
effectively in this capacity, and then invite them to join you in studying the topic
of healing from a scriptural and historical point of view. Coach them on their
role in the service. Teach them how to pray publicly, and encourage them. Their
ministry should not be limited to healing services within the four walls of the
church alone; empower them to travel to hospitals, nursing homes, prisons—
anywhere people are restricted but are still in need of God's healing touch.

Attributes for Presiding

As you prepare to preside at services of healing, think about what attributes
would make you effective.

- Knowledge of your people. Having a keen sense of who your people are
  will go a long way in maintaining the effectiveness of the service as well
  as its tone. Some people will need to be encouraged to request prayers for
  healing; others may seek to draw attention to themselves on such occasions. The more time you spend getting to know your people, the better
  you will be at involving people properly in the healing service.
- Demeanor. Let your tender side show. Don't be afraid to be vulnerable.
  Praying for healing can be emotional at times. While you will seek to
  maintain a calm presence and self-control, be authentic. Weep with those
  who weep; laugh with those who laugh.
- Patience. As you preside during the service, lead at a careful pace. Don't
  feel rushed. Allow for quiet prayer times, reflection, moments of silence.
  In short, don't worry about "empty spaces" in the service. Take it easy,
  and don't feel that you need to fill every minute with activity or sound.

Administration

Providing regular opportunities for healing involves very little administration. But here are a few suggestions to keep things running smoothly.

- Keep a small vial of oil on hand. Always have one handy in the pulpit or in your office so that you can be ready to pray and anoint when appropriate. Consider carrying one with you in your car as well. Occasionally you will be glad you had it available when calling on the sick at home, nursing homes, or hospitals.

- When feasible, you may wish to have a pre-healing service meeting for those who plan to receive prayer. The purpose of this meeting is to explain healing and to allow for confession of sin. If you choose this option, announce that this meeting will take place prior to the service.

- Train leaders in the church to assist you. Keep a record of trained leaders and potential future leaders for this ministry. Don't forget to thank those who participate.

- Follow up with those who have received prayers for healing. Call them, encourage them, answer any questions they may have, and offer continued prayer for them.

- Keep a record of all occasions you have offered opportunities for healing—either a time of prayer within a regular service or stand-alone services of healing. This will hold you accountable for providing regular healing opportunities.

Special Considerations

Exceptionally Difficult Circumstances

We recognize that there are some unanswered questions surrounding praying for the sick. Yet we should not refrain from following in our Master's footsteps simply because there are things we don't understand. Mentioned below are a few things that will challenge any honest leader. These issues are raised with the intent that you will begin to reflect on and resolve, to the best of your human ability (and with the Spirit's aid), those issues that confound us.

The Terminally Ill

How does one pray for an individual who is obviously losing the battle with a life-threatening illness? While miracles certainly occur to serve God's gracious purposes, we have all known someone who has not recovered from a severely debilitating illness. Prayers are still welcome on behalf of the one who suffers. It may not be inappropriate to continue to pray for physical healing; your pastoral experience and guidance by the Holy Spirit will direct you as to when such a prayer is best laid aside for another. It is *always* appropriate to pray for strength, courage, hope, and, most of all, peace in the midst of the situation. These types of prayers are also prayers for healing—that God will bring wholeness of mind and spirit so the afflicted one may embrace what is ahead with faith that he or she rests in the hands of a loving God. Many times Christian leaders feel uncertain as to how to pray in this or similar circumstances. I urge the leader to *pray about what they should pray about.* Spend sincere time in prayer seeking God's perspective. When praying for others, pray out of your own time with God. You will have greater assurance that you are praying in a manner that is pleasing to God.

Children

Very young children are not able to ask for prayers for healing. Parents or guardians should be encouraged to "call for the elders of the church" to offer anointing with oil and prayers for healing on behalf of children. The Gospels record incidents that clearly encourage bringing children for blessing and healing (Matt. 9:18–26; Mark 10:13–14). Bring the children for healing. This will happen more naturally in your church if you have been faithful to sound teaching regarding healing. Whether by means of parents, guardians, pastors, or other church leaders, it is appropriate to be the voice of the voiceless in calling for divine power to bring wholeness to these young lives.

Exorcism

Confusion abounds concerning the casting out of demons (exorcisms). Unfortunately, erroneous conclusions are drawn equating demon possession with mental illness or depression, among other things. While Satan and his army of demons are real (Eph. 6:12), they are generally not the cause of illnesses; the minister should normally not associate illness of any kind with demon possession. Having said that, demon possession could be an occasion for healing prayer, perhaps in the form of exorcism. However, I agree with Frederick Gaiser.

> In the Bible, demons are a reality, but a penultimate reality—darkness not light. They should be taken as seriously as darkness, but only as seriously as darkness. To spend overmuch time speculating about demons—writing and preaching about them, immersing oneself in the culture of demonology—is to give them in practice more power than they have in reality. It is to sin against the admonitions of Deuteronomy and to court illness—surely theological illness, but perhaps physical illness as well. The testimonies of both Testaments are clear: demons, though dangerous, are for driving out. In the face of God and in the light of Christ, they are gone. And once dismissed, the less said about them the better.[39]

In the ancient church, exorcisms were performed at stages of preparation for baptism, not as an antidote for illness. Here exorcisms had nothing to do with illness, but rather with putting the devil in his place. Remnants of the same language from these early baptismal rituals are found in many current baptismal liturgies used today. Gaiser sums it up well.

> Christians ought not turn to exorcism too quickly as a remedy against disease. Not only might it give too much credence to the world of darkness, but also it may overlook less exotic but much more effective treatments. For most Christians, the fundamental exorcism in baptism will be sufficient for a lifetime: "Do you renounce the devil and all the forces that defy God?"[40]

When Someone Doesn't Want Healing

The Scriptures are clear that one condition in which healing may occur is when the one who is ill is a willing participant in the event. Public prayer in the context of a healing service should not be offered for the healing of someone who does not wish for prayer on his or her behalf. On these formal occasions for prayers of healing, the persons who are ill must present themselves (at a church, hospital, nursing home, and so on) as viable participants in the process. No one should ever be coerced. Of course, apart from a service of healing, you should always feel free to pray for anyone who is ill, even if he or she seems to resist prayers for healing. However, note that in the Gospels there is no record of Jesus healing anyone who did not seek it or cooperate with him on the matter. Holy power—divine unction—is a profound gift offered only to those who have some measure of faith (James 5:15).

When Healing Doesn't Happen

Perhaps the most difficult question universally posed is simply, "Why not?" Why wasn't an individual healed when the instructions from Scripture were followed and prayer was offered in faith? It is natural to want an answer. There is also unspoken pressure to be able to explain why some folks are healed and others are not. Do not resort to irrational or unbiblical rationale when something simply cannot be explained. Do not be afraid to answer, "I don't know," for that is the honest truth. Healing does not result from following the instructions; healing comes as a gift from God. Remember that (1) healing comes in many forms, (2) healing comes in God's time, (3) healing from God's perspective may be quite different from our perspective, and (4) healing is God's prerogative. Our inability to answer the "why" questions should not discourage us from engaging in services for healing. God invites us to pray for healing. We must simply leave the results where they belong—with a good God whose ways are not our ways, whose thoughts are not our thoughts (Isa. 55:8).

Ethical Considerations

Everyone recognizes that much poor theology and malpractice has been associated with praying for the sick. False prophets claiming to have the gift are nothing new (Acts 13:6–10; 19:13–17). Great care must be given to maintain the integrity of this ministry of pastoral care. Seek to establish an honorable reputation for yourself and your church (not to mention God!). Consider these things:

- Don't make promises. Avoid making any outright claims about particular persons and their circumstances. Keep silence about matters that are difficult (Prov. 29:11).
- Don't heal by proxy. Don't have someone "stand in" for someone else's prayer for healing. There is no biblical precedent for this,[41] and there is really no reason whatsoever for this to be done. If the one requesting prayer cannot attend a church service of healing, go to him or her or arrange for someone to go. Gather a few saints wherever the sick person resides and proceed.
- Never accept money. Pastors or other Christian leaders should never accept money or any type of gift for offering prayers for healing. This is a dire violation of the gospel, in particular, and a serious breach of pastoral ethics, in general. The gifts that come from God are offered and received freely.

Conclusion

Laura asked her dad to attend the healing service at Allison's church. The whole idea was new to both of them, but they felt strangely drawn to see what it was all about. It was just as Allison described—a relatively small group of people who devoutly gathered to hear the Scriptures, sing, and pray for the sick. Ron felt comfortable enough, even in an unknown setting, to go forward for the anointing with oil, the laying on of hands, and the prayer of faith. He looked forward to healthier days as a result. But until then, a peace had come over not only himself but also his daughter, Laura. They left the church greatly encouraged, not only physically but emotionally and spiritually as well. They agreed that they would return to this service again.

Key Terms

chrism The blessing of the oil.

exorcism Casting out evil spirits; accompanied in the early church by the anointing with oil.

extreme unction The Roman Catholic practice of anointing with oil and of confession of sin to prepare for death; performed in extreme cases of grave illness or when death is imminent.

unction From the Latin word referring to the anointing with oil as a religious rite; especially connected to the receiving of the Holy Spirit.

To Learn More

Dudley, Martin, and Geoffrey Rowell, eds. *The Oil of Gladness: Anointing in the Christian Tradition*. Collegeville, MN: Liturgical Press, 1990.

Gaiser, Frederick J. *Healing in the Bible: Theological Insight for Christian Ministry*. Grand Rapids: Baker Academic, 2010.

Wagner, James K. *Healing Services*. Just in Time! Nashville: Abingdon, 2007.

Engage

Review the two types of prayer unique to the healing service. Also review the form and content of the invocation and benediction. (See appendix A to review some forms.)

Try writing three prayers and a benediction that could be used in a service of healing at your church:

- An invocation
- A prayer of thanks for the oil
- A general prayer for healing
- A benediction

Qualities of prayer to remember (four Ss):

- Keep them *short*.
- Keep them somewhat *simple*.
- Make them *scriptural* in content.
- Make them theologically *sound*.

7

The Foot Washing Service and the Love Feast

Before reading chapter 7, reflect on your own experience of foot washing.

- Have you ever participated in a foot washing service? If so, describe it in detail.
- Do you imagine that it would be more difficult to wash someone's feet or to have someone wash your feet? Why?
- From personal experience or using your imagination, is there any type of person whose feet you would find difficult to wash?
- What is or would be the benefit of participating in a foot washing service *for you*? (Be honest and specific.)
- If Christ commanded his disciples to wash one another's feet, why do you suppose it is not universally practiced among Christians?

Now that you have begun to reflect on foot washing, expand your thinking by reading chapter 7.

Expand

Tyler jogged by the old church on his evening run. He noticed light from the basement windows and casually glanced toward it. What he saw took him aback; in fact, he completely stopped and peered inside as his curiosity got the best of him. Why were people kneeling down beside large pans of water? Was the dusty window clouding his vision—or were they actually washing feet? Everyone seemed at ease, yet how could anyone be comfortable with such a strange gesture? He stayed longer, not able to tear himself away from the scene. He needed to catch his breath anyway. There were laughter and embraces, singing and readings from a book. What in the world was going on? Was this some sort of weird cult? He had no explanation. Tyler leaned closer to the window, hoping to hear what was being said. But the glass was thick, and no sound made it to the street. He would have to make do with what he saw, but it was indeed bizarre! He resumed running, making a mental note to see whether the group would still be there when he doubled back at the end of his route. Maybe someone would be around, and he could ask them about this puzzling scene.

What Tyler witnessed could have been taking place in any number of churches today: Church of the Brethren, the Brethren Church, Mennonite, Brethren in Christ, or Churches of God General Conference, to name a few. All told, more than one hundred denominations practice foot washing as a meaningful and viable ritual for the church today.[1] Even some churches that do not regularly practice foot washing hold services of foot washing periodically. Yet while many Christians have practiced foot washing throughout the centuries and continue to do so, it has never been universally practiced within the Christian faith. Some have found it irrelevant in today's culture, or downright odd. Still, it remains a significant ritual for the church, possessing much character that commends itself for contemporary communities.

The term for this ritual varies; the two main terms are "foot washing" and "feet washing."[2] Some groups feel strongly that both feet should be washed, while others believe that washing only one foot is needed, suggesting that the symbolism is more important than the number of feet! Oddly, the word used doesn't necessarily indicate how many feet are involved, for some groups that refer to the event as "foot washing" do, in fact, wash both feet. For our purposes, we will use the term "foot washing" throughout this chapter; it may refer to washing one or both feet, a detail to be determined by the participants.

Those Protestant denominations that have historically embraced foot washing as normative typically practice a threefold event which includes (in varying order)[3] foot washing, Communion, and love feast (more on the latter below). These three aspects of one event share some things in common: (1) all involve material in some way (water/feet/towel; bread/wine; simple cake/water); (2) all involve particular words ("the peace of Christ be with you"; "take and eat"; and "if you know these things, blessed are you if you do them"); and (3) all involve gestures (kneeling and solemn embrace; take, bless, break, and give; passing food and drink at a simple meal). The integration of material items, words, and gestures forms a powerful experience in the ritual. As Eleanor Kreider remarks, "The material, the words, and the gestures are bound up with an inward will or disposition which can direct or change lives."[4]

The inaugural occasion that undergirds the rationale for foot washing in contemporary practice is found in the story of Jesus, who, while observing Passover with his disciples on the night before he died, washed their feet (John 13:1–17). The purpose of the foot washing service is to encourage believers to follow Jesus's example by humbling themselves in order to mutually serve other believers. Foot washing today portrays identification with Christ in expressing egalitarian relationships, for "servants are not greater than their master, nor are messengers greater than the one who sent them" (John 13:16).

Laying the Foundations

Biblical Foundations

First let's briefly examine the few New Testament passages that mention the ritual washing of feet. As mentioned, the primary passage concerning foot washing, John 13:1–17, forms the basis for its ongoing practice over time. The context for the event is Jesus's celebration of the Passover meal with the disciples on the night before he was crucified. This evening meal that John describes, where Jesus washes feet, is taken to be the same meal referred to in the Synoptic Gospels where Jesus institutes the new covenant by assigning new meaning to bread and wine. Interestingly, the episode of foot washing is *not* included in the Synoptic Gospels' accounts of the Lord's Supper, and the Lord's Supper is not included in John 13. But together they flesh out the story of that evening's events.

In John 13 we note several important features.

- Jesus washed feet as one of his final acts before returning to the Father (v. 3).
- He washed the feet of every disciple, even one who resisted (vv. 8–9) as well as his betrayer (vv. 2, 21).
- He taught them that if he, as Lord and Teacher, would stoop to wash their feet, they certainly should wash one another's feet (vv. 14, 16).
- He considered his action to be an example that they should follow (v. 15).
- He promised a blessing for those who wash feet (v. 17).

The story in John 13 is significant because it takes the act of washing feet, so common in Mediterranean culture of the time, and lifts it to an action rich with spiritual significance instituted by Christ for his followers. As such, it serves a greater purpose than mere cleanliness, as Jesus indicates to Peter (v. 10). A common action is now infused with new meaning and becomes a ritual for future believers. Jesus establishes the act of washing one another's feet to communicate profound truths concerning the nature of Christian community—and he does so as one of his last (and therefore evidently significant) acts with his followers. During Jesus's time, foot washing was an act both of hospitality and of service; naturally, these two meanings are virtually inseparable. By washing the feet of his disciples, Jesus portrays himself as both host *and* servant—a remarkable, ironic picture of the character qualities he was instilling in those who would lead the church after his ascension.

Beyond these meanings is the overarching view that the real point of the foot washing is for the disciples to have a "share" in Jesus's life, not only in the present, but in the future.[5] Hence, a concrete act in Jerusalem that depicts mutual service as the expectation of a soon-to-be departing Lord is likewise an eschatological act, one that foreshadows the share Jesus's disciples will have in the Father's home (John 14:2). "One's share with Jesus, then, is the gift of full relationship with him, which he offers in the foot washing, a relationship that opens the believer to Jesus' eschatological gift of eternal life."[6]

There are only two other references to washing feet in the New Testament. Luke 7:36–50 tells the story of another meal, at which a sinful woman bathed Jesus's feet with her tears and dried them with her hair, all the while anointing and kissing them. At one level this event portrays an individual act of devotion. On another level Jesus uses it as a teachable moment to note to the guests gathered for the meal that what is a common act, when rendered with faith and sincere devotion, becomes an occasion for the forgiveness of sins and pronouncement of peace. A common ritual yields uncommon results. While this beautiful story speaks volumes, it is not instituted by Jesus on this occasion as a practice to be taken up by future disciples. Nevertheless, it stands as a witness to the power of Christ to turn everyday rituals into life-transforming events.

The only other New Testament passage that mentions the washing of feet is found in 1 Timothy 5:9–10, which contains a list of qualifications for widows who should receive care and support from the community. Given the relative inability for most unmarried women in first-century Palestine to provide for their own basic needs, the Judeo-Christian value of communal care (offered by way of either biological nuclear families or the wider community of local congregations) is clear. Paul teaches that the widow who has no one else and therefore "has set her hope on God" (1 Tim. 5:5) should be cared for by the community of believers. Criteria are established, however, for these widows, and on the list is "one who has . . . washed the saints' feet." It is unclear whether this act was a matter of "social courtesy or possibly a quasi-liturgical act."[7] Either way, it implies selfless hospitality and service in the name of Christ. On the basis of these few references, some scholars believe that it is fair to deduce that during the first century foot washing was practiced at least in Ephesus and in the Johannine community.[8]

I have started with the New Testament passages concerning foot washing because the ritual expression of the church is most directly linked to these (especially John 13). But the Old Testament is not without relevant passages. There are several references to foot washing as a standard cultural practice of general hospitality (see Gen. 18:4; 19:2; 24:32; Judg. 19:21; 1 Sam. 25:41). However, references to *ritual* foot washing are somewhat minimal. The priests were required to wash hands and feet from a bronze basin at the entrance to the tent of meeting prior to entering (Exod. 30:17–21; 40:30–32). This instance is ceremonial for the priests, but not an action undertaken by the community.

Historical Foundations

While there is no record of the universal practice of foot washing in the history of the church, there is a continuous one. Foot washing was a part of both Jewish and Greco-Roman cultures in the ancient Mediterranean world.[9] It had three primary functions: personal hygiene, an expression of hospitality, and a cultic act.[10] The washing of feet was normally performed by the guests themselves or by servants/slaves on behalf of the host.[11] Basins of water were often provided by the host for this purpose.

There is notable mention of foot washing among the church fathers, though the details concerning its practice are not entirely specified. Early writings with at least passing reference to foot washing include those of Irenaeus, Cyprian, Tertullian, and Clement of Alexandria.[12] Athanasius charged bishops to wash the feet of "weak priests" three times per year, following Easter, Pentecost, and baptismal feasts.[13] Ambrose of Milan, while noting that it was not a practice of the Roman Church, nevertheless links foot washing to postbaptismal rites and "asserts that 'it is a sacrament and means of sanctification.'"[14] The connection between baptism and foot washing continued for centuries. "Exhortations recalling Christ's action in John's Gospel as the warrant for baptismal foot washing are also found in many eighth-century Gallican, Frankish, Spanish, and Italian sacramentaries," states Nathan Mitchell.[15] "As an icon of selfless service, foot washing not only molded the Last Supper narrative in John's gospel; it also shaped the liturgy of Christian baptism in many Western Christian churches," he continues.[16] Other church fathers mentioning ritual foot washing include Augustine and Chrysostom.[17] By the ninth century, postbaptismal foot washing waned in local parishes, but foot washing remained alive and well in medieval monasteries as attested to in St. Benedict's Rule,[18] and by writings of Bernard of Clairvaux.[19]

In addition to the various practices of foot washing mentioned above, it was observed as a part of ecclesiastical and secular court rituals for the coronation of kings and emperors.[20] The service for the installation of popes also included the head of the church washing the feet of twelve old, poor laypersons or priests as a sign of humility.[21] In time the Roman Church came to observe the practice only during Holy Week by including the ritual act within the Maundy Thursday service, reminiscent of the night Jesus instituted it. Foot washing is practiced on Maundy Thursday in many traditions today, including the Roman Catholic Church, the Anglican Communion, and many mainline denominations and Anabaptist groups.

Other Reformers, such as Martin Luther, opposed foot washing,[22] and the state churches of the Reformation did not adopt foot washing.[23] However, one of the primary Reformation movements to emerge in the early sixteenth century—the Anabaptist tradition—was quick to identify foot washing as a significant ritual expression and continues to embrace the practice today.[24] The first extant record of an Anabaptist foot washing occurred in Waldshut, South Germany, as early as 1525.[25] While foot washing has not been observed universally among Anabaptists, it has been a significant feature of many churches within the tradition for the last five hundred years. Anabaptist historian Harold Bender notes, "The rite fitted in well with their tendency toward communalism, their Biblical fundamentalism, and their emphasis on self-effacing equalitarianism among the members."[26] Interestingly, Anabaptist Reformer Menno Simons mentions it rarely in his writings; however, other early leaders, such as Pilgram Marpeck and Dirk Philips, emphasized the practice. Marpeck "makes repeated mention of footwashing as a Christian ordinance on a par with other ordinances."[27] Indeed, on the basis of Jesus's words "You also should do as I have done to you" (John 13:15) and "If you know these things, you are blessed if you do them" (John 13:17), a significant number of denominations within the larger Anabaptist tradition have elevated foot washing to the level of ordinance,[28] thereby practicing *three* ordinances (Lord's Supper, baptism, and foot washing).

While foot washing was a significant worship act among Anabaptists, no highly developed, standardized liturgy emerged, likely because of their protest against set liturgies of the Roman Church and because they highly value Free

Church worship practices.[29] Nevertheless, there are some common general features shared among Anabaptist groups. Perhaps the most uniform feature of the foot washing service is its connection to the Lord's Supper, harking to John 13. Standard practices include the embrace or holy kiss, and words of peace, reconciliation, or Christian love after two people have washed each other's feet. Offerings for the poor (almsgiving) are also commonly collected at the conclusion of the service.

The Anabaptist practice of foot washing is connected to ethical themes— those of humility, discipleship, reconciliation, fellowship, and service. The Mennonite Confession of Faith states it well.

> We believe that Jesus Christ calls us to serve one another in love as he did. Rather than seeking to lord it over others, we are called to follow the example of our Lord, who chose the role of a servant by washing his disciples' feet. . . . Believers who wash each other's feet show that they share in the body of Christ. They thus acknowledge their frequent need of cleansing, renew their willingness to let go of pride and worldly power, and offer their lives in humble service and sacrificial love.[30]

Theological Foundations

A number of themes related to foot washing hold rich potential for deepening the spirituality of believers; such themes include humility, cleansing, forgiveness, discipleship, service, reconciliation, mutuality, and love. Two of these are particularly central to the ethos of foot washing: humility and service. While numerous themes are appropriate for interpreting the meaning of foot washing, none are more closely tied to Jesus's own interpretation of the event than these two. When Jesus donned his outer clothing once again and returned to his place at the table, he seized the poignant, teachable moment to interpret the significance of what the disciples had just witnessed. As any wise rabbi would do, he posed a critical question to his followers for contemplation: "Do you understand what I have done to you?" (John 13:12). The Rabbi answered his own question, focusing on the qualities of humility and service:

> You call me Teacher and Lord—and you are right, for that is what I am. So if I, your Lord and Teacher, have washed your feet, you also ought to wash one another's feet. For I have set you an example, that you also should do as I have done to you. Very truly, I tell you, servants are not greater than their master, nor are messengers greater than the one who sent them. If you know these things, you are blessed if you do them. (John 13:13–17)

Humility and service are always closely woven together in function and purpose. Humility is the virtue through which service is most sincerely rendered. It takes a humble person to *truly* serve, and service is most honoring to God when expressed by a humble person. When we kneel to wash someone's feet, it is a humbling act. Both the act of kneeling and the gesture of washing dirty, smelly feet require humility. In essence, we bow before another (a gesture of humility) and cradle an "unlovely" part of the human body in our hands to perform a ministry to someone (an act of service). Very few acts are as humbling as this one, and those who hold themselves in high esteem will struggle to lower themselves to do as Jesus did the night before he died. It is hard enough to wash the feet of those we love, harder still to do so for an enemy, as Jesus did. Still, with the washing of feet we demonstrate the remarkable reality that all sisters and brothers are equal in God's sight; no one is above another. The apostles encouraged believers to pursue humility as one of the attributes of God's chosen ones. Paul urged the Colossians to "clothe yourselves with compassion, kindness, humility, meekness, and patience" (Col. 3:12); Peter echoes Paul's instructions in writing that members of the body of Christ "must clothe yourselves with humility in your dealings with one another, for 'God opposes the proud, but gives grace to the humble'" (1 Pet. 5:5).

Service was the primary mission of Jesus. He made it clear that his purpose in coming to earth was to serve (Mark 10:45). Service is, therefore, the mark of discipleship for the Jesus-follower. When two of his disciples, James and John, asked for positions of influence in his coming kingdom, Jesus responded that "whoever wishes to become great among you must be your servant, and whoever wishes to be first among you must be slave of all. For the Son of Man came not to be served but to serve" (Mark 10:43–45). "Slave of all" was the theme Jesus taught in Galilee and the theme he would demonstrate so breathtakingly in the upper room with only hours remaining in his earthly life. As stated in a minister's manual,

> We must note that the servanthood assumed by Jesus in this drastic act is related to the dedication of his coming. It is eternally bound to the cause for which he came and died. As the bread and cup are symbols of the sacrifice and giving of his life, so the kneeling to wash one another's feet is the symbol of the purpose and the living of his life.[31]

Foot washing, therefore, demonstrates humble service. With humility and service unified, humble service is the way we are to live daily in the world for the glory of God. While these may represent laudable attitudes and activities, the primary virtue is love. During the same meal and while Jesus was issuing last-minute instructions to the Twelve, he said, "I give you a new commandment, that you love one another. Just as I have loved you, you also should love one another. By this everyone will know that you are my disciples, if you have love for one another" (John 13:34–35). Humble service is the act; love is the ultimate virtue.

Some New Testament scholars view Jesus's institution of foot washing as significant for its unifying of the two sacraments/ordinances of baptism and the Lord's Supper. Biblical historian Oscar Cullman sees strong baptismal allusions in the ritual of foot washing.[32] The exchange between Peter and Jesus regarding how much of Peter's body should be washed (John 13:6–9) "can surely have only this meaning; he who received Baptism, even when he sins afresh, *needs no second Baptism*, for one cannot be twice baptized. The reference of the word 'bathed' to Baptism is the more convincing that Baptism in early Christianity did actually consist of dipping the whole body in the water."[33] That the washing of feet occurred during the meal of the Passover feast in which Jesus instituted the Lord's Supper as an ongoing ritual of the church is noteworthy, for in this way the Gospel of John illustrates that "one and the same event, Baptism and Lord's Supper . . . are formally placed together."[34] The act of foot washing, then, may be perceived not as a third ordinance but as a unifying gesture that emphasizes the two sacraments of baptism and Lord's Supper.[35]

A more technical issue is open for investigation and interpretation. Should a community practice Communion first, followed by foot washing, or vice versa? Denominations that historically practice foot washing disagree on the sequence. Some groups insist that Communion comes first, on the basis of earlier translations of John 13:2; for instance, "And supper being ended . . . [Jesus] riseth from supper" (John 13:2, 4 KJV), and then he performed the foot washing. More accurate renderings indicate that the Passover meal was in progress ("And during supper . . . [Jesus] got up from the table" [John 13:2, 4]) and the foot washing took place before the institution of the new covenant.[36] Yet for those believers who practice the threefold service of Communion, foot washing, and love feast, it is less important that the events reflect a literal historical sequence than that the spirit of the threefold service is maintained.

Today foot washing is not practiced at all among many Christian communities. Some argue that since washing feet is not practiced in modern cultures, the ritual is so uncommon as to be outdated. To such an argument, one minister's handbook responds, "That is true, but we are not seeking to learn a common lesson, rather a deep one."[37] Others try to modify the ritual by finding alternative practices, such as washing hands instead of feet. This act is discouraged for two reasons: (1) it cannot possibly demonstrate humble service at the same level as washing feet, and (2) the ritual of hand washing may represent a *different* sentiment—for instance, that of rejecting a person or idea, just as Pilate washed his hands at Jesus's trial to rid himself of all responsibility. Finding substitutes for a ritual established by Jesus Christ is questionable at best. In some Christian circles foot washing is making a comeback. As mentioned earlier, many groups that historically embraced foot washing as important to their faith have had an erratic history of its practice over the centuries. However, some of those who have neglected this "third ordinance" are indicating renewed interested in reclaiming its vital expression of discipleship among their communities.[38]

Building the Structure

When the foot washing service is offered for a local Christian community, it can be approached in one of several ways. First, the service may stand alone as simply a service of foot washing when designed with a combination of appropriate worship acts that create a thoughtful, communal experience for worshipers. The order of service that appears below is an example of such a service, though it could easily be incorporated into a service consisting of more parts with only slight alterations. You will note how minimal the liturgy seems; this is in keeping with the natural simplicity of the event, given its roots historically. The sample service here may be offered at any appropriate time other than Sunday morning (a special evening service, a camp or retreat setting, a special service of the Christian year such as Maundy Thursday, and so on). Second, a foot washing service can be combined with one or more related worship events, such as Holy Communion and/or the love feast (addressed later in this chapter). It could also occur, under the right circumstances, as a Response to the Word within the fourfold order of service on the Lord's Day. Each service would be nuanced a little differently to fit the setting.

The structure for a service of foot washing, while including several appropriate worship acts, is centered in three primary actions: the washing of feet, the embrace, and the speaking of words of peace. These basic parts are surrounded with a few other relatively optional elements of worship that do, however, serve to embellish the service if desired. The elements shown with titles on the left side of the page are considered essential to the service; the elements shown with centered titles within brackets [] are considered optional. If the service of foot washing is an extension of a longer service, a transitional congregational song and/or words spoken by the leader will form a bridge into foot washing.

The Order of the Foot Washing Service

The basic outline alone appears in appendix B.

Pre-service Music

Note: Maintaining complete silence can be an alternative way to mark the beginning of this service.

Greeting/Welcome

This should be scriptural in content and pastoral in tone.

A Hymn of Preparation
Invocation
Scripture Reading

Read John 13:1–17.

Read other passages appropriate to the ritual as desired (see below in "Installing Doors and Windows").

Note: Creative options include these ideas:

- Read from a contemporary translation of the Bible that captures well the drama of the story.
- Perform a dramatized enactment of John 13.
- Offer John 13 in reader's theater format.[39]

[Call to Humility]

Use a passage of Scripture or thoughtfully prepared words to invite the community to pursue the humble life as exemplified in Jesus's washing the disciples' feet.

Note: John 13:13–16 is a perfect passage to be incorporated as part of the call to humility:

"You call me Teacher and Lord—and you are right, for that is what I am. So if I, your Lord and Teacher, have washed your feet, you also ought to wash one another's feet. For I have set you an example, that you also should do as I have done to you. Very truly, I tell you, servants are not greater than their master, nor are messengers greater than the one who sent them."

[Time of Silence]

Silence is offered as a time of self-examination.

Note: It is recommended that true silence is kept. Avoid the use of background music.

[A Song of Reflection]

Reflection/Exhortation

The leader offers brief thoughts concerning the meaning of foot washing and encourages the community in its practice.[40]

Note: As is the case for the healing service, I recommend that these remarks not be a full sermon or even a homily; they are best kept very brief.

[Remembering Our Story]

The leader reads a brief statement from an official denominational source stating the purpose of the event for worshipers historically. This may be taken from a denominational handbook, an approved creedal-type statement, and so on.[41]

Confession of Sin

Invite the congregation to confession of sin. Pray a prayer of confession. (See appendix A.)

A Song of Assurance or Reconciliation

Invite the congregation to sing a hymn or song that emphasizes the worshiper's union with God and others.

Prayer of Preparation

See below in "Installing Doors and Windows."

The Washing of Feet

Invite the community to wash one another's feet.
Note: Several aspects of this service are listed below for your consideration.

- Instruct the participants as to the logistics of foot washing:
  - Kneel before someone sitting on a bench or chair.
  - Hold one of their feet in your hands, gently splashing water over it.
  - Dry with a towel.
  - Wash and dry the other foot (optional).
  - Trade places and repeat the action.

- ○ Stand and embrace.
- ○ Exchange words of peace (such as "The peace of Christ be with you," "God bless you," "God loves you and so do I," or any extemporaneous words of encouragement and fellowship).
- Have attendants (servers, deacons) posted at a table to empty basins and refill with warm water from large pitchers of water. As each set of partners come to wash feet, they will approach the refill station for fresh water and towels.
- Have hand cleanser in the room to use following the washing of feet.
- Select one of the service options below to facilitate this modest act, and explain it to the congregation.
  - ○ *Open-ended.* Whenever ready, an individual goes to another worshiper and asks if they may wash their feet.
  - ○ *Rows.* Seated in rows, the first person washes the feet of the person on their right, who in turn washes the feet of the person to their right, and so on.[42]
  - ○ *Separated.* Women and men are dismissed to two separate rooms for purposes of modesty. A dismissal is given after the foot washing portion is concluded, and the two groups reconvene to continue in unified worship. If separated, make sure you have adequate supplies and leaders for each room.
  - ○ *Leaders' foot washing.* Decide in advance when each of the leaders will wash worshipers' feet, including the attendants at the supply table. Leaders may go first as a form of modeling, or last as a sign of servanthood. In some traditions "the ministers wash each other's feet first, and then wash the feet of all the brethren in turn, the ministers' wives doing the same for the sisters."[43]
- Set up several washing stations in the space. Think about various options to suit your community, including several stations across the front, stations in the middle of a circle, and so on.
- Have the congregation sing hymns/songs while feet are washed. A leader may stand off to the side to assist the people in singing. Songs may be accompanied by organ, piano, or other instruments well suited to support congregational singing. Singing without accompaniment is also beautiful for this service, especially if there is an able leader and the people are able to ad lib four-part singing.
- Consider washing feet in complete silence, with only the sounds of the water in the basins and the exchange of peace spoken by participants.

Prayer of Thanksgiving and Petition

The leader offers a prayer of thanks for the blessings received in this holy act and for the privilege of serving one another as Christ did. The leader prays that participants will continue to live in humility as they serve the world in the name of Jesus.

[Testimonies Are Shared]
(An opportunity is given for spontaneous testifying and exhortation.)

A Hymn of Benediction

A closing song is an excellent way to conclude the service.

The Benediction

A benediction is pronounced upon the people.
Note: A scriptural benediction is encouraged.

[Offering for the Poor][44]
(A collection for those in financial need is made.)

It is common (and appropriate) to conduct a service of foot washing in conjunction with the Lord's Supper and/or the love feast; indeed, there is much precedent for doing so, as has been noted. The sequence in which the parts of the service appear (foot washing, Lord's Supper, love feast) should remain flexible; a case can be made for any order. If your worshiping tradition has a standard order, follow it; if not, or if there is freedom to do otherwise, arrange the order as best suited to your service.

Installing Doors and Windows

Some songs, Scriptures, prayers, and symbols add to the foot washing service. Unfortunately, very few songs, relatively speaking, are explicitly about washing feet in the context of worship. A few will be listed below. To add to this list, be looking for other songs that carry the same general theological themes relevant to foot washing (service, humility, reconciliation, and so on). Remember that songs, prayers, and symbols provide a means for worshipers to interact with God and one another. They encourage the corporate nature of the foot washing service by providing a means of full participation.

Songs

Here is a brief list of relevant hymns/songs for the foot washing service.[45] Those songs that directly reference foot washing are listed first; those with more general themes related to foot washing are listed next.

Songs Directly Referencing Foot Washing

As in That Upper Room You Left Your Seat (Timothy Dudley-Smith)

Extol the Love of Christ (Samuel Frederick Coffman)[46]

Father of Earth and Heaven (Charles Wesley)

Jesu, Jesu (words: Tom Colvin; music: Ghana folk song)

Jesus, Greatest at the Table (Stephen P. Starke)

Love Consecrates the Humblest Act (S. B. McManus)[47]

Our Noble Master, Brave and Strong (Constance Cherry)[48]

Songs with General Themes Related to Foot Washing

Christ, You Call Us All to Service (Joy Patterson)

Let Your Heart Be Broken (Bryan Leech)

Make Me a Servant (Kelly Willard)

Who Is My Mother, Who Is My Brother? (Shirley Erena Murray)

Scripture Passages

In addition to the obvious passage in John 13, there are several relevant Scripture passages appropriate for the foot washing service. Here are a few with which to begin your own list of Scripture passages to use.

Mark 10:35–45	Colossians 3:12–16	1 John 4:7–21
Luke 22:24–27	Colossians 3:17–24	
John 15:9–17	1 Peter 5:1–11	

Prayers

Prayers are often offered extemporaneously in the foot washing service; this is typical for an act rooted in the Free Church tradition. Nevertheless, listed below are a few samples of types of prayers appropriate for this service.

Prayer of Preparation

"Eternal Creator and Loving God,
In the act of kneeling to wash one another's feet,
    may we kneel also in our hearts
      so that our lives may bow in service
      to your will and not our own.
In allowing our feet to be washed,
    may our lives be cleansed with your forgiveness

so that we may go forth
    freed from the bonds of guilt and despair
    to live in freedom and hope.
O Lord,
In our washing of feet,
    cleanse our relationships with one another as well.
May we, in washing one another's feet,
    forgive and accept forgiveness from one another
    for any hurts or wrongs or misunderstandings
    that have passed between us,
    so that we may rise to sit together at your table
    in a renewed and strengthened fellowship in your love. Amen."[49]

Prayers of Thanksgiving and Petition

"O Jesus Christ, our Lord and Teacher,
    we give you thanks for inviting us, as your disciples,
    to take up the basin and towel in serving one another.

Thank you for counting us worthy to follow in your footsteps.

Thank you for the new commandment you have given to us
    to love one another in the same manner in which you love us.
Empty us of self.
Fill us with the very love with which you
    loved your disciples of long ago,
    and continue to love your followers today.
Give us the Spirit's strength to serve and love others in your name,
    to the glory of God the Father. Amen."[50]

Our dear Lord Jesus Christ,
    we praise you that, having loved your own,
    you showed the full extent of your love by humbling yourself,
    becoming obedient to death—even death on a cross.
May our service to one another this [evening/day]
    be pleasing in your sight.
Look on us, your disciples,
    and rejoice that your followers
    remember to do for others what you first did for us.
Give us faith to follow you always
    until we, like your first disciples,

see for ourselves your nail-scarred hands,
which on the night before their piercing,
cradled and washed the feet of weak and faithless followers
to demonstrate your unconditional love.
May our lives reflect this same love to others—
both friends and enemies—
so that all people will know that we are your disciples.
We pray this through your power at work in us by your Spirit. Amen.[51]

Meditation for Foot Washing

"Feet!
Just plain, ordinary, tired feet.
Jesus cared about feet.
He didn't ignore the head, the heart and the soul—
spectacular things like that.
But I'm especially glad that he cared about feet.
How many Messiahs ever did that?
You can wax eloquent and be beautifully abstract
about people's heads and hearts and souls.
But it is hard to be removed from human need
when you're kneeling down on the floor washing another's feet.
Dusty roads are scarce and very few sandals are worn now.
But feet trapped in leather are just as tired and just as ignored.
There still aren't many messiahs around who care about feet."[52]

Symbols

Some of the symbols and gestures representative of foot washing include the following:

- Towel
- Basin
- Pitcher of water
- Kneeling
- Embrace
- Holy kiss
- A table set with meal items reminiscent of the Passover meal and/or the Last Supper

The Christian Year

The service of foot washing may be held at any time during the Christian year; however, Maundy Thursday is especially appropriate in remembrance of the occasion when Jesus instituted the ritual act of foot washing. Several traditions, from Roman Catholic to Mennonite, highly recommend its observance during Holy Week.

Serving as Hospitable Host

A service of foot washing is an unusual service in many ways. In some respects, the role of host is quite remarkable, for she or he engages in one of the very acts of hospitality offered in first-century Palestine—literally! Use your imagination; think of how a host in that era would receive guests arriving for a visit. "Get your welcome on" and consider each worshiper to be your own personal guest for the day or evening. Help them feel at ease in what is a somewhat vulnerable situation. Be certain that those who assist you are fully prepared to make things flow smoothly. Hosts generally set the tone for any event; make sure the spirit you hope to prevail at this service is evident in your leadership from beginning to end.

Duties

A number of duties are related to conducting a service of foot washing. First, make sure everyone understands the nature of this service. Announce it well in advance and explain through bulletins, newsletters, and spoken announcements what will happen at this service. Communicate *why* this service will be observed, and do so with enthusiasm! Next, think through the logistics. Consider such things as

- whether or not there will be a separation of genders for the actual washing of feet;
- who is permitted to participate (what age, baptized or not, and so on);
- how foot washing partners will be determined;
- what space is best suited for the event;
- how many basins, pitchers, buckets for dirty water, towels will be needed;
- how many assistants will be needed (to change water, provide fresh towels, and so on);
- making sure the water is very warm (it will cool off quickly);
- having hand disinfectant available;
- who will clean up the space afterward.

As you prepare the order of service, consider which worship leaders are needed in order to help facilitate the worship elements.

Attributes for Presiding

As you prepare to host a foot washing ritual, you will find certain attributes to be effective.

- Be aware of those for whom this may be their first service of foot washing. First-timers may feel awkward or unsure. Put novices at ease by simply stating that this service is a fellowship service—such as, "We're here because we're family." Tell them not to worry about how to participate; you and others around them will guide them through it.

- Be calm and confident in your demeanor. This is a low-key service in tone. Though worship is always cause for enthusiasm, refrain from overly animated gestures and speech.

- Don't overlead. As leader, it is not necessary for you to maintain a presence that is front and center, as you would while presiding at the Table. Instead, stay in the background; move to the side and simply oversee the proceedings, stepping in as needed.

- Be prayerful. Maintain an ongoing prayer for the worshipers as they participate. No doubt you will notice some interesting dynamics among those who are washing feet—perhaps moments of real reconciliation are taking place or someone appears to be in deep conviction, thought, or prayer. Let the Holy Spirit do the Spirit's work while you maintain a prayer vigil over the service. Don't interfere; let the service unfold naturally. Extend pastoral care *after* the service if appropriate.

Administration

Very little administration is necessary as it relates to services of foot washing, but keep track of such things as

- making sure plenty of supplies are on hand and in good shape (clean towels, basins, pitchers, and so on);
- training deacons to facilitate at the services;
- keeping a record of those who assist, so that you may rotate the privilege among the members of the community;
- keeping a record of the dates you offer foot washing to ensure that it is being provided for according to your community's priority.

Exceptionally Difficult Circumstances

A few circumstances may prove challenging. Anticipate these to the best of your ability.

- Issues related to modesty. Women, in particular, may feel sensitive about removing stockings in mixed company. Some participants (perhaps older people) may feel awkward washing the feet of someone of the opposite sex. The key here is to *know your community*. If you are committed to having all participants in the same room to emphasize unity in community, one small adaptation can easily be made: stay in the same room, but ask men and women to sit in sections. Again, the important thing is to do what is best for your community.
- Embarrassment about one's feet. Some people are very self-conscious about their feet. An appropriate remark during instructions can remind everyone in the room that no feet are pretty! If one is embarrassed concerning the appearance of one's feet, all the more reason to humble oneself to let someone else wash them.
- Health issues. Occasionally persons suffer from foot diseases of various kinds. This may be addressed in one of two ways: (1) for mild, noncommunicable diseases, provide clear plastic gloves for the one who is washing, or (2) indicate that it is perfectly fine for anyone to "pass" when invited by someone to come to the basin. Urge such people to contribute to the other acts of worship during the service.

Ethical Considerations

One ethical consideration is to provide for modesty during this service. In earlier generations it was generally not customary for men and women to wash each other's feet due to issues related to modesty. While times have changed, and men and women washing feet together is more common, nevertheless be sensitive to any concerns that may arise with both genders participating. For instance, folks may be more comfortable if everyone is advised to wear slacks to the service (avoiding shorts or skirts).

A second consideration involves issues of power. Be aware of power plays (intentional or unintentional). It is possible that someone could abuse the purpose of foot washing by choosing or not choosing certain people with whom to partner. The leader does not control who washes whose feet but may feel led to later confront suspected power plays in the spirit of fostering true unity, which is the purpose of the service in the first place.

The Love Feast

The love feast, also referred to as "the agape meal," has a long and distinguished history in conjunction with feet washing. It is beyond the parameters of this chapter to offer a lengthy and detailed account of its history, theological foundations, and practices—valuable as this would be. What I will attempt, however, is a simple introduction to the love feast so that the reader will understand the basic purpose and nature of this special service, especially its association with the foot washing service.

Have you ever noticed that food and fellowship seem to go hand in hand with Christian community? It seems that it has been this way from the beginning. Jesus's ministry among his disciples often entailed eating together. Examples of the importance of being at the table together abound in the Gospels. In the earliest days of the infant church, believers met often, even daily, in one another's homes to "break bread." It is likely that this involved a common meal that also included the Eucharist. The frequent meals believers shared in this setting were essentially fellowship meals celebrating the sheer joy of being together as followers of the Way. At some point (it is not known exactly when) these regular dinners were separated from the ritual act of Eucharist. Some have suggested that during the time of severe persecution of Christians in the second century, it would not have been safe to hold public gatherings in homes, so the fellowship dinners ceased.[53] Laying aside exactly when the separation occurred, it is pertinent to this discussion to note simply that agape meals have been a part of Christianity from its inception.

Rooted in the significance of believers eating together, the love feast developed as a special type of worship service involving a simple meal. Love feasts held in conjunction with Holy Communion have been a long-standing tradition among Anabaptists, as noted earlier in this chapter. Fast-forward seventeen hundred years to 1727, when the modern history of the love feast began among the Moravians in Germany.[54] Count Zinzendorf introduced an intimate service of worship involving sharing simple food, prayer, religious conversation, and hymn singing.[55] John Wesley became acquainted with the love feast as a result of his associations with the Moravians. Wesley, in turn, adapted the practice to suit the eighteenth-century evangelical revival in England. Love feasts played a prominent role among the societies, class meetings, and bands of Methodism, in both Great Britain and America. Wesley felt that attendance at love feasts should be restricted to active members of these Methodist formation groups, so that the purity of worship and level of fellowship that occurred in their private worship services could be maintained. Of greatest concern for maintaining privacy at love feasts was "the desire to safeguard the atmosphere so participants felt able to speak freely in testimony."[56] This was especially significant so as to allow women to speak, "since some non-Methodists opposed women speaking in the church."[57] Another rationale for private love feasts was the

Wesleyan view "that God was uniquely present in their midst when they gathered as God's distinct people."[58] Therefore, to include nonbelievers at love feasts would be to compromise the setting in which God's presence is especially real. In order to restrict participation, entrance was monitored by a doorkeeper who allowed admittance by way of a ticket to the regular society meeting, a written note of special permission, or someone verifying one's credibility. "Simply put, Methodists believed that what they frequently experienced in these restricted rituals was nothing less than a foretaste of the quality of life in heaven."[59] Love feasts were common on the American frontier for closing worship at camp meetings; Methodists also included them in annual conferences.

Today, depending on one's tradition, love feasts are held with or without the Lord's Supper. Either way, it is important to note that the two should never be confused. The Lord's Supper includes the bread and the cup instituted by Jesus as the ongoing sacrament/ordinance for his disciples; the love feast is an extended meal wherein fellowship is fostered beyond the bounds of the Lord's Supper.

A love feast is composed of a group of believers (a church community) sitting at tables, sharing simple items of food and drink. Most often bread, crackers, or plain cakes are served in baskets—finger food, so to speak. Water is typically the beverage of choice, though tea or other light drink may be used. One of the acts of fellowship is the serving of one another during the meal; to accomplish this, leaders may arrange for the food and drink to be served at tables in small groups. It is important *not* to use food and drink too similar to that which would be used for the Lord's Supper; the distinction is an important one.

The content of the service—songs, testimonies, Scriptures, prayers—takes place *during* the eating of the meal. The meal and the service can take place separately, but the chances are much greater that conversation will more explicitly cover topics related to spiritual matters if the two aspects overlap. The meal/service may begin with a song, an invocation, or a blessing for the meal. Give some simple instructions and simply begin a series of alternating opportunities for singing of the Christian faith, sharing testimonies, exhortation, and so on. Lean heavily on singing and testimonies—they are the heart and soul of the love feast. If your church members tend toward the timid side, ask a few leaders in advance to be ready to share their testimony "spontaneously" at different points, so as to encourage others to do the same. An actual sermon should be avoided. Having hymnals or minimal materials needed on each table facilitates the worship greatly. If you are in a setting with projection capabilities whereby everyone can see the screen(s), take advantage of that, not only for words, but also for graphics. Typically, anyone can preside at a love feast; so it is a flexible addition to the Lord's Supper, especially where ordained pastors are at a minimum, as is the case in some regions of the United States and the world.

The Christian Year

These services are appropriate at any time in the Christian year, but especially during Holy Week or in conjunction with John Wesley's Covenant Service (often observed around the beginning of a new calendar year). A love feast may have a theme if desired. Choose hymns and songs according to the theme (Holy Week, renewing our covenant to follow Christ, and so on).

Conclusion

Tyler took the same route home as he finished his evening run. As luck would have it, a few folks were leaving the church, so he slowed down, hoping to make eye contact. A couple of men not much older than him greeted him with a wave. Tyler decided to go for it; he asked them about what he had observed through the window. Sitting on the church steps on this warm spring evening, Tyler had a fascinating conversation with complete strangers—but they didn't seem like strangers at all; they were among the most warmhearted people he had ever met. He doubted that anyone in his world would be willing to lower themselves to the point of washing someone else's feet as an act of service. It was so countercultural. Yet there was something radically refreshing about the whole idea. He would do an internet search when he got home to learn more. And maybe—just maybe—he would time his evening run to encounter his new friends again.

Key Terms

agape meal A fellowship dinner that developed among the first generation of Christians to foster community in Jesus Christ; originally included Eucharist as a part of the meal.

anteroom Side room or other alternative space in which participants may carry out foot washing for purposes of modesty or to facilitate a large crowd.

holy kiss A sign of fellowship as practiced in New Testament times; used often by the apostles. (See Rom. 16:16; 1 Pet. 5:14.)

washing of the saints' feet An older term for the service of foot washing.

To Learn More

For All Who Minister: A Worship Manual for the Church of the Brethren. Elgin, IL: Brethren, 1993.

Stutzman, Paul Fike. *Recovering the Love Feast: Broadening Our Eucharistic Celebrations.* Eugene, OR: Wipf & Stock, 2011.

Engage

Here are some practical things you could do to further explore the meaning and practice of foot washing:

1. Locate someone who has participated in foot washing on a fairly regular basis as a way of participating in his or her church's stated ordinances. Interview this person as to the meaning he or she finds in this liturgical act.
2. Write a "Prayer of Thanksgiving and Petition" using the examples above as a model.

8

Child Dedication
and Alternative Rites

Explore

Before reading chapter 8, reflect on child dedication services.

- Does your church practice the dedication of children? Why or why not?
- If your church **does** practice child dedication, who are the primary partici-pants, as you recall? What role does each participant play?
- Is child dedication a very elaborate ceremony? Describe it in detail, as best you remember it, as if to someone who has never witnessed a child dedication.
- If your church **does not** practice child dedication, why do you suppose some churches do observe this ceremony?
- In what ways might child dedication be different than infant baptism? In what ways might they be similar?
- Do children play a prominent role in the primary worship service(s) of your church? Why or why not?

Now that you have begun to reflect on child dedication, expand your thinking by reading chapter 8.

Expand

Erin is nine years old. She attends church almost every Sunday with her fam-ily. She really looks forward to seeing her friends, and she smiles when the pastor presses a mint into her hand when she leaves the church. She enjoys the smell of fresh coffee brewing in the fellowship hall as she enters the building. She hears the clanging of metal hangers on the coat rack near the entry as the draft from the door causes the empty hangers to bump into each other. She wonders how long it will be until she can drink coffee and reach the hangers to hang up her own coat. Even though church seems mostly to be for adults, she likes being there. The songs make her happy, and the prayers help her feel closer to God. She enjoys putting the coins her dad gives her into the offering plate; and even though she is told she wouldn't understand the sermon and needs to leave for children's church, some weeks she'd really like to stay in the sanctuary to be with everyone else. Today Erin gets to stay in "big church" a little bit longer, because there will be a child dedication, and the children's leader said it would be fine for all the children to watch as the Harper family brings their children forward to be given to God. Erin doesn't remember it, of course, but her parents told her that they did the same thing soon after she was born: *she* was dedicated to the Lord. Erin sometimes wonders whether her dedication means that she might have to leave home soon in order to serve God somewhere far away. Maybe today she would get some answers. Erin plans to listen very carefully to see what the Harper kids are in for.

Erin and her family attend one of a large number of churches that have practiced child dedication for many years.[1] The service is typically held once or twice a year—whenever newly born babies or young children arrive on the scene in a local church community. This brief "service within a service" occurs within the framework of Sunday worship and serves as recognition of the birth of a child and a religious rite for the parents. While many denominations observe child dedications, many do not. The difference generally lies with the view a church holds concerning infant baptism. Those churches that hold to infant baptism rarely practice child dedication; conversely, those who dedicate children do not generally practice infant baptism. (Infant baptism is addressed in chapter 4.)

Laying the Foundations

This chapter will offer some historical perspective on child dedication by identifying three historical practices, other than baptism, associated with the acknowledgment and welcoming of young children into the life of the church throughout the centuries. To these I will add an additional alternative rite, endorsing its potential viability for practice today. These four types of "child dedication" practices will be briefly compared and contrasted to child dedications as performed currently among Free Church traditions.[2] Biblical and theological foundations will follow, helping to formulate our thinking into appropriate options for child dedications today. As in the preceding chapters, some model services are offered, representing three alternative rites.

Historical Foundations

The historical practice of rites related to the birth of children in the Christian community is somewhat complicated but not without valuable and credible sources that shed some light on the subject. As mentioned, these rites cannot be considered independently from the development of infant baptism, for the rites, historically speaking, either deeply and intentionally foreshadow baptism or stand apart from baptism altogether. With this in mind, we begin by noting that historians differ on when exactly infant baptism began to be in widespread practice.[3] Nevertheless, we may with fair certainty conclude from the evidence that during the fourth century, with the large numbers of adult baptisms resulting from Constantine's support of Christianity, there was a period of time with little to no indication of infant baptism being normative.[4] As church historian David F. Wright states, "All historians of the development of early Christian baptism are agreed that for a period of several decades in the fourth century the children of most Christian parents were not baptized in infancy."[5] Wright concludes that though historians "may not be of one mind in their accounts of baptismal practice before this period or of how long it lasted, nor indeed of how to explain it and hence how to speak about it," nevertheless evidence supports the fact that "during at least half a century . . . the offspring of Christian parents . . . were not given baptism."[6]

The significance of this conclusion for our purposes is to raise the question, What *did* happen during this period with respect to infants born to Christian parents? At least three rites made their way into practice, with varying degrees of popularity (and historical documentation). First, some evidence suggests that perhaps there was a regular liturgical practice of giving thanks for the birth of a child. In a second-century work *Apology* of Aristides, we find: "And when a child has been born to one of them [a Christian], they give thanks to God."[7] In his analysis of this reference within *Apology*, Wright concludes, "The variety of settings in which 'thanking God' occurs . . . strongly suggests a non-baptismal but possible liturgical usage. We have here then a thanksgiving for the birth of a child."[8] Assuming Wright is correct, this suggests one possible option for an alternative rite to the contemporary practice of child dedication: a service of thanksgiving for the birth of a child.

A second historical model that emerged during the fourth century was the enrollment of infants in the catechumenate, with baptism to follow upon personal declaration of faith during adulthood. Here we have a more substantive record to go on. Many of the church fathers of the late fourth and early fifth centuries fell into this category, including Basil of Caesarea, Gregory of Nanzianzus, Gregory of Nyssa, John Chrysostom, Augustine, Jerome, Ambrose, and others.[9] Indeed, the point could be made that the approach to child dedication during this period yielded remarkable leaders of the church—leaders who were dedicated to God by virtue of infant enrollment in the catechumenate, with baptism following as an adult. Augustine is a prime example.[10] The sign of the cross and the seasoning with salt[11] were rituals of enrollment in the catechumenate, not baptism,[12] and "would have constituted a kind of dedication of the baby Augustine to Christ and his church."[13] Wright concludes, "The commencement of his catechumenate was equivalent to his infant dedication to the church, and implicitly also to a pledge of intent by his parents . . . to his Christian upbringing."[14] Wright believes this practice "must have been extremely common" and that "it seems reasonable to regard such entry into the status of catechumen at birth as a form of infant dedication."[15] It is clear that the rite of enrollment in the catechumenate was not confused with infant baptism and stood apart as a distinct rite.

A third development belongs to this general time period, that of dedicating infants—even before birth—to lives of virginity for the purpose of vocational service to the church.[16] This tended to occur among the wealthier class, who leaned toward asceticism. Ambrose was particularly supportive of this approach to child dedication, even urging parents to train their daughters to follow this path; Jerome was familiar with this practice also.[17] In addition, there are "sufficient attested instances of infant boys being vowed, by their parents . . . to the clerical service of the church for us to regard it as another form of infant dedication in the church of late antiquity."[18] The Second Council of Toledo (AD 527) testifies to this practice by regulating the treatment of those who have entered the office of clergy by virtue of parental intent from infancy.[19] It is perceived that "the dedication of the newborn to virginity serves somewhat as Augustine's initiation into the catechumenate did at Tagaste in AD 354—to mark at the outset of life a parental commitment that the child become a servant of Christ."[20] Germane to our discussion is that infant baptismal rites do not seem to be normative for those pledged very early to virginity or clerical ministry.[21]

The result of this brief historical overview points to a profitable conclusion for child dedications. Wright says that "we cannot miss the significance that, mostly during the period when all parties agree infant baptism was normally not administered, other, albeit varied, forms of pledging infants to God were being observed."[22] We have here historical rationale for some type of child dedications. But is it the type with which we are most familiar in the Free Church practice of the twenty-first century?

The ritual of child dedication, *as we see it performed today*, is a fairly recent development. At the time of the Reformation, there were a few notable exceptions to the all but universal practice of infant baptism. The Anabaptists were among the exceptions, as noted in chapter 4, delaying baptism until personal profession of faith was made. However, it is important to note that the Anabaptists had no prebaptismal rite for infants,[23] whereas other groups practicing believer's baptism provided rites for infants that were viewed as a precursor to baptism;[24] the connection was clearly made in the liturgy between the rite for the child and future baptism. One can see that these rites were vastly different in content and purpose than the child dedications we often witness today. These earlier communities understood these rites for infants to be the first "installment" of a process resulting in baptism; therefore, the content was markedly different than the dedication of a child, which generally makes no mention of future baptism and is not viewed as a precursor to baptism explicitly. Instead, children are "given to the Lord" as parents pledge themselves to the Christian upbringing of the child. In fact, one order of service for the dedication of a child suggests that the ritual "be included in the offertory, as an act signifying the offering of the child to God. As the gifts are brought forward a representative of the congregation escorts the parents and the child to a place before the table."[25]

The modern beginnings of child dedication are not easy to pinpoint with any degree of accuracy; hence, exactly when and how they originated is not altogether clear. It is much easier to identify denominations or movements that practice child dedication as opposed to infant baptism. Child dedications tend to be performed widely in denominations from within the Free Church tradition that baptize believers exclusively and which do not view either rite—child dedication or baptism—as sacramental in nature. Various Baptist denominations, the Christian Church/Churches of Christ, Assemblies of God, Church of God (Anderson), most Pentecostal groups, and many others are representative of those denominations that currently practice child dedication. Even some denominations stemming directly from the influence of John Wesley, who favored infant baptism, have opted for child dedication over infant baptism, including the Church of the Nazarene, the Wesleyan Church, the Free Methodist Church, and more.[26]

Biblical Foundations

Congregations that affirm child dedication today commonly appeal to the same biblical passages for the foundations on which they ground this practice.[27] The most commonly cited passages include Hannah's presentation of young

Samuel to the Lord (1 Sam. 1:24–28), Joseph and Mary's presentation of Jesus in the temple when he was eight days old (Luke 2:22–24), and Jesus's blessing of children during his earthly ministry (Mark 10:13–16). In the first two instances, it becomes obvious that the action is instigated and taken by the parent(s) of the child. However, the child is not *dedicated*; rather, the child is *presented* in order that parents fulfill their spiritual obligations (they dedicate themselves, so to speak). Hannah made a vow to God that if her barrenness was reversed and she bore a son, she would present him to God for a lifetime of religious service in thankfulness for this miracle. Hannah's gift of Samuel to the priest Eli was a means of keeping *her* vow. It does not represent a normative practice expected of all parents and all children in Old Testament times, since few parents made this vow. Note that Samuel wasn't dedicated; he was presented as an offering to fulfill a vow made by his mother as a result of *her* dedication.

As for the instance of Joseph and Mary, their presentation of Jesus in the temple was also the result of parental faith. In this case they were fulfilling three requirements of the Mosaic law: first, all males were to be circumcised on the eighth day after birth (Gen. 17:12); second, the couple's gift of doves or pigeons was the required sacrifice for Mary's purification (women were considered "unclean" after childbirth; see Lev. 12:8); and third, as the firstborn male of the family (the Levites being the exception), a fee of redemption would have needed to be paid (see Num. 3:44–48).[28] On this occasion, like that of Hannah, *parents* exhibited *their dedication* as they presented their child for God's purposes. What we see modeled in these instances is not the dedication of the child (as we think of it today); rather, we see parents who desire to live out their faithfulness to God and God's laws. In light of all of this, it seems more in keeping with these passages to think of "parent dedication," rather than "child dedication." Here we see that both Samuel and Jesus were presented by means of ritualistic sacrifices (1 Sam. 1:24–25; Luke 2:22–24) that were undertaken by their parents for the purpose of offering themselves to the Lord for the benefit of the child.

The two occasions cited above share some features common to infant baptism: the prominence of the parents' faith and the offering of themselves to the Lord for the benefit of the child, as is evident in the pledges found in the baptismal service for infants (see chapter 4). With these commonalities noted, the marked distinction remains: child dedications are largely centered in human acts offered to fulfill God's expectations for raising children in the faith. While child dedication is not technically an ordinance, it is nevertheless most appropriate for sisters and brothers holding the ordinance view as explained in chapter 1. Infant baptism, however, is viewed primarily as God's activity of grace for with the parents' role as integral (appropriate for sisters and brothers holding the sacramental view).

In Mark's passage, parents seek a blessing for their children. They do not bring their children for dedication purposes; instead, they simply want Jesus to place his hands upon them and to bless them. Here again, the faith of the parents is the key. They long for the great teacher and miracle worker to impart a special blessing; after all, like most parents, they want the best for their child. Dedication is not implied anywhere in this passage. What *is* explicitly affirmed is that Jesus loved and valued young children. Consequently, he desired that they should not be prevented in any way from coming to him, whereupon he would hold them in his arms, place his hands upon them, and pronounce a blessing. Jesus loves the little children.

What may be drawn from these passages often used to undergird the practice of child dedication is that the ritual centers on what the parent(s) will do to raise the child in the Christian faith. This is seen upon examining the rites of contemporary examples of child dedication services.

Theological Foundations

In the paragraphs below I would like to suggest the circumstances around which child dedication seems to make sense; then I will describe three approaches to child dedication that may be pastorally and theologically appropriate.

Under what circumstance might child dedication seem to make sense? Child dedication may be appropriate if one's family belongs to a church that practices believer's baptism exclusively (a church where infant baptisms are never performed). In this case, when a newborn child theoretically has a number of intervening years between birth and her or his personal experience of salvation followed by baptism, it may be beneficial to have a service of child dedication. Under these circumstances, a child dedication can serve several purposes: (1) an occasion for the child and family to receive a blessing from God; (2) a recognition of the gift of life; (3) welcoming the child into the local Christian fellowship; (4) emphasizing the child's importance to the fellowship; and (5) celebrating with the parent(s), for the church always seeks to rejoice with those who rejoice (Rom. 12:15). A child dedication could also be profoundly significant if parents rededicate themselves by renewing their Christian vows publicly as a means of accepting their spiritual parental duties as prescribed by God (Deut. 6:6–9; Prov. 22:6; Eph. 6:4). These purposes for child dedication will be seen in the various services outlined below as alternative rites. If child dedication serves these purposes, I urge the pastoral leadership to consider using the alternative terms for the services (explained below) as a means of stressing that the weight of the responsibility falls on the parent(s) rather than focusing on the child.

Under no circumstances should *both* a service of child dedication and a service of infant baptism be offered to the same child, because *the purposes fulfilled in a service of child dedication are also cared for in the service of infant baptism* (though not vice versa). A service of infant baptism, in addition to other things, pronounces a blessing on the child, welcomes the child into the church universal, and affirms the child's importance to the local fellowship. The services are redundant (and confusing) if both are administered for a child. However, we must not make the mistake of thinking that because they are redundant, they are the *same*. The *sacrament* of baptism offers grace to the recipient; the *ordinance* of baptism is done out of obedience to Christ's command. A service of child dedication, however, does not administer grace, nor does it fulfill a command of our Lord. It is, rather, an optional, occasional service of pastoral benefit to a nuclear family in connection with its spiritual family—its local church body.

What are the theological underpinnings, then, of child dedication? First, child dedication is not baptism. Baptism signifies several important truths (see chapter 4), one of which is that it is the primary rite of initiation into Christ's holy church. (This is true for both infant and believer's baptisms.) Membership in the church universal is achieved on the basis of the covenant. We become heirs of this covenant through baptism. Child dedication is neither a sacrament nor an ordinance; therefore, it cannot be performed as a sign of the covenantal relationship established between God and God's people. To confuse child dedication with becoming a child of the covenant is to drastically mix the meaning of two very distinct rituals. One signifies initiation into Christ's holy church (baptism); the other signifies a parental pledge to pursue Christlikeness in order to influence their young child (or children) toward Christian faith. Every effort should be made to clearly differentiate between the acts of baptism and alternative rites. For this reason, the features clearly associated with baptism should be avoided during a rite of child dedication. Water must be reserved for a baptismal service and therefore is not used symbolically in any way for a dedication. Also, Trinitarian formulations are necessary as part of the baptismal service (Matt. 28:19) but only end up confusing the issue when applied to the child dedication service.

Second, child dedication today (within the Free Church tradition) is not an offering of the child for full-time Christian service, as was the case for Hannah and for the ascetics in the late fourth and early fifth centuries, discussed above. While parents may have aspirations that their girl or boy will enter the ministry or other avenue of vocational service, that is not theirs to determine. Pray for it, yes, if they feel led; offer their young child without her or his consent, no. The Scriptures testify to people who are called from birth;[29] however, these are unusual circumstances, and the vast majority of servants of God become *personally* convinced that God is calling them as a result of the Holy Spirit's direct work in their lives. Parental prayers may be effective in the vocational calling of their children, but it takes a willing and obedient child to answer the call. A child dedication service alone does not constitute a call to ministry.

Rites to Recognize the Birth of a Child

For those congregations that do not practice infant baptism, here are some foundations to consider regarding child dedication services.

Rethinking the Emphasis of Child Dedication Services

If a service of child dedication is desired under the circumstances outlined above, what purpose should it serve? What form should it take? Child dedications are advisable theologically and offer real pastoral merit if they are *reframed and renamed*. Let me explain.

Given that child dedication is not explicitly demonstrated or commanded in Scripture, one might be quick to conclude that it serves no purpose and should be disposed of. But there may be enough precedence by way of scriptural implication to commend it when infant baptism is not an option. However, some reorientation in thinking about its purpose and participants is needed. I see three different types of "child dedication" services that have value under the right circumstances. I give each type of service a new name to more accurately describe its nature. The first and third alternative rites mentioned below make no real connection to future baptism. The second alternative rite is strongly connected to the future baptismal event.

A Service for the Blessing of a Child

First is "The Blessing of a Child" (or "The Blessing of Children"). There are several biblical instances of the ritual blessing of children. When John the Baptist was born, his father, Zechariah—a priest—pronounced a "prophetic blessing" on the baby; in fact, his blessing seems to be among the first words he spoke when he was finally able to do so after being struck mute for his disbelief concerning the circumstances of Elizabeth's pregnancy (Luke 1:20). While Zechariah's words are viewed as prophetic in nature (Luke 1:67), they are also a blessing directly pronounced on the child.

> And you, child, will be called the prophet of the Most High; for you will go before the Lord to prepare his ways, to give knowledge of salvation to his people

by the forgiveness of their sins. By the tender mercy of our God, the dawn from
on high will break upon us, to give light to those who sit in darkness and in
the shadow of death, to guide our feet into the way of peace. (Luke 1:76–79)

What greater blessing could there be than to be identified as the prophet of
the Most High? Evidence of this blessing of the child is seen as Luke comments,
"The child [John] grew and became strong in spirit" (Luke 1:80). Jesus later
confirms John the Baptist's status as premier prophet when he speaks to his
disciples about him: "A prophet? Yes, I tell you, and more than a prophet. . . .
Among those born of women no one is greater than John" (Luke 7:26, 28). The
blessing received at John's birth held promise that was realized for all Israel.

Jesus also received a blessing as a newborn. Simeon, a righteous and devout saint who was in the temple when Joseph and Mary presented Jesus for
circumcision, took Jesus in his arms and praised God in the form of offering
a "prophetic blessing" similar to that of Zechariah: "Master, now you are
dismissing your servant in peace, according to your word; for my eyes have
seen your salvation, which you have prepared in the presence of all peoples, a
light for revelation to the Gentiles and for glory to your people Israel" (Luke
2:29–32). That this is a blessing becomes crystal clear as Luke writes, "Then
Simeon blessed [the family]" (Luke 2:34), continuing with more prophetic
words (see Luke 2:34–35).

Jesus not only *received* a blessing as a baby; he *gave* blessings to little ones.
An important incident is reported in Mark's Gospel that shows Jesus's love
and concern for little children: Jesus "took them up in his arms, laid his hands
on them, and blessed them" (Mark 10:16). There is ample incidence of the
blessing of a child in Scripture.

What does a blessing involve? A cursory look at occasions of blessing in
the Bible seems to suggest several key components to any blessing. Normally
blessings are

- pronounced (announced directly *to* the individual, not a prayer *over* the
  individual);
- composed of good words for well-being (shalom);[30]
- accompanied with gestures (holding the child in one's arms, laying hands
  on the child's head, and so on);
- performed in community and most often in a sacred space.

A blessing is not a magical incantation to ensure that the wishes of others
come true. But it is a God-breathed expression for peace and well-being to
be a reality for God's child.

So far I have proposed that "child dedications" make sense if the emphasis shifts from *dedicating* the child to *blessing* the child. With this shift in purpose, renaming the ritual also makes sense: "The Blessing of a Child" (or other similar title of your choice) is more in keeping with the event than "Child Dedication." An example for an order of service for "The Blessing of a Child" appears below as Service 1. *Note that this alternative is not viewed as a precursor to baptism, as is the case for the second alternative rite.*

A Service of Welcome for the Young Disciple

A second alternative rite exists for rethinking child dedication. Instead of focusing on the blessing of a child, this service officially enrolls the infant as a "disciple-to-be"; it functions as a sort of first step toward baptism, which would occur years later upon personal confession of faith. This service may be referred to as "A Service of Welcome for the Young Disciple."[31]

Geoffrey Wainwright recommended this type of service decades ago as a viable option for those parents, pastors, and other leaders who prefer that baptism be administered upon confession of faith of the one baptized.[32] Every Christian denomination, even those that regularly baptize infants as the preferred approach, provides for the baptism of someone old enough to personally profess faith in Jesus Christ. If it is determined by those responsible for a child that baptism be delayed until personal conversion, the question is then raised as to the infant's official relationship to the church. Wainwright notes that while a baptismal service exists for those who are able to profess Christ for themselves, "no service is set forth for use meanwhile in the case of infants whose parents, while favouring for the sake both of their own children and of the whole Church the postponement of their offspring's baptism, yet desire that the entry of their children into the Church should be begun in infancy in some appropriate way."[33] A ceremony whereby the child is received as an official member of the church and whereby he or she is identified as a candidate for baptism in the earliest stage of progression is advantageous here. Wainwright points out that this is not unlike the catechumenate process of the ancient church (as discussed earlier in this chapter).[34] In early Christianity, a potential believer was enrolled as a catechumen, underwent years of spiritual preparation and intentional discipleship, and then, as a culmination of the process, upon his or her sincere profession of faith, was baptized.

A few instances of this approach exist in modern practice. One example is found in the Reformed Church of France during the mid-twentieth century. This denomination normally expresses a deep and long-standing commitment to infant baptism, but it devised a nonbaptismal rite of initiation for infants.

During the rite, infants are presented and blessed; also explicit in the liturgy is language that makes it perfectly clear that this rite is viewed as the first step toward baptism—an event to be forthcoming upon the catechumen's request in the future. As such, the infant is welcomed into Christ's church and comes under the official care of the church for guidance, nurture, and discipleship. In this service, "parents and Church alike recognize their responsibility to educate the child in the Gospel of Jesus Christ,"[35] and the child is blessed. An interesting aspect of the service reflects God's prevenient grace toward the child. The officiant speaks these words to the child:

> Little child, before you can understand and believe it, we declare, with your parents, that your life is in the hands of your Lord: for you Jesus Christ came upon earth, fought and suffered; for you he went through the agony of Gethsemane and the darkness of Calvary; for you he cried, "It is finished"; for you he died and for you he overcame death; yes, for you, little child, and you know nothing about it yet! So is the word of the apostle confirmed: we love God because he first loved us.[36]

Similar services in different traditions have been developed that make it clear that the infant is considered to be at the earliest stage of the catechumenate process and en route to baptism. The strong connection between this type of service and future baptism is what sets this service apart from a standard child dedication as we know it today. It is also the primary difference between "A Service of Welcome for the Young Disciple" and "The Blessing of a Child."

A Service for Parental Renewal of Baptism

The first two types of services mentioned thus far, though perhaps not very widely practiced, have historical precedent and, I would argue, real possible value to Christian communities that embrace the idea of believer's baptism and yet wish to give attention to the relationship between the youngest members of the community and the church. A third way to think about child dedications may be an option that is new. Instead of emphasizing the blessing of the child or his or her trajectory toward baptism, this third way emphasizes the parents' role of spiritual nurture, thus becoming a sort of "parent dedication" rather than a "child dedication." The emphasis in this service is one of recommitment by the parents of their allegiance to Christ and their intention to continue with new resolve their pursuit of holiness so that the child in their care is influenced in becoming a true disciple of Jesus Christ. This service may be referred to as "A Service for Parental Renewal of Baptism."[37] In reflecting on how this would look, let us return to the idea of the remembrance of baptismal vows discussed in chapter 4.

A remembrance of baptism service helps believers remember the importance of baptism in their daily lives. So many times we view our baptism as a one-time event, and the significance is quickly forgotten. In fact, persons who were baptized as an infant *cannot* remember their baptism in the literal sense. A remembrance of baptism service reminds believers that their baptism matters every single day. As the apostle Paul describes it, "We have been buried with [Christ] by baptism into death, so that, just as Christ was raised from the dead . . . so we too might walk in newness of life" (Rom. 6:4). To "remember our baptism" is to "walk in our baptism"—every moment of every day. The idea of the renewal of one's baptismal vows is similar to the renewal of wedding vows. When couples decide to renew their marriage vows, they are not getting remarried (we don't get rebaptized); they are simply remembering that every day of their married life they hope to take the vows just as seriously as they did on their wedding day.

When a baby is born to or adopted by Christian parents, it is a perfect opportunity for the parents to reexamine their walk with Christ. A remembrance of baptism service for the parents could hold profound meaning as they publicly accept the responsibility for raising their young child—a gift from God—by virtue of their baptism. With baptism comes responsibility; this is true for all believers. As a result of our baptism, we increase in faith, grow in love for God and others, and commit to greater service in the kingdom of God. These virtues become all the more important when the shaping of new generations of believers is at stake. Perhaps as parents renew their baptismal vows in light of raising their children—as they dedicate themselves anew to pursuing the character of Jesus especially in light of family life—young children may be spiritually formed with greater intentionality and love than ever before. The greatest benefit a child can receive is that of parents who daily walk in their own baptism to the glory of God.

A word of caution is in order when speaking of a remembrance of baptism service for parents. Though in the context of this service parents or guardians will make personal statements of intent about how they intend to raise their child, this service should *always be viewed as a corporate service*. It does not necessarily have to be a remembrance of baptism service for the whole congregation (though that too would be fitting and even encouraged), but it certainly must be a corporate service in that the community is called on to participate fully throughout the liturgy. Care must be taken to ensure that the community does not simply watch as parents remember their baptism but that community members are active in the event, reflecting upon their baptisms as well. As mentioned in chapter 4, care must also be given that there is no confusion between rebaptism and remembering one's baptism. If water is used symbolically to enrich the service (which is very common), it must not be used in any way to suggest rebaptism.

With this third shift in emphasis regarding child dedication, we have moved from dedicating the *child* to dedicating the *parents*. An example of "A Parental Renewal of Baptism" service is offered below.

If your church has historically been part of a tradition that dedicates children/infants, you can find many resources to support the traditional service. Check especially in the minister's handbooks of various denominations that favor child dedication. A number of interdenominational minister's handbooks may also be found in major publishers' catalogues or Christian bookstores. There is much available to help you shape a standard child dedication service. But if you would like to explore alternative rites related to the birth of a child that are distinctly different from traditional child dedications of recent years, perhaps one of these three services described here will serve you well. Each of these services is also perfectly suited for adopted children (or any number of other scenarios) with little or no adaptations.

Building the Structure

Three separate services are described below. You will observe some overlap in the content of these three services. That is okay; the key is in what the services emphasize.

Service 1: An Order of "The Blessing of a Child"

The basic outline alone appears in appendix B.

For those churches that do not practice infant baptism, a separate but different rite may be pastorally helpful when an infant or very young child is new to a local church community.[38] The following service for "The Blessing of a Child" is not a child dedication service. Rather, it is a service of thanksgiving for and blessing on a newborn child belonging to Christian parents, either biologically or by adoption. Because a service like this is not private but always done in community, it becomes a part of the normal Lord's Day worship. This "service within a service" assumes that a worship service is under way, consisting of the Gathering and the Word (now completed) and leading to the Blessing of a Child, which is viewed as the Response to the Word. Feel free to be somewhat flexible in the order of service to suit your purposes. Though this service is not an ordinance or sacrament requiring an ordained person to officiate, it is most fitting for the ordained pastor to conduct it.

Note: The elements shown with titles on the left side of the page are considered essential to the service; the elements shown with centered titles within brackets [] are considered optional.

Song (Transitioning from the Sermon)

An appropriate song is sung by the congregation. (See song suggestions below.)

Note: Parents and other family members may come to the front during the song.

Statement of Purpose

The pastor makes a simple statement as to the special nature of this service.

Samples

- Sisters and brothers, we have a new member of the family to celebrate—[*full name of child*]! We recognize that [*first name of child*] is a gift not only to the [*last name of family*] family but to us as well. And so we gather to rejoice and to ask God's blessing upon [*child's name*] and [*her/his*] family. This is a special day! May God's presence abound as we express Christian love to our newest member of the household of faith and pray God's blessing upon [*her/him*].[39]

- Members of the household of faith, we are gathered in God's presence to rejoice and give thanks for the gift of new life. [*Name of child*] was born [*date of birth*] to [*names of parents*]. What a happy day that was, not only for the [*last name of family*] family, but for us too—members of the family of God. All life is a gift from God. How precious is this newly born child in the sight of God and of [*her/his*] spiritual family, the members of [*name of church*]. Because we rejoice with those who rejoice, today we will offer a blessing upon this child. We will also dedicate ourselves anew to living as true disciples of Jesus Christ so that [*name of child*] will become acquainted with our Savior and come to follow him too.[40]

Invocation

Offer a brief prayer inviting the presence of God's Spirit as we worship God for the most generous gift of life.

Samples

- Jesus, lover of the children, remind us that you who scooped little ones up into your arms to bless them are with us during these moments to do the same. Come, make your presence known in a special way so that just as you spoke words of welcome in Galilee so long ago, we will hear your voice once again saying, "Let the little children come to me." We worship you by welcoming the little ones with the same passion which you displayed so long ago. We pray this in your name. Amen.[41]

- "God, as a mother comforts her children, you . . . sustain and provide for us. As a father cares for his children, so continually look upon us with compassion and goodness. We come before you with gratitude for the gift of this child, for the joy that has come into this family, and the love with which you surround them and all of us. Pour out your Spirit. Enable your servants to abound in love, and establish our homes in holiness; through Jesus Christ our Lord. Amen."[42]

Opening Words from Scripture

An appropriate Scripture passage is read. (See scriptural suggestions below.)

Note: A youth who has been well prepared may be an excellent choice to read the Scripture.

[Litany of Thanksgiving]

Sample

Pastor: This is the day the Lord has made; let us rejoice and be glad in it!

People: We rejoice in God's goodness.

Pastor: This is the day we celebrate the innocence and beauty of young children.

People: We rejoice in God's goodness.

Pastor: This is the day we fling our arms wide open to embrace this precious child.

People: We rejoice in God's goodness.

Pastor: This is the day our community offers the blessing of God upon [*name of child*], trusting that God's shalom will abound in [*her/his*] young life always.

People: We rejoice in God's goodness.

Pastor: This is the day the Lord has made.

All: Let us rejoice and be glad in it![43]

[Parents' Intent[44]]

The pastor asks the parents publicly what their hopes and prayers are for their child.

The parents respond by mentioning a spiritual grace for which they pray for the child. It is also possible that the parents may wish to claim a Bible verse as a word of direction for their child's life—a "life verse" that will guide the parents as they pray for their little one in the future.

Note: The entire service, and especially this section, should be discussed prior to the service. The pastor should guide the parents so that they are thoughtful and prayerful concerning these matters, and to avoid any inappropriate choices.

Sample

Pastor: What are your hopes for this child?

Parents: We pray that God will fill [*name of child*] with love for God and others. [Love is used here as an example; other virtues may be chosen, such as courage, gentleness, peace, boldness, prayerfulness, and so on. Only one virtue should be given. The "life verse," if chosen, will relate to the virtue.]

Note: Either naming hopes for the child or selecting a verse of Scripture may be done or both.

Pastor: Is there a verse of Scripture you choose to pray in the coming years for [*name of child*]?

Parents: We hope that [*name of child*] will especially live out this verse from Matthew: "You shall love the Lord your God with all your heart, and with all your soul, and with all your strength, and with all your mind; and your neighbor as yourself" (Luke 10:27).[45]

The Blessing

The pastor takes the child into her or his arms and speaks a blessing on the child.

- Position yourself so that the community as well as the family members may see your action.
- It is meaningful to invite worshipers to stretch their hands toward the child at this moment.
- If the parents have identified a particular virtue to abound in their child, include reference to this virtue in the blessing.
- If the parents have selected a "life verse," try to shape the blessing in that general direction.
- Memorize and use a scriptural blessing/benediction.
- *Pronounce* the blessing; do not *pray* the blessing (direct it upon the child).

- Look into the face of the child; place your hand on her or his head.
- Avoid Trinitarian formulations so as not to confuse with baptism.
- Invite the congregation to participate in the "Amen."[46]

Prayer for the Parents

The pastor or other lay leader offers prayer that the parents will be strengthened to care for and lead this child in the ways of Jesus Christ.

- These may be spontaneously offered by one or more persons.
- It is appropriate to lay hands on the parents during the prayer.

Introduction of the Child

While continuing to hold the child, the pastor moves closer to the congregation (and may even choose to stroll down the center aisle), introducing the child to the people. This is an informal moment with spontaneous words of introduction. The purpose in this gesture is to remind the congregation that this child is in relationship not only with the biological family but with the local family of God as well.

[Spontaneous Praises]

The congregation is invited to offer very brief, spontaneous words of praise to God for the child and the family.

Closing Prayer

The pastor closes this part of the service with a brief prayer. This prayer should be distinctly different than the blessing. Avoid the word "blessing" and avoid placing hands on the child's head.

Sample

Loving Jesus, you express great love and concern for young children. As we hold [*name of child*] in our arms, remind us that it is really you who are holding [*her/him*]. Let us be your gentle hands, your cheerful voice, your kindly face as we welcome [*name of child*], giving thanks to God the Father for this magnificent gift of a little one. Good Shepherd, enfold us all in your care this day, that together we will know the Shepherd's voice and follow you ever more faithfully. Through Christ, our Lord. Amen.[47]

[The Lord's Prayer]

Song (Celebrating Relationships)

A song related to community, spiritual unity, the family of God, and so on is fitting.

The worship service continues with the Sending.

Service 2: An Order of "A Service of Welcome for a Young Disciple"[48]

The basic outline alone appears in appendix B.

Note: The elements shown with titles on the left side of the page are considered essential to the service; the element shown with a centered title within brackets [] is considered optional.

Song (Transitioning from the Sermon)

An appropriate song is sung by the congregation. (See song suggestions below.)

Note: Parents and other family members may come to the front during the song.

Statement of Purpose

The pastor makes a simple statement as to the special nature of this service.

Samples

- Sisters and brothers, from the earliest days of Christianity, it was the church's solemn duty to proclaim the good news to those not yet professing Christ and, upon their expressed interest, train them in matters of discipleship until they for themselves publicly stated their resolve to follow Jesus devotedly and were baptized. Today, we as the household of faith at [name of church] start [name of child] on [his/her] journey toward faith in Christ, culminating in baptism. How long this will take we do not know; but God knows. So until that time when [name of child] professes personal faith in Christ and enters the waters of baptism, we, like many disciples throughout the centuries of the church, will dedicate ourselves anew to living as true disciples of Jesus Christ so that [name of child] will become acquainted with our Savior and come to follow him too.[49]

- Dearly beloved, the call to follow Jesus was first issued to Simon and Andrew, James and John. On that day when Jesus called fishermen to be his disciples, he commissioned them to fish for people. Since then, the church of Jesus Christ has done the same, inviting all people to believe, to repent, to be baptized, and to make other disciples. Today we come before God to declare our intent to continue the mission Jesus established long ago. We begin a spiritual journey on behalf of [*name of child*]—even before [*he/she*] is aware of the importance of this moment. We have come to formally place [*him/her*] under the nurture and care of the church so that when the Holy Spirit's work is brought to fullness and [*name of child*] declares faith in Jesus Christ, [*he/she*] will be baptized and the church will rejoice not only in the salvation of [*name of child*] but that we were counted worthy to journey with [*him/her*] along the way."[50]

Invocation/Prayer of Thanksgiving

Offer a brief prayer inviting the presence of God's Spirit as we worship God for the most generous gift of life.

Samples

- Holy God, Giver of Life: we welcome your presence as this moment we rejoice in the gift of new life—the birth of your precious child, [*name*]. We praise you that you made us in your image, that you have crowned us with glory and honor, and entrusted us with the care of your creation. In these holy moments, we ask that you will meet us through your Spirit as together we acknowledge that you have entrusted [*name*] to our care as the family of God. Lead us as your church to walk with [*him/her*] from this day forward until [*he/she*] is a new creation through faith in Christ, and we celebrate that the old has gone and the new has come! We praise you that all of this is from God, who reconciled us to himself through Christ and has given to us the ministry of reconciliation. Through Christ we pray. Amen.[51]

- Holy Jesus, lover of the children, we come to you with joy and thanksgiving in our hearts that we may welcome a child as you welcome children. We praise you for the gift of life! We praise you for the gift of this life, a child made in the image of God. Send the Holy Spirit to anoint these moments, as we pledge ourselves to accompany [*name*] from physical birth to spiritual rebirth—from being born into the world until [*he/she*] is born again through water and the Spirit. This is the Lord's doing; it is marvelous in our eyes. This is the day that the Lord has made; let us rejoice and be glad in it. Through Christ, our Lord. Amen.[52]

Opening Words from Scripture

An appropriate Scripture passage is read. (See scriptural suggestions below.)

Note: An official lay representative from the congregation is an excellent choice to read the Scripture.

Parents' Intent[53]

The pastor leads the parents in declaring their intent that their child is raised in the Christian faith as expressed through the church so that in time the child will express personal faith and desire to be baptized.

Note: The liturgy for "A Service of Welcome for a Young Disciple" should be discussed with the parents/guardians prior to the service so that they are prepared to make sincere and prayerful responses.

Sample Words of Intent

Pastor: Is it your intent that [name of child] will become a disciple of Jesus Christ?

Parent(s): It is [our/my] sincere desire.

Pastor: Is it your intention to provide consistent spiritual nurture in your home—to pray and read the Scriptures often as a family, to attend worship in this community regularly, and to do all in your power to acquaint [name of child] with the Christian faith?

Parents: It is our intent, God helping us.

Pastor: Do you seek the participation of the whole church in influencing your child toward personal acceptance of Jesus Christ as Savior and Lord?

Parents: We know we need the help of our sisters and brothers of this faith community.

Pastor: Do you intend to guide [name of child] toward Holy Baptism?

Parents: We do.[54]

Congregational Pledge

The members of the local church community are asked to accept their role as co-nurturers in the Christian faith.

Sample Words of Intent for the Congregation[55]

Pastor: Do you understand the significance of your role in providing spiritual nurture for [name of child]?

People: We do.

Pastor: Will you love and accept this child unconditionally?

People: We will.

Pastor: Will you fulfill your spiritual duty to lead [him/her] in [his/her] love of the church's worship, of the holy Scriptures, of the blessing of prayer, and of serving others?

People: We will, God helping us.

Pastor: Will you joyfully accept your duty to provide spiritual nurture and care for [*name of child*] until [*he/she*] accepts for [*himself/herself*] Jesus as Savior and Lord, and follows Jesus in baptism?

People: With God's help we will proclaim the good news and live according to the example of Christ. We will surround [*him/her*] with a community of love and forgiveness, that [*he/she*] may grow in [*his/her*] trust of God, and be found faithful in [*his/her*] service to others. We will pray for [*him/her*], that [*he/she*] may be a true disciple who walks in the way that leads to life.[56]

Charge to the Congregation

The pastor charges the congregation.

Sample Charges

- "Beloved, build yourselves up on your most holy faith; pray in the Holy Spirit; keep yourselves in the love of God; look forward to the mercy of our Lord Jesus Christ that leads to eternal life. And have mercy on some who are wavering; save others by snatching them out of the fire; and have mercy on still others with fear" (Jude 1:20–23).
- Jesus left his disciples with these words: "All authority in heaven and on earth has been given to me. Go therefore and make disciples of all nations, baptizing them in the name of the Father and of the Son and of the Holy Spirit, and teaching them to obey everything that I have commanded you. And remember, I am with you always, to the end of the age" (Matt. 28:18–20).

Enrollment in Covenant Discipleship[57]

This is a brief but meaningful worship act that indicates the formal covenant between the child, the parents/guardians, and the church. It consists of two basic parts: (1) the naming of the child and (2) writing her or his name on a certificate of covenant discipleship. The purpose is to formalize the covenant between the seeker (the child) and the congregation (the covenant community), resulting in profession of faith and baptism when the child comes of age. While the certificate commemorates the covenant, I recommend that there be a formal record of those baptismal candidates who are under the ongoing care of the church beginning in infancy.[58]

Note: Only the first and middle name are given in the naming of the child, consistent with normative baptismal practice (see chapter 4).

Pastor: What is the Christian name of this child?
Parents: [*First and middle names.*]

Note: The pastor or other official lay representative gives a certificate of covenant discipleship to the parents, indicating that their child is officially enrolled in the care and nurture of the church.

Prayer of Invocation for the Child

The pastor takes the child into her or his arms and offers a prayer invoking the presence of the Holy Spirit upon the child.

- Position yourself so that the community as well as the family members may see your action.
- Invite worshipers to stretch their hands toward the child at this moment.
- Place your hand on her or his head.
- Avoid Trinitarian formulations so as not to confuse with baptism.
- Invite the congregation to participate in the "Amen."[59]

Sample Prayers of Invocation

- "Holy Spirit, surround [*name*] with your powerful presence. Work in [*his/ her*] life from this day forward to guide [*him/her*] into all truth. Bring [*him/her*] to the place where [*he/she*] will do what can only be done by your great power—proclaim with [*his/her*] lips, 'Jesus is Lord!' Protect and keep [*name*], body, mind, soul, and spirit, until that day when [*his/ her*] name is written in the Lamb's book of life, securing residency in the city not made by human hands. Amen."[60]
- "Gracious God, from whom every family in heaven and on earth is named: Out of the treasures of your glory, strengthen us through your Spirit. Help us joyfully to nurture [*child's name*] within your church. Bring [*him/her*] by your grace to [*baptism/Christian maturity*], that Christ may dwell in [*his/her*] heart through faith. Give power to [*child's name*] and to us, that with all your people we may grasp the breadth and length, the height and depth, of Christ's love. Enable us to know this love, and to be filled with your own fullness; through Jesus Christ our Lord. Amen."[61]

Sealing of the Holy Spirit

The pastor makes the sign of the cross on the forehead of the child.[62]

Benediction

The pastor, still holding the child, pronounces a benediction upon the child.
Note: This is not a prayer but a spoken blessing upon the child. Therefore, look directly into the face of the young disciple while speaking the benediction.

Sample Benedictions

- "Now to him who is able to keep you from falling, and to make you stand without blemish in the presence of his glory with rejoicing, to the only God our Savior, through Jesus Christ our Lord, be glory, majesty, power, and authority, before all time and now and for ever. Amen" (Jude 1:24–25).
- "The LORD bless you and keep you; the LORD make his face to shine upon you, and be gracious to you; the LORD lift up his countenance upon you, and give you peace." Amen (Num. 6:24–26).

[Introduction of the Child]

While continuing to hold the child, the pastor moves closer to the congregation (and may even choose to stroll down the center aisle), introducing the child to the people. This is an informal moment with spontaneous words of introduction. The purpose in this gesture is to remind the congregation that this child is in relationship not only with the biological family but with the local family of God as well.

Song (Celebrating Discipleship)

A song related to discipleship, community, spiritual unity, the family of God, or similar is fitting.

The worship service continues with the Sending.

Service 3: An Order of "A Parental Renewal of Baptism"

The basic outline alone appears in appendix B.

A third rite to recognize the birth of a child is "A Parental Renewal of Baptism." Here the emphasis is on the dedication of the parents by virtue of remembering their own baptismal vows. The Parental Renewal of Baptism service is rooted in several biblical events where devoted parents fulfilled holy vows previously taken. (See 1 Sam. 1:1–28 and Luke 2:21–24.) Like the services outlined above, this service is integrated into the regular, primary worship service of a local congregation, it serves as the Response to the Word, and it is conducted by an ordained pastor. It is appropriate for the infant to be present (held by a parent, other family member, or church leader), though the service will center not on the child but the parents. Again, the elements shown with titles on the left side of the page are considered essential to the service; the elements shown with centered titles within brackets [] are considered optional.

Song (Transitioning from the Sermon)

An appropriate song is sung by the congregation. (See suggestions below.)
Note: Parents and other family members may come to the front during
the song.

Statement of Purpose

The pastor makes a simple statement as to the special nature of this service.

Samples

- Members of the household of faith, we are gathered to participate with
  and support [name] and [name] as they desire to reaffirm the vows stated
  at their baptism. They especially desire to publicly declare their faith
  and intent because of the birth of [name], their young child. It is their
  prayer that by reaffirming their promises at baptism and by rededicating
  themselves to living lives consistent with the aspirations for holy living
  set forth in Scripture, they will be empowered to witness of God's love
  and mercy to [name of child] all the days of their life.[63]

- "Brothers and sisters, from time to time we experience a new beginning
  in our faith journey, when the Holy Spirit breaks into our lives to inspire
  us, to lead us, and to deepen our commitment to Christ. Today, we praise
  the Lord for what has been happening in [name] and [name] lives.[64] We
  rejoice in the gift of [name of child] which brings them to the place of
  dedicating themselves anew to God's purposes. As God's people we affirm
  that this is an occasion for seeking the Holy Spirit's work of renewal in
  [name] and [name], and in so doing we dedicate ourselves with them, as
  fellow believers, to live lives worthy of the gospel."[65]

Invocation

Offer a brief prayer inviting the presence of God's Spirit as we worship
God in this service of renewal.

Sample

Triune God, Father, Son, and Holy Spirit, we joyfully welcome your presence here and now. As your people, together with you, we witness our brother
and sister, [name] and [name], as they affirm once again their intention to
follow you as true disciples. May you be glorified as together we offer you
worship through this act of remembrance and dedication. Through Christ,
our Lord. Amen.[66]

Opening Words from Scripture

An appropriate Scripture passage is read. (See below for scriptural suggestions.)

The Reaffirmation of Baptismal Vows

The pastor leads in reaffirming the baptismal vows.

- These may be given to either just the parents or the entire congregation. If the congregation participates in the vows, they should stand.
- Those persons reaffirming their vows respond with the words in bold type.

Pastor: I invite you now to remember God's promise, to turn away from all that is evil, and to reaffirm your faith in Jesus Christ and your commitment to Christ's church. Do you renounce Satan and all the spiritual forces of evil that rebel against God?
People: I renounce them!
Pastor: Do you renounce all sinful desires that draw you from the love of God?
People: I renounce them!
Pastor: Do you turn to Jesus Christ?
People: Yes! I trust in him as my Lord and Savior.
Pastor: Do you intend to be Christ's faithful disciple, trusting his promises, obeying his Word, honoring his church, and showing his love, as long as you live?
People: Yes! God helping me.[67]

Profession of Faith (All Worshipers)

Pastor: As the church of Jesus Christ, let us profess our faith.
People: (Recite the Apostles' Creed or other appropriate affirmation of faith in unison.)

> **I believe in God the Father almighty,**
> **creator of heaven and earth.**
> **I believe in Jesus Christ his only Son our Lord,**
> **who was conceived by the Holy Spirit,**
> **and born of the Virgin Mary.**
> **He suffered under Pontius Pilate,**
> **was crucified, died, and was buried;**

he descended into hell.
The third day he rose again from the dead.
He ascended to heaven
and is seated at the right hand of God the Father almighty.
From there he will come to judge the living and the dead.
I believe in the Holy Spirit,
the holy catholic church,
the communion of saints,
the forgiveness of sins,
the resurrection of the body,
and the life everlasting. Amen.[68]

Remembrance with Water

The pastor will pour water from a pitcher into a font or bowl. He or she may dip his or her hands into the basin and lift some water, letting it run back into the basin, saying the words, "Remember your baptism and be thankful."

The pastor will invite the parents renewing their baptismal vows to come forward, dip their hands into the water, and raise some water to let it drip back into the bowl. A further option would be to make the sign of the cross on their foreheads before drying the hands. Others who are renewing their baptisms are invited to come forward and do the same. The one who presides stands at the station, repeating words to those who come: "Remember your baptism and be thankful."

Note: Congregational singing is very effective during this time.

Prayer for the Parents

The pastor or lay leader offers prayer that the parents will be strengthened to walk in their baptism daily, being faithful disciples of Jesus Christ, so that they may live the Christian life consistently, thereby witnessing to their child the love and grace of God.

- These prayers may be spontaneously offered by one or more persons.
- It is appropriate to invite the parents to kneel while others lay hands on the parents (though not the child) during the prayer.

Sample

"O Lord, uphold [*names*] by your Holy Spirit.
Daily increase in [*him/her/them*] your gifts of grace:
the spirit of wisdom and understanding,

the spirit of counsel and might,
the spirit of knowledge and the fear of the Lord,
the spirit of joy in your presence,
both now and forever. Amen."[69]

Prayer of the Parents

The parents offer petitions to God for strength and grace to live lives worthy of their calling before their young child. They may include prayers for the child. This prayer may be prepared or spontaneous.

[The Lord's Prayer]

Pledge of the Community

The pastor asks for a verbal pledge of support for the parents.

Sample

Pastor: People of God, do you pledge to uphold these parents in their efforts to live out their baptism daily? Will you surround them with prayer and encouragement? Will you extend your sense of Christian community to include this child in every way?[70]
People: We will, God helping us.

[Words of Encouragement]

The congregation is invited to offer very brief, spontaneous words of encouragement to the parents, offering their assistance, love, and support.

Closing Prayer

A prayer closing this part of the service is offered.

Sample

"God of life and goodness,
we praise you for claiming us through our baptism
and for upholding us by your grace.
We remember your promises given to us in our baptism.
Strengthen us by your Spirit,
that we may obey your will and serve you with joy;
through Jesus Christ our Lord. Amen."[71]

The worship service continues with the Sending.

Installing Doors and Windows

As is the case for each corporate ritual, songs, Scriptures, prayers, and symbols enrich the service by creating avenues for people to connect with God and others. As is the case for the healing service, resources with direct references to the three types of services described above are somewhat slim in number. A few relevant hymns/songs are offered here.[72]

Songs for "The Blessing of a Child" Service

Because He Lives (Gloria and William Gaither; stanza 2)
Children of the Heavenly Father (Carolina Sandell Berg)
For the Beauty of the Earth (Folliott S. Pierpoint; stanzas 1, 4, 6)
Go, My Children, with My Blessing (Jaroslav J. Vajda)
Hymn of Promise (Natalie Sleeth)
I Want to Walk as a Child of the Light (Kathleen Thomerson)
Jesus Loves Me! This I Know (Anna B. Warner)
Lord, for the Gift of Children (Duane Blakley)
Lord, We Bring to You Our Children (Frank von Christierson)
On Eagle's Wings (Michael Joncas)
Savior, Like a Shepherd Lead Us (Dorothy A. Thrupp)
Take, O Take Me as I Am (John Bell)
Tell Me the Stories of Jesus (William H. Parker)

Songs for "A Service of Welcome for a Young Disciple"

Come, Let Us Use the Grace Divine (Charles Wesley; stanzas 1, 2)
I Want to Walk as a Child of the Light (Kathleen Thomerson)
Lift High the Cross (George W. Kitchin)
Lord, I Want to Be a Christian (traditional spiritual)
Take, O Take Me as I Am (John Bell)
Tell Me the Stories of Jesus (William H. Parker)
We Are an Offering (Dwight Liles)

Songs for "A Parental Renewal of Baptism" Service[73]

A Charge to Keep I Have (Charles Wesley)
Come, Let Us Use the Grace Divine (Charles Wesley; stanzas 1, 2)

Come, Thou Fount of Every Blessing (Robert Robinson)

Jesus Calls Us o'er the Tumult (Cecil F. Alexander)

Lift High the Cross (George W. Kitchin)

Lord, I Want to Be a Christian (traditional spiritual)

O Jesus, I Have Promised (John E. Bode)

Spirit of the Living God (Daniel Iverson)

We Are an Offering (Dwight Liles)

Scripture Passages

A few Scripture references appropriate to these services are listed below. Some are appropriate for more than one service; some are more appropriate for a particular service.

Sample Scripture Passages (The Blessing of a Child)

- Psalm 8   • Matthew 18:1–14   • Mark 10:13–16

Sample Scripture Passages (A Service of Welcome for a Young Disciple)

- Deuteronomy 6:4–9 • Deuteronomy 31:12–13 • Galatians 4:1–7

Sample Scripture Passages (A Parental Renewal of Baptism)

- Deuteronomy 6:4–9   • Romans 6:3–4
- Deuteronomy 31:12–13   • Ephesians 2:19–22
- 1 Samuel 1:9–11, 20–28   • Ephesians 5:8–20
- Micah 6:8   • Ephesians 6:4
- Luke 2:21–40

Prayers

The prayers that are helpful in these types of services include the invocation, petitions for help to live the godly life, and the benediction,[74] among others. A few sample prayers are offered here.

Petitions for the Parent(s)

"Lord, uphold [*names of parents*] by your Holy Spirit.
Daily increase in them your gifts of grace:
    the spirit of wisdom and understanding,
    the spirit of counsel and might,

the spirit of knowledge and the fear of the Lord,
the spirit of joy in your presence,
both now and forever. Amen."[75]

"Faithful God,
in baptism you claimed us,
and by your Spirit you are working in our lives,
empowering us to live a life worthy of our calling.
We thank you for leading [name(s)]
to this time and place of reaffirming the covenant
you made with [him/her/them] in [his/her/their] baptism.
Establish [him/her/them] in your truth,
and guide [him/her/them] by your Spirit,
that, together with all your people,
[he/she/they] may grow in faith, hope, and love,
and be [a faithful disciple/faithful disciples] of Jesus Christ,
to whom, with you and the Holy Spirit
be honor and glory, now and forever. Amen."[76]

"God, like a good shepherd searching for a lost lamb,
like a woman looking for a lost coin,
like a father redeeming his son,
your love is rich beyond our deserving.
You never forsake us, no matter how far we move from you.
We thank you for all you have done for [name(s)].
Strengthen [him/her/them] by the Holy Spirit,
that [he/she/they] may grow in faith and increase in love for you.
May [his/her/their] service and witness bring you honor and glory,
In the name of Jesus Christ. Amen."[77]

Symbols

A few symbols may be helpful to facilitate worship for the community. Use your imagination to add to this brief list.

The Blessing of a Child

• Single rose (white)   • Open Bible

A Service of Welcome for a Young Disciple

• Rainbow   • Open Bible   • Cross

A Parental Renewal of Baptism

- Water in a bowl, basin, or font   • Cross
- Open Bible

The Christian Year

The Christian year holds some interesting opportunities to help worshipers connect with the alternative rites for child dedication. These special services are appropriate at many places throughout the Christian year; however, historically baptism is associated with Easter especially, and it is also associated with Pentecost. Therefore, "Aa Parental Renewal of Baptism" would be appropriate at these times as well. Other days that are also fitting for this service include the first Sunday of Epiphany and the Sunday that Jesus's baptism is celebrated.

Serving as Hospitable Host

Blessing children and reaffirming baptisms are joyful times for the pastor; these are celebrative occasions. Serving as a host at these rites requires a few duties.

Duties

Begin your ministry immediately on the birth of a child in your congregation. Give attention and express concern to both the newborn and the parents. Offer support, visit them, and pray with them. Consider the baby to be an important new member of your local church family.

If you come from a tradition that does not baptize infants, within a reasonable amount of time after the birth of the child, discuss with the parent(s) their interest in one of these other types of services. Explain, if need be, the difference between a child dedication and a child blessing, between a baptism and a renewal of baptism. Suggest that these types of rites are helpful to both the family and the local church community.

Once the service is agreed upon, plan the service carefully, working with the parent(s) to bring about meaningful worship acts for everyone.

Attributes for Presiding

Your primary attributes as leader will center on your pastoral role. Portray a loving and caring spirit as you preside at these rites. Be patient and don't rush the liturgy. "Tease out" the worship acts so that they will form a significant part of the service. Share the joy by including a representative of the congregation in a formal role; this will emphasize the corporate nature of the rite.

Administration

One of the primary administrative duties for the pastor is record keeping. Maintain accurate records of the dates of births for all children and also the date when a child blessing or other dedicatory-type service is held. Consider sending a yearly note to individual children, once they are old enough to read, to remind them that they are a valued part of the community—that God loves them and so do you, their pastor.

Exceptionally Difficult Circumstances

Recognize that celebrations related to a newborn could be difficult for would-be parents who have struggled with infertility, have lost a child, are in the midst of custody battles, or are attempting a drawn-out adoption. These situations should not hinder our joy at these occasions; at the same time, be pastorally aware so that you can minister to those who might need a little extra attention, be it a prayer, a hug, or a home visit. One time while serving as pastor, I was greeting people at the end of the service on Mother's Day. Some gentlemen were passing out flowers to all mothers. Unfortunately, I overheard one careless man take back a flower that had been given to a young woman, because he discovered she was not yet a mother. Her husband and she had prayed for children for years but had not been able to bear children. Mother's Day is hard enough for some folks; taking back the flower only drove the loss deeper into their hearts. Be pastorally aware.

Ethical Considerations

Be careful in your pastoral care of children. First, pay attention to all children equally. Avoid the impression that you have favorites. Honor and love them all. Second, put safety measures in place to protect them completely. Evaluate your facility and grounds. What modifications might need to be done to secure their safety? Many agencies, perhaps even your denomination, can provide materials and consultants who can guide congregations to take extra precautions in protecting their children. Third, make sure that all children's workers—including you, the pastor—have had training in the complicated but important area of child sexual abuse. Insist that all those who work with children are screened and educated. Create child protection policies, and keep them updated. Join other churches to establish continuing education for issues related to children. Children are precious members of the family of God; do all in your power to ensure their sense of safety and welcome in the house of God.

One of the premier ways that leaders can demonstrate their conviction that children are valued members of the family of God is to design Lord's

Day worship in a manner that welcomes their presence. Today, very often children are either overlooked or relegated to age-specific alternative activities during corporate worship. There are a number of reasons given for this relatively recent development. Some have suggested that the child will learn more in a group designed just for them. But have you not marveled at what young children have, in fact, comprehended by attending an "adult" service?

I believe that worship is best when it is intergenerational. I am convinced that much of worship is *caught* rather than *taught*. Children need to *experience* the saints at worship; in so doing they are likely to become worshiping saints themselves. I fear that many churches will pay a very high price in the near future for segregating young disciples out of their primary services of corporate worship. Not only is it to children's great benefit to be welcomed participants in worship; it is to the benefit of the adults as well. I readily admit, indeed rejoice in, my need for the presence of little ones and what their simple faith contributes to the community at worship. I marvel at their innocent praise of their Creator, their simple prayers, their displays of affection. What's more, all ages worshiping together is a physical witness of the universality of the body of Christ, a theological truth made flesh.

This will mean more work, of course, for leaders will need to pay closer attention to what is said and done so that people of all ages and various stages of faith may enter in. This will not require dumbing down worship; I do not mean to suggest that every young child must be able to comprehend every aspect of worship. But it will require rituals architects to be intentional in providing moments within each service that afford young worshipers an opportunity to participate in this truly corporate event, without patronizing them or putting them on display. I know of one church in my local community that includes "The Young People's Blessing" as an alternative to the children's sermon every Sunday. Following the pastoral prayer and Lord's Prayer, all the children, from toddlers to teenagers, come forward, make a line across the front, and receive an individual blessing from the pastor. The pastor places her hand on each child's head, looks into his or her eyes, and speaks a very brief, spontaneous, personal blessing on his or her life. It's as routine as the taking of the offering, but these young people, and indeed every worshiper, view it as far from routine. Those young people are highly valued in that worshiping community.

Conclusion

Erin really enjoyed watching the Harper family come forward to dedicate their children to God. They weren't given away after all! Instead, their names were written on a special certificate, and the people in "big church" promised to make sure the children understood who Jesus is as they grew up. Mr. and Mrs. Harper smiled a lot. Today it felt like everyone there belonged to one big, happy family. Though Erin couldn't possibly remember when she was dedicated, she was pretty sure that her parents had smiled a lot too.

Key Terms

catechumenate The historical process of spiritually forming Christians in stages, from inquirers/seekers to well-formed disciples of Jesus Christ.

dedication The act of setting something or someone apart for God's divine use.

reaffirmation, renewal, remembering Terms signifying the recalling of one's earlier baptism.

To Learn More

Wright, David F. *Infant Baptism in Historical Perspective: Collected Studies.* London: Paternoster, 2007.

Engage

Historically, what kinds of worship rites has your church observed on the birth of a child? Do you use more than one? Do you give the parents options? Is it clear to everyone what these rites mean?

As a pastoral leadership team, strategize your response under the following circumstances.

Scenario One

Your church regularly practices child dedications. Jared and Alisha come from different church backgrounds and are somewhat divided over whether their son should be dedicated or baptized. How would you guide them in this matter?

Scenario Two

Pedro and Mercedes are expecting their first child, a girl. They always dreamed of their child's baptismal day at church. However, recently they visited a different local congregation when Pedro was invited to hear his golfing buddy give his testimony. They witnessed a child dedication service on that Sunday, and Pedro found it meaningful. They have an appointment to meet with you, the pastor, to discuss this as an option. What would you do?

9

Serving as a Rituals Architect

How to Create Meaningful Rituals for Corporate Worship

Introduction

Throughout this book we have examined in detail seven significant events for Christian worship. Each one employs particular content and features, both historical and contemporary, with the intent that the worshiping community will encounter God with greater awareness and be formed by God's Spirit in the act of worship.

However, these seven events are in no way the only occasions for services that reach beyond normative Lord's Day worship.[1] They only represent the many other events that will naturally rise as any local congregation shares life together. Other types of dedications will be needed, such as dedicating a mission team going out from the church to serve for an extended time, dedicating local church workers and officers, dedicating additions to the building and significant church furnishings such as a pulpit, and so on. There are relational rituals that may be of value, such as a service of racial reconciliation, a public confession of sin, the renewal of wedding vows, and so on. There may also be services related to other life passages, including transitioning to college or moving into an extended care facility.

No book can cover every foreseeable scenario for which the community may wish to create an act of worship. What I would like to provide in this chapter is a way for the rituals architect to create meaningful worship vignettes that are faithful to principles described in this book and are context specific—appropriate for one's local worshiping community. I also offer some practical considerations whereby any pastor or other worship leader may design fitting experiences for worship of a particular nature.

At one level, creating liturgies can seem like a daunting task. There are many reasonable questions to ask. How does the worship leader balance form and freedom, corporate and individual expression, vertical and horizontal direction, orthodox Christian tradition and local denominational expression, the verbal and the symbolic? Prayerful study and experience will answer these questions over time. I pray that the considerations I offer below will aid rituals architects in this process of discovery as they plan for and preside at various rituals in their vocational service.

Five Dimensions of Sacred Rituals for Corporate Worship

As you create rituals for your local worshiping community, consider these five dimensions to every ritual for worship.[2] I will simply state each assertion followed by recommendations.

The Corporate Dimension

Rituals are corporate in nature because they occur in public worship for the glory of God. Rituals are best performed when the community gathers for the stated purpose of worshiping God. Private rituals for the sake of being private are not appropriate. Though some rituals may occur with only a few people, the small gathering should consist of representative members of the congregation. For example, a healing service provided by the church may occur in a hospital room in the presence of very few members—but it is corporate because those who surround the one to be anointed and prayed for do so on behalf of the church.

Recommendations:

- Use corporate pronouns throughout the liturgy.
- Involve more than one leader as appropriate.
- Plan for as much corporate participation as possible, involving the people in the prayers, pledges, songs, Scripture readings, use of symbols, and so on.

- Set the liturgy within the wider context of Christian practice, drawing on historical worship content of the church universal when able (for instance, using the Lord's Prayer, creeds, and so on).

The Formational Dimension

Rituals are formational in nature, because when we place ourselves under the influence of sacred texts and actions with prayerful and sincere expectations that we are meeting with God, we will be changed by our encounter with God in community. It may take time to discover in what way this transformation has occurred; nevertheless, by faith we believe that God is at work in worship in general, and in sacred actions in particular, to mold us into the image of Jesus Christ. Sacred actions enable worship as a corporate spiritual discipline. When rituals architects create services for a specific occasion, they must do so aware that they are fashioning the means through which people are changed as they surrender themselves freely to God for his purposes. In this way persons place themselves in the paths of disciplined grace together, so that God's Spirit will work to transform individuals for the sake of Christ's church.

Recommendations:

- Spend significant time in prayer prior to shaping the service. Seek the Holy Spirit's direction in your thoughts and ideas.
- Reflect on how the particular ritual can be thought of as a spiritual discipline (something we offer to God for God's intentions).
- Emphasize the "surrender moment." Carefully and prayerfully think how you will go about inviting all participants to yield themselves to God for God's purposes as it relates to the event you are preparing. Make sure that every ritual has a time devoted for believers to offer themselves anew—individually and corporately—to God in full surrender. Abandonment to God is a key feature of every true Christian ritual.

The Symbolic Dimension

Rituals are symbolic in nature because spiritual truths are too profound to be captured in words alone. Throughout Scripture symbols are used to communicate the great dimensions of profound realities. Verbal communication is extremely important but limited in scope. A picture is worth a thousand words, as they say. Many of the symbols connected to certain sacred actions are specified in Scripture; these symbols are authoritative and should not be replaced. Other symbols have emerged over time; they may be highly useful while not, perhaps, as authoritative in nature. The symbol of the cross, for example, is not directly set forth as a symbol for Christians in Scripture but emerged in later centuries as a sign of salvation and faith. Remember that symbols are not only pictures, drawings, or objects. Symbols also consist of elements such as gesture, color, sound, and time.

Recommendations:

- Identify all known symbols in Scripture that relate directly to the particular ritual at hand.
- Consider several ways that each symbol may be used prominently in the liturgy.
- Consider the dominant placement of symbols. Don't marginalize them, but place them where they can create full visionary impact.
- Symbols may not only be placed but may also be enacted. For instance, the font is centered in the worship space to hold the water of baptism; the water is also heard and felt.
- Reflect on an additional symbol that may be useful to communicate a profound truth in a simple item. If you use a symbol in the course of designing a particular ritual, make sure that it is understood universally by your participants. Be certain that its meaning is clean (unencumbered with other meanings) and clear (comprehended by all). At the same time, avoid overexplaining the meaning of a symbol verbally. If you have to work too hard at making the symbolic value clear, the symbol probably is not a good choice.

The Christo-centric Dimension

Rituals are Christo-centric in nature, because Jesus Christ is always the center of worship.[3] The ritual action flows in and through Christ, empowered by the Spirit, to the glory of God the Father. Christ has been assigned a priestly role by God in our worship (see Heb. 7–9). As our priest, Jesus mediates our worship (our various rites), transforming our human efforts of worship into offerings acceptable to the Father. As we engage in sacred actions that mark our spiritual journeys, we do so in and through Jesus, our perfect High Priest. Jesus is what makes rituals *Christian* rituals. Also remember that Christ's work is at once past, present, and future. Well-formed rituals portray a sense of not only what has happened in the past but what is happening presently in the sacred action and how this relates to the fulfillment of God's purposes through Christ when the kingdom of God fully and finally comes.

Recommendations:

- Pay attention to the "God language" of each ritual. Make sure there are appropriate references to Jesus Christ, while being faithful to the Trinitarian ethos of biblical worship.
- Review Christ's biblical role in similar events where possible. Let your ritual reflect the type of ministry Christ performed in Scripture.
- Pray *to* Christ when appropriate.
- Sing *to* Christ when appropriate.
- Pray authoritative prayers in the name of Jesus Christ (prayers having to do with the primary action[s] of the ritual).
- Situate the ritual in the past/present/future vision of the kingdom of God where Jesus is Lord.

The Proclamation Dimension

By nature, rituals are for others, because the point of any ritual is to bring us to conformity to Jesus Christ *so that the world may know* that Jesus was sent from God (John 17:23). Well-conceived rituals have proclamation power—they witness to the grace and love of God. When Christians gather to enact sacred actions representing this grace and love of God, we do so not ultimately for our own satisfaction but so that we may "proclaim the mighty acts of him who called [us] out of darkness into his marvelous light" (1 Pet. 2:9). We enact sacred actions in order that we may tell God's story.[4] While the postmodern worldview supports the viability of multiple metanarratives of equal value, Christians believe in one metanarrative—one grand story that proclaims truth. In the rituals of Christian worship, we proclaim God's story unapologetically, not only as a means for keeping our sacred history intact, but to announce—through actions, words, gestures, and symbols to all who will behold—the greatness of our God and the reality (God's story) to which these rituals point.

Recommendations:

- Make sure that the liturgy takes full advantage of proclamation. Fashion the text especially to announce the gracious action(s) of God.
- See that the liturgy connects the brief, local ritual to the grand story of God's purposes.
- Include prayer that explicitly intercedes for others who will benefit as a result of our faithfulness in worshiping God through this particular ritual.

Other Considerations

The five dimensions of sacred rituals are necessities for sacred actions in Christian worship.[5] Here are a few other considerations.

The Christian Year

Whenever possible, think through how any particular ritual you are creating may relate to the current day or season of the Christian year. If there
is a strong connection to a certain season without forcing the issue and the
event is not urgent, take advantage of celebrating the ritual in the context of
the Christian year of which it is most naturally a part. After all, the purpose
of the Christian year is to tell God's story. Relating the ritual with a part of
God's story is especially powerful.

Biblical Language

The texts of any liturgy for Christian worship are especially strong when
rooted in Scripture. To the degree possible, draw heavily on Scripture passages
for the actual language of the liturgy—its statement of purpose, prayers,
litanies, and so on. Paraphrase and incorporate appropriate passages from
the Bible (while being careful to avoid proof-texting). Shape the liturgy in the
shape of Scripture. This yields an "organic" dimension to the event.[6]

Style

When developing any sacred action, always begin with the content first.
What needs to be proclaimed? What needs to be celebrated or accomplished?
What words need to be spoken? What actions need to be taken? First, make
sure that the content and form of your service represent authentic, biblical,
and pastoral integrity. After you have prayerfully thought through these aspects of the ritual, interpret your content in a style appropriate to your given
context. It is risky to begin with style, for in doing so sometimes the content
gets inadvertently modified for the sake of capturing a certain worship style.
The content can be expressed in any number of ways that will help it resonate
in the voice of your people. Think of style as language. The content of what
is said may be said in a myriad of languages. The purpose of language is to
communicate; the purpose of worship style is to place your content (liturgy)
in a language that communicates to your congregation.

The General Order of Sacred Actions

As a rituals architect, you will think through a logical order for the elements
of worship you have determined are needed. The order in which things occur
should simply make sense; they should be logically placed to serve the purpose
of the event. It will probably not be so much a matter of right versus wrong

as deciding what sensibly moves the liturgy forward. That being said, I have found that very often the fourfold order of worship that undergirds the general Lord's Day order of worship makes a great deal of sense for the "service within the service."[7] When creating a particular ritual for worship, think about Gathering, Word, Response, and Sending. As you begin the ritual, think of Gathering: calling the people to engage with God, stating the purpose of the ritual, inviting God's presence for this moment of the service, and so on. Next, think of the Word: read a passage of Scripture and offer *brief* words of a devotional nature based on the passage.[8] Then, focus on the Response to the Word: design moments where the participants (both the primary participants and the congregation) will pledge themselves anew to God's purposes as related to the ritual at hand. Last, focus on Sending: end the ritual with a missional tone, choosing worship elements that help the participants view this event for the sake of others—with God's greater purposes in mind.

To be honest, I have not come across a sacred action for which this fourfold plan doesn't work beautifully. I heartily recommend it as you craft organic liturgy. Rituals architects need not slavishly hold to this order if another order works better at a certain point in time; but this is a great place to start.

Dedications

Dedications of one type or another often arise in the life of a church; they may relate to people, objects, property, offerings, service, and so on. Dedications generally unfold with four general movements: presentation, thanksgiving, petition, and consecration.[9] Various worship elements are selected to accomplish this sequence of worship movements. First, whatever is being dedicated is formally presented to God for God's use. It is freely given—no strings attached—so that people or possessions may be used for the advancement of the kingdom of God. Next, thanksgiving is given for the gift of what is being dedicated (thanksgiving is offered for people or things presented to God's service). Petitions are then made for God's strength, support, faithfulness, and so on. Last, prayers of consecration are offered as people or possessions are sanctified for God's holy use. At this moment we surrender ourselves or an item to the greater purposes of God.

This sequence of dedicatory acts is seen, in a general way, in Solomon's dedication of the temple (see 1 Kings 8). First, there is the presentation of the ark and holy vessels as they are moved to the temple site (8:1–13). Next, Solomon blesses the assembly and gives thanks for God's faithfulness (8:14–26). The king then asks God's favor on the people and that the temple would serve as the centerpiece of Israel's worship (8:27–61). Last, he offers sacrifices of consecration (8:62–64). Perhaps these very aspects of dedications will help you as you think through dedications in particular.

Ten Basic Steps in Designing Sacred Actions for Corporate Worship

In conclusion, here are ten steps you may find useful as you approach the design of any sacred action.[10]

1. Pray for the Holy Spirit to influence your thoughts.
2. Review the real purpose and focal point of the ritual.
3. Reflect on any possible connection to the Christian year.
4. List your "givens" (those elements that must be in the liturgy).
5. Brainstorm a few ideas for appropriate worship elements.
6. Select the best ideas from your list. (Warning: little is much.)
7. Arrange the elements you have chosen into logical order, considering the fourfold order.
8. Think about transitions. What precedes and follows your ritual in the larger service that surrounds it?
9. Interpret your worship elements stylistically.
10. Check for levels of participation. How much are all worshipers involved, and at what levels?

Conclusion

May your community encounter God in fresh and powerful ways as you faithfully lead your people in significant moments along their spiritual journey—moments of critical life passages, the sacraments/ordinances, and other occasions that mark God at work. And may all of this be done by the Spirit's power to the glory of God and for the sake of the world Christ came to redeem.

Appendix A

Prayer Forms

Certain standard prayer forms will be of use repeatedly in creating and leading the sacred actions for Christian worship. A simple explanation and template is provided below for those most commonly used.[1]

The Invocation

Purpose. The purpose of the invocation is to invoke and/or welcome God's presence at the beginning of a service of sacred action.

Template.
1. Address God by name. Draw on the myriad of possibilities for names/ titles that exist in the Scriptures.
2. Offer a divine attribute. Announce the nature of God by referring to one or more of God's attributes or promises, establishing his divine character.
3. Make a petition related to God's presence in worship. Call on God to do something for the community at worship.
4. State the intended result. Formulate the "so that" of the petition. Don't just call on God to be present, but say why we would invite God's presence.
5. Conclude with a brief doxology, praying in the name of Jesus, or use a Trinitarian ending.

The Prayer of Confession and Assurance of Pardon

Purpose. In light of God's holiness and humanity's sinfulness, the prayer of confession serves to make us right with God so that our worship can continue unobstructed by sin.

Note: Confession consists of three movements: [1] a scriptural invitation to confess sin, [2] the confession, and [3] the assurance of pardon.

Template.
1. Address God.
2. Admit we have sinned.
3. Acknowledge that God is holy.
4. Express sorrow for sin.
   (Optional silence for confession of personal sins.)
5. Thank God for patience and mercy.
6. Pray for help to stand against sin.
7. Conclude.

The prayer of confession must be followed by an assurance of pardon—words of promise reminding worshipers that they can trust the mercy and grace of God for complete forgiveness and reconciliation.

There are several things to note regarding the assurance of pardon.

- It is spoken to the people; it is not a part of the prayer.
- The leader looks directly into the faces of the congregation and pronounces them forgiven on the basis of God's promise.
- A Scripture passage (memorized) is the best source for the assurance.

The Pastoral Prayer

Purpose. The pastoral prayer serves as one type of primary intercessory prayer.

Template.
1. Offer general praise/adoration/thanksgiving/exaltation for who God is.
2. Confess sin (unless there is an earlier prayer of confession).
3. Make petitions for persons, ministries, and needs related to the sacred action.
4. Make intercessions for the world in relation to the sacred action.
5. Submit to God's will and offer ourselves again to God's service.
6. Conclude (a Trinitarian ending is preferred).

The Prayer of Illumination

Purpose. The prayer of illumination asks for divine power so that the community will be attentive to the word of God and gain understanding.

Template.
1. Address God the Holy Spirit.
2. Make a request concerning the hearing of the Word.
3. Give the purpose of the request.
4. Conclude.

The Prayer of Consecration

Purpose. The prayer of consecration sets persons or things apart for God's holy use.

Template.
1. Present people or things to God.
2. Give thanks for the person(s) or thing(s) being presented.
3. Invite God's Spirit to bless the giving of these persons or items to serve God's purposes.

The Benediction

Note: Though I have listed the benediction under common prayers in worship, it is technically not a prayer, because it is directed to worshipers rather than to God.

Purpose. The benediction sends people from the worship service with the knowledge that God's presence is with them and all will be well.

Template.
1. May the Lord bless the people in some way.
2. May the Lord grant peace.

Appendix B

Orders of Services

The complete orders of services contained in the various chapters of this book are provided here without commentary so that the reader may easily visualize the most basic order of service for each sacred action. In each case the worship elements shown with titles on the left side of the page are considered necessary to the service; the elements shown with centered titles within brackets [ ] are considered optional.

The Order of the Christian Wedding

Gathering

Pre-service Music (Prelude)
The Processional
Greeting
Call to Worship
Invocation
Statement of the Meaning of Marriage
Declaration of Intent
Affirmation of the Families
Affirmation of the Congregation

[A Congregational Hymn or Song]
[A Corporate Prayer of Confession and Assurance of Pardon]

Word

The Reading of Scripture
The Homily

Response to the Word

The Exchange of Vows

> [The Exchange of Rings or Tokens]
> [A Congregational Song or Vocal Solo]
> [Holy Communion]

Prayer of Consecration

> [The Lord's Prayer]

Sending

Charge to the Couple
Declaration of Marriage

> [Closing Congregational Hymn]

The Benediction
The Recessional

The Order of the Christian Funeral or Memorial Service

Gathering

Pre-service Music (Prelude)
Greeting
Opening Words from Scripture
Statement of Purpose
Invocation
Opening Hymn/Song
Naming

> [Eulogy]

Word

Scripture Lesson
Prayer for Understanding
Homily

Response to the Word

Prayer of Intercession
Other Response-Oriented Worship Acts

Sending

Closing Hymn/Song
Closing Prayer

The Order of the Christian Committal Service

Scripture
The Committal
The Commendation
The Prayer of Offering (Concluding Prayer)
The Lord's Prayer

[Hymn/Song]

Benediction
Charge
Greet the Family

The Order of Christian Baptism of an Infant

[Song]

Opening Words from Scripture
Statement of Purpose
Presentation of Candidate(s)
Invocation
The Pledges of the Parents
The Pledge of the Community
A Corporate Affirmation of Faith

The Prayer for the Candidate(s)
The Baptism

[The Anointing with Oil]

The Blessing of the Candidate(s)

[Presentation of Token]

Introduction to the Community
A Song of Faith

The Order of Christian Baptism of Believers

[Song]

Opening Words from Scripture
Statement of Purpose
Presentation of Candidate(s)
Invocation
The Testimony of the Candidate(s)
The Pledge of the Candidate(s)
The Pledge of the Church
A Corporate Affirmation of Faith
The Baptism

[The Anointing with Oil]

The Blessing for the Newly Baptized

[Presentation of Token]

A Song of Faith

The Order of the Table of the Lord

[A Creed/Affirmation of Faith]
[Song]

Invitation to the Table
Confession of Sin
Assurance of Pardon

[The Passing of the Peace]
[Offering]

The Prayer of Thanksgiving
The Words of Institution
Consecration of the Elements

[The Lord's Prayer]
[The Breaking of the Bread]

The Distribution and Partaking
Concluding Prayer
OR
Benediction

[A Song of Praise]

The Order of the Healing Service

[Pre-service Music]
OR
[Enter in Silence]
[Greeting/Welcome]

Scripture Reading/Call to Worship
Invocation

[Congregational Song]

Confession of Sin
Assurance of Pardon

[The Passing of the Peace]
[Reading of a Biblical Account of Healing]
[Homily]

Brief Scriptural Basis for Healing and Instructions
Thanksgiving for the Oil

[Congregational Song]

Call for the Elders (or Leaders)
Invitation to Receive Prayer for Healing
Anointing with Oil
Prayer for Healing
Prayer of Thanksgiving

[Testimonies/Informal Sharing]

Song of Hope
Benediction

The Order of the Foot Washing Service

Pre-service Music
Greeting/Welcome
A Hymn of Preparation
Invocation
Scripture Reading

[Call to Humility]
[Time of Silence]
[A Song of Reflection]

Reflection/Exhortation

[Remembering Our Story]

Confession of Sin
A Song of Assurance or Reconciliation
Prayer of Preparation
The Washing of Feet
Prayer of Thanksgiving and Petition

[Testimonies Are Shared]

A Hymn of Benediction
The Benediction

[Offering for the Poor]

Service 1: An Order of "The Blessing of a Child"

Song
Statement of Purpose
Invocation
Opening Words from Scripture

[Litany of Thanksgiving]

[Parents' Intent]

The Blessing
Prayer for the Parents
Introduction of the Child

[Spontaneous Praises]

Closing Prayer

[The Lord's Prayer]

Song (Celebrating Relationships)

Service 2: An Order of "A Service of Welcome for a Young Disciple"

Song
Statement of Purpose
Invocation/Prayer of Thanksgiving
Opening Words from Scripture
Parents' Intent
Congregational Pledge
Charge to the Congregation
Enrollment in Covenant Discipleship

Prayer of Invocation for the Child
Sealing of the Holy Spirit
Benediction

[Introduction of the Child]

Song (Celebrating Discipleship)

Service 3: An Order of "A Parental Renewal of Baptism"

Song
Statement of Purpose
Invocation
Opening Words from Scripture
The Reaffirmation of Baptismal Vows
Profession of Faith (All Worshipers)
Remembrance with Water
Prayer for the Parents
Prayer of the Parents

[The Lord's Prayer]

Pledge of the Community

[Words of Encouragement]

Closing Prayer

Notes

Introduction

1. James F. White, *The Sacraments in Protestant Practice and Faith* (Nashville: Abingdon, 1999), 120.

2. Church historian James White cites two distinguishing features of "Free Church" worship: freedom to reform worship exclusively on the basis of local interpretation of Scripture, and freedom to operate autonomously when ordering worship. See James F. White, *Protestant Worship: Traditions in Transition* (Louisville: Westminster John Knox, 1989), 172.

Chapter 1

1. Simon Chan, *Liturgical Theology: The Church as Worshiping Community* (Downers Grove, IL: IVP Academic, 2006), 88.

2. Ibid.

3. The categories of "life passages" and "spiritual life passages" are not mutually exclusive, of course. Nor do I mean to suggest a secular-versus-sacred paradigm. I intend to indicate only that there are various types of sacred rituals that have a particular focus.

4. This is an operational definition for our purposes in studying the sacred actions of the church. Social scientists use the term in a slightly different way. In fact, the meaning of "ritual" is disputed even within the social sciences community. Here I am simply offering a working definition to be used throughout the book.

5. Some did carry forward, such as the connection Jesus and Paul made between the Jewish Passover and the new feast (see Luke 22:15–16; 1 Cor. 5:7–8).

6. In this opening chapter I will most often use the term "Lord's Supper" for its widespread understanding. However, in chapter 5 we will explore other appropriate terms for this ritual as well.

7. The word "rite" is also used in the larger sense to refer to the worship practices of a particular region or theological point of view, for instance a Celtic rite.

8. Nathan D. Mitchell quoting Avery Dulles in *Models of Revelation* (Garden City, NY: Doubleday, 1983), 141.

9. A term especially used for the whole (eucharistic) service by Eastern Christians.

10. Nathan D. Mitchell, *Meeting Mystery: Liturgy, Worship, Sacraments* (Maryknoll, NY: Orbis Books, 2006), 153.

11. A clear-cut example of the interchangeability of the terms "liturgy" and "rite" is found in *The Catholic Encyclopedia*: "So liturgy means rite; we speak indifferently of the Byzantine Rite and the Byzantine Liturgy" (http://www.newadvent.org/cathen/09306a.htm).

12. There is a plethora of minister's handbooks available that are extremely helpful. Many large denominations provide their own handbook for clergy. Be aware that this large inventory of handbooks covers the gamut of theological vantage points; nevertheless, for the discerning and wise leader, there is much help to be found by researching various rituals from a sampling of these resources.

13. Churches that use more or less than these two sacraments/ordinances are discussed in corresponding chapters.

14. The term "sacrament" is used at first; "ordinance" is defined shortly.

15. While the Orthodox Church officially recognizes seven sacraments, it is not limited to seven and may consider other rituals to be sacraments on occasion as well.

16. James F. White, *The Sacraments in Protestant Practice and Faith* (Nashville: Abingdon, 1999), 18.

17. Ibid., 19.

18. Ibid.

19. Ibid., 21.

20. Articles of Religion XXV, *The Book of Common Prayer* (New York: Oxford University Press, 2006), 872.

21. Peter Lombard in *Lombard's Sentences* IV.1.2.

22. *Webster's New Universal Unabridged Dictionary*, 2nd ed., s.v. "sacrament."

23. Mitchell, *Meeting Mystery*, 141.

24. Even the ordinance view can have a range of perspectives. Reformer Ulrich Zwingli is often credited as being the father of the ordinance view, yet he did not view them as so purely symbolic as do some of his followers.

25. "President" is a term used in many of the earliest church documents when referring to the administration of the sacraments.

26. Some highly unusual circumstances may prove to be an exception. Apart from these, rituals are corporate acts of worship.

27. Of course, there are times and places when believers are isolated due to special circumstances. Prisoners come to mind. I am speaking here of the normative expectation of Scripture that believers gather weekly for worship.

28. Attributed to fifth-century monk Prosper of Aquitaine and widely adopted.

29. Mitchell, *Meeting Mystery*, 235.

30. Though the approach is informal, it is certainly hoped that it is nonetheless intentional. Worship leaders must think carefully about the content and practices of whatever liturgies they employ, knowing that a liturgy *will* affect the faith of the worshipers to a profound degree.

31. I am not using it in the sense of Christian education.

32. M. Robert Mulholland, *Invitation to a Journey: A Road Map for Spiritual Formation* (Downers Grove, IL: InterVarsity, 1993), 12.

33. Dallas Willard, *The Spirit of the Disciplines: Understanding How God Changes Lives* (New York: HarperCollins, 1988), 158.

34. Ibid.

35. This "longer" view of sanctification does not discount the "shorter way" of sanctification. God's prerogative to achieve sanctification in the believer is simply that—*God's* prerogative.

36. Chan, *Liturgical Theology*, 94.

37. Richard Foster, *Celebration of Discipline* (New York: HarperCollins, 1978), 166.

38. "Symbol" and "sign" are sometimes used interchangeably, but there is a difference. A sign indicates a more rational, specific meaning than does a symbol, which tends toward the more abstract.

39. Mitchell, *Meeting Mystery*, 67.

40. Gail Ramshaw, *Christian Worship: 100,000 Sundays of Symbols and Rituals* (Minneapolis: Fortress, 2009), 16.

41. *Webster's New Universal Unabridged Dictionary*, 2nd ed., s.v. "symbol."

42. Franklin M. Segler and Randall Bradley, *Christian Worship: Its Theology and Practice*, 3rd ed. (Nashville: B & H, 2006), 197.

43. I am indebted to Mark Torgerson for some of these points concerning symbols.

44. Mitchell, *Meeting Mystery*, 37.

45. Louis-Marie Chauvet, *Symbol and Sacrament: A Sacramental Reinterpretation of Christian Existence*, trans. Patrick Madigan and Madeleine Beaumont (Collegeville, MN: Liturgical Press/A Pueblo Book, 1995), quoted in Mitchell, *Meeting Mystery*, 38.

46. The biblical understanding of remembrance is found in the Greek word *anamnesis*, "remember." The Greek sense of the word depicts an active remembrance—the present, the past, and the future come together as that which has been fulfilled, that which is being fulfilled, and that which will be fulfilled.

47. Mulholland, *Invitation to a Journey*, 12.

48. Mitchell, *Meeting Mystery*, 59.

49. Ibid.

50. Ibid., xv.

Chapter 2

1. Michael Fowler, "Historical Origins and Development of Christian Marriage," in *The Complete Library of Christian Worship*, ed. Robert E. Webber (Nashville: Star Song, 1993), 6:275.

2. *A Service of Christian Marriage*, Supplemental Worship Resources 5 (Nashville: Abingdon, 1979), 14–15.

3. Ibid., 14.

4. Ibid., 16.

5. Marriage is considered a sacrament in both the Catholic Church and the Orthodox Church.

6. In the next section, Eucharist is discussed in relation to weddings as a truly *corporate* element of worship.

7. Be cautious to choose songs that are approved for *Christian* worship. The wedding worship service is not the time for popular love songs. Consider using these at the reception if the couple wishes.

8. Some couples are choosing to move away from this option, believing that the idea of the woman moving toward the man suggests subordination of the woman.

9. A gesture that some view as suggesting a marriage of equals.

10. The Presbyterian Church (USA), *Book of Common Worship* (Louisville: Westminster John Knox, 1993), 842.

11. Constance M. Cherry, 2012.

12. This part of the service is reminiscent of the legal dimensions of a contract.

13. *Book of Common Worship*, 843.

14. Constance M. Cherry, 2012.

15. *Book of Common Worship*, 844.

16. Only first names are used (as in baptism).

17. *The Wesleyan Pastor's Manual for Pastors and Local Churches*, 5th ed. (Indianapolis: Wesleyan Publishing House, 2002), 59.

18. *Book of Common Worship*, 845.

19. *The United Methodist Book of Worship* (Nashville: United Methodist Publishing House, 1992), 121.

20. *Book of Common Worship*, 847.

21. Constance M. Cherry, 2012.

22. Note that the *rings* themselves are not blessed, but the *giving* of the rings is.

23. If Communion is included in the service, the elements are to be distributed to all believers.

24. *Book of Common Worship*, 851.

25. Ibid., 850.

26. Constance M. Cherry, 2009.

27. *Wesleyan Pastor's Manual*, 61.

28. See www.hymnary.org for information on most of these hymns.

29. Constance M. Cherry, 2009.

30. *United Methodist Book of Worship*, 123.

31. To examine an excellent resource for premarital counseling, see www.prepare-enrich.com.

32. Women leaders have the additional caution of dressing modestly. The wedding (or other occasions at which they preside) is not a time for tight clothing, low-cut necklines, and short skirts. It's not about fashion or one's "right" to look a certain way. It is about respect and not drawing attention to oneself as one leads.

Chapter 3

1. For a fascinating and succinct overview of early Christian ceremonies for the dead, see chapter 4 in Thomas G. Long, *Accompany Them with Singing: The Christian Funeral* (Louisville: Westminster John Knox, 2009).

2. *A Service of Death and Resurrection: The Ministry of the Church at Death*, Supplemental Worship Resources 7 (Nashville: Abingdon, 1979), 23–24.

3. Unfortunately, the same has become true for the Christian wedding, an issue similarly discussed in chapter 2.

4. Long, *Accompany Them with Singing*, 24.

5. Ibid., 6.

6. Ibid., 24.

7. Ibid.

8. Memorial services (discussed below) sometimes expand beyond these venues, especially if cremation is involved.

9. The figures pertaining to standard funeral/burial and cremation costs are provided by the National Funeral Director's Association for 2009, the latest figures available at the time of this writing, and do not include *all* costs, such as cemetery costs, monuments or markers, special urns, published obituaries, printed materials for the viewing or service, etc. Additional expenses could easily push the average cost to around ten thousand dollars.

10. Long, *Accompany Them with Singing*, 23.

11. Ibid., 24.

12. *Service of Death and Resurrection*, 28.

13. Long, *Accompany Them with Singing*, 67.

14. Because this practice evolved into the giving of the elements of the Lord's Supper *after* death, it was condemned in the late fourth century. See Long, *Accompany Them with Singing*, 68–69.

15. The Episcopal Church U.S.A. would be one exception.

16. See, for example, *The United Methodist Book of Worship* (Nashville: United Methodist Publishing House, 1992).

17. *Service of Death and Resurrection*, 24–25.

18. For instance, there would be no formal procession at the funeral home, the casket already being in place.

19. Be cautious to choose songs that will not automatically signal highly emotional responses.

20. Some traditions suggest that the cross precedes the Christ candle. I believe either order is fitting.

21. Other appropriate passages may be found later in this chapter. See "Installing Doors and Windows."

22. Constance M. Cherry, 2012.

23. Ibid.

24. Sometimes a memorial service is followed by a service at the columbarium, especially when the columbarium is at or near the place of the service. The same basic service is used, with slight adjustments made in words spoken, such as committing "ashes" instead of "body." Be sure to think through any necessary adjustments that may be needed prior to the service.

25. *Service of Death and Resurrection*, 27.

26. Note that the verses at the committal are slightly different in content than those at a funeral, though they are not mutually exclusive. The committal passages tend to have direct reference to bodily resurrection, among other differences.

27. You will notice that most "committal of remains" wording includes the word "commend," though the actual prayer of commendation follows. The emphasis on the committal, while using the word "commend," is on the elements (earth to earth, etc.).

28. Joseph Buchanan Bernardin, *Burial Services* (New York: Morehouse Gorham, 1941), 25–26, quoted in *Service of Death and Resurrection*, 89.

29. Ibid.

30. *The Discipline of the Wesleyan Church* (Indianapolis: Wesleyan Publishing House, 2004), 384.

31. *The Book of Common Prayer* (New York: Oxford University Press, 2007), 464.

32. Ibid., 465.

33. Ibid., 99.

34. *Evangelical Lutheran Worship* (Minneapolis: Augsburg Fortress, 2006), 284.

35. Upon the conclusion of the first funeral/committal service I ever conducted, the funeral director suggested to me that I consider offering peace to the family by saying, "The peace of God/Christ be with you." In his opinion it was the most helpful thing for the family to hear as the final words of the event. I have done so ever since.

36. Calls increase in number if the survivors are not recovering normally; calls may be made less frequently if there are healthy signs of normal recovery.

37. Women leaders have the additional caution of dressing modestly. The funeral (or other public leadership occasions) is not a time for tight clothing, low-cut necklines, and short skirts. It's not about fashion or one's "right" to look a certain way. It is about respect and not drawing attention to oneself as you lead.

38. Long, *Accompany Them with Singing*, 137–39.

39. It is interesting that while many funerals do not include the use of palls, we still use the term "pall bearer."

40. Wakes are more common in some regions than others, and among some subculture groups than others.

Chapter 4

1. See chapter 1 for a discussion of the terms "sacrament" and "ordinance."

2. Attributed to Rupertus Meldenius, a German Lutheran Reformer.

3. See Matt. 3:1–17; Mark 1:9–11; Luke 3:21–22; John 1:29–34.

4. Grant R. Osborne, "Baptism," in *Baker Encyclopedia of the Bible*, ed. Walter A. Elwell (Grand Rapids: Baker Books, 1988), 257.

5. Ibid., 257–58.

6. Ibid., 258.

7. Walter Bauer, *A Greek-English Lexicon of the New Testament and Other Early Christian Literature* (Chicago: University of Chicago Press, 1979), 131.

8. One can turn to a myriad of sources to find these same themes, because there is widespread consensus concerning them, given they are extracted from Scripture. Here I have drawn from

and adapted James White's baptismal themes. See James F. White, *A Brief History of Christian Worship* (Nashville: Abingdon, 1993), 20–22. White acknowledges that there are other themes but cites these as the primary ones. See also James F. White, *The Sacraments in Protestant Practice and Faith* (Nashville: Abingdon, 1999), and *Baptism, Eucharist and Ministry* (Geneva: World Council of Churches, 1982).

9. White, *Sacraments*, 58.

10. This statement is explained in light of infant baptism later in this chapter.

11. John Wesley, quoted in White, *Sacraments*, 70.

12. As indicated in chapter 1, I hold the sacramental view of baptism and the Lord's Supper and therefore, while respecting the ordinance view, will most often refer to these events as sacraments.

13. *Webster's New 20th Century Dictionary*, 2nd ed., s.v. "prevenient."

14. Ibid.

15. From *Blessed Sacrament of Baptism* in *Luther's Works*, vol. 35, as quoted in White, *Sacraments*, 34.

16. Robert E. Webber, *Journey to Jesus: The Worship, Evangelism, and Nurture Mission of the Church* (Nashville: Abingdon, 2001), 157–58.

17. White, *Brief History*, 46.

18. Ibid., 37.

19. "Circumcision," in *Baker Encyclopedia of the Bible*, ed. Walter A. Elwell (Grand Rapids: Baker Books, 1988), 462.

20. I speak to what is normative here, though there are exceptions to most things. On are some occasions someone other than the parent makes the pledge; for instance, a godparent who has vital and ongoing input in the rearing of the child. The greater principle is this: parents who are not seriously committed followers of Jesus Christ cannot take baptismal pledges on behalf of their child(ren). Under these circumstances, it is best for the child to be baptized on her or his own confession of faith.

21. Generally speaking, the Lutheran view is more amenable to regeneration.

22. Friedrich Rest, quoted in John H. Armstrong, ed., *Understanding Four Views on Baptism* (Grand Rapids: Zondervan, 2007), 198.

23. This is a somewhat arbitrary age but commonly mentioned in sources related to baptism.

24. To emphasize, every denomination that practices infant baptism also practices believer's baptism. In addition, the mid-twentieth-century Roman Catholic development of the Rite of Christian Initiation of Adults underscores the church's commitment to the baptism of new converts not previously baptized as infants.

25. Armstrong, *Understanding Four Views on Baptism*, 25.

26. Albeit the personal confession in the case of the infant is made at a later time, when he or she is able to make a personal response to Christ as a result of the Spirit's keeping and the diligence of faith-filled parents and community.

27. I am indebted to *Baptism, Eucharist, and Ministry*, 4, for these examples.

28. *The Didache* or *The Teaching of the Twelve Apostles*, trans. Tim Sauder, www.scroll publishing.com/store/Didache-text.html, chap. 7.

29. White, *Sacraments*, 46.

30. Ibid., 47.

31. There may be extreme situations that require a baptism administered apart from a worship service, but these are truly rare and should not be considered except under the most unusual and urgent of circumstances.

32. Dom Gregory Dix, *The Shape of the Liturgy*, new ed. (London: Continuum, 2005), 341.

33. White, *Brief History*, 20.

34. The Orthodox Church also requires immersion of infants. The Roman Catholic Church today practices immersion as well as other modes.

35. White, *Sacraments*, 60.

36. Many helpful materials can be found for baptismal renewal services in mainline denominational resource books and online. I especially recommend the resources in *The Worship Sourcebook* (Grand Rapids: Calvin Institute of Christian Worship, Faith Alive Christian Resources, and Baker Books, 2004), 286–304.

37. *Anamnesis* is a noun derived from the Greek verb that means "to remember."

38. Constance M. Cherry, *The Worship Architect: A Blueprint for Designing Culturally Relevant and Biblically Faithful Services* (Grand Rapids: Baker Academic, 2010), 208.

39. Other appropriate passages may be found later in this chapter. See "Installing Doors and Windows."

40. Constance M. Cherry, 2012.

41. This sentence is taken from *Worship Sourcebook*, 249.

42. Constance M. Cherry, 2012.

43. Ibid.

44. Or those who are approved to answer for the child.

45. *Wesleyan Pastor's Manual for Pastors and Local Churches*, 5th ed. (Indianapolis: Wesleyan Publishing House, 2002), 18.

46. This part of the baptism rite is an ancient treasure, as evidenced from the very earliest records of Christian baptism available. The renunciation of Satan was a dramatic portion of the vows taken by the early catechumens. It has been recently reclaimed by many denominations in their pursuit of worship renewal.

47. *The United Methodist Book of Worship* (Nashville: United Methodist Publishing House, 1992), 88.

48. Constance M. Cherry, 2012.

49. *United Methodist Book of Worship*, 88.

50. *Wesleyan Pastor's Manual*, 18–19.

51. *United Methodist Book of Worship*, 89.

52. A seventeenth-century Huguenot baptismal formula, quoted in William A. Dyrness, *A Primer on Christian Worship: Where We've Been, Where We Are, Where We Can Go* (Grand Rapids: Eerdmans, 2009), 117.

53. *United Methodist Book of Worship*, 91.

54. Unless otherwise indicated, the content of this entire liturgy was composed by Constance M. Cherry, 2012.

55. This part of the baptism rite is an ancient treasure, as evidenced from the very earliest records of Christian baptism available. The renunciation of Satan was a dramatic portion of the vows taken by the early catechumens. It has been recently reclaimed by many denominations in their pursuit of worship renewal in recent decades.

56. *United Methodist Book of Worship*, 88.

57. Ibid.

58. Ibid., 89 (adapted).

59. Detailed instructions for immersing adults are given at the end of the chapter.

60. *United Methodist Book of Worship*, 91.

61. See appendix A for the traditional form for the invocation.

62. *Evangelical Lutheran Worship* (Minneapolis: Augsburg Fortress, 2006), 230.

63. For other fine examples of this prayer, see *Book of Common Prayer* and www.bit.ly /kiddbaptism.

64. *Worship Sourcebook*, 279.

65. Archaeologists have discovered a large amount of artwork in catacombs, in ancient churches, and on ordinary household items depicting the shell as an instrument for pouring water during baptism. Much evidence exists for the practice of pouring as a popular mode of baptism in the early days of the church. Very early baptisteries, including one excavated in Jesus's hometown of Nazareth, could facilitate pouring but not immersion. The artwork depicts adults

standing or kneeling in a pool; the one who is baptizing is often shown dipping a shell into the water to pour over the head of the candidate. The traditional symbol of the baptismal shell is shown with three drops of water dripping from the shell, symbolic of the Trinity. See www .christiananswers.net/dictionary/baptism.html.

66. White, *Brief History*, 47.

67. Ibid.

68. Dix, *Shape of the Liturgy*, 341.

69. Some exceptions include certain Anabaptist groups and other denominations with a lay emphasis.

Chapter 5

1. For example, the Salvation Army, Friends, and Quakers do not generally observe the Lord's Table.

2. Charles Wesley, *Come, Sinners, to the Gospel Feast*, 1747 (stanzas 1, 2, 5). Public domain.

3. A sense of celebration is not mutually exclusive to those who hold the ordinance or sacramental view; I only suggest that each view perhaps tends to lend itself to a certain tone for the service more naturally than another.

4. The view of Roman Catholicism.

5. The Lutheran view, sometimes referred to as consubstantiation, has become so confusing that many Lutherans now avoid the term. See chapter 3 in John H. Armstrong, ed., *Understanding Four Views on the Lord's Supper* (Grand Rapids: Zondervan, 2007).

6. Though nuanced differently, this view is held by Reformed, Anglican, and Wesleyan traditions.

7. This is not to say that God in Christ does not minister to us at the Table; it is simply to say that the Table has historically involved much response-oriented worship, as shown throughout this chapter.

8. See Carmine Di Sante, "The Berakhah or Blessing," in *The Complete Library of Christian Worship*, ed. Robert E. Webber (Nashville: StarSong, 1993), 1:141–42.

9. *Webster's New Universal Unabridged Dictionary*, 2nd ed., s.v. "sacrament."

10. Satan's ultimate power is destroyed, though his destructive forces are permitted some license on the earth until the end.

11. Robert E. Webber, *The Majestic Tapestry: How the Power of Early Christian Tradition Can Enrich Contemporary Faith* (Nashville: Thomas Nelson, 1986), 30.

12. The Divine Liturgy and the Mass refer to the whole divine service of worship, of which the Table is the central, primary piece. It is so central that the Table and the whole service cannot be separated.

13. Parts of this section are adapted from Constance M. Cherry, *The Worship Architect: A Blueprint for Designing Culturally Relevant and Biblically Faithful Services* (Grand Rapids: Baker Academic, 2010), 87–89.

14. Francis Foulkes, "The Lord's Supper," in *Baker Encyclopedia of the Bible*, ed. Walter A. Elwell (Grand Rapids: Baker Books, 1988), 1355.

15. Ibid.

16. William A. Dyrness, *A Primer on Christian Worship: Where We've Been, Where We Are, Where We Can Go* (Grand Rapids: Eerdmans, 2009), 82.

17. Ibid.

18. The Passover also extended to Gentiles within the household who were accepted by virtue of their formal relationship to their Jewish hosts.

19. Ben Witherington III, *Conflict & Community in Corinth: A Socio-Rhetorical Commentary on 1 and 2 Corinthians* (Grand Rapids: Eerdmans, 1995), 251.

20. The Enlightenment eventually also had a hand in dismissing the supernatural and embracing that which was more rational, a development that did not encourage frequent Eucharist.

21. For this analysis I am indebted to John Weborg, "Guidelines for Preparing Communion Prayers," in *The Complete Library of Christian Worship*, ed. Robert E. Webber (Nashville: Star Song, 1993), 5:258.

22. Other appropriate passages may be found later in this chapter. See "Installing Doors and Windows."

23. For purposes of this order of service I have chosen to offer a brief and modified form of the Great Thanksgiving so as to make this service more accessible for a wider variety of liturgical families, including those from the Free Church tradition.

24. *The Worship Sourcebook* (Grand Rapids: Calvin Institute of Christian Worship, Faith Alive Christian Resources, and Baker Books, 2004), 324.

25. *The United Methodist Book of Worship* (Nashville: United Methodist Publishing House, 1992), 38.

26. *The Wesleyan Pastor's Manual for Pastors and Local Churches*, 5th ed. (Indianapolis: Wesleyan Publishing House, 2002), 46–47.

27. Other terms for this prayer include the Great Prayer of Thanksgiving, the Eucharistic Prayer, the anaphora, and the canon.

28. Dom Gregory Dix, *The Shape of the Liturgy*, new ed. (London: Continuum, 2005), 156.

29. Ibid., 158.

30. Ibid., 159.

31. *At the Lord's Table: A Communion Service Book for Use by the Minister*, Supplemental Worship Resources 9 (Nashville: Abingdon, 1981), 11.

32. Dix, *Shape of the Liturgy*, 156.

33. The elements in this section are summarized from *At the Lord's Table*, 11. There are many sources that substantiate this outline. See also Keith Watkins, *The Great Thanksgiving* (St. Louis: Chalice, 1995), 134–46.

34. Known as the *sursum corda* ("lift up your hearts").

35. Watkins, *Great Thanksgiving*, 136.

36. Known as the *sanctus* (Latin for "holy").

37. Known as the Memorial Acclamation.

38. The Greek word *anamnesis*, "remembrance," is used to recall an occasion not as a past event fully concluded but one that is ongoing in scope—past, present, and future all at once.

39. Known as *epiclesis*, calling upon the presence of a deity to be present.

40. A less sacramental version of the invocation would invite the Holy Spirit upon the congregation but not the elements.

41. *Worship Sourcebook*, 325.

42. Ibid.

43. Technically, World Communion Sunday is not a part of the Christian year, in that it does not signify a true chapter in God's story. Nevertheless, it signifies an important spiritual reality worthy of observance.

44. There are a number of exceptions, such as the Christian Church or Disciples of Christ (whose elders may preside at the Table), most Anabaptist groups, Plymouth Brethren groups, and so on.

45. One worship pastor recently told me that he took consecrated bread home, baked bread pudding with it, and served it to a church member who was going through a difficult divorce. They ate it together and prayed. It reminded him of an ancient love feast.

46. *Eucharistia* is used in these passages, signaling the *berakhah* noted earlier in this chapter.

47. This wording of the institution is taken from *The United Methodist Book of Worship*, 52.

48. There may be extreme cases when bread and wine are truly not available; that is a different issue, and thoughtful substitutions may be made. What is addressed here is the objectionable, arbitrary substitution of elements to somehow contemporize the Table or make the Table "relevant." This very idea shows an uninformed and callous disregard for what is actually occurring when we follow Christ's command: "Do this in remembrance of me."

49. Armstrong, *Understanding Four Views on the Lord's Supper*, 93.

50. Ibid.

51. Ibid.

52. For instance, if a blatant unbeliever wishes to blaspheme the holy act in some way.

Chapter 6

1. Denominations that have included templates and rubrics for services of healing in recent, official worship books include the Evangelical Lutheran Church of America, the Presbyterian Church (USA), and the United Methodist Church, to name a few.

2. One exception is Matt. 9:18, where a synagogue leader seeks Jesus's help to revive his daughter who has just died. Another biblical exception is the Roman centurion requesting healing for his servant (Matt. 8:5–13).

3. Robert G. Tuttle, Jr., "John Wesley and the Gifts of the Holy Spirit," The Unofficial Confessing Movement Page, ucmpage.org/articles/rtuttle1.html (accessed April 22, 2012).

4. Jeffrey John, "Anointing in the New Testament," in *The Oil of Gladness: Anointing in the Christian Tradition,* ed. Martin Dudley and Goeffrey Rowell (Collegeville, MN: Liturgical Press, 1993), 56–57.

5. Ibid., 49.

6. Geoffrey Wainwright and Karen B. Westerfield Tucker, eds., *The Oxford History of Christian Worship* (New York: Oxford University Press, 2006), 121.

7. John Halliburton, "Anointing in the Early Church," in *The Oil of Gladness: Anointing in the Christian Tradition*, ed. Martin Dudley and Goeffrey Rowell (Collegeville, MN: Liturgical Press, 1993), 78.

8. Ibid., 86.

9. Ibid., 89.

10. Ibid.

11. Ibid., 78.

12. John, "Anointing in the New Testament," 59.

13. Thomas G. Long, *Accompany Them with Singing: The Christian Funeral* (Louisville: Westminster John Knox, 2009), 115.

14. Ibid.

15. John, "Anointing in the New Testament," 51.

16. Halliburton, "Anointing in the Early Church," 89.

17. Ibid., 87–88.

18. Ibid., 86.

19. Ibid.

20. Ibid., 85.

21. Wainwright and Tucker, *Oxford History of Christian Worship,* 813.

22. John, "Anointing in the New Testament," 58.

23. Ibid., 59.

24. Other appropriate passages are found later in this chapter. See "Installing Doors and Windows."

25. In the expanded order, which includes a homily, it is also appropriate, if desired, to move the confession of sin and assurance of pardon after the homily, as it may inform the content of the prayer of confession.

26. Most Christian supply stores carry inexpensive vials of olive oil for this purpose; they may also be purchased at internet sites.

27. A memorized or written prayer for healing is not inappropriate by any means; however, the intimacy of this service benefits from more personal, extemporaneous prayers. If extemporaneous, I nevertheless urge the leader to prepare her or his thoughts prior to the service. Spontaneous prayers generally run a higher risk of theological error than prepared prayers.

Great care should be given to voice only that which is affirmed by the church to be true concerning healing.

28. *The Book of Common Prayer* (New York: Oxford University Press), 456.

29. Ibid., 456–57.

30. Wainwright and Tucker, *Oxford History of Christian Worship*, 814.

31. Dennis G. Michno, *A Priest's Handbook: The Ceremonies of the Church*, 3rd ed. (Harrisburg, NY: Morehouse, 1998), 237.

32. See "A Service of Healing I," in *The United Methodist Book of Worship* (Nashville: United Methodist Publishing House, 1992), 615–21.

33. The last name of an author, composer, or other reference note is offered in parenthesis to help you locate the hymn or song. A most helpful website to assist you in locating these songs is www.hymnary.org.

34. The benediction is significant to this service also, though it is not technically a prayer.

35. *Book of Common Prayer*, 455.

36. *United Methodist Book of Worship*, 620.

37. *The Worshipbook: Services and Hymns* (Philadelphia: Westminster Press, 1972), 32–33.

38. *United Methodist Book of Worship*, 621.

39. Frederick J. Gaiser, *Healing in the Bible: Theological Insight for Christian Ministry* (Grand Rapids: Baker Academic, 2010), 149.

40. Ibid., 150.

41. A few occasions exist in the Gospels that seem to resemble healing by proxy, but these are quite different in principle. There were occasions when a parent asked healing for a child (who was too young to ask healing for herself) or when the centurion asked healing for a servant (who would presumably be unable to come to Jesus), but on no occasion did Jesus touch the ambassador on behalf of the one who was ill, asking them to "pass it on" vicariously. There is one odd reference to cloth articles that, having touched the apostle Paul's skin, brought healing to others when they in turn came in contact with the items (Acts 19:11–12). I regard these as "extraordinary miracles," however; I do not consider them a rationale for healing by proxy.

Chapter 7

1. Keith Graber Miller, "Historical Developments and Origins of Footwashing," in *The Complete Library of Christian Worship*, ed. Robert E. Webber (Nashville: Star Song, 1993), 6:341.

2. The term appears in various historical documents in at least five forms: foot washing, foot-washing, feetwashing, feet washing, and feet-washing.

3. For instance, the Mennonites do Communion followed by foot washing; the Grace Brethren do foot washing followed by Communion. Some exceptions to these practices no doubt occur.

4. Eleanor Kreider, *Communion Shapes Character* (Scottdale, PA: Herald, 1997), 158.

5. *The New Interpreter's Bible*, vol. 11 (Nashville: Abingdon, 2000), 723.

6. Ibid.

7. Ibid., 820.

8. Keith Graber Miller, "Mennonite Footwashing: Identity Reflections and Altered Meanings" (www.anabaptistnetwork.com/book/export/html/311).

9. *New Interpreter's Bible*, 722.

10. Ibid.

11. Ibid.

12. Irenaeus, "Against Heresies," trans. Alexander Roberts and William Rambaut, *Ante-Nicene Fathers* 1, ed. Alexander Roberts, James Donaldson, and A. Cleveland Coxe (Buffalo, NY: Christian Literature, 1885), IV.23.1; Clement of Alexandria, "The Stromata," trans. William Wilson, *Ante-Nicene Fathers* 2, IV.22; Tertullian, "The Chaplet," trans. S. Thelwall, *Ante-Nicene Fathers* 3, XIII; Cyprian, "The Epistles of Cyprian," trans. Ernest Wallis, *Ante-Nicene Fathers* 5,

V.2; and "Three Books of Testimonies Against the Jews," trans. Ernest Wallis *Ante-Nicene Fathers* 5, XII.2.39.

13. Athanasius, *The Canons of Athanasius of Alexandria*, ed. and trans. Wilhelm Riedel and W. E. Crum (London: Williams and Norgate, 1904), Canon 66.

14. James F. White, *A Brief History of Christian Worship* (Nashville: Abingdon, 1993), 48.

15. Nathan D. Mitchell, *Meeting Mystery: Liturgy, Worship, Sacraments* (Maryknoll, NY: Orbis Books), 245–46.

16. Ibid., 245.

17. Augustine, "Book II of Replies to Questions of Januarius," trans. J. G. Cunningham, *Nicene and Post-Nicene Fathers*, First Series, vol. 5, ed. Philip Schaff (Buffalo, NY: Christian Literature, 1887), XVIII.33, and "Homilies on the Gospel of John," trans. John Gibb and James Innes, *Nicene and Post-Nicene Fathers*, First Series, vol. 7, LV–LVIII; John Chrysostom, "Homilies on Saint John," trans. Philip Schaff, *Nicene and Post-Nicene Fathers*, First Series, vol. 14, LXX–LXXI.

18. St. Benedict's Rule is mentioned in Harold S. Bender, "Footwashing," in *The Mennonite Encyclopedia* (Scottdale, PA: Mennonite Publishing House, 1956), 2:348.

19. Bernard of Clairvaux is mentioned in Daniel Webster Kurtz, "Washing of Feet," NET Bible Learning Environment, classic.net.bible.org/dictionary.php?word=Washing%20Of%20Feet (accessed October 22, 2012).

20. Bender, "Footwashing," 348.

21. Kurtz, "Washing of Feet."

22. *The Encyclopedia of Christianity*, ed. Erwin Fahlbusch et al. (Grand Rapids: Eerdmans, 2001), 2:322.

23. Bender, "Footwashing," 348.

24. "Anabaptist" refers to "again-baptizers"—those who did not accept infant baptism as initiation into the Christian community and therefore rebaptized adult believers upon their own confession of faith, a highly controversial approach during this time period. Foot washing was one practice that gave Anabaptists an identity as members of "the true Church."

25. Henry C. Vedder, *Balthasar Hubmaier: The Leader of the Anabaptists* (New York: AMS Press, 1971), 108–12.

26. Bender, "Footwashing," 348.

27. Ibid.

28. In my research I found no denomination that refers to foot washing as a sacrament, though admittedly one could exist.

29. James White considers the Anabaptist movement to be the first of the Free Church Traditions. (See chapter 5 in *Protestant Worship* by James F. White [Louisville: Westminster John Knox, 1989]).

30. Article Thirteen of the Mennonite Confession of Faith, *Confession of Faith in a Mennonite Perspective* (Scottdale, PA: Herald, 1995), 53.

31. "Feetwashing in the Church of the Brethren," www.anabaptistnetwork.com/node/312 (accessed March 28, 2012), adapted from *For All Who Minister: A Worship Manual for the Church of the Brethren* (Elgin, IL: Brethren, 1993), 183–226.

32. Oscar Cullmann, *Early Christian Worship,* trans. A. Stewart Todd and James B. Torrance (London: SCM Press), 108.

33. Ibid.

34. Ibid.

35. This raises interesting questions as to whether or not baptism is required to participate in either the Lord's Supper or foot washing. A number of traditions require baptism for participation in Communion (as do most Mennonite groups) but not for participation in foot washing.

36. John Winebrenner, "The Ordinance of Feet Washing, Part II: The Proper Time and Manner of Observing It," www.mun.ca/rels/restmov/texts/believers/wineord/ORD02B.HTM.

The New Revised Standard Version and the New International Version, among others, indicate that the Passover meal was under way when Jesus washed the disciples' feet.

37. *For All Who Minister*, 191.

38. I have recently had several conversations with long-term members of various Anabaptist denominations who substantiate renewed interest in foot washing among their groups.

39. *The Dramatized New Testament*, ed. Michael Perry (Grand Rapids: Baker, 1994) is a handy resource, with this passage and many others divided into parts for assigned readers according to characters in the story.

40. Minister's manuals/handbooks or worship books of denominations that have a long tradition of foot washing are especially helpful for the leader.

41. If your denomination has practiced foot washing historically for centuries, do not overlook the power inherent in hearing how this event connects with your story.

42. Traditionally referred to as "row washing."

43. Bender, "Footwashing," 347.

44. It was customary among some Anabaptists to collect monetary gifts for charities (almsgiving).

45. The last name of an author, composer, or other reference note is offered in parentheses to help you locate the hymn or song. A helpful website to assist you with information on these songs is www.hymnary.org.

46. This is a historic hymn associated with foot washing, found in early Mennonite hymnals.

47. This is another historic hymn associated with foot washing found in early Mennonite hymnals.

48. For permission to use this text, simply visit the website of Hope Publishing Company (www.hopepublishingcompany.com).

49. *For All Who Minister*, 226.

50. Constance M. Cherry, 2012.

51. Constance M. Cherry, 2012.

52. *For All Who Minister*, 225.

53. Although agape meals faded, the Eucharist remained as a frequent, even weekly, observance.

54. *United Methodist Book of Worship* (Nashville: United Methodist Publishing House, 1992), 581.

55. Ibid.

56. Lester Ruth, *A Little Heaven Below: Worship at Early Methodist Quarterly Meetings* (Nashville: Kingswood Books, 2000), 63.

57. Ibid.

58. Ibid., 63–64.

59. Ibid., 60.

Chapter 8

1. This ritual is referred to as either infant dedication or child dedication, since age is not an urgent matter. For the sake of ease, the term "child dedication" will be used throughout this chapter.

2. Church historian James White cites two distinguishing features of Free Church worship: freedom to reform worship exclusively on the basis of local interpretation of Scripture, and freedom to operate autonomously when ordering worship. See James F. White, *Protestant Worship: Traditions in Transition* (Louisville: Westminster John Knox, 1989), 172. Many Free Church groups, such as the Anabaptists, Congregationalists, and Baptists, are noted for believer's baptism. The groups that do not practice infant baptism have tended to develop services of child dedication over time. Hence, today child dedications tend to be practiced primarily among Free Church groups.

3. James White is emphatic that "infants were certainly being baptized by the beginning of the third century, if not long before that." See James F. White, *A Brief History of Christian*

Worship (Nashville: Abingdon, 1993), 51. David F. Wright, however, claims that it is all but impossible to pinpoint "the first known child of Christian parents who are baptized routinely, i.e., not clinically, as a newborn." See David F. Wright, "Infant Dedication in the Early Church," in *Infant Baptism in Historical Perspective: Collected Studies* (London: Paternoster, 2007), 118–19. Wright continues, "The absence of mention of baptism in contexts where modern investigators expect it is a repeated feature of early Christian literature" (121).

4. David F. Wright asserts that there is very limited record concerning the half century wherein offspring of Christian parents did not receive baptism. He states, "I find no more than the occasional footnote or paragraph" (ibid., 116).

5. Ibid.

6. Ibid.

7. "The Apology of Aristides the Philosopher," Early Christian Writings, www.earlychristian writings.com/text/aristides-kay.html (accessed May 16, 2012).

8. Wright, "Infant Dedication," 125. Wright admits that some have interpreted this passage to imply infant baptism—a viewpoint Wright rejects as a result of historical debates he cites in his chapter.

9. Ibid., 124.

10. See also David F. Wright, "Augustine and the Transformation of Baptism," in *The Origins of Christendom in the West*, ed. Alan Kreider (Edinburgh: T&T Clark, 2001).

11. Two of the ceremonies for entrance into the catechumenate were the sign of the cross and the taste of salt. The sign of the cross was made on the forehead to indicate that the catechumen now belonged to Christ. The symbol of tasting salt suggested for Augustine that the candidate was preserved and seasoned in the faith. See J. Wm. Harmless, *Augustine & the Catechumenate* (Liturgical Press, 1995), 150.

12. Ibid.

13. Wright, "Infant Dedication," 117.

14. Ibid., 118.

15. Ibid., 123.

16. Our discussion is limited to the church in the West, though there are similar practices in the ancient Eastern church also.

17. Wright, "Infant Dedication," 128, 131.

18. Ibid., 135.

19. Ibid.

20. Ibid., 128.

21. Ibid., 136.

22. Ibid., 137.

23. This is not to say that the early Anabaptists had no rite of welcoming a child into the community; it is to say that if this were the case, it would not have been viewed as a step in the baptismal process.

24. The Waldensian Church in Italy and the Adoptionist Paulicians of ninth-century Armenia are such examples. See Geoffrey Wainwright, "The Need for a Methodist Service for the Admission of Infants to the Catechumenate," *London Quarterly and Holborn Review* (January 1968), 53–54.

25. John E. Skoglund and Nancy E. Hall, *A Manual of Worship*, new ed. (Valley Forge, PA: Judson Press, 1993), 202.

26. While these denominations favor child dedication over infant baptism, they do not forbid infant baptism, which was Wesley's practice.

27. In researching child dedication services, I found overwhelming use of the same three biblical passages cited in this section. Deuteronomy 6:4–9, which will be discussed later in the chapter, also appears somewhat prominently but less often than the three mentioned here.

28. Even if someone tried to build the case for child dedication on the basis of the firstborn male in Israel belonging to the Lord (dedicated to Yahweh, so to speak), the argument falls apart, for (1) it applied only to males, (2) it applied only to *firstborn* males, and (3) it was negated in New Testament practices as a result of Christ's atonement.

29. In addition to the story of Samuel (see 1 Sam. 1), see also Jeremiah (Jer. 1:4–10) and Samson (Judg. 13:2–5).

30. A blessing is also a benediction. The English word "benediction" is derived from Latin words, "*bene*" (good) and "*diction*" (speech/words). A blessing (benediction) is speaking good into another's life.

31. Perhaps you will find a different name for the service to suit your community, such as "A Service of Initiating Discipleship" and so on.

32. See Wainwright, "Need for a Methodist Service," 51–60.

33. Ibid., 52.

34. Ibid., 53. Wainwright offers the church father, Augustine, as an example of this.

35. Ibid., 54.

36. "Présentation ou Bénédiction d'un enfant in Liturgie" *en liturgie* (Paris: Editions Berger-Levrault, 1963), 246–49, quoted in Wainwright, "Need for a Methodist Service," 55.

37. Again, feel free to find a different name for the service, such as "Parent Dedication on the Birth of a Child" and so on.

38. To reiterate, this service is redundant if the infant or very young child is or will soon be baptized.

39. Constance M. Cherry, 2012.

40. Ibid.

41. Ibid.

42. *The United Methodist Book of Worship* (Nashville: United Methodist Publishing House, 1992), 586.

43. Constance M. Cherry, 2012 (referencing Ps. 118:24).

44. "Parents or guardians" is intended throughout.

45. The section "Parents' Intent" is developed by Constance M. Cherry, 2012.

46. Avoid the lead-in "And all God's people said" if possible. Rather, tell them in advance to join you in the "Amen." It doesn't matter whether it is performed in perfect synchronization. Allow the people to agree with your prayer by stating, "Amen."

47. Constance M. Cherry, 2012.

48. Four of the primary elements of this service are attributed to Geoffrey Wainwright: thanksgiving for the birth of the child, admission to the catechumenate, invocation of the Holy Spirit upon the child, and a physical gesture that expresses the action being performed. See Wainwright, "Need for a Methodist Service."

49. Constance M. Cherry, 2012.

50. Ibid.

51. Ibid. (referencing 2 Cor. 5:17–18).

52. Ibid. (referencing John 3:3–5 and Ps. 118:23–24).

53. "Parents or guardians" is intended throughout.

54. Constance M. Cherry, 2012.

55. Ibid., except for the final paragraph.

56. Adapted from the *United Methodist Book of Worship*, 89.

57. Or "Admission to the Catechumenate."

58. This procedure is not unlike the former traditional practice of enlisting infants in the church's "Cradle Roll." It was widely popular, particularly among those in the Free Church tradition, to officially enroll children in the Sunday school program beginning with the nursery department. Other, more liturgical, churches also have a cradle roll tradition with enrollment upon baptism or christening.

59. Avoid the lead-in "And all God's people said" if possible. Rather, tell them in advance to join you in the "Amen." It doesn't matter whether it is performed in perfect synchronization. Allow the people to agree with your prayer by stating, "Amen."

60. Constance M. Cherry (referencing John 16:13 and 1 Cor. 12:3).

61. *United Methodist Book of Worship*, 586–87.

62. This should be a "dry" sign. Reserve water and oil for baptism.

63. Constance M. Cherry, 2012.

64. *The Worship Sourcebook* (Grand Rapids: Calvin Institute of Christian Worship, Faith Alive Christian Resources, and Baker Books, 2004), 289 (adapted).

65. The second part of the prayer is an addition by Constance M. Cherry, 2012.

66. Constance M. Cherry, 2012.

67. *Worship Sourcebook*, 286.

68. Ibid., 295.

69. John D. Witvliet, "A Liturgy for the Renewal of the Baptismal Covenant," in *The Complete Library of Christian Worship*, ed. Robert E. Webber (Nashville: Star Song, 1993), 6:201.

70. Constance M. Cherry, 2012.

71. Witvliet, "Liturgy for the Renewal of the Baptismal Covenant," 201.

72. The last name of an author, composer, or other reference note is offered in parentheses to help you locate the hymn or song. A most helpful website to assist you in locating these songs is www.hymnary.org.

73. These suggestions are more generally suitable, given the lack of songs directly related to one's renewal of baptism.

74. The benediction is not technically a prayer but is included here for organizational purposes.

75. *Holy Baptism and Services for the Renewal of Baptism*, Supplemental Liturgical Resource 2 (Louisville: Westminster John Knox, 1985), 413.

76. *Worship Sourcebook*, 299.

77. Ibid.

Chapter 9

1. I consider the Table of the Lord to be normative for every Lord's Day but account for the fact that the majority of Protestant congregations do not celebrate weekly Eucharist.

2. See chapter 1 for elaboration on these five dimensions of sacred ritual.

3. For an expanded discussion of this central principle of worship, see chapter 2 in Constance M. Cherry, *The Worship Architect: A Blueprint for Designing Culturally Relevant and Biblically Faithful Services* (Grand Rapids: Baker Academic, 2010).

4. See Robert E. Webber's culminating work, *Who Gets to Narrate the World? Contending for the Christian Story in an Age of Rivals* (Downers Grove, IL: InterVarsity, 2008).

5. I do not consider this to be an exhaustive list of dimensions to sacred rituals. Feel free to embellish this list as appropriate.

6. For an excellent guide to "organic liturgy" (liturgy shaped from Scripture), see F. Russell Mitman, *Worship in the Shape of Scripture* (Cleveland: Pilgrim, 2001).

7. See chapter 1.

8. A homily would be too much in most cases. I am simply suggesting a few moments of brief reflection on the passage.

9. These may work with the fourfold order just mentioned, or replace it.

10. This list is adapted from appendix A in Cherry, *Worship Architect*.

Appendix A

1. Adapted from Constance M. Cherry, *The Worship Architect: A Blueprint for Designing Culturally Relevant and Biblically Faithful Services* (Grand Rapids: Baker Academic, 2010), chapter 9.

Index

All Saints' Day, 86
Ambrose of Milan, 223
Anabaptists
  and foot washing, 224–25
  and infant baptism, 247
  and the love feast, 239
anamnesis, 151
anointing with oil, 206
  in the Bible, 196–97
  and Communion, 184–85
  Greek verbs for, 197
  and healing, 195
Apology (Aristides), 245
Apostolic Constitutions, 198
Apostolic Tradition (Hippolytus), 172, 198
Aristides, 245
Augustine, 246

baptism, 29–30, 32, 95–96
  administered, how, 113, 138
    and candidate's name, 115–16
    mode of, 113–14
    one time, 116–17
    and quantity of water, 114
    and Trinitarian formula, 114–15
    and worship context, 115
  administered, when, 109–11
  administered, where, 111–13
  biblical foundations of, 97–98, 107, 109,
    114–15
    as act of initiation, 98–99
    and receiving the Holy Spirit, 99–100

as recognition of new birth, 99
    and union with Christ, 98
  and catechumenates, 99
  and the Christian year, 134
  as communal event, 112–13
  and confirmation, 106–7
  as covenant, 104–5
    and circumcision, 104–5
  in Cuba, 110–11
  historical foundations of, 99, 101–2, 104,
    107–8, 111–12, 245
  ordinance view of, 100–101
  and pastor serving as host, 134
    and administration, 138
    attributes for presiding, 137–38
    and credentials, 135
    duties before, 135–36
    and follow-up, 136–37
    and logistical details, 139
    preparation for service, 136
    and unusual circumstances, 138–39
  Protestant differences regarding, 96, 100,
    114
  and "Remembering Your Baptism," 117
  as sacrament, 20–21, 100–102
  and service for parental renewal of baptism,
    254–56
  structure of service, 117
    order of believer's baptism, 123–30
    order of infant baptism, 117–23
  suggested prayers for service, 131–33
  suggested Scriptures for service, 131

suggested songs for service, 130–31
suggested symbols for service, 133
what is, 97–102
who gets
    and believer's baptism, 107–9, 249–50
    infants, 103–7, 245–47
why do, and baptism of Jesus, 102–3
baptism, infant, 103–7, 245–47, 253
    and Anabaptists, 247
    vs. child dedication, 249–50
    order of infant baptism, 117–23
Bender, Harold, 224
berakhah, 151
blessing, 252
Book of Common Prayer, The, 112
breaking of bread. *See* Lord's Supper; love feast

Calvin, John, 115, 160, 186
    on sacraments, 20
catechumenate, 99, 110, 161, 245–46, 253, 254
Chan, Simon, 27–28
child dedication service, 243–45
    biblical foundations of, 247–49
        and birth of Jesus, 248–49, 252
        and birth of John the Baptist, 251–52
        and Hannah and Samuel, 248–49
    and the Christian year, 274
    and different Protestant practices, 247
    historical foundations of, 245
        and dedication to virginity, 246
        and enrollment in catechumenate, 245–46
        and infant baptism, 245–47
        and thanksgiving service, 245
    and pastor serving as host
        administration, 275
        attributes for presiding, 274
        and difficult circumstances, 275
        duties, 274
        and ethics, 275–76
    and rites to recognize birth of child, 251
        purpose for, 251
        service to bless child, 251–53
        service for parental renewal of baptism,
            254–56
        service of welcome, 253–54
    structure for
        service to bless child, 256–61
        service for parental renewal of baptism,
            266–70
        service of welcome, 261–66
    suggested prayers for service, 272–73
    suggested Scriptures for service, 272
    suggested songs for service, 271–72
    suggested symbols for service, 273–74
    and theological foundations for, 249–51
        and infant baptism, 249–50
        and relationship to believer baptism,
            249–50
children, Jesus's acceptance of, 106–7, 252
Christian year
    and baptism, 134
    and child dedication, 274
    and healing service, 211
    and foot washing service, 235–36
    and the Lord's Supper, 174–76
    and love feast, 241
    and ritual architect, 284
    and weddings, 52
chronos, 174–75
Church of England, 20–21
"Come, Sinners, to the Gospel Feast" (Wesley),
    147
Communion. *See* Lord's Supper
Council of Toledo, 246
counseling, premarital, 53
Cyril of Jerusalem, 198

death, biblical view of, 64
    and the soul and body, 64–65, 69
dedication of temple, Solomon's, 285–86
Didache, 111–12
Duba, Arlo, 114
Dyrness, William, 157

Eucharist. *See* Lord's Supper
eucharistia, 151
exorcism, 214–15

foot washing, 28
foot washing service, 219–21
    biblical foundations for, 221–23
        and John 13, 221–22, 225–27
    and the Christian year, 235–36
    historical foundations of, 223–25
        and Anabaptists, 224–25
        and Maundy Thursday, 224
    and the Lord's Supper, 227
    and the love feast, 220, 238–41
    and pastor serving as host
        administration, 237
        attributes for presiding, 237
        and difficult circumstances, 237–38

duties, 236
and ethics, 238
structure of, 228
order of, 229–32
suggested prayers for service, 233–35
suggested Scriptures for service, 233
suggested songs for service, 232–33
suggested symbols for service, 235
theological foundations for, 225
and differing views, 227–28
and humility and service, 225–27
funeral, Christian, 61–62. *See also* death,
biblical view of
burial vs. cremation, 68–69
characteristics of good, 93
and the Christian calendar, 86
and Communion, 71–72
and evangelism, 66
historical foundations of, 62, 71–72
location of, 67
vs. memorial, 69–70
for non-Christian, 90–91
open vs. closed casket, 70–71
and pastor serving as host, 86–87
administration, 89–90
attributes for presiding, 88–89
and difficult circumstances, 90–91
duties, 87–88
and ethical considerations, 91–92
purpose of
as witness, 64
as worship, 63–64
and rites of fraternal order, 71
structure of, 72–73
and gathering, 73–76
and response to word, 76–77
and sending, 77–78
and word, 76
suggested prayers for service, 85
suggested Scriptures for service, 85
suggested songs for service, 83–84
suggested symbols for service, 85
and technology, 67–68
and transition to final resting place, 78
graveside service, 79
service of committal, 78–83

Gaiser, Fredrick, 214
Great Thanksgiving Prayer, 132, 151, 171–72,
183
example of, 172–74
history of, 172

Halliburton, John, 196–97
healing service, 191–93
and anointing with oil, 195, 206
in the Bible, 196–97
biblical foundations for, 192, 199–200, 202, 214
and principles, 193–96
and Christian year, 211
and confession, 195
and ethical considerations, 216
and extreme unction, 198
and faith, 195, 201–2
and faith-healers, 201–2
historical foundations of, 196–98
and pastor serving as host, 211
administration, 212–13
attributes for presiding, 212
and children, 214
and difficult circumstances, 213
duties for, 211–21
and exorcism, 214–15
and terminally ill, 213–14
and prayer, 194–95
structure of, 202–3
order of, 203–7
suggested prayers for, 210
suggested Scriptures for, 209–10
suggested songs for, 208–9
suggested symbols for, 211
theological foundations for, 198–99
and dependence on Holy Spirit, 201–2
and God as healer, 199
and God's sovereignty, 200
and God's welcome, 199
and purpose of suffering, 201
and when healing does not happen, 215
and when healing not wanted, 215
Hippolytus, 172, 198

individualism, and worship, 24–26

James, book of, on healing, 192–96, 197, 199
John, Jeffrey, 199–200
Justin Martyr, 172

kairos, 174–75
Kreidor, Eleanor, 221

lex orandi, lex credenda, 25
liturgy
and the body, 18
definition of, 17–18
and prayer, 18

Long, Thomas, 63, 64–65, 69, 93, 197
Lord's Supper, 16, 32, 143–44
    and anointing with oil, 184–85
    biblical foundations for, 144–45, 148, 152–53,
        155, 156, 158, 180
    and catechumenate, 161
    and challenging circumstances
        and children, 185
        and refusing communicant, 186
        and weddings, 185–86
    and the Christian year, 174–76
    as dialogical worship, 149–50
        and Word and Table, 149–50
    and different approaches/names, 155
        breaking of bread, 156–57
        Communion, 156
        Eucharist, 155
        Lord's Supper, 155–56
    and fourfold action of Jesus, 180–82, 285
    and Great Thanksgiving prayer, 151, 171–72,
        183
        example of, 172–74
        history of, 172
    historical foundations of, 149–50, 156–57,
        158, 160, 162
    how bread and cup to be taken, 163–64
    key motifs of, 150
        anticipate kingdom, 152
        celebrate Christus Victor, 153–55
        communing, 152
        remembering, 150–51
        renew covenant, 152–53
        thanksgiving, 151
    and the love feast, 240
    as a meal, 144–45, 156–57
    and pastor serving as host, 176
        attributes for presiding, 179–82
        communicating with servers, 178
        credentials for, 176
        post-communion duties, 178–79
        pre-communion duties, 177
        words spoken at Table, 182–83
    relational essence of, 157–58
    as sacrament, 20–21
    structure of, 164–65
        order of, 165–70
        and warrant vs. narrative form, 165
    on substituting elements, 183–84
    suggested prayers for service, 171–74
    suggested Scriptures for service, 171
    suggested songs for service, 170–71

    suggested symbols for service, 174
    what it is, 145
        and transubstantiation, 148–49
        and Memorialist view, 147–48
        Protestant views on, 146–47, 149
        sacrament/ordinance, 145–49
    when offered, 162–63
    where offered, 163
    who may eat, 159–62
        different denominational approaches, 161
        Paul on, 160–61
    why celebrate, 158–59
love feast, 220, 238–39
    and Anabaptists, 239
    and the Christian year, 241
    description of, 240–41
    and the Lord's Supper, 240
    and Methodism, 239–40
Luther, 20, 115
    on baptism, 101

Marpeck, Pilgram, 224
marriage, Christian
    and Christ, 38
    and covenant, 37
    and creation, 36–37
    and the kingdom, 38–39
    as sacrament, 39
Mennonite Confession of Faith, 225
Mitchell, Nathan, 26, 223–24
Moses, 152–53
Mulholland, M. Robert, 27, 33

officiate, 24
ordinance
    definition of, 22
    vs. sacrament, and Lord's Supper, 23, 145–49
Osborne, Grant R., 97

Paul, 21, 43, 74, 154
    on baptism, 98, 99, 105, 255
    on foot washing, 222–23
    and healing, 195, 199–200, 201
    on Lord's Supper, 16, 151, 156, 160–61
    on marriage, 36, 38, 39
Pentecost, 97, 134
Peter, 97
    on Lord's Supper, 159–60
preside, 24

Reformed Church of France, 253–54
rite, definition of, 16–17, 18

ritual, sacred, 12–13
  and the church, 12
  definition of, 14–16, 18
  dimensions for
    Christo-centric, 31–32, 282–83
    corporate, 24–26, 280–81
    formational, 281
    proclamation, 283
    symbolic, 281–82
  education by, 24–26
  and formalization, 16
  general order for, 284–85
  and the Lord's Supper, 16
  and the New Testament, 14–15
  and the Old Testament, 14
  power of, 15
  and relationship with God, 12
  and repetition, 15
  and rubrics, 19
  and spiritual formation, 26–28
  symbolic nature of, 28–31
    and meaning, 31
    and mystery, 29
  vocabulary of, 13–24
  for the world, 33
ritual architect, 279–80
  and biblical language, 284
  and Christian year, 284
  and dedications, 285–86
  dimensions for
    Christo-centric, 282–83
    corporate, 280–81
    formational, 281
    proclamation, 283
    symbolic, 281–82
  and general order for action, 284–85
  and style, 284
  ten basic steps for, 286
routine, 11–12
rubric, definition of, 19–20

sacrament
  definition of, 20–21
  as "means of grace," 22
  vs. ordinance, and the Lord's Supper, 23,
    145–49
  and Protestantism, 20–21
    and differing views, 21–22
Scaer, David P., 184
Solomon, 285–86

spiritual formation, 26–28
symbols
  and baptism, 133
  and child dedication, 273–74
  and healing service, 211
  and foot washing service, 235
  and the Lord's Supper, 174
  and weddings, 52

Wainwright, Geoffrey, 253
Webber, Robert, 72
  on baptism, 101–2
  on Christus Victor, 154
weddings, Christian, 35–36. See also marriage,
    Christian
  and the Christian year, 52
  and difficult cases, 58
    and divorce, 58
    and ethical issues, 59
  historical foundations of, 36, 40
  and pastor serving as host, 52
    and administrative issues, 57–58
    attributes of officiating, 56
    and ceremonial duties, 54–55
    and post-wedding duties, 55–56
    and pre-wedding duties, 53–54
  planning the ceremony, 53–54
  and pre-Christian practices, 40
  and related services, 59
  structure of, 41–42
    and gathering, 42–45
    and ordering of service, 42
    and response to Word, 46–47
    and sending, 47–48
    and the Word, 45–46
  suggested prayers for service, 51–52
  suggested Scriptures for service, 50–51
  suggested songs for service, 49–50
  suggested symbols for service, 52
  and wedding rehearsal, 54–55
  as worship service, 39
    and Communion, 41
    and location of, 40–41
Wesley, Charles
  on Lord's Table, 147
Wesley, John
  on baptism, 100, 112
  on grace, 22
  on Lord's Table, 147
  and the love feast, 239–40, 241

White, James, 3, 20, 98, 103–4, 114
worship. *See also* ritual architect
  and baptism, 115
  corporate, 24–26, 255–56
    five dimensions for, 280–83
    ten basic steps for, 286
  funeral as, 63–64
  and individualism, 24–26
  as intergenerational, 276

and the Lord's Table, 149–50
and spiritual formation, 26–28
and weddings, 39–41
Worthington, Ben, 161
Wright, David F., 245–46

Zinzendorf (Count), 239
Zwingli, Ulrich, 104
  on Lord's Table, 148